RAISING CONSUMERS

POPULAR CULTURES, EVERYDAY LIVES

ROBIN D. G. KELLEY AND JANICE RADWAY, EDITORS

POPULAR CULTURES, EVERYDAY LIVES

ROBIN D.G. KELLEY & JANICE RADWAY, EDITORS

Interzones: Black/White Sex Districts in Chicago and New York in the Early Twentieth Century.
Kevin J. Mumford

City Reading: Written Words and Public Spaces in Antebellum New York.
David M. Henkin

Selling Suffrage: Consumer Culture and Votes for Women.
Margaret Finnegan

Ladies of Labor, Girls of Adventure:
Working Women, Popular Culture, and Labor Politics at the Turn of the Century.
Nan Enstad

Telling Bodies, Performing Birth: Everyday Narratives of Childbirth.
Della Pollock

From Bomba to Hip-Hop: Puerto Rican Culture and Latino Identity.
Juan Flores

Taking the Train: How Graffiti Art Became an Urban Crisis in New York City.
Joe Austin

Shaky Ground: The Sixties and Its Aftershocks.
Alice Echols

A Token of My Affection: Greeting Cards and American Business Culture.
Barry Shank

RAISING CONSUMERS

Children and the American Mass Market
in the Early Twentieth Century

Lisa Jacobson

COLUMBIA UNIVERSITY PRESS

NEW YORK

COLUMBIA UNIVERSITY PPRESS
PUBLISHERS SINCE 1893
NEW YORK, CHICHESTER, WEST SUSSEX

Library of Congress Cataloging-in-Publication Data
Jacobson, Lisa
Raising consumers : children and the American mass market in the early
twentieth century / Lisa Jacobson.
p.   cm.
Includes bibliographical refererences and index.
ISBN 0-231-11388-9 (cloth : alk. paper)
1. Child consumers—United States—History—20th century.   2. Market
segmentation—United States—History—History—20th century.   3. Target marketing—
United States—History—20th century.   4. Advertising and children—United States—
History—20th century.   I. Title.

HF5415.33.U6J33 2004
339.4'7'0830973—dc22
2004045638

Columbia University Press books are printed on permanent and durable acid-free paper
Printed in the United States of America

c 10 9 8 7 6 5 4 3 2 1

References to Internet Web Sites (URLs) were accurate at the time of writing. Neither the
author nor Columbia University Press is responsible for Web sites that may have expired
or changed since the articles were prepared

For John and Sam

CONTENTS

ILLUSTRATIONS

ACKNOWLEDGMENTS

THIS PROJECT BEGAN AS A DISSERTATION at UCLA nearly a decade ago. In the years between the composition of my raw dissertation proposal and the submission of the finished manuscript, I incurred many debts that I am delighted to acknowledge now. I benefited immensely from the advice and support of my dissertation committee. Joyce Appleby pushed me to carefully consider precisely what was new about consumer culture in my time period, and her suggestion that I investigate school savings banks pointed me in a fruitful direction. Mary Yeager peppered me with numerous questions that prodded me to think more carefully about advertisers' motivations and strategies. Deborah Silverman introduced me to important works of European cultural history that helped shape some of the fundamental questions I investigated. In similar fashion, Cecile Whiting helped me to navigate the complexities of cultural theory, and she offered excellent suggestions for revising the dissertation for publication.

I owe an especially big thanks to my mentor, Regina Morantz-Sanchez, whose own work and teaching on gender history and family history had a great influence on me. Gina has been a steadfast supporter and engaged critic of my work. She read multiple drafts of the manuscript in its various incarnations as a dissertation and as a book, sometimes on short notice to help me meet a pressing deadline. Her comments improved the manuscript immeasurably, and her enthusiasm sustained me through the moments of doubt that afflict every writer.

Many others provided crucial feedback and support. Sue Gonda, Alison Sneider, and Anne Lombard offered excellent suggestions that improved various dissertation chapters. Margaret Finnegan read multiple drafts of dissertation chapters, as well as the entire book manuscript. Her insightful comments and conversations with me about consumer culture made this a much better book, and her friendship carried me through the many ups and downs of writing.

Numerous scholars influenced my writing and thinking as the dissertation evolved into a book. I was very fortunate that Miriam Forman-Brunell and Gary Cross read the manuscript for Columbia University Press. Their input made this a much better book. Leslie Paris, who read both the dissertation and the book manuscript, helped me to clarify key points and to think about children's culture in new ways. My work also benefited tremendously from the criticisms and suggestions of colleagues at UCSB, especially Mary Furner, Erika Rappaport, and Laura Kalman. Mary's perceptive reading of the entire manuscript pushed me to situate my work in broader historical contexts. At various conferences and colloquia, many individuals commented on my work. In this regard, I would especially like to thank George Lipsitz, Susan Douglas, Regina Blaszczyk, Michael Nash, Roger Horowitz, Jennifer Scanlon, Eileen Boris, Ann Plane, Robert Davidoff, Kelly Schrum, Lauren Lessing, Danielle Swiontek, Sarah Case, and Jay Carlander.

Securing permissions to reproduce the illustrations that appear in this book proved more challenging than I had imagined. The author and publisher made every effort to identify, obtain permission from, and acknowledge the companies whose work appears in this publication. More than one company expressed concern that granting permission might be misconstrued as an endorsement of marketing practices no longer sanctioned by that company. Daisy Outdoor Products, for example, noted that the reproduction of the vintage King Air Rifles ad (figure 3.5) does not reflect the manner in which air rifles are currently marketed. I am extremely grateful to Steven Rosen, an attorney with the University of California's Office of the General Counsel, for his diligence in helping me obtain some permissions.

My research was facilitated by funding from a Rosecrans Dissertation Fellowship and a history department dissertation fellowship at UCLA, as well as by grants from the Hagley Museum and Library and the Hartman Center for Sales, Advertising, and Marketing History at Duke University. A generous bequest from Ruth Teiser, my friend and mentor at the Regional Oral History Office, also aided my graduate studies. Several librarians and archivists provided valuable assistance in locating sources. I would like to thank in particular Jacqueline Reid and Ellen Gartrell at the Hartman Center and Lynn Catanese and Jon Williams at the Hagley Library. A tip from Kelly Schrum led me to wonderfully rich documents on the Philadelphia Savings Fund Society's school savings bank program that are housed at the Hagley Library. Other individuals kindly shared their recollections of growing up in the early twentieth century. Beth Plotnik deserves special thanks for helping me to arrange interviews with several of her cohorts.

I would also like to thank the *Journal of Social History* for allowing me to reprint sections of an article ("Revitalizing the American Home: Children's Leisure and the Revaluation of Play, 1920–1940," 30 [Spring 1997]: 581–596) that appear in chapter 5. Chapter 3 reprints portions of "Manly Boys and Enterprising Dreamers: Business Ideology and the Construction of the Boy Consumer, 1910–1930," *Enterprise and Society* 2 (June 2001): 225–258, which benefited from the excellent suggestions of Angel Kwollek-Folland, David Sicilia, and two anonymous readers.

The love and encouragement of my family kept me going through the long and often lonely process of writing. For their interest and support, I thank my sisters, Melanie and Karen Jacobson, my brothers-in-law, Jim Pearson and Jerry Schwartz, and my parents, Vivienne and Charles Jacobson. My parents, as it happened, also contributed directly to the book by sharing recollections of their own childhood consumer fantasies and experiences during the Great Depression. My deepest gratitude goes to my husband, John Majewski, who helped me in countless ways, from critiquing papers and listening to half-formed ideas to caring for our son, Sam, during my research trips. John read more drafts of dissertation and book chapters than anyone and did so with a sharp critical eye for better ways to focus my argument and tighten my analysis. His intellectual engagement, patience, good humor, and wit made writing this book possible. Sam, himself now a budding consumer, provided his mom with many joyful distractions and the support that only a vibrant, happy five-year-old can. It is to John and Sam that I dedicate this book.

ABBREVIATIONS

Ayer Collection	N. W. Ayer and Sons Advertising Agency Records Collection, Archives Center, National Museum of American History, Smithsonian Institution
Coolidge Papers	Calvin Coolidge Papers, Library of Congress, American Memory Website http://memory.loc.gov
DMB&B Collection	D'Arcy, Masius, Benton & Bowles Advertisement Collection, Hartman Center for Sales, Advertising and Marketing History, Duke University
Ellis Collection	Wayne P. Ellis Collection of Kodakiana, Hartman Center for Sales, Advertising, and Marketing History, Duke University
JWT Archives	J. Walter Thompson Company Archives, Hartman Center for Sales, Advertising, and Marketing History, Duke University
PSFS Archives	Philadelphia Savings Fund Society Archives, Hagley Library and Museum
Warshaw Collection	Warshaw Collection of Business Americana, Archives Center, National Museum of American History, Smithsonian Institution

RAISING CONSUMERS

IN OUR COLLECTIVE POPULAR MEMORY, the child consumer is a product of the television age and postwar affluence. Yet the notion that television was midwife to the "Youth Market" is as technologically overdetermined as it is chronologically imprecise. More than half a century before television enchanted the baby boom generation, middle-class children had become targets of advertising and prominent figures in corporate dreams of market expansion. Business courted their patronage in the advertising pages of juvenile magazines and enlisted their aid as selling agents within the home. Movie palaces tempted children with thrilling celluloid adventures, dime stores and candy shops drained spending allowances and spare change from their pockets, and department stores enveloped them in a juvenile dreamworld of lavish toy departments and stylish clothing.[1] To the delight of American business, children were becoming full-fledged participants in the burgeoning consumer economy.

If child consumers ignited corporate fantasies of widening profit margins, they also stirred fears that American families were losing control over the socialization of children. From the penny candy days of grade school through the identity-seeking phases of adolescence, children's consumer desires alerted parents, child experts, educators, and reformers to the challenges of raising responsible and respectable consumers. *Raising Consumers* examines how children were imagined and socialized as consumers during the decades between 1890 and 1940, a period that saw the flowering of modern consumer society and the gradual emergence of a distinctive children's consumer culture. The rich historical literature on consumer culture in this pivotal period, which privileges the historical experiences of adults, has understudied the cultural significance of children's consumption.[2] More than simply reperiodizing the emergence of children's consumerism, this study explores the social, cultural, and economic transformations that made the child consumer such a meaningful cultural invention. As historians of childhood have long recognized, the concept of childhood has different meanings in different times and places, and can thus tell us much about the anxieties and aspirations of the adults who conceived what it meant to be a child.[3] The child consumer proved compelling to late-nineteenth- and early-twentieth-century Americans in part because the child is such a liminal figure—ever in the process of becoming, seemingly more open to enlightenment or corruption and seemingly more vulnerable to the forces of historical change. Americans who valorized child consumers as conduits of novelty and progress, or who maligned them as impulsive spendthrifts, often projected their greatest hopes and deepest fears about the burgeoning consumer society onto the child. Child consumers thus figure in my story not only as economic actors and social beings, but also as cultural icons that helped Americans grapple with the promises and perils of consumer capitalism at a moment when its legitimacy was still contested.

Because Americans have lived since 1945 in what historian Lizabeth Cohen calls a Consumer's Republic—"an economy, culture, and politics built around the promises of mass consumption"—it is easy to forget that consumer culture was an alternative culture before becoming a dominant one.[4] Consumer culture's emphasis on pleasure and self-fulfillment challenged traditional nineteenth-century Protestant, middle-class injunctions against spending, immediate gratification, and loss of self-restraint. Perhaps most threatening of all, the new culture suggested that everyone—regardless of age, class, gender, or race—was entitled to desire whatever they pleased. Though consumer culture's democratic promises were never realized in practice, it nevertheless threatened to unravel older traditions of restraint as well as older hierarchies of status and respect between parents and children, husbands and wives, and elites and ordinary Americans.[5] Understandably, children's encounters with consumer culture compelled Americans to contemplate how they should prepare the nation's youngest citizens to greet the allures and dangers of this newly emerging moral order.

Child consumers also prompted Americans to think anew about the meaning of childhood itself. Many early-twentieth-century Americans found children's consumption unsettling because it raised profound questions about what constituted a protected childhood in an age of mass culture and mass consumption. Paradoxically, even as child labor laws imposed new taboos on the commercial exploitation of children, child consumers were increasingly exposed to the selling pressures of the marketplace and the sensual allures of mass culture. Some observers wondered how children could learn to live in consumer society without succumbing to its vulgarities. Others asked how children could be taught economic responsibility without also making them overly "money conscious" and de-

priving them of a carefree childhood. If twentieth-century American culture seemed more than ever to exalt the sentimental worth of all children—
to embrace children, in sociologist Viviana Zelizer's words, as "economically 'worthless' but emotionally 'priceless'"—it also made sentimental
conceptions of childhood innocence harder to sustain.[6] The Victorian notion of the child as a guileless innocent whose spiritual gifts could rescue
fallen adults gave way to a more candid recognition of children's selfish impulses and beguiling manipulations. The once celebrated child redeemer
had become, as one commentator lamented at the turn of the twentieth
century, a "mercenary little wretch."[7]

Such constructions of the child consumer underwent many subsequent
revisions, each a barometer of wider transformations in the family, the
economy, and the meaning of childhood itself. These broad shifts in discourse about children's consumption often registered across many cultural forms and texts—in literature, advertising, art, advice columns, industry
trade presses, and government publications—an important measure of the
child consumer's cultural resonance. One important shift occurred in the
mid-1920s and 1930s. By then, child experts had become more inclined to
see children's spending impulses as benign and manageable rather than
dangerous and insatiable. In childrearing literature and popular culture,
the savvy child consumer, disciplined not just to save but to spend judiciously, often garnered more praise than the thrifty child banker. Indeed, in
the eyes of many child experts, the overly thrifty child suffered more from
a deficit of imagination and personality than a surplus of virtue. *Raising
Consumers* seeks to explain how this positive revaluation of children's consumer identities in the 1920s and 1930s came about.

For the past twenty-five years, scholars have devoted much energy to
analyzing why consumer culture came to play such a dominant and defining role in twentieth-century American society. At the heart of these discussions have been debates about the relationship between culture and the
economy. Some Marxists have argued somewhat conspiratorially that corporate elites used advertising to create a mass market of compliant consumers for their surplus production and to channel frustrations with the
workplace into dissatisfaction with one's possessions and body.[8] Other
historians, finding business less concerned with social control than control
of the market, have also viewed the expansion of consumer markets largely as the result of corporate strategies to rationalize demand.[9] This dynamic is certainly not absent in *Raising Consumers*. American business had
much to gain by reclassifying children, a whole segment of society, as consumers. Not only were advertisers eager to open new domestic channels
for mass-produced goods, but they also embraced children as allies who

could help them consolidate national markets through their influence on family purchasing.

These top-down interpretations, however, miss the extent to which advertising strategies evolved in response to broader social and cultural transformations. Simply put, cultural change did not merely reflect the economic imperatives of corporate elites. Rather, *Raising Consumers* stresses how dynamic interactions between the market and new family ideologies, including new notions of play, helped to shape and ultimately legitimize children's consumer culture. In so doing, it also restores agency to the noncorporate elites—children, parents, educators, child experts, and reformers—who played a crucial role in both moderating and fostering a culture of consumption. In this sense, my study is broadly sympathetic with the approaches of other cultural historians who have argued that consumer culture's alliance with older and newer cultural traditions was vital to its success. Neither mass merchandisers' tantalizing strategies of enticement nor the development of national markets and distribution networks could by themselves account for the emergence of a culture of consumption.[10] The prism of children's consumption, however, focuses our attention on a different set of players and ideologies that helped consumer culture acquire such great cultural legitimacy in the twentieth century.

The study of children is a rich area for understanding the development of consumer culture, if only because examining the socialization of children gives us important insights into how American capitalism reproduces itself at particular historical moments. A variety of groups and institutions had a stake in children's development as consumers. The family, traditionally the primary institution of child socialization, faced an array of new competitors who sought to put their own imprint on children's acculturation to consumer capitalism. Advertisers, children's magazine publishers, public schools, child experts, and children's peer groups alternately collaborated with, and competed against, the family in its quest to define children's identities. At stake in these conflicts and collaborations, as some key players saw it, was the future direction of American consumer society—would children's consumer training rein in hedonistic excesses or merely contribute to the spread of pecuniary values?

Reproducing consumer capitalism was complicated by the fact that children's experiences of capitalism in the late nineteenth and early twentieth centuries varied considerably by class, gender, race, and even age cohort. Unlike their urban middle- and upper middle-class counterparts, many working-class and farm families expected children to contribute their labor to the family economy. Although working-class and immigrant children often waged pitched battles to retain a portion of their earnings for spending on movies, candy, and other consumer delights, limited discretionary funds constrained their ability to participate fully in the consumer economy. Working-class and immigrant children sometimes asserted an independent consumer identity as patrons of mass commercial amusements and the bargain basement, but often they were producers first and foremost and consumers on the sly.

By contrast, throughout much of the nineteenth century, white middle-class children had experienced childhood as a period of prolonged dependency freed from labor and adult responsibilities. They consumed rather than augmented the family income. Even so, consuming family resources was not the same as possessing a consumer identity. A consumer identity endowed middle-class children with a certain sense of entitlement, new ways of defining themselves in relation to peers, and new means of asserting independence from parental authority. This new child identity, I argue, emerged around the turn of the twentieth century but developed most perceptibly in the middle class during the 1920s and 1930s, when family democratization and the growing salience of peer relationships awakened mass marketers to the lucrative potential of catering to children's wants and desires.

Popular conceptions of child consumers both reflected and reinforced the different ways children experienced capitalism. When advertisers imagined the child consumer, they typically envisioned a white, middle- to upper middle-class child, somewhere between age nine and nineteen. Such a child was prosperous enough to subscribe to an advertising-laden juvenile magazine or well-enough connected to borrow a friend's. In advertisers' ideal world, the child consumer was also a boy. Boys, advertisers and children's magazine publishers thought, were the most exuberant consumers, eager to spend their allowances or earnings on radio batteries, bicycles, or whatever the newest technology happened to be. Boys were also the favored consumer caste because advertisers perceived girls to be far more flexible and boys far more rigid in their gender identification. Even as they sought the allegiance of both boys and girls, advertisers routinely privileged boy culture, expecting girls to embrace male heroes and male interests as their own. Because the realm of consumption was itself traditionally coded as female, advertisers took special care to associate boys' enthusiasm for consumer goods with manly enthusiasms for business endeavors, technological innovation, and modernity itself. By contrast, advertisers invoked more stereotypical notions of the other-directed female consumer when addressing the adolescent girl. While advertisers paid tribute to new models of girlhood that celebrated athleticism and adventure seeking, they also worked at deeper levels to encourage a conformist, peer-directed self. Adolescent girls who absorbed the lessons of advertisers and advice columnists—to say nothing of their own peer culture—learned that victory in the competitive game of dating was more likely to win peer approval than victory in academics, athletics, or entrepreneurial ventures.

Some children, of course, were excluded altogether from advertisers' pantheon of vaunted child consumers. Lacking both personal and family resources, black and other minority children did not attract the interest of national advertisers. Indeed, the only signs of black children in the world of advertising were the buffoonish pickaninnies that appeared as demeaning trademark characters in soap and cereal advertisements. Kornelia Kinks, the trademark character for H-O Cereal Company, for example, was forever getting caught in her attempts to sneak off to devour a box of Korn Kinks. Such depictions reinforced the idea that African-Americans were unfit to become full-fledged citizens and consumers. Consumer culture thus preserved many existing hierarchies among children, even as it enshrined the place of white middle-class child consumers at the center of the American dream of material abundance.

Although working-class children drew little attention from national advertisers, they were nevertheless often the focal point of popular concerns about children's dangerous consumer excesses. If the white middle-class boy was the quintessential wholesome child consumer, the working-class boy was the quintessential problematic child consumer. During the Progressive Era, working-class children became the objects of a wide variety of child-saving campaigns that sought to reduce, if not eliminate, child labor and children's unsupervised access to commercialized leisure—practices that flouted the middle-class ideal of a sheltered childhood. Progressive-Era innovations such as compulsory schooling laws attacked the exploitation of child workers, but other reforms—the creation of supervised public playgrounds and school savings banks, and bans on unaccompanied minors at movie theaters—aimed to regulate children's consumption by channeling their play into more wholesome outlets than movie theaters, penny arcades, pool halls, and even candy shops.

Supported by thrift advocates, home economists, the Women's Christian Temperance Union, and the American Bankers' Association, the school savings bank movement established roots in major urban public schools in the northeast, west, and Midwest during the first two decades of the twentieth century. Through the weekly ritual of Bank Day, in which children deposited coins into a school savings account, reformers hoped not only to limit opportunities for "foolish spending" but also to transform children into self-supporting citizens. In the minds of school savings bank promoters, children from all classes needed to curb their spendthrift ways, but lessons in saving and self-control were especially imperative for working-class and immigrant children who spent their nickels and dimes at potentially corrupting sites of commercialized leisure. As Progressive-Era reformers saw it, the best way to reform the problematic working-class child consumer, it seemed, was to suppress the formation of a strong, independent consumer identity in the first place.

Not surprisingly, the distinctive children's consumer culture that emerged during the interwar years replicated many of the class, racial, and gender stratifications of the wider society. National advertisers recognized white, urban, middle-class children as the most fully enfranchised child consumers, with boys leading the way. During the 1930s children's consumer culture became somewhat more democratized, as radio advertising extended consumer culture's reach to rural and working-class children. No longer limited to the typically urban, middle- and upper middle-class readers of juvenile magazines, radio advertisers made children's consumer culture a truly national phenomenon. At the very historical juncture that working-class children "joined their middle-class counterparts in a new nonproductive world of childhood," thanks to child labor taboos and compulsory schooling, they also joined the ranks of a national children's consumer culture.[11] However, while consumer culture provided children a common cultural reference point, it certainly did not grant them equal access to its rewards. Indeed, even as child labor laws erased a major fault line between working-class and middle-class childhoods, the mass market's growing role in shaping children's peer cultures made other markers of class distinction more visible and palpable. Children who heard radio sponsors' enticements to accumulate box tops for enviably bigger and better rewards quickly learned that purchasing power buys rank. Similarly, adolescents who matriculated at large urban high schools were all too painfully aware of how fashion and other consumer possessions impinged on their social standing. The "democratization of luxury" did not characterize children's consumer culture in the 1930s nearly so much as the democratization of consumer envy and consumer disappointment.

Although constructions of childhood often take center stage, this study also locates child consumers at the intersection of social and cultural history, examining them not only as evocative symbols of historical change but also as historical actors in their own right. Accessing children's perspectives and experiences presents a number of challenges, as few children left written records documenting their childhood. To compound matters, market research on children's consumer practices and consumer preferences was still rudimentary in the 1920s and 1930s. Advertising agencies often relied on crude measures, such as counting coupon returns, to assess consumer receptivity, and most often sought children's input by staging contests that asked children to write sample advertisements touting the virtues of a particular branded good. While social scientists conducted some extensive studies of the media's influence on children, most famously the Payne Fund studies of children's moviegoing, market research interviews with children did not appear until the late 1930s. Although limited in volume, market research interviews and contest data illuminate children's outlooks, aspirations, and consumer behavior as well as the criteria that advertisers used to size up their juvenile audience. Sociological studies and surveys offer both quantitative and qualitative information about children's spending and saving practices as well as their consumer ambitions and consumer frustrations. Autobiographies and oral histories, although they are adult reminiscences shaded by the passage of time, allow for more expansive commentary and reflection than most surveys. More traditional sources also enhance our sense of children as agents of historical change. Albeit written by adults, children's magazines, childrearing literature, and the advertising trade press all offer glimpses of children's consumer practices that won adults' approval or scorn.

These varied sources have yielded important findings that change how historians should look at children and consumption. One finding of fundamental importance is that children were conceived as consumers and became targets of advertising much earlier than historians have thought. During the decades between 1880 and 1910, advertising to children was quite limited and done mostly to imprint lasting impressions on future adult buyers. But even during this very tentative phase of children's marketing, advertisers began to toy with the idea that children possessed a consumer consciousness. Turn-of-the-century advertising iconography, trading on new cultural ideals of childhood that prized children as much for their spunk and savvy as their innocence, often celebrated the child's discerning, if not somewhat greedy, consumer appetites. Such images paved the way for even bolder departures in advertising during the 1920s. By then, advertisers had conceived of middle-class children as a more definable and viable group of consumers. Advertisers' enthusiasm for developing child markets stemmed in part from the recognition that modern childhood itself had become more organized around peer activities, thanks to compulsory schooling and the rise of youth organizations like the Boy Scouts, Girl Scouts, and Camp Fire Girls—all of which published their own advertising-laden magazines. Although advertisers sometimes misjudged children's aspirations, neither they nor most parents for that matter failed to recognize the growing autonomy of children's peer culture. This awareness emboldened advertisers to cater to children's sense of their own distinctiveness from adults as they attempted to discern, however imperfectly, the norms and expectations of children's peer groups. Increasingly, children's culture became inextricably intertwined with the mass market: just as the peer cultures of children and adolescents helped to shape the mass market, so too did the mass market help in turn to shape the peer cultures of children and adolescents.

Owing partly to their own middle-class backgrounds, admen and adwomen also sensed new opportunities to capitalize on the growing egalitarianism of urban middle-class families. During the decades between 1890 and 1920, rising divorce rates, relaxed sexual mores, and expanding opportunities for women outside the home made older family ideals based on sexual repression and patriarchal authority seem outmoded. At the same time, middle-class men, faced with routinized corporate jobs and dwindling opportunities for economic autonomy, increasingly turned to the home for pleasure and personal fulfillment. As middle-class men and women invested the family with new burdens and expectations, the hierarchies of the Victorian family were gradually replaced by more democratic and less formal relationships among family members.[12] Unlike its Victorian predecessor, the middle-class companionate family granted children greater freedom from parental control and greater latitude for self-expression. In many cases such egalitarianism also meant that children enjoyed their own allotment of spending money and a voice in family spending decisions. Poised to exploit these trends toward greater family democracy, advertisers no longer confined their interest in children to cultivating the brand loyalty of future buyers, nor even to expanding juvenile markets. They also aimed to enlist children as active selling agents within the home.

Middle-class families were hardly passive in the face of children's growing consumer clout and attraction to consumer culture. At the behest of child experts and educators, parents embraced new methods of parenting and money training that promised to restrain children's consumer excesses while simultaneously accommodating their consumer desires. Child-rearing experts endorsed allowances to give children training in spending as well as saving and justified them as an economic and educational entitlement in keeping with modern ideals of family democracy. As child experts saw matters, creating a play-centered home was just as crucial as systematic money training to children's development as judicious consumers. During the 1920s and 1930s, as middle-class children increasingly experienced the pleasures of mass commercial amusements outside the supervision of adults, parents and child experts grew ever more anxious about the growth of an autonomous youth culture and the erosion of family ties. To combat the allures of mass culture, child experts and other progressive reformers sought to revitalize the domestic sphere and modernize parent-child relationships. Rather than reject commercial culture outright, child experts exhorted parents to embrace its ethos of salesmanship and enticement in constructing a wholesome alternative playworld within the home. Experts advised parents to equip their homes with playrooms and educational toys, and to forsake their authoritarian ways for more companionable relationships with their children. By so doing, parents could transform children into respectable middle-class consumers who favored edifying amusements over cheap trinkets and passive spectatorship. Greater permissiveness, in other words, was the ticket to greater parental influence over children's consumption.

Such appropriations of commercial culture for conservative ends were emblematic of the symbiotic relationship between the mass market and new family ideologies. Just as the companionate family bred changes in marketing, the burgeoning consumer culture fueled and reinforced changes within the companionate family. *Raising Consumers* thus complicates our understanding of the dynamic interactions between the family and the mass market that helped to erode boundaries between the public and private spheres. Ironically, as parents and child experts sought to reclaim the home and family as the primary agents of children's socialization, the private realm lost much of its distinctiveness from the outside world of commercial amusements. Once viewed primarily as a place of moral uplift and spiritual rejuvenation—a sacred refuge—the middle-class home was now redefined as a realm of pleasure and emotional satisfaction.[13]

This blurring of boundaries between private and public life was part of a larger historical process that took many forms in the early twentieth century. Historians have documented the declining influence of separate spheres ideology in political discourse and public policy.[14] Innovations in architectural designs, such as the merging of inside and outside space in bungalow cottages and ranch-style homes, gave physical expression to the assimilation of public and private. More dramatically, domestic life increasingly began to merge with the public world of commercial amusements, as new technologies such as radio and later television moved spectatorship from the movie palace and the public theater to the privacy of the home.[15]

Some family historians have seen the erosion of boundaries between public and private life primarily as a story about external interventions that weakened the authority of the family. As schools, social welfare agencies, and professional experts assumed more of the family's socializing functions, Christopher Lasch has argued, the family also became more vulnerable to market values and ceased to exist as a "haven in a heartless world."[16]

Although the boundaries between middle-class family values and market values had never been impenetrable, the expansion of consumer capitalism in the early twentieth century certainly made them more permeable. Even so, Lasch's conception of the modern family as overrun by outside forces oversimplifies the mechanisms of change. As *Raising Consumers* demonstrates, the family was less a passive victim of historical change than an active, albeit sometimes unwitting, agent of change. Paradoxically, even as parents and child experts sought to shore up the shaky boundaries between public and private, they often weakened them in the process. The revitalized home might zone out the vulgarities of commercial culture, but not without incorporating some of its ethos of pleasure and play. Efforts to temper consumer culture's influence in the end only reaffirmed its hegemonic authority.

Children's consumer culture has sometimes been described as a liberating realm that provided compensatory satisfactions for parents and children alike. In Peter Stearn's formulation, children's expanding consumer freedoms compensated for the increasing discipline imposed upon them by more vigorously enforced school attendance, ever more demanding homework assignments, and the proliferation of adult-guided extracurricular activities. Parents willingly acceded to an expanding children's consumer culture, others have argued, because it allowed adults to participate vicariously in the playful, even primitive, pleasures of childhood that adults had long ago learned to repress and control.[17] Put another way, in yielding to children's consumer desires, parents were also nurturing their own "inner child."

By no means, however, did the compensatory allures of children's consumer culture entail the sacrifice of parental authority. In ironing out the proper balance between children's autonomy and parental control, *Raising Consumers* argues, middle-class families concealed more subtle and manipulative forms of domination within the more enticing promises of pleasure, play, and spending freedom. New ideologies of permissive parenting, so often credited to the post–World War II influence of Dr. Benjamin Spock, initially acquired salience during the interwar years, when children's consumption exposed deep tensions within the companionate family over the boundaries of children's new freedoms. Nowhere were these tensions more apparent than in family conflicts over spending money. Family experts recommended allowances as both an educational tool and a compensatory economic entitlement that could ease children's resentment of their prolonged dependency. Only by relaxing patriarchal control of the family purse strings, child experts contended, could modern, democratic families hope to keep spending money disputes at bay.

Children readily invoked the democratic rhetoric of family experts to argue for a greater share of the family's spending money, but parents all too happily embraced democratic reforms to serve their own interests. Beneath the greater permissiveness of allowances and the play-centered home lay a conservative impulse to reassert parental control and the primacy of middle-class aesthetics. After all, allowances gave children practice in spending so they might ultimately learn to save for better things that could be had only by deferring present wants. Likewise, play with the "right" kinds of toys in the "right" kinds of settings promised to strengthen children's allegiance to middle-class consumer ideals.

The bounded nature of children's expanding consumer freedoms within the family partially explains how children's consumer identities gained legitimacy during the interwar years. To be sure, children's growing consumer clout signaled increasing comfort with new cultural values that valorized spending, self-fulfillment, and pleasure seeking. But as recent scholarship by Jackson Lears and Lendol Calder has observed, the rise of consumer culture did not invariably lead to a hedonistic ethos.[18] Indeed, consumer culture's legitimacy hinged in part on its ability to remain in dialogue with the past—to suggest ways in which the consumer ethos of spending and self-fulfillment could be reconciled with older producer values that valorized self-control, hard work, and thrift. In the early-twentieth-century advertising imagination, no figure better illustrated how consumerism could balance the tensions between hedonism and control than the idealized boy consumer. Admen and children's magazine publishers glorified the boy consumer's expansive consumer appetites, but in courting the boy, admen imagined that they were selling to enterprising dreamers who used consumer goods to further worthy, entrepreneurial ambitions. Possessing none of the alleged excesses and irrationalities of the feminine consuming masses, the celebrated boy consumer studied manufacturing trends and favored rational advertising copy over emotional appeals. For the boy consumer, being up-to-date was simply the natural outgrowth of being a good businessman. His consuming passions offered proof that the consumption ethic need not undermine the work ethic.

This construction of the boy consumer has important historiographical implications, as it extends our understanding of the gendered discourses that framed how Americans evaluated the promises and perils of consumer culture. Much has been written about the long-standing associations of consumption with feminine excess and dependency in Western culture. Such views had softened somewhat in the nineteenth century, when women gained cultural authority as expert shoppers and arbiters of taste, yet stereotypes of the emotion-driven, weak-willed woman consumer persisted well into the twentieth century.[19] These negative stereotypes coexisted, of course, with more positive assessments that valorized the woman shopper as a rational, scientific consumer.[20]

But the much-vaunted boy consumer bespoke even bolder departures from traditional gendered discourses of consumption. New ideals of masculinity in the early twentieth century helped to disentangle consumption from its problematic associations with effeminacy and to construct positive masculine consumer identities for boys and men. Toy retailers and entertainment entrepreneurs such as Fred Thompson, who created Coney Island's Luna Park and other mass amusements, promoted what historian Woody Register has called "Peter Pan manhood," the idea that "a man, in order to achieve and enjoy the full benefits of American life, should never stop playing or being a boy."[21] But if the architects of a culture of consumption encouraged overly regimented middle-class men to rediscover the joys of eternal childhood, they also transformed the consumer exuberance of real middle-class boys into a manly virtue. Advertisers and children's magazine publishers imagined the boy consumer less as a joyfully irresponsible Peter Pan than as a cunning Tom Sawyer who used his powers of persuasion to satisfy acquisitive and entrepreneurial ambitions. In his enthusiasm, passionate loyalty, and eager salesmanship, the boy consumer embodied new ideals of masculinity that characterized both the successful corporate team player and the effervescent consumer, a personality that easily straddled the worlds of work and consumption. The complex interactions between consumer capitalism and new ideologies of masculinity thus preserved but softened traditional divisions between work and consumption and between men and boys. By legitimizing enthusiasm for consumer goods as a manly virtue befitting real American boys, admen and children's magazine publishers heralded the increasingly widespread acceptance of consumer culture in the early twentieth century.

The legitimization of the child consumer is also part of a larger story about the waning cultural authority of Victorianism. By the end of the Great Depression, when *Raising Consumers* concludes, the Victorian taint of sin associated with consumer desire had largely faded. Although many political and economic history narratives of the interwar years paint a sharp contrast between "the roaring twenties" and "the somber thirties," the histories of childrearing and consumer culture do not easily yield to such dichotomies.[22] The Depression, in fact, accelerated and reinforced the legitimization of children's identities as consumers. Advocates of thrift education, who had long struggled to reinvigorate the crumbling Victorian moral order of saving and self-restraint, found themselves on the defensive, as many parents and child experts concluded that lessons in wise spending were more valuable than lessons in habitual saving. Support for allowances grew even stronger during the Depression, partly because they were seen as a way to moderate children's demands during economic hard times, but also because childrearing experts came to see consumer desire as a sign of healthy psychological adjustment. This positive revaluation of consumer desire also reflected the shifting priorities and demands of the nation's political economy. At a moment when child experts championed spending's psychological merits, economists and New Deal liberals trumpeted the social and economic virtues of consumer spending.

The 1930s are also significant as a moment when children and advertisers began to gain the upper hand in the struggle to define children's consumer identities. While conventional histories of children's consumerism have mostly focused on how advertisers exploit children's gullibility and shape them into obedient consumers, *Raising Consumers* moves away from this model of consumer passivity and instead explores how children invested goods and spending money with meanings that reflected their own needs, values, and experiences.[23] Not surprisingly, children's consumer behavior did not always conform to adult expectations. However much advertisers and parents vied for the allegiance of child consumers, neither group could completely control children's own imaginative uses of consumer culture. As we shall see in chapter 6, during the depression-ridden 1930s, millions of children satisfied yearnings for autonomy and recognition when they joined radio-inspired clubs like Little Orphan Annie's Secret Circle or Post Toasties' Junior Detective Corps and received "free" premiums in exchange for proofs of purchase. Armed with secret passwords, decoding devices, and mysterious languages impervious to adult comprehension, children embraced the privileges of club membership as a road to empowerment. Membership in such clubs, however, also afforded many children their first lessons in consumer disappointment, when long-awaited premiums failed to live up to advertisers' hype. Children exercised their own limited form of consumer payback in choosing cash contest prizes over dubious premiums and in mocking exaggerated advertising claims. As childhood edged into adolescence, ridiculing exaggerated advertising claims became something of a teenage rite of passage—a proud proclamation of childhood innocence lost. Yet children's vaguely subversive appropriations of consumer culture were at best a muffled protest alongside the widening ideological supports for consumer culture.

Ultimately, *Raising Consumers* hopes to show that children, so often relegated to the margins along with those who hold little formal power, have a profound bearing on the mainstream. Not only did children become important players in the development of modern consumer society, with its increasing investment in market segmentation, but they also spawned a host of innovations in vital American institutions—the family, the public schools, and the corporation—as Americans struggled to come to terms with children's consumer identities. Children's consumption brought into focus all that Americans found unsettling and exhilarating about modern consumer society, and illuminated what various Americans most prized and despised in themselves.

CHAPTER 1

"Big Sales from Little Folks":
The Development of Juvenile Advertising

IN A JANUARY 1916 ISSUE OF THE advertising trade journal *Printers' Ink*, the well-established children's magazine *St. Nicholas* publicly chided "a certain food manufacturer (and his agent)" for failing to advertise within their magazine. Taking out a full-page advertisement, the magazine boasted that an impressive number of companies—"Campbell, Swift, Libby, Kellogg, Quaker Oats, American Sugar, Walter Baker, National Biscuit, Beech-Nut, Genesee, Hills, Borden's Post, Welch, Red Wing or Hungerford Smith"—relied upon *St. Nicholas* to expand markets and build brand consciousness among its nine- to seventeen-year-old readership. Educated to "buy by name," the magazine's young readers readily recognized trademarks because "they *study* St. Nicholas advertisements until they *know.*" Nor, the ad promised, could advertisers find a better way "to create active 'consumer demand' instead of 'passive consumer acceptance.'" For children invariably "have a way of . . . getting what they set their hearts on. There's nothing passive about *them!*"[1]

Seeking to awaken American business to the lucrative potential of children's advertising, *St. Nicholas* set forth a tantalizing vision of the child as an unproblematic consumer. Impressionable yet loyal, the *St. Nicholas* reader was decidedly brand conscious. More boldly still, *St. Nicholas* implied that children, with their knack for loosening parental purse strings, were critical allies in mass marketers' quest to expand and consolidate national markets for branded goods. After all, children could stimulate flagging demand where previously there had been only "passive consumer acceptance." *St. Nicholas* was not alone in voicing these claims. By the early 1910s, *American Boy* magazine was trumpeting the untapped potential of the boy market and the dynamic salesmanship of the boy consumer in the advertising trade press. Children's magazine publishers continued to press their case during the interwar years, when the child consumer became the focus of numerous articles in the advertising trade press and the target of advertising campaigns for everything from breakfast cereal and toys to big-ticket items such as radios and automobiles.

According to one estimate, by 1928 magazine advertisers were reaching approximately 12 million children, ranging in age from 10 to 20.[2] Children and adolescents encountered advertisements in movie magazines, confessional tabloids, and mainstream periodicals that enjoyed a primarily adult audience, but they also found ads in a growing number of magazines written explicitly for younger readers. Reaching a predominantly white, middle- and upper-class juvenile audience, *St. Nicholas, American Boy, American Girl, Open Road for Boys, Youth's Companion,* and *Boy's Life* enjoyed circulations that ranged from 80,000 to 500,000—all easily surpassing the 50,000 minimum needed to attract the lucrative accounts for nationally advertised branded goods.[3]

The Depression transformed the marketing landscape for juvenile advertisers. In 1933 *American Boy*'s advertising revenues fell from a 1929 high of $750,000 to $200,000, where they remained until the periodical shut down its presses in 1941.[4] *St. Nicholas* folded just two years later. The changing fortunes of children's magazine publishers, however, did not spell the demise of children's marketing. American businesses found they could advertise more economically through the radio and reach children younger and less affluent than those who typically subscribed to juvenile magazines. The Depression, despite causing the financial doldrums of children's magazines, broadened the child constituencies sought and reached by the mass market.

Despite such enthusiasm for developing child markets, historians have generally ignored or dismissed the importance of early-twentieth-century children's advertising.[5] Identifying the 1950s as the pivotal historical moment, scholars instead have argued that greater affluence, less rigid childrearing, and the advent of television awakened advertisers' interest in children's consumer socialization.[6] Such technological and economic determinism, however, obscures a host of earlier efforts to inculcate brand consciousness, ranging from school "enrichment" materials and advertising jingle books to magazine and radio advertising. While early-twentieth-century juvenile advertisers undoubtedly had fewer veins to mine than their 1950s counterparts, the veins they did exploit were nevertheless quite rich.

More important still, advertisers' early-twentieth-century courtship of child consumers illuminates important transformations in the culture of childhood and middle-class family life. Advertisers' initial conceptions of children as consumers traded on new cultural ideals that prized children as much for their spunk and savvy discernment as their innocence. Moreover, the emergence of the middle-class companionate family and the growing salience of children's peer relationships convinced advertisers that children had influence over spending decisions that far outweighed their limited ability to earn. Rejecting the strict hierarchies that governed Victorian families, the companionate family granted children more freedom from parental control, a greater say in family decision making, and in many cases their own allotment of spending money. Sensing these changes most profoundly in the 1920s and 1930s, juvenile advertisers no longer simply aimed to cultivate the brand loyalty of future generations, as they had since the late nineteenth century, but to enlist children as active selling agents within the home. With the aid of children's magazine publishers, advertisers trained children to recognize brand names and distrust goods that were not advertised in their favorite magazines. Advertisers also educated children in the arts of salesmanship, teaching them how to exploit parental sentimentality and the new egalitarianism of the companionate family. Children's advertising was thus not simply the outcome of strategies conceived in corporate boardrooms to manipulate consumer demand, but rather the product of dynamic interactions between the market and new family ideologies.

Advertising to children was nonetheless fraught with tensions and contradictions. In courting children as a separate consumer constituency, advertisers celebrated consumer goods as essential accouterments of a sheltered childhood while enmeshing children ever more deeply in the world of money and commerce. Some historians go so far as to argue that age-segmented marketing undermined the family's authority and pitted children against parents.[7] Advertisers' willingness to capitalize on children's growing independence and assertiveness certainly stretched and tested the egalitarian boundaries of the emerging companionate family. But advertisers also recognized that they could ill afford to sacrifice parental good will in their quest for children's consumer affections. Mindful of the tenuous balance between parents' concerns and children's desires, advertisers struggled to accommodate the interests of multiple constituencies within the consumer household. Ultimately, theirs was not a campaign to divide family allegiances but rather to romance the companionate family.

THE DISCOVERY OF THE CHILD CONSUMER IN TURN-OF-THE-CENTURY ADVERTISING

While a market for children's goods—books, toys, clothing, and furniture—had existed since at least the eighteenth century, market awareness of children as consumers and persuaders took much longer to emerge.[8] The first hint of this development occurred during the 1870s and 1880s, when national advertisers began supplying retailers with colorful trade cards that included a decorative picture on the front (sometimes bearing no relation to the advertised product) and the manufacturer's message on the back. Company salesmen distributed the trade cards to storekeepers as a means of building brand recognition, seeking to undercut older shopping traditions of buying in bulk or relying on the grocer's recommendation.[9] Storekeepers, in turn, handed the cards "to customers after a purchase or included [them] in the manufacturer's package as a kind of bonus."[10]

Some national advertisers hoped that children would also digest the advertising messages on the backs of trade cards, or at least serve as intermediaries in bringing advertisements to their mother's attention. The back of a Magnetized Food Company trade card, for example, instructed "the lively little card collector" to show the card to their mother, promising that the tasty children's medicine was "far better for their health than nasty pills, oils, and powders."[11] Many national advertisers, however, did not conceive of such advertising as a form of early consumer training. In the highly competitive cotton thread market, business leaders theorized that alluring trade cards, judiciously placed on store countertops, would help children decide which brand to buy, if their mother had neglected to specify one when she sent them on a shopping errand. To entice untutored child shoppers, Clark's O. N. T. Spool Cotton created small pamphlets of advertising jingles based on parodies of Mother Goose rhymes, hoping, as one advertising veteran later explained, that the appeal of a booklet or a "brightly colored picture to go with the spool of thread would decide the issue." Clark's goal, like its competitors', was to stimulate sales at the point of purchase rather than to convert children into selling agents or even inculcate brand consciousness.[12]

Children incorporated advertising into their play and their memory banks even before advertisers firmly embraced children as a consumer constituency in their own right. Directing such play from the sidelines, some clothing companies produced trade cards from which children could cut paper dolls and paper outfits representing the latest fashions.[13] Children enjoyed imaginary adventures with a cake of Fairy Soap in N. K. Fairbank Company's *Fairy Tales*, a complementary booklet of didactic verses issued in three separate editions between 1898 and 1903.[14] Other companies entertained children with mildly subversive little ditties, such as the one that appeared in an advertising jingle book published by clothier Max Baum in 1896:

> For seven years she spanked this boy
> With all her might and main,

But he wore a pair of "Hopkins" pants
And he didn't feel the pain.[15]

More often, advertisers encouraged scrapbook making—a favorite childhood pastime, especially among girls—by producing a set or series of collectible trade cards.[16] Even after advertising in mass-circulation magazines had largely supplanted the use of trade cards during the 1890s, trade card collecting continued to be a popular children's hobby. In a survey of 1,200 California school children conducted in 1907, psychologist G. Stanley Hall found that advertising cards ranked third among girls' favorite type of collection, just behind stamps and seashells, and eighth among boys.[17] Children valued trade cards for their luxurious color images, themselves a novelty thanks to advances in chromolithographic printing, and for the status that an unusual card or fine collection conferred on its owner. Competitive collecting sometimes even transformed children into volunteer salesmen who worked on advertisers' behalf. One enterprising schoolboy "became the envy of the schoolyard" when he amassed the first complete fifty-card set of Arbuckle Coffee's travel and history cards—a feat he accomplished by knocking on doors and beseeching housewives to purchase Arbuckle Coffee.[18]

At the turn of the century the advertising trade largely dismissed children as members of the buying public, but readily embraced the notion that children constituted the future buyers of tomorrow. Theorists of advertising psychology such as Harlow S. Gale and Walter Dill Scott argued that buying was less influenced by rational arguments than by unconscious decision making, including "suggestions" that advertisers implanted in the consumer's mind.[19] The plasticity of young minds made children especially valuable targets of advertising. If repeatedly exposed to trademarks and brand names, children could, imperceptibly and unconsciously, acquire brand preferences that would last a lifetime.[20] In the new advertising psychology, historian Ellen Garvey succinctly explains, "Childhood became the repository of a commercial unconscious, where early habits left their untraceable mark on adult behavior."[21] This alone made children's advertising a worthy long-term investment.

Such psychological insights hardly constituted a revolution in children's advertising, but they did point to a new way of imagining the sheltered child in relation to the market. The whole notion that children possessed a consumer consciousness long before they possessed purchasing power circulated broadly in turn-of-the-century advertising iconography. In magazine advertisements and trade cards read by adults and children alike, admakers depicted children as product endorsers, discerning shoppers, and voracious consumers. These portraits toyed with and sometimes even subverted more traditional iconographic representations of childhood innocence and purity. Already accustomed to advertisements that used testimonials from famous endorsers—the actress Sarah Bernhardt, for example, vouched for Pears' Soap—trade card collectors and magazine readers must have been amused by testimonial-style ads that endowed children with a consumer consciousness.[22] Here, after all, were the voices of the innocent, not the eminent or the powerful, urging and exhorting consumers to follow their advice. Combining purity and precocity, angel-faced babes championed the virtues of everything from Mennen's Borated Talcum Baby Powder and Clinton Safety Pins to Ivorine and Wool laundry soaps.[23]

Such advertisements suggest how the spread of consumer culture simultaneously buttressed and revised familiar constructions of childhood innocence. On the one hand, turn-of-the-century advertisers eagerly appropriated the innocent child to bolster their own public image, conflating the purity of childhood with the purity of advertised goods.[24] A reassuring emblem of industrial progress and benevolence, the figure of the innocent child helped to ease widespread concerns about adulterated foods and unsanitary factories. Yet advertising representations of children as product endorsers prized children as much for their savvy and discernment as their innocence. The precocious child, it turned out, was also a discriminating consumer. In a 1906 ad captioned "A Fair Judge," *McClure's Magazine* readers saw a bespectacled white girl, dressed as a magistrate and seated beside an empty cereal bowl, poring approvingly over an advertisement for Cream of Wheat (fig. 1.1). Early-twentieth-century ad readers might well have interpreted the ad's racial imagery—Rastus, the subservient black chef and Cream of Wheat trademark, has served the little girl—as further testament to the superior intellect of the child consumer. Here whiteness and savvy consumership go hand in hand.[25]

Indeed, what made child consumers such effective advertising icons was their seemingly magical blend of innocence and precocity. Too inquisitive to passively accept advertising hokum but too guileless to be anything less than trustworthy advertising spokesmen, a boy and girl featured in another ad let their pet bull dog attempt to rip an arm seam from their father's jacket to determine the veracity of the advertiser's claim that Belding silk thread was "an insurance policy against ripping."[26] Departing from Victorian idealizations of the passive, dutiful child—one who was meant to be seen but not heard—the children who inhabited early-twentieth-century advertising were far more decisive in asserting their will and their pleasures. These children were meant to be seen *and* to be heard.

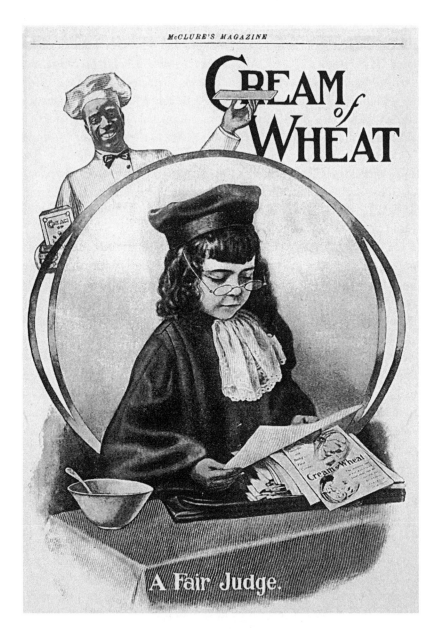

1.1 CREAM OF WHEAT ADVERTISEMENT IN MCCLURE'S MAGAZINE (1906).
Early-twentieth-century advertisers portrayed the child as a discerning consumer.
Reproduced with permission of KF Holdings. CREAM OF WHEAT® is a registered trademark
of KF Holdings. Courtesy Warshaw Collection.

The spunky, precocious child consumer that appeared in turn-of-the-century advertising hinted at a subtle but profound adjustment in the norms and expectations of middle-class childhood. Throughout the nineteenth century, the middle-class had sought to prolong childhood as a special period free from adult responsibilities and worldly corruption. Valuing children as "economically 'worthless' but emotionally 'priceless'" Progressive-Era reformers attempted to extend that ideal of sheltered childhood to working-class children through legal measures such as compulsory schooling, child labor laws, and evening curfews.[27] Children's induction as consumers into the world of commodities was thus potentially fraught with peril, as the sacralization of childhood fostered expectations that children should be shielded from commercial exploitation of any kind.[28] Yet exposure to the world of commerce hardly seemed to taint children's innocence when advertisers depicted children incorporating branded goods into their playtime and their school lessons. Maude Humphrey, a celebrated painter of child life, created a full-color poster of a little girl who used Ivory Soap to "launder" doll clothes.[29] Advertisements for Shredded Wheat, Cream of Wheat, and Pettijohn's showed little girls and boys spelling out the name of their favorite breakfast cereal with alphabet blocks and inscribing brand names on the school blackboard (fig. 1.2).[30] Such sentimental portraits of children's play at home and at school—the primary sites of sheltered childhood—suggested that children's engagement with commerce could serve wholesome, even edifying, ends, free from any taint of worldly corruption. In the advertising imagination, tutoring the child's "commercial unconscious" merged seamlessly with the child's wholesome world of play.

Other turn-of-the-century advertisements proved more transgressive in portraying children as discerning consumers with bountiful and insistent consumer appetites. Consider, for example, the tyrannical tot in a 1913 ad who shouts, "NO MORE EXCUSES! I Want A Penny NOW—for WRIGLEY'S SPEARMINT," as he commands his mother to "Buy It by the Box! Then you'll have it when I want it!" (fig. 1.3).[31] Such decidedly unsentimental portraits, intended as satire for adult magazine readers, humorously acknowledged—and even celebrated—the baser passions that animated children's interest in branded consumer goods. In a 1902 advertisement, a boy furtively devouring a box of Whitman's Chocolates and Confections was, according the ad's caption, "A BAD BOY but A GOOD JUDGE" (fig. 1.4).[32] A toddler girl, too short to reach the Mackintoshs's Toffee tin without using a hefty book for a stepping stool, had a "good excuse for getting into mischief," another ad claimed.[33]

Though devious, the child consumer might be seen as lending the consuming passions a more wholesome veneer by associating them with the in-

"This is the way I spell BREAKFAST"

Shredded Wheat

It spells HEALTH and STRENGTH for OLD and YOUNG, for WORK or PLAY. ALL THE "MEAT" IN THE GOLDEN WHEAT.

1.2 SHREDDED WHEAT ADVERTISEMENT, 1910.

In early-twentieth-century advertising iconography, the brand-conscious, yet wholesome, child consumer suggested that engagement with the world of commerce need not taint childhood innocence. Reproduced with permission of KF Holdings. SHREDDED WHEAT® is a registered trademark of KF Holdings. Courtesy Warshaw Collection.

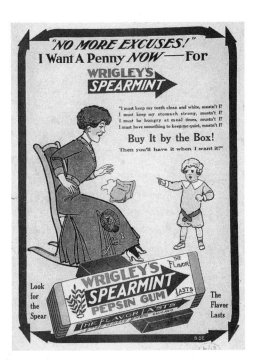

1.3 WRIGLEY'S GUM ADVERTISEMENT IN MCCALL'S MAGAZINE (FEBRUARY 1913). Advertisers sometimes imagined the child consumer as a demanding tyrant. Reproduced with permission of the Wm. Wrigley Jr. Company. Courtesy Warshaw Collection.

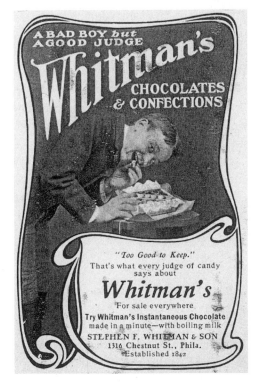

1.4 WHITMAN'S CHOCOLATES AND CONFECTIONS TRADE CARD ADVERTISEMENT, 1902. In advertisers' eyes, the covetous child consumer was discriminating, even if a bit naughty. Reproduced with permission of Whitman's Candies. Courtesy Ayer Collection.

nocent pleasures of childhood. But the mischievous child consumer imagined in turn-of-the-century advertising had greater parallels in the celebrated "bad boys" of late-nineteenth- and early-twentieth-century children's fiction. From Mark Twain's *Tom Sawyer* and *Huckleberry Finn* to Thomas Aldrich's *The Story of a Bad Boy*, the naughty, cunning prankster figured as an emblem of the spiritedness and spontaneity that many found lacking in middle-class culture. Simply put, parents preferred a little spunk in their child. Unlike their mid-century Victorian counterparts, who sometimes revered children as spiritual "redeemers" of adults, middle- and upper-class parents were now likely to view "moral precocity" with suspicion.[34] As Kate Douglas Wiggin, the author of *Rebecca of Sunnybrook Farm*, warned, "We must not expect children to be too good. . . . Beware of hothouse virtue."[35] Instead of prizing children for their spiritual gifts, many turn-of-the-century Americans exalted childishness as a repository of virtues that "overcivilization" and Victorian decorum too often stifled. Some antimoderns became fascinated with the Middle Ages as the "childhood of the race" and sought to recover the playfulness, spontaneity, emotional vitality, and capacity for intense experience they associated with childhood and medieval mentalities.[36] Advertisers spoke to such fascinations when they associated children's brand preferences with children's instinctive desires and natural impulses—even if such desires and impulses occasionally led to harmless mischief.[37]

By contrast, racist advertising caricatures of black children may have made white children's unbridled devotion to branded goods seem more laudatory to turn-of-the-century ad readers. As the trademark character for H-O Cereal Company, Kornelia Kinks, a pickaninny with bulging white eyes and exaggerated white lips, became the subject of a postcard series entitled the "Jocular Jinks of Kornelia Kinks." Repeatedly foiled in her attempts to abscond with a box of Korn Kinks cereal, Kornelia, unlike the precocious white children in other advertisements, never manages to get her way.[38] Kornelia Kinks symbolically attested to the allure of branded goods, but like the pickaninnies in minstrel shows and vaudeville theaters, her blackness made her a buffoon to laugh at rather than laugh with.

CHILDREN'S MAGAZINE PUBLISHERS AND THE EMERGENCE OF NEW CHILD MARKETS

By the second decade of the twentieth century, advertising had secured a welcome place in the middle-class home as a source of "news," humor, and even imaginative play.[39] A generation of magazine readers and trade card collectors had encountered images of children, if not actual real-life children, who actively identified with branded goods and incorporated trade names into their memories and their play. Eager to build on that legacy, children's magazine publishers began to push for a broader view of children's marketing significance—one that more firmly acknowledged children as consumers with distinct needs and interests, and the power to influence the spending of family and peers.

Several children's periodicals joined *St. Nicholas* in promoting advertising to children not just as a long-term investment but as a surefire sales booster. In a 1909 advertising trade press ad, *Boys' World*, a Christian weekly with a circulation of 300,000, promised advertisers access to readers who "absorb [the paper's] contents greedily" and "consider seriously" the goods advertised within its pages.[40] Its feminine counterpart, *Girls' Companion*, guaranteed advertisers an equally strong return on their investment. The "bright, intelligent" girls who eagerly devoured the weekly would not only retain "the graphic description of an advertised article," but "may eventually . . . purchase . . . that particular article."[41] By far the most aggressive promoter of children's consumer clout, however, was *American Boy*. From the 1910s through the 1920s, the periodical hounded the advertising trade press with ads celebrating the exuberance of boy consumers and their influence over family purchasing. As we shall see in greater detail in chapter 3, *American Boy* contended that modern, democratic families routinely consulted boys about family purchases and readily yielded to boy expertise on new consumer technologies such as cars, radios, cameras, and batteries. By advertising in its pages, *American Boy* claimed, firms thus not only secured an opportunity to make "their indelible impression" on future consumers but also gained access to "loyal, enthusiastic and responsive readers" who were "a mighty power NOW in helping to decide what shall be bought for the home."[42]

American Boy's promotional efforts paid off handsomely. During the mid-1910s *American Boy* began to swell with ads for bicycles, erector sets, rifles, and breakfast cereals, and by 1920 annual advertising revenues for the magazine had reached half a million dollars.[43] Perhaps it should not surprise us that *American Boy*'s claims found a receptive audience. After all, advertising images of children as product endorsers and discerning shoppers had accustomed the magazine-reading public to imagining the child as a consumer since the turn of the century. Similarly, the years between 1890 and 1920 witnessed a revolution in toy merchandising and department store retailing that had, according to historian William Leach, "place[d] the 'child world' on par with the adult in strategic marketing importance."[44] During World War I, the American toy industry owed at least some of its dramatic success to juvenile advertising campaigns that nurtured children's patriotic zeal for American toys. The Toy Manufacturers of the U.S.A., a national trade association seeking to squeeze out the already dwindling German competition, announced in juvenile magazines that toy dealers would distribute red, white, and blue American-Made Toy Brigade buttons to any "regular, dyed-in-the-wool, 100 percent American" child who pledged to play only with American toys. By the second and third year of the campaign, dealers reported that children often entered stores wearing their entire collection of buttons, "proudly showing that their patriotism was not of recent birth."[45]

It was the 1920s, however, that proved to be a major turning point in the field of juvenile advertising. Children's magazine publishers continued to sing the praises of the child consumer, but now the advertising trade itself had joined the chorus. A contributor to a 1920 issue of *Printers' Ink* acknowledged the growing importance of children's advertising, observing that "many advertisers of products ordinarily used by grown-ups have taken to the juvenile publications with the idea of 'catching 'em young' and 'bringing 'em up in the way they should go.'"[46] Egging on others to reap the rewards of promoting goods to children, the trade congratulated itself for "cashing in" on what had been a long neglected field. "It is within easy memory when young folk were not taken very seriously by the advertiser," *Printed Salesmanship* observed. "To advertise to them seriously, was a will-o'-the-wisp luxury, never certain of any definite, traceable results."[47] Results, in fact, were just what juvenile magazine advertising was yielding. "Not so very long ago," *The Printing Art* observed in 1924, "a manufacturer of batteries would not think of spending large sums of money in advertising to children . . . today, with the youth of the land mechanically inclined, it is one of the most profitable of markets."[48] J. Walter Thompson's 1922 advertising campaign for Keds shoes in newspapers and juvenile magazines proved so successful that the country's largest department stores— the Fair of Chicago, the Grand Leader of St. Louis, Filene of Boston, Wanamaker of Philadelphia, and Gimbel of New York—all clamored to identify themselves as the Keds retail headquarters for their particular city.[49]

The advertising trade's newfound enthusiasm for child consumers was not driven by immediate profits alone. Indeed, the old argument that advertising to children formed lasting impressions among the buyers of tomorrow continued to gain adherents.[50] Girls' magazines in particular urged advertisers not to pass up their "opportunity with the 'Mrs.' of the future."[51] However, the most striking development in the 1920s was a new willingness among advertisers to contemplate the short-term benefits of targeting children. Advertisers discovered that they could generate immediate returns not only by enlisting children to badger their parents but also by tapping children's own purchasing power. More and more children, a contributor to *Printed Salesmanship* observed in 1928, had spending money of their own, and could be "persuaded to 'save up' for a desired article."[52] Thanks to a rising standard of living and new ideals of family democracy, children, sociologist Robert Lynd noted, were now "buying more things . . . unassisted by their parents."[53] As the fashion editor of *Child Life* put it, "the child is no longer 'the customer of tomorrow' but of today."[54] Eventually, even "dubious" advertisers came around to the idea that children's advertising could yield "outstanding" results. An astonished food products manufacturer who advertised solely for the purpose of building "good will" among future generations reported an annual sales increase of $60,000 thanks to a $1,000 advertising investment in *American Girl*.[55]

Recognition of children as valued customers prompted retailers to think carefully about how their sales personnel could best tap children's independent economic resources. The successful retailer, a children's fashion editor contended, treated the child as an "exacting" customer, "to whom they must cater as they would to the grownup."[56] To meet the demands of child shoppers, some department stores began adding fitting rooms where young girls could try on clothing, as was already customary in adult sections, and hired college-aged sales clerks better acquainted with children's likes and dislikes.[57] Eastman Kodak proved just as unwilling to forfeit the spending resources of any potential child customer. Because spending "hard won coin" was a matter of enormous pride, child customers, *The Kodak Salesman* insisted, deserved "to be treated with even more dignity than is accorded to grown-ups." For this very reason, Kodak counseled its salesmen to avoid the common blunder of addressing child customers as "kid" or by any moniker that smacked of condescension.[58] Kodak retailers even sent letters to children who had received Brownies as Christmas gifts, alerting them to photo finishing services and film supplies that could be purchased from their local Kodak store.[59]

ADVERTISERS AND THE
NEW MIDDLE-CLASS FAMILY

A variety of parallel social transformations—the democratization of middle-class family life, the increasing salience of children's peer relationships and peer group activities, and the growing independence and assertiveness of children themselves—convinced many in the trade that advertisers and retailers stood poised on the threshold of a new historical moment. "The child of the hour is not so unsophisticated as in the older days," a contributor to *Printed Salesmanship* insisted. Better educated, "the youngster of ten knows as much of life, in general, as did the child of fifteen or eighteen when Grandmother was a girl."[60] Clothing merchandisers also believed that they were "dealing with a new type of child," one more worldly, "self-reliant and observant" than a generation ago. According to the manager of a children's and infants' wear shop, "Children are no longer passive buyers, to be shoved into whatever garments or hat their parents might choose for them."[61] Today's children demanded clothes that fit their own sense of style. Much to parents' dismay, such style consciousness seemed to afflict children at younger and younger ages. As Robert and Helen Lynd reported in *Middletown in Transition*, their mid-1930s study of Muncie, Indiana, third graders sported "rouge and brightly colored fingernails" as well as "Shirley Temple permanent waves." Worse still, family disputes over the appropriate age to get a permanent had become commonplace in Middletown homes.[62]

These disputes—implying that children had a real voice in family spending—were in part the product of the democratization of middle-class family life. During the half-century between 1880 and 1930, the urban middle-class family underwent a series of changes that came to the fore most dramatically and perceptibly in the 1920s. The trend toward smaller families of one to three children, most notable by 1910 among urban professionals and business groups, helped to break down rigid definitions of family roles.[63] Parents could now devote more personalized attention to each child, permit greater self-expression, and impose less strict discipline and obedience.[64] As children and childrearing assumed greater prominence in such families, rigid hierarchies gave way to more egalitarian relations patterned on ties of affection and companionship. Children's autonomy also expanded as middle-class families focused more intensely on satisfying the emotions of its members.[65] The new, more permissive childrearing practices advocated by child experts in *Parents' Magazine*, government bulletins, and women's periodicals called for "guidance rather than punishment . . . and a sympathetic understanding of children."[66] Children nurtured in such environments, in turn, came to expect greater sympathy from their parents. The Lynds found that high school teenagers ranked "respecting children's opinions" high as a desired quality in parents, especially so in fathers, who typically discharged family discipline.[67] Unlike their rural counterparts, urban middle-class children enjoyed not only greater latitude for self-expression, but more unsupervised time with their peers and their own share of the family's spending money.[68] Greater family democracy thus translated into very real changes in both the freedoms and the expectations of middle-class children.

Advertising authorities and merchandisers readily grasped such social transformations—owing partly to their own middle-class backgrounds—and often attributed children's consumer clout to the democratization of the modern family. Marshall Fields, a pioneer in child-oriented merchandising, justified its efforts with the observation that "children these days are listened to by parents much more than used to be the case. If a child is a firm friend of Marshall Field he can do wonders in bringing his parents around to the same view."[69] Advertising authority Charles Muller also related the rationale for children's advertising to the child-centeredness of the modern family. The strategy of using children "as bait with which to catch the adult consumer" worked, Muller contended, because "the boy and girl in the home occupy a position of respect" and "adults listen carefully to youngsters' preferences," often denying themselves for their children.[70] Parental selflessness on behalf of children's consumer desires proved a boon to manufacturers even in hard times. As a contributor to a 1933 issue of *Printers' Ink Monthly* reported, "Anyone who saw how sales of velocipedes, roller skates and similar products kept up last Christmas realizes that the younger generation isn't going to be held off by any thought of chaos or depression."[71]

By advertisers' lights, children, with their infinite powers to badger and cajole, were uniquely positioned within the family circle to jump-start adult consumption. "To use good old circus parlance," a *Printers' Ink* contributor wrote, "every parent is a sucker when it comes to children."[72] Throughout the 1920s and 1930s, reports of children's dynamic consumer salesmanship abounded in industry trade journals. Children's reputations as influential lobbyists for goods inspired *The Kodak Salesman* to enthuse over the prospect of gaining "an active salesman in each home" once Kodak distributors invited neighborhood children to an in-store demonstration of the Kodatoy children's movie projector.[73] The Charles Francis Press, a specialist in children's advertising, promoted its services to business executives who wanted to add the nation's 37 million children under age fifteen to their "sales force."[74] Merchandisers reveled in the notion that parental sentimentality rendered adults powerless before the demands of children. A railway promoter, confessing his reliance upon children to win "the undivided attention of an adult audience," told his advertising colleagues that "the oft repeated, 'please can I?' of the child often outsells more mature forms of salesmanship."[75]

To many merchandisers and advertising authorities, children's capacity to loosen parental purse strings seemed to work its magic best on mothers. As the family's chief purchasing agents, mothers proved particularly important agents of democratized family spending. While mothers once "bought according to their own judgment, regardless of the child's opinion," one advertising expert asserted, they now were "very much influenced by the child's desires in the matter of style." In light of such maternal deference to children's wishes, makers of children's undergarments and shoes, who previously confined their selling talk to mothers, shifted the focus of their appeal to children.[76] That mothers now relinquished some control over shopping to their children amply testified to the family's new democratic spirit.[77] Guaranteeing "BIG SALES from LITTLE FOLKS," an advertising firm specializing in juvenile appeal promised that its colored nursery rhyme picture cards would help business "Reach today's market—the Mother—through tomorrow's market . . . her Children."[78] Margaret Bartlett, testifying from her own experience as a mother of two boys under six, informed *Printers' Ink* readers that targeting mothers "may—and may not—reach its mark. But an advertisement that arouses a great desire on the part of the children themselves can hardly fail of results—for who can long resist the appeal of a child filled with a great desire?"[79]

Exploiting the full potential of the family's new consumer democracy, of course, involved more than simply milking maternal sentimentality. Advertisers conceived of children as a more definable and viable market in the 1920s and 1930s partly because modern childhood itself had become more organized around peer activities. Burdened by fewer chores and less parental supervision, the urban, middle-class child's leisure was, according to the Lynds, increasingly organized "not by parents and home, but by a variety of 'youth' agencies."[80] The fact that many of these organizations—the Boy Scouts, the Girl Scouts, and the Camp Fire Girls—published their own magazines provided advertisers a ready means of reaching a national audience of boys and girls with common interests. Even farm children began attracting the attention of national advertisers in the mid-1920s, when child membership in the nation's 4-H Clubs reached half a million, a critical mass indeed.[81] Advertisers frequently capitalized on children's peer affiliations by suggesting that their products could be used to earn scouting merit badges or enhance camping experiences. Even the "worst" camp cook could impress his fellow Boy Scouts if he took Aunt Jemima pancake mix on the next hike, an ad promised *Boy's Life* readers.[82] With a little help from Fab suds, *Everygirl's* readers learned, Camp Fire Girls could earn credit for a Home Craft honor bead.[83] Girl Scouts who washed dishes with Lux Soap, another ad pledged, received the added bonus of "beautifully smooth and white" hands while working toward their Homemaker badge (fig. 1.5).[84] By keeping girls germ-free, Lifebuoy Soap even promised to help Girl Scouts retain the stamina they needed to pursue multiple merit badges.[85] Though

Girls··
if you want pretty hands, *wash dishes!*

Betty says she "can't abide" doing the dishes—it makes her hands look *horrid!*

Now beauty experts have good news for Betty and all other girls!

For the Dean* of the National Schools of Cosmeticians, the best-known beauty schools in the country, says washing dishes *with Lux* keeps hands beautifully smooth and white!

These beauty schools use, in manicuring, the very same Lux suds you can use for the dishes! They find Lux so gentle to the hands!

Try washing dishes this beauty-wise way! Just a few Lux flakes are enough to make a dishpanful of bubbling suds. And how pretty and white your hands look afterward! Lux costs so little—less than a cent a day for lovely hands!

* Mrs. Pearl Ecker Hubbell

HOME-MAKER

Lovely hands for less than a cent a day

1.5 Lux advertisement in American Girl (July 1928).

Juvenile advertisers aligned themselves with children's organizations and children's peer interests by suggesting, for example, how their product could be used to achieve Girl Scout merit badges.

Reproduced with permission of Cheesebrough-Pond's, Inc.

American Boy lacked the institutional affiliations of these other magazines, its publisher proudly presented the magazine as "the principal organ in the formation and development of boy opinion."[86] As both shapers and purveyors of children's culture, juvenile magazines offered advertisers not just an avenue for reaching child consumers but a means of mobilizing peer interests into a definable juvenile market.

Eastman Kodak calculated that children's peer culture would prove an effective consumer stimulus when it announced in Sunday newspapers and mass magazines that on May 1, 1930, in commemoration of its fiftieth anniversary, the company would give away 500,000 free cameras to any child who turned twelve that year. Anticipating that "news of the gift [would] be the main topic of childhood's talk on the way to school, at every lull in their play," Kodak instructed its salesmen to prepare for an onslaught of new business from children of all ages.[87] As it happened, even Kodak was unprepared for the public's overwhelming response. Newspapers across the country covered Kodak's anniversary celebration as a major news event. In some communities, dealers ran out of free cameras in the first hours of business, even though May 1 fell on a school day. As predicted, however, demand for Hawk-Eyes, Brownies, and Boy Scout and Girl Scout Kodaks skyrocketed among youngsters of many ages.[88]

None of these broader social transformations—the democratization of family life and the increasing peer orientation of children's leisure—would have been as compelling if advertisers did not believe that children themselves possessed valued consumer attributes. In championing child consumers, commentators in the advertising trade press often delighted in the progressive spirit of youth itself. Nowhere was the construct of progressive youth embraced more enthusiastically than in the popular discourse of modern advertising. Much as "youth" today represents "a consuming vision for Americans of all ages," "youth" in 1920s advertising discourse represented a consuming attitude as much as an age.[89] "Youth is spendthrift, middle-age conservative," Ray Giles wrote in a 1922 issue of *Printers' Ink*. "Youth buys quickly, maturity brings a more judicial frame of mind into its buying."[90] Unlike a generation ago, Giles argued, today's clothes-conscious young men declined "father's leftovers." Equally responsive to stylistic obsolescence, young women paid more for gloves, hosiery, and undergarments than did their mothers. All this, Giles advised his colleagues, suggested that "youth—not the older-folks—should be the bull's-eye of your own advertising target."[91] *The Printing Art* even concluded that advertisers would be remiss not to capitalize on "this independence of spirit" and "begin working on tomorrow's market, while it is still in its toddling stage."[92]

As boosters of children's advertising liked to point out, not only did children constitute a more responsive market than adults, but they also helped to counter the consumer complacency of adults. Businesses designed marketing strategies around precisely such assumptions. In the 1930s, for example, Chrysler Motor Company relied upon children to break down adult resistance to the streamlined design of their new De Soto model. Giving away 150,000 miniature reproductions, Chrysler aimed not only to impress the brand name upon the children who played with the diminutive De Soto but to accustom the less progressive adults of the household to the new streamlined body styles through repeated exposure to the child's toy.[93] Businesses also found that children stimulated adult demand more directly. Furniture merchandisers, for example, viewed daughters as ambassadors of progress and beauty who refused to let their mother lag behind. Were it not "for the prods of the daughter who is ashamed to bring her friends into the house," a furniture advertiser observed, middle-aged folks would keep their furniture "forever."[94] Likewise, an experienced car salesman found that supplying the son or daughter with selling points usually assured a sale. "Father has the cash but the youngster has the real buying impulse. Father could easily worry along with the old boat for a year longer—son calls it a coffee-mill and daughter thinks it looks like an old barn."[95]

Advertisers' enchantment with the progressiveness of youth inspired even grander fantasies about using children to remake tradition-bound immigrants into exuberant American consumers. Some commentators in the trade press held out hope that immigrant children, once reconstructed through the public schools as progressive consumers, could wield influence over the "hundreds of thousands of foreign-born families" upon whom advertising messages were lost. "*They*, as a class, can be taught buying habits which are peculiarly of the United States," and, *The Printing Art* surmised, then teach their "sluggish" parents, ignorant of American customs, to buy more progressively.[96] Such ambitions anticipated the story lines of postwar television situation comedies like *I Remember Mama* and *The Honeymooners*, which performed much the same function of schooling ethnic and working-class audiences in the virtues of installment buying and spending rather than saving.[97]

Children also enchanted advertising authorities with their seemingly instinctive receptivity to advertisers' messages.[98] Unlike adults, who were "apt to talk back," children, *Printed Salesmanship* insisted, were "more plastic, more open to reason and argument."[99] A paragon of consumer pliancy, the impressionable child consumer became the object of numerous advertising fantasies. The Charles Francis Press promised the trade that children could be reached "with the least possible mental resistance."[100]

Though seemingly at odds, children's malleability did not undercut their precocity in the eyes of advertising trade writers. Impressionable but not naive, children were portrayed as discriminating consumers who resented being misled or treated with condescension. Uthai Vincent Wilcox warned advertisers who might exploit children's earnest receptivity that children, being "literalists," would "never quite forgive the magazine or advertiser who takes advantage of them and supplies them with an inferior article."[101] Nor, according to *Printed Salesmanship*, would children tolerate "shabby, hastily put together" advertising that lacked high-quality artwork and copy writing.[102] Ironically, admen and adwomen liked to imagine the unjaded child consumer as virgin territory for advertising messages, yet, as Wilcox intimated, this very innocence made children all the more primed for bitter disappointment when advertisers failed to satisfy their expectations. To avid readers of the advertising trade press, cultivating the brand loyalty of children must have seemed at once a delicate proposition and an opportunity not to be missed.

CULTIVATING BRAND-CONSCIOUS CHILD CONSUMERS

In the early twentieth century, advertisers and magazine publishers alike initiated numerous games, contests, and educational ventures to teach children an appreciation of advertising and train them in brand-conscious shopping. Publishers' investment in this project was at least as deep as advertisers'. As mass magazines came to depend more on advertising revenues than subscription sales, magazine publishers themselves became important players in the marketing system. Their economic survival hinged on their ability to deliver the right kinds of consumers to the right kinds of advertisers.[103]

One strategy magazine publishers used to attract advertising dollars was to supply advertisers who purchased space in their magazine with complementary copy that extolled the virtues of advertising. Mass magazines like *Ladies' Home Journal, Colliers,* and *Good Housekeeping* published essays that offered lessons in advertising fundamentals and credited advertising with having made significant contributions to material and cultural progress.[104] In the juvenile field, no institution more aggressively promoted the virtue and value of advertised goods than *American Boy*. To gain credibility as a profitable advertising medium, *American Boy* informed prospective advertisers that it was educating its readers in "the whys and wherefores of advertising" through "a series of articles . . . in its columns."[105] Having built up expectations within the trade about the exuberance of boy consumers, *American Boy* worked hard to make sure that its much-heralded readers did not disappoint. From May 1917 to March 1918, the boys' magazine published a series of monthly "Advertising Talks," which lauded advertising as a progressive force in American business. Signed by "the American Boy Ad-visor," the talks sought to educate *American Boy* readers about the workings of the market and to promote confidence in the trustworthiness and superior economic value of advertised goods.

American Boy made no effort to conceal the self-interested motives of its advertising boosterism. Informing its readers that advertising reduced subscription prices and funded the finest stories, serials, and illustrations, the editors urged boys to buy from *American Boy* advertisers and mention the magazine's name when writing away for special offers.[106] The magazine also made known its policy to refuse all advertisements for liquor, tobacco, cigars, cigarettes, and playing cards, promising its readers that *American Boy* accepted only those advertisements that honored the good character and best interests of its readers.[107] Advertisements that did make their way into the magazine, the editors assured, were valuable sources of information about new technologies and commodities.

Time and again the *American Boy*'s Advertising Talks stressed the trustworthiness of advertising and advertised goods. Only firms with the best products could afford to advertise because advertising put a company's reputation on the line.[108] "The success of advertising presupposes that the goods will be right," *American Boy* argued, "and if they are not right you can avoid them."[109] Since consumers were the ultimate arbiters of whether advertising lived up to its claims, business really could not afford to be dishonest. Honest advertising, the magazine argued, was simply sound business practice.[110] Such tributes to advertising's honesty attempted to dissolve traditional suspicions of advertising as an art of deception—a view muckrakers reinforced in their accounts of corrupt influence and exaggerated claims. In response to such attacks, advertisers launched truth-in-advertising campaigns and redefined themselves as "public relations experts" who informed and educated the public.[111] *American Boy*'s advertising talks corroborated the trade's rationale for professional legitimacy. Advertisements, boys were told, were objective representations of reality, untainted by carnivalesque excess or psychological manipulation.

At the same time that *American Boy* encouraged faith in nationally advertised goods, the magazine also fueled suspicion of unadvertised and unbranded goods. Analogizing the purchase of advertised branded goods to "doing business with an old friend," the *American Boy* suggested that any savvy businessman "would rather make a trade with a fellow that [he] knew very well and knew to be honest than with a fellow that [he] did not know and had never even heard of before."[112] Virtually no aspect of unadvertised goods could withstand comparison to advertised goods. While a trademark guaranteed the uniform quality of advertised goods, the same standardization was by no means assured when boys purchased unbranded goods. "The only way a poor product can be sold continuously," the *American Boy* argued, "is unnamed and unmarked."[113] Nor were unadvertised goods any less expensive. Advertising made goods cheaper, the *American Boy* contended, because it increased demand, thereby putting into motion the engines of mass production and distribution which invariably lowered unit costs and stabilized prices.[114]

American Boy was certainly not the only juvenile publication to underscore advertising's benefits to consumers. In 1928 and 1929 *Scholastic* ran its own ten-part series on advertising fundamentals to enlighten careerseekers and curious teens about advertising's "powerful" role in "modern economic life." The advertising industry clearly saw something of value in preaching their gospel to high school students, as each monthly installment was written by a leading national advertising agency or trade organization.[115] In learning about advertising's contributions to modern economic life, children were also learning important lessons about their own roles as consumer citizens. Advertising editorials taught children to see themselves as part of a national network of intelligent consumers whose patronage of advertised goods helped to lower prices and improve quality.[116] Such empowering rhetoric gave children nothing less than a stake in maintaining the national standard of living.

Another promising, if sporadic, venue for advertising boosterism was the letters-to-the-editor column in children's magazines. *American Boy* and *American Girl* used children's letters to remind readers not to ignore advertisements and to model good ad-reading habits. In an August 1929 issue of *American Boy*, boys who turned to the "In the Morning Mail" section could find a letter from Roger E. Lewis Jr., who so enjoyed the advertisements that he "read every one, and . . . some twice." Following Lewis's letter, they could read another missive from a subscriber testifying to the trustworthiness and educational value of advertisements: "They helped me a lot when I needed pictures for land, water, and air transportation in my science work at Junior High," Carl Weidner wrote. "I've sent away for a lot of things advertised, too, and found them just as good as advertised—and sometimes better!"[117] Letters from *American Girl* subscribers proved just as enthusiastic. In an October 1929 issue, Marie Louise Bell praised the ads as "the best ever!" while Charlotte Tyrus delighted in "discover[ing] something . . . of real benefit" from them. Eager to underscore the value of reading advertisements, the editor praised the two letters for suggesting how *American Girl* readers could get the "thicker magazine" they all wanted. "When we get more subscriptions we will have more advertising," the editor explained, "and that will mean more good stories and articles."[118]

Children's letters suggested that some magazine readers evaluated advertisements not as promotional literature but as straight news, undifferentiated from any other part of the magazine. As Celeste Gillette told the *American Girl*, "The advertising *articles* have helped me very much decide what to buy" [emphasis mine].[119] Publishers seemed eager to foster such misperceptions. In the September 1929 issue of the *American Boy*, the editors awarded the prize for the best letter "In the Morning Mail" to Harry Hess, who praised advertisements for their instructional and entertainment value. Hess wrote that he read the ads from cover to cover, even before reading any stories. "They are news. I believe the editors of the magazine want them to appeal to their readers as much as the stories." In Hess's mind, advertising even obviated the need for the science department that some subscribers wanted in the magazine. "Practically every ad contains something in the line of science, not only in the reading material but in the pictures used to illustrate them," Hess wrote.[120]

Magazine publishers redoubled their efforts to buoy confidence in advertised goods during the Depression, when advertising budgets tightened and public faith in corporate benevolence dissipated. *American Boy* ran another series of advertising talks, which appeared sporadically throughout the 1930s, to tout the dependability and superior value of advertised goods—attributes that acquired added significance during economic hard times.[121] Some advertising editorials even seemed aimed at rehabilitating public faith in the corporation as an institution that could be safely entrusted with consumers' interests. In language reminiscent of Depression-era corporate public relations campaigns, one talk urged boys to depend on advertisers as valuable "economic scouts" and "purchasing advisers" who would help them "get the last cent's worth for every dollar."[122] Though ostensibly directed at child readers, *American Boy*'s advertising editorials were also intended to reassure nervous advertisers, whose investment in children's periodical advertising declined rapidly during the 1930s. Advertisers and children's magazine publishers were particularly eager to vilify the purchase of less expensive substitutes for nationally advertised goods. In a talk entitled "Step a Little Closer, Folks!," the *American Boy* contrasted the veracity of corporate-sponsored national advertising with the exaggerated claims of sidewalk salesmen.[123] Such editorializing buttressed the claims of juvenile advertisers, who repeatedly stressed the "true economy" of branded goods.[124]

Juvenile magazine publishers also worked to gain advertisers' confidence by sponsoring contests and games that trained children to pay close attention to advertising. As early as 1904, *St. Nicholas* began asking child readers to create their own advertisements or solve puzzles using phrases and pictures found in the advertising sections at the front and back of the magazine. Encouraging the whole family to get in on the fun, one "*St. Nicholas* contest even invited its readers to create a shadow family of sorts: the Uptodates, who had experiences 'with modern advertised articles.'"[125] Continuing that tradition, *Child Life* staged a "detective contest" in the early 1930s, asking its grade school readers, with the help of their parents, to identify advertised goods shown on a page, write a letter explaining which they liked best, and list the products used by the family. The magazine then announced the results in the trade press as proof that advertising had reached its mark.[126] *American Girl* suggested that its Girl Scout readers try out a new game at their next troop meeting to determine who could remember the most brand names from a list of thirty-odd household goods.[127]

Advertisers, of course, employed their own gimmicks and games for building brand consciousness. Within the home itself, advertisers seized upon children's playtime as an opportunity to mold lifelong consumer habits. If so inclined, mothers could turn their child's playroom into a virtual "advertising nursery," furnished with lithographed cutouts, miniature stoves and dishes, doll clothing and bed linens, and other novelty samplers of branded goods—all supplied upon request from the manufacturer. "It is really possible nowadays," one jubilant mother exclaimed, "to outfit a nursery with things that delight children simply by . . . answering advertisements."[128] Her enthusiasm was apparently not unique. Ninety thousand mothers responded to Libby Service Page advertisements in women's magazines to request their special premium offer of a toy grocery store stocked with Libby's canned foods.[129] Miniature boxes of cereals and soap cakes reportedly enjoyed a "tremendous vogue" among children, who used them for "doll houses."[130] No miniature, however, could surpass the "Junior Store" as an instrument for building brand recognition. Equipped with play money, counter space for nationally advertised goods, and thirty-two empty packages furnished by the cooperating sponsors, the Junior Store gave children hands-on training in counting change and purchasing products by name (fig. 1.6). Every month, juvenile play store owners received an issue of the "Junior Storekeeper," which taught apprentice shoppers how to buy on a budget and reminded them to accept no substitutes for their favorite brand.[131]

Advertisers' efforts to inculcate brand consciousness even extended to children who had not yet reached school age. To lure such young prospects, advertising agencies sought the best creative talent in the business. Well-known writers of children's verses and illustrators of children's books commanded substantial salaries as ad agency hires—as much as $50,000 annually in one copywriter's case.[132] For maximum child appeal, admakers incorporated brand names into advertising story booklets that fashioned fairy tales and heroic adventure stories in rhymed verse. As testament to their allure, more than 50 percent of coupons requesting advertising story booklets bore the signature of a child.[133] These strategies were not entirely new in the 1920s. Since the turn of the century, admakers had created alphabet primer books lined with advertising messages and nursery rhyme jingles that preserved just enough of the original to be recognizable.[134] Advertisers hoped that children too young to read would recognize the nursery rhyme verses as "their own form of story" and demand that the ad be read to them.[135] Eventually, a *Printers' Ink* contributor observed, children began repeating the reformulated rhymes "with all the gusto they have had in quoting their old nursery verses."[136]

Advertisers also fostered brand consciousness by sponsoring contests that encouraged play with advertising. In 1929 Shredded Wheat awarded cash prizes to children for the best painted alphabet primer. How could

1.6 "THE JUNIOR STORE."
Children's toys helped to inculcate brand consciousness.

Shredded Wheat's name not become emblazoned in memory after coloring twenty-six separate entries, each with its own alphabet-inspired sales pitch—"G is for GROW. Which we all want to do. Eat SHREDDED WHEAT and grow healthy too"?[137] Prize contests for the best testimonial letters or sample advertisement proved especially popular with advertisers. One benefit of such contests, Ellen Garvey perceptively argues, was that they "prompted readers to try on the advertiser's role, and thus see themselves as having interests in common with advertisers."[138] Advertisers also used the contests as an important market research tool for learning more about the consumer preferences of their juvenile audience. Though unstated, this objective was plainly evident in the formulation of essay topics for prize contests. Daisy Air Rifles wanted to learn "Why the Daisy is the Favorite Boys' Gun" and offered prizes to boys whose ideas about interesting targets or new shooting games were worthy of passing on to other boys.[139]

Advertisers did not simply envision children as passive consumers whose wants could be molded at will, but rather attempted to discern their tastes and aspirations. In the end, some prize contests may have amounted to little more than consumer flattery—a form of homage to the hackneyed advertising refrain that in a consumer democracy children's votes really mattered. Nevertheless, many advertisers relied on contests to help them craft campaigns that, in the words of one advertising trade writer, "call[ed] to Youth in its own language."[140]

"ENRICHMENT" FOR THE PUBLIC SCHOOLS?

Advertisers discovered yet another promising venue for raising brand consciousness in the public schools. By supplying schools with "enrichment materials," advertisers cast an even wider net over the domain of children's consumption, reaching masses of immigrant and working-class children, who typically did not read juvenile magazines. Though ostensibly limited by the conventional boundaries of the school curriculum, advertisers spared little effort in getting their messages into the classroom and via the classroom into the home. Presenting themselves as teachers' helpmates, advertisers offered booklets, exhibits, and charts that promised to transform run-of-the-mill lessons into livelier fare.[141] A chart tracing Shredded Wheat's development from harvest through various stages of production and distribution became the foundation of geography lessons.[142] Commercially sponsored tooth brush drills and Lifebuoy washup charts assisted lessons in health and hygiene.[143] Coloring-jingle books featuring different varieties of Skookum apples and Flower Puzzle Booklets distributed by a national florists' organization enlivened nature-study classes.[144] All told, such exhibits transformed the classroom into a site for building faith in advertised goods and the corporations who made such wonders possible.

As envoys from the world of mass culture, advertisers infused their instructional materials with a potent blend of didacticism and entertainment. Procter and Gamble's elaborate "Cleanliness Crusade" spiced up character-building lessons with adventure stories and art projects. Teachers launched the crusade with "A Trip to Ivorydale," a story about soap production at Procter and Gamble plants, then treated children to "The Cruise of the Ivory Ship," an illustrated fairy tale laden with the "imperial rhetoric" and racial overtones common to many early-twentieth-century soap advertisements.[145] Dramatizing the adventures of Betty Snow and Bobby White on a cannibal island inhabited by "Muddy Men," the story celebrates the triumph of civilization over savagery when the child heroes tie up filthy natives and scrub them with Ivory Soap. For the crusade's coup de grace, teachers taught children how to create floating yachts, animals, and other sculptures from Ivory Soap.[146] Other advertisers tried to recreate the spectacular atmosphere of a vaudeville theater by hiring stuntsmen to hawk their goods before filled school auditoriums. The manufacturers of Toddy drink mix, for instance, employed an athlete to perform "physical culture stunts" and lecture students on how healthful food products such as Toddy contributed to athletic prowess.[147]

Teachers and teaching organizations proved remarkably receptive to corporate-sponsored innovations in the curriculum. Because restrictive school budgets often curtailed the use of visual aids, teachers were ever on the lookout for inexpensive materials to invigorate lessons.[148] Shredded Wheat, in fact, received fifty to one hundred requests a day after taking out a small ad in a school journal, and within "a very short time" had distributed about 5,000 school charts describing the cereal's production and distribution.[149] Advertising trade writers reported that many advertisers found themselves unprepared for "the avalanche of requests" they received. The demand for "industrial education material" proved so great, one writer noted, that "many teachers, not being able to get the sort they want, [made] up their own by cutting illustrations from current advertisements and arranging them . . . to tell a story."[150] Teachers even initiated the creation of corporate-sponsored education materials. In response to requests from schools for information about gum and its manufacture, Wrigley created a booklet, "Chewing Gum—What It Is and How It Is Made," for use in seventh-grade geography classes.[151]

Advertisers proved equally inventive in getting their messages from the schoolroom into the home. Advertisements placed on school-book covers not only carried sales messages into the home, but, as one manufacturer noted, they "stay[ed] on the job for the entire school year."[152] More typically, advertisers relied upon direct social pressure from teachers and children to enlist the consumer patronage of mothers. Palmolive distributed cards that asked children to sign a pledge that could not be fulfilled without adding the soap to mother's shopping list: "Dear Teacher: I promise to wash my face and hands with my little cake of Palmolive Soap before every meal and before going to bed until it is all used up."[153] The extent of voluntary teacher-advertiser collaboration in matters of health and hygiene was quite impressive. The education journal *Normal Instructor—Primary Plans* placed several advertisements in *Printers' Ink* announcing that teachers would co-operate with manufacturers of products that benefited the child's health and hygiene—"even to the extent of advocating its use in the home."[154]

In the late 1920s, teachers in some 70,000 schools across the country did just that when they embraced Cream of Wheat's plan to encourage regular consumption of hot breakfast cereals. The program required little preplanning, as Cream of Wheat supplied an instruction manual, graded contest devices, prizes, and breakfast charts free of charge.[155] At the end of a month-long trial period, teachers asked mothers to return a card affirming that their children had eaten a hot breakfast cereal three times a week.[156] Guided by concern for children's health and enlightened self-interest, teachers saw the plan as a way to make children more attentive and better behaved.[157] An intensified national interest in improving children's health during the 1920s, sparked by reports of the poor health of many World War I draftees, undoubtedly made selling the plan easier.[158] Leaving nothing to chance, however, Cream of Wheat launched a massive advertising campaign to promote the plan in leading women's magazines and newspapers (fig. 1.7).[159] Cream of Wheat presented itself as a benevolent corporate adjunct to the Parent-Teacher's Association, eager to help mothers and teachers find solutions to common childrearing problems, but its methods were highly manipulative.[160] Failure to cooperate could prove embarrassing, the ads implied, as every day, "in thousands of schools" teachers asked for a show of hands to determine how many children "had their *hot, cooked* cereal this morning."[161]

School advertising was not without its critics. In newspaper editorials and some education circles, business came under attack for diverting "school facilities to its own selfish purposes." Though operating under the guise of promoting public welfare, business, by its own admission, eagerly sought the brand loyalty of school children and their families. Even defenders of school advertising conceded that business crossed the line when they offered cash prizes to students who wrote the best essays on behalf of their product.[162] What most galled critics about corporate education materials,

Now a Daily Question in Thousands of Schools

"How many have had their hot, cooked cereal this morning?" In thousands of schools this question is now asked every day. Hot, cooked cereal for breakfast has become Rule Number One in many school health programs.

Children Asked to Report Every Morning on This Care Which Mothers Give

Few mothers have realized that children are actually handicapped both at study and at play when this precaution is overlooked. Now it has become the center of interest in a nation-wide health campaign.

In over 70,000 school rooms this slogan today hangs on the walls:

"Every boy and girl needs a hot cereal breakfast"

Day after day teachers are asking their pupils to answer this question: "Did you have your *hot, cooked* cereal this morning?"

Only a *hot, cooked* cereal, so tests in many cities have shown, can give children the energy needed to meet the strain of school work.

For over 30 years, authorities have recommended one *hot, cooked* cereal children love—Cream of Wheat.

It supplies in abundance just the mental and physical energy needed most by little minds and bodies. And Cream of Wheat, since it contains none of the harsh indigestible parts of the wheat, is quickly and easily digested even by the most delicate stomach. Give it to your children regularly. Cream of Wheat Company, Minneapolis, Minn.

Children are often slow to learn and inattentive simply because they have not eaten the right kind of breakfast. That is why school authorities everywhere are now urging a hot, cooked cereal for youngsters every morning

---

1.7 CREAM OF WHEAT NEWSPAPER ADVERTISEMENT, JANUARY 1928.
Cream of Wheat involved mothers and teachers in its national campaign to make children's consumption of hot breakfast cereal a daily routine. Reproduced with permission of KF Holdings. CREAM OF WHEAT® is a registered trademark of KF Holdings. Courtesy JWT Archives.

however, was not their thinly disguised sales promotion but their "production-mindedness." Students were taught about the manufacturing processes of everything from gum and cereal to shoes and cars, but nothing about how to measure quality, durability, or fair pricing.[163] Even in home economics courses, "traditional household productive skills such as canning, baking, and sewing" received more attention than instruction in smart shopping.[164] Until the mid-1930s, when the consumer education movement got underway, schools themselves provided no substantive counterpoint to the claims of modern advertising. In a 1932 article boldly headlined "CRITICIZING THE ADVERTISEMENTS," *Scholastic* magazine, the high school weekly, taught readers how to identify effective advertising layouts and artful graphic design. *Scholastic*'s advertising "criticism" was in reality a lesson in advertising appreciation. Not surprisingly, Consumers' Research, a leading consumer education group, charged that the schools churned out young people "who cannot select tooth powder intelligently or . . . refrain from urging his parents to purchase the latest model radio or pseudo-streamlined car."[165]

While advertising trade writers concurred that it was unwise to overstress the advertising viewpoint in education materials, the standard for measuring what constituted "out-and-out" advertising was remarkably flexible.[166] John Allen Murphy, for example, upheld "A Day in the Palmolive Factory" as a model effort, arguing that it was "by no means an advertising publication," even though the company name and its products were mentioned throughout the booklet. Nor did he fault Lever Brother's campaign to promote Lifebuoy Soap, even though it was conceived as a way to accustom children to the soap before they developed a prejudice against its distinctive smell—an odor produced by the presence of carbolic acid.[167] Indeed, advertising practitioners like Evalyn Grumbine, the advertising manager for *Child Life*, continued to insist that advertisers provided a valuable public service by recognizing childhood as a "golden age" for arousing lifelong interests.[168] As a devotee of psychologist Alfred Adler, Grumbine came by her interest in nurturing children's developmental needs honestly. In the end, however, advertisers' devotion to stimulating children's lifelong interests belied a much stronger commitment to nurturing children's developmental progression as consumers.

IMAGINING THE CONSUMER HOUSEHOLD

When early-twentieth-century advertisers began imagining children as consumers in their own right, they confronted a dilemma that, to varying degrees, has plagued them ever since: how to master the art of winning "juvenile good will" without sacrificing "the good will of the parent."[169] Admittedly, one advertising trade writer observed in 1920, children were "allowed much greater latitude" in their spending allowances and choices than a generation ago, but parents still had "a very natural objection to letting their children get expensive ideas into their heads."[170] Even so, there were dangers in bowing too deeply to parental authority. As the J. Walter Thompson *News Bulletin* argued, advertisers needed to acquire "a sympathetic understanding of the . . . innermost desires and . . . rooted aversions" of each family member in the consumer household.[171] Advertisers who used the same appeal to reach Mrs. Consumer as they did to reach "the oldest Consumer boy, an adolescent of sixteen," or the youngest child could not possibly hope to "crystallize" the child's "buying *appetite*."[172]

Early-twentieth-century advertisers saw the family as a consumer democracy in which both children and adults had a say, but they also struggled to strike the right balance in addressing children's desires and parents' concerns (fig. 1.8). Overt parental appeals that linked children's consumption to nutrition and achievement often appeared in children's advertising, in sharp contrast to the utopian emphasis on pleasure and antiauthoritarian values that predominated in late-twentieth-century children's advertising.[173] Yet in many respects, juvenile advertising in the 1920s and 1930s was remarkably bold in its efforts to empower children within a consumer democracy. Advertisements in children's magazines literally instructed children how to lobby their parents for new purchases, supplying them with sales ammunition that appealed to pressing parental concerns. An advertisement for Structo engineering toys put a boy's manhood and future success on the line when it instructed boys to "Tell Dad you want STRUCTO because it will teach you to think for yourself, to create ideas of your own, to make you think as *men* think."[174] Similarly, an ad listing "10 Reasons Why You Should Have 'Chicago' Rubber Tire Roller Skates" provided girls with health and beauty arguments to use on their parents. "Tell Daddy and Mother," the ad urged, that skates help "build sturdy bodies and stronger ankles" as well as develop "poise and graceful actions."[175]

While advertising trade guidelines in the late twentieth century advised advertisers not to urge children "to ask parents or others to buy products," early-twentieth-century advertisers exhibited no such compunctions.[176] With boldfaced headlines like "Please—Father—Please" screaming from the top of the page (fig. 1.9), advertisements routinely sanctioned begging and the old childhood standby—buttering up mom and dad.[177] A comic-strip advertisement narrating "How Tom Got His Train," for example, depicted Tom offering a light for his father's cigarette before pointing out the coveted train in a catalog.[178] Elgin watch ads urged girls to corner Dad

1.8 PUFFED GRAINS CEREAL ADVERTISEMENT IN YOUTH'S COMPANION (MAY 20, 1920).

Advertisers depicted the family as a consumer democracy in which children and adults had an equal say. Reproduced with permission of The Quaker Oats Company. Courtesy Security Pacific Collection, Los Angeles Public Library.

1.10 Cartoon in American Boy (December 1939). Though unwilling to promote particular brands, children's magazine publishers sanctioned the practice of lobbying parents for goods by offering children tips on bargaining strategies, as this cartoon does.

after dinner, when he was comfortably settled in "his big easy chair."[179] Recommending the use of flattery and pragmatic appeals, Elgin scripted a sales pitch destined to win over dad:

> Suppose you whispered to Dad tonight, "Mother ought to have a new ELGIN watch" . . . And suppose *he* said, "Humph! Is that *so*! And what makes you think *that*, young woman?" . . . And suppose *you* said, "Because Mother is the nicest person in the world . . . except maybe you . . . And then besides *I'd* be able to have the watch Mother wears now. And *you'd* be giving two gifts for the price of one!"[180]

Ads like these transformed what it meant to be an enterprising child in the early twentieth century. The iconography of success increasingly centered on feats in the realm of consumption, as the clever child exercised his or her pluck and wit through determined salesmanship inside the family circle (fig. 1.10).

Advertisers would not have dared compose such specific family dialogues had children's requests not already become an accepted part of middle-class family dynamics. Even so, advertisers' detailed instructions suggest that they may have needed to stretch the boundaries of the democratic family further than was customary. Carefully scripted sales pitches gave children permission and encouragement to pester their parents and made parental resistance harder to sustain. That late-twentieth-century advertising trade guidelines urged advertisers to avoid such tactics may ultimately be less a testament to improved advertising scruples than a measure of just how deeply entrenched patterns of child begging and parental acquiescence eventually became.[181]

The impact of advertisers' new tactics undoubtedly fell hardest on the family breadwinner. Although fathers had traditionally borne the responsibility to provide for their families, the emerging culture of consumption, historian Robert Griswold has observed, "gave new meaning to this obligation and put middle-class fathers to the test."[182] Advertisers advised boys and girls to play on the breadwinner's vulnerability in distinctively gender-appropriate ways. While boys could lobby dad directly on their own behalf, hint-dropping became the favored way for "nice little girl[s]" to get what they wanted "without even asking." In the Elgin watch ads "clever" girls even made it seem as if they were lobbying on others' behalf. Bargaining for a new watch for mother and mother's old watch for herself allowed the girl solicitor to retain the semblance of self-sacrificing femininity (fig 1.11).[183] But it also suggested that mother-daughter consumer alliances posed a particularly formidable threat to the breadwinner's prerogatives.

This Little Girl has just thought how to get a wrist watch!

Sometimes, if you're *very* clever, you can get things without even asking for them. This little girl has just thought of a happy plan for having a watch of her own. She's going to whisper to Daddy to give Mother a new wrist watch. Then *she* will inherit the watch Mother has now. So everybody will be happy. Isn't that a good idea?

You see, ELGIN watches really are the loveliest, smartest, finest watches of all. So any mother would be tickled pink to have one. And they come in such a variety of grades . . . all the way from diamond set cases at $260. down to the new, *chic* Parisiennes at $35. So Father will have a wide choice and can give Mother just the watch he feels he can afford . . . and whichever one he chooses, it will be beautiful.

So you'd be doing Father a favor, too . . . helping him select such a perfect gift. And Mother will be delighted . . . and *you* will have Mother's present watch to wear for your very own!

15 jewel movement . . . exquisite mesh strap instead of the usual ribbon $55

Parisienne, designed by Louiseboulanger. In blue or black and white enamel $35

1.11 ELGIN WATCH ADVERTISEMENT IN CHILD LIFE (APRIL 1929).

According to this ad, clever, enterprising girls learned to get what they wanted through gender-appropriate means: by asking indirectly rather than bargaining aggressively. Reproduced with permission of M Z Berger.

In justifying the pressure children exerted on fathers, juvenile advertisers heralded the arrival of a new kind of dad—one at once more generous and sympathetic. "The Dads of today," a 1932 American Flyer train catalog insisted, "are different—they plan on their boys having better things than they had."[184] By the same token, fathers' failures to provide were equated with failures of fatherly understanding. One ad, showing a boy longingly watching two other boys ride bicycles, laid blame on the father for the lonely plight of the bike-deprived boy. "Left all alone again—cut off from his friends—denied their healthy, boyish fun and companionship! If this is *your* fix," the ad deplored, "show this to dad!"[185]

While some parents may have deplored advertisers' encouragement of begging and lobbying as cynical manipulation, commentators in the advertising trade press proffered a much more benign interpretation of advertisers' motives. Far from seeking to circumvent parental authority, advertisers claimed they were really out to promote companionate family relations. "One of the most pleasing aspects of these special campaigns in children's magazines," *The Printing Art* contended, "is the spirit of comradeship engendered in the parents and their children—the get-together spirit . . . Children are invited to 'talk things over with Dad,' or to 'take their little problems to mother.'"[186] Even if *The Printing Art* conflated means and outcomes, the journal nonetheless captured a key dynamic of children's advertising in the early twentieth century: advertisers courted children not as rebels against parental authority but as seekers of parental companionship. In contrast to the cultural stereotype of flappers flouting tradition, the iconography of the child lobbyist generated images of intergenerational harmony and cooperation. Numerous advertisements, captioned "Show this to Father" or "Talk it over with Dad," represented the child lobbyist as a boy seated next to his father, engaged in friendly discussion of a magazine advertisement (fig. 1.12).[187]

Nowhere was the celebration of companionate family values more evident than in advertising campaigns that celebrated father-son companionship. Throughout the 1920s and 1930s, family experts advocated new models of parenting that idealized the father as a playmate to his children.[188] Advertisers promised to help turn those ideals into reality for every boy. Membership in "The Father and Son Library," one bookseller told boys, could transform patriarchal fathers from aloof grown-ups into the pals that every boy desired. Since joining the reading club, one boy's father, never before inclined "to take a hand in fixing up the swimming hole, or taking that hike Saturday," had become, to the boy's delight, "one of the bunch."[189] Train catalogs promised similar rewards: "Thousands of Dads and sons better understand each other and more fully learn the value of

Talk it over
with Dad

Dad wants you to be a leader now in your school, in your club, and in everything you do.

And he hopes that some day you will become a leader of men.

Boys everywhere find that the Remington Portable typewriter assists them greatly in their school work. Many make money by doing typing for others. The fact that they have Remingtons makes them the envied ones of their crowd. In addition to the fun they are having now by doing all of their writing on a Remington Portable, they are laying a most substantial foundation for future years.

Your Dad knows the importance of the typewriter in the business world. Tell him you want to be a leader of boys now, and a leader of men later. Tell him you need a Remington Portable. He'll be pleased that you're showing such interest in yourself. Let us send you "For You—For Everybody".

Address Department 66
REMINGTON TYPEWRITER COMPANY
374 Broadway, New York

See the Keys

This is the Portable Typewriter with the one and only complete keyboard — exactly like the big machines. Compact, light and easily carried in a handy case.

Sold by all Remington branches and over 3,000 dealers. Easy payment terms if desired.

REMINGTON
Portable Typewriter

THE RECOGNIZED LEADER—IN SALES AND POPULARITY

1.12 REMINGTON TYPEWRITER ADVERTISEMENT IN AMERICAN BOY (MAY 1924).

Playing to the new companionate family ideal, the iconography of the child lobbyist generated images of intergenerational harmony and cooperation, especially between fathers and sons.

each other's companionship through the building and operating of American Flyer railroad systems."[190] Advertisers clearly spoke to boys' yearnings for more egalitarian relationships with their dads, but their tributes to father-son companionship also strove to melt patriarchal resistance to the more expensive ideas advertisers put in boys' heads. A 1932 electric trains catalog, for instance, urged boys to "Take Your Dad into Partnership [and] Make Him Your Pal" by getting his help in building a fully accessorized Lionel railroad system—cleverly eliding the distinction between financial partnership and father-son fellowship in play.[191] Through their romance of the companionate family, advertisers discovered how to unite juvenile and parental appeals, but in the process they also further blurred the boundaries between market values and family values.

Juvenile advertisers' romance of the companionate family also required an attentive courtship of mothers, as they often designed advertising to be read aloud by mothers to their youngest charges. *Child Life*, a magazine for younger children, saw tremendous advantages in selling mothers and children through the same ad. Advertising in its pages was "sure to be effective," *Child Life* told prospective advertisers, "because the mother will see it when she is reading to fascinated kiddies" and "certain to be in a receptive mood, her mind attune to the needs of her little ones."[192] Factor in children's own curiosity, and advertisers were virtually guaranteed success. "The profit circle widens," *Child Life* informed toy manufacturers, "when Child Life Magazine brings your toy story to its Mother-Child, all-prospect audience."[193]

To win the good favor of mothers, however, advertisers had to walk a fine line between stimulating children's desires and addressing parental concerns. Creators of advertising story booklets recognized that mothers would be unlikely to read rhymed verses to their children if they did not approve of their moral message.[194] Since only repeated readings guaranteed that an advertiser's message would be absorbed, Twinkies shoes took care to weave "pointers on morals and behavior" into their advertising fairy tale booklet. Not only did the well-behaved elfin Twinkies say their prayers and give thanks for their blessings, but they also practiced good health and hygiene.[195]

Juvenile advertisers also attempted to befriend mothers by promising to ease their workload. In the early twentieth century, the tasks assigned to middle-class housewives became both more demanding and more time-consuming, thanks to a shortage of household servants, rising standards of cleanliness fostered by advertisers themselves, and new childrearing philosophies that urged mothers to devote more individualized attention to each child.[196] Some juvenile advertisers aligned their own interests with mothers' by encouraging daughters to be more helpful around the house.

"Mothers think it's pretty fine when their daughters begin to take some of the responsibility of keeping the home in order," a Hoover vacuum ad counseled. "Even if it is only one little thing that you do, if you . . . can be *depended* upon, it helps a lot."[197] Other juvenile advertising schemes vowed to reduce the burdens of childrearing and free mothers for other pursuits. Advertisers' complementary coloring booklets, puzzle books, and bedtime stories all aimed, one advertising authority wrote, to fill that "ever-present parental need" for materials that "educate and amuse and temporarily subdue the irrepressible spirits of the very young."[198]

For all of its novelty, what is perhaps most striking about early-twentieth-century children's advertising is how little organized opposition it faced. To be sure, some critics raised their voices to protest the self-interested advertising "enrichment materials" used in public schools and consumer education programs that failed to teach students the basic principles of smart shopping. Others, as we shall see in chapter 6, were troubled by the specter of children's radio advertisers' preying on impressionable minds. Nevertheless, despite its shameless encouragement of begging, despite its invasion of the schoolroom, and despite its efforts to mold even the tiniest tots into brand-loyal consumers, children's advertising was often embraced and accepted. Ironically, juvenile advertisers successfully exploited the increasingly permeable boundaries between family values and market values because consumerism proved so compatible with the ideology of the sacred child and the companionate family. They did so by aligning themselves with the very institutions of early-twentieth-century childhood that sought to sequester childhood as a wholesome, play-centered stage of life. Advertisers secured the cooperation of the public schools in promoting advertising-based instruction in health and hygiene. They supported the Boy Scouts, Girl Scouts, and Camp Fire Girls by allotting much-needed advertising dollars to their magazines and promoting branded goods as adjuncts to scouting activities. Most critically, they wore down parental resistance by romancing the companionate family and associating their products with children's developmental needs and mothers' quests for more leisure.

Yet, as the following chapters will show, the seductive powers of children's consumer culture did not go uncontested. The public schools and child experts promoted new methods of money training to teach thrift and wise spending. Middle-class mothers and fathers, armed with new parenting strategies, battled the allures of consumer culture with captivating manipulations of their own. Finally, during the Great Depression, the uneasy alliance among parents, children, and advertisers threatened to unravel when overzealous radio advertising exposed the inherent tensions in simultaneously courting parental and juvenile goodwill.

CHAPTER 2

From Thrift Education to Consumer Training:
Reforming the Child Spender

AT THE TURN OF THE TWENTIETH CENTURY, when advertisers had just begun to envision children as discerning and demanding consumers, America's urban children were becoming increasingly enmeshed in a burgeoning culture of consumption. For mere pennies, working-class children could satisfy their sweet tooth at the candy shop, learn their fortune from a slot machine, or glimpse flickering images through the kinetoscope at the penny arcade. One nickel afforded them an afternoon of celluloid adventures at the neighborhood nickelodeon, two bought them cheap gallery seats at the vaudeville theater.[1] For more affluent children, a trip to the department store opened the door to an enticing "new child's world" of dolls and toys, while advertisements in children's magazines alerted them to a host of new items that merited inclusion on mother's shopping list. Even from afar, if only in fantasy, rural children paging through the Sears or Marshall Fields catalog could enter the tantalizing realm of children's fashions and playthings housed in the city's grand "palaces of consumption."[2]

While advertisers found much to admire in this new class of consumers, many other turn-of-the-century Americans found much to despair over in children's newfound consumer enthusiasms. Thanks in part to the new temptations of the city, American children were acquiring a reputation distinctly at odds with the Victorian paeans to their angelic natures. No longer the guileless innocent, the modern American child, commentators complained, was instead becoming a "mercenary little wretch." In 1900 a contributor to *Harper's Bazaar* suggested that American children, like their parents, had become afflicted with the national passion for rapid accumulation and extravagant spending. "The mind of a child," Carolyn Benedict Burrell wrote, "veers between the love of acquiring and the love of spending. It delights to hoard, to shake its bank and feel its increasing weight, and to spend recklessly until it is bankrupt."[3] Parents, too, recognized the force of such acquisitive instincts, and fretted over their children's nasty habit of

begging for money. Summing up the problem, an Iowa mother's club concluded in 1900 that "the commercial instinct among . . . children does not
require stimulating, but curbing and directing into right channels."[4]

The image of the child as an impulsive spendthrift fueled debate in the
late nineteenth and early twentieth centuries over how to teach children
economic responsibility and respect for money. Women's magazines, parenting guidebooks, and education journals disputed how, and to what extent, parents and teachers should develop children's money sense. For
some, the spendthrift habits of children called for money training to teach
proper discipline. Yet the widespread idealization of childhood as a carefree
period often stirred resistance to such training. Many worried that early development of children's money sense might in itself be corrupting. Would
school savings banks teach children valuable lessons in thrift, an editorial-
ist wondered in 1897, or merely exacerbate the "mercenary tone" of American civilization?[5] How could children learn to be "economically responsible" without also becoming overly "money conscious"?[6] Such concerns
underscored the difficulty parents and child experts faced in resolving one
of the central dilemmas of twentieth-century childhood: how to prepare
children for their encounters with the outside world while still protecting
their cherished innocence.

From the turn of the century through the Great Depression, educators
and childrearing authorities chipped away at parents' sentimental attach-
ments to a carefree childhood to sell them on the virtues of school savings
banks and weekly allowances. Though both approaches aimed to teach
children responsibility and respect for money, they employed different
means to reform child spending and, to a degree, targeted different class
constituencies. From their modest beginning in the mid-1880s, school savings banks gradually gained support across the country, taking root in predominantly urban areas with high concentrations of children from
working-class and immigrant families. The school banks required children
to deposit money on a weekly basis in hopes that regular practice in saving
would eventually become habit. Backed by the American Bankers Association, school banks proved particularly popular with moral reformers who
embraced compulsory saving as a way to reduce children's access to commercial culture, Americanize immigrant children and their families, and
stem the growth of pauperism and welfare dependency.

Allowance advocates made their pitch to the largely middle-class readers of women's magazines and parenting guidebooks. Though restraint in
the use of money was certainly one aim, allowance proponents also wanted to teach children how to spend—an aspect of money training that
school banks typically ignored. As allowance boosters saw matters, teach-

ing children the value of money meant teaching them to be wise consumers.[7] Such views gained authority among child experts, parents, and even some school officials during the 1920s and became more deeply entrenched during the depression-ridden 1930s. By then, the ideal of the thrifty child banker had given way to a new ideal of the savvy child consumer—disciplined not merely to save but to make discriminating choices in the marketplace.

This chapter explores the social and cultural transformations that legitimized this reconception of the child consumer during the 1920s and 1930s. Modern psychology and child-centered pedagogy facilitated this reconception by stressing the need to educate children's consumer desires rather than curb them. Casting aside earlier views of children's spending impulses as dangerous and insatiable, psychologists and Freudian popularizers interpreted children's desire for things more sympathetically and reconceived consumer desire as a vital component of a well-adjusted personality. Consumer-oriented money training got a further boost from New Dealers and other economists who dethroned thriftiness as the preeminent economic virtue in the 1930s. Shifts in children's money training thus paralleled broader shifts in the national political economy.

Internal struggles within the consumer household also contributed to the legitimization of the savvy child consumer. The contradictions of the middle-class ideal of a sheltered childhood, with its isolation of children from work but not the allures of the marketplace, compelled parents, children, and child experts to grapple with family relations of power and affection in new ways. As proponents of "democratic" parent-child relationships, child experts affirmed children's right to a regular share of the family spending money as an economic and educational entitlement. Beneath the greater permissiveness of allowances, however, lay a conservative impulse to reassert parental control and an ethic of self-restraint—an impulse that children themselves sometimes sought to thwart. Children's money training was thus the site of contested attempts to delineate both the boundaries of consumer desire and the boundaries of family democracy.

SCHOOL BANKING AND THE GOSPEL OF THRIFT

With Benjamin Franklin as its patron saint and the crusading spirit of Progressive-Era reform its guiding sensibility, the school savings bank movement attempted to reform children's spendthrift ways and a host of related societal ills by inculcating habits of saving at an early age. In 1885, when John H. Thiry, a Belgian-born American, launched the first public school banking program in Long Island, Americans were already latecomers to the school banking idea. School banking originated in France in 1818 and had spread to several other European countries, including Italy, Hungary, Great Britain, Switzerland, and Belgium by the second half of the nineteenth century.[8] Those successes gave school bank advocates like Thiry the ammunition they needed to bring school administrators on board. By 1890, school banking programs had been instituted in 31 eastern cities and 158 schools.[9] Enthusiasm for school banking spread in large eastern, midwestern, and West Coast cities during the decades between 1890 and 1920, as the cause gathered momentum and inspiration from the Progressive reform energies that swept the country. But school banking's greatest influence came during the 1920s, when more and more banks recognized school savings programs as a valuable "advertising medium" and public relations tool.[10] By the decade's end, the number of participating schools had climbed from 2,736 to 14,610.[11]

Historians of education have often stressed how child-saving reformers envisioned public education as the means to help children, especially working-class boys, adjust to the new industrial economy. Through Progressive-Era curricular innovations such as manual training, vocational guidance, student government, and student extracurricular activities, children would be, in historian David Nasaw's apt phrase, "schooled to order"—trained to fit the economy as productive factory workers and team-playing organization men.[12] Bankers, educators, and thrift advocates promoted school banking in very much the same vein—as a means to cultivate self-supporting citizens endowed with a strong producer ethic. Garnering support among thrift advocates in home economics departments, women's clubs, and the Women's Christian Temperance Union, educators envisioned compulsory saving as a barrier against the "alarming increase" in crime, pauperism, intemperance, and welfare dependency.[13] School banking advocates evinced distinctly modern attitudes in nurturing optimism that education could advance social progress and combat the chaos that accompanied rapid industrialization, mass immigration, and urbanization. Yet, like so many Progressive-Era reformers, they also engaged in a backward-looking quest to reinvigorate a crumbling Victorian moral order.[14] In the end, these tensions made school banking less an adjustment to the new economic order than a defense of the Victorian culture of thrift.

Instead of training children to navigate the temptations of consumer culture, school banking sought to isolate children from it by draining their pockets of nickels and dimes on a regular basis. Under the Thiry school banking system, urban school children participated in a weekly ritual of depositing coins in a school account each Monday morning. Bank Day, as it was called, typically began with the teacher's roll call asking each student to bring forward his or her deposit. Deposits could be as small as a penny or as grand as the sum of a newspaper boy's weekly earnings, though they rarely exceeded a quarter.[15] Teachers recorded the weekly deposits on a savings bank card, which students kept as a receipt and a reminder to save for the next week's deposit, and the principal took charge of getting the collective deposits to the bank.[16] The entire procedure usually required fifteen to thirty minutes of class time. In some school banking programs, like the one established by the Philadelphia Savings Fund Society, junior high schools broadened the learning experience by enlisting student tellers to take charge of collecting and recording deposits (fig. 2.1).[17]

Teachers and program administrators relied on a series of carrots and sticks to ensure student compliance. One inducement was that student bankers gained the banking privileges enjoyed by adult depositors. In the 1890s local banks cooperating with public schools issued students bank books once they accrued a sum of fifty cents or one dollar. Students also earned three percent interest, then the going rate, when they accumulated

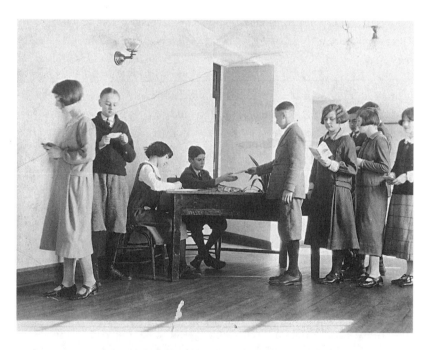

2.1 PHILADELPHIA SAVINGS FUND SOCIETY SCHOOL BANKING PROGRAM IN ACTION.
Student tellers in this Philadelphia junior high school, photographed in the 1920s, record their classmates' deposits. Courtesy of Hagley Museum and Library.

three dollars.[18] The appeal of such adult entitlements was very real. Some adults, recalling their school banking experiences in the 1920s and 1930s, underscored the pride they felt in possessing their own bank book and account (fig. 2.2).[19] The economic autonomy that might have accompanied such banking privileges, however, was limited, if not illusory. Both by precept and policy, schools strongly discouraged students from withdrawing money. Some required parental consent on withdrawals larger than twenty-five cents.[20] Others prohibited withdrawals before Bank Clearing Day around Christmas.[21]

Such policies were thoroughly grounded in what historian Lendol Calder calls the "Victorian money management ethic." Popularized in the nineteenth century by Benjamin Franklin's "The Way to Wealth," this ethic stressed the importance of cultivating new moral and mental disciplines of self-control. Frugality, thrift, planning, spending within one's means, and avoiding consumptive debt were all considered crucial economic virtues—testaments to one's character and integrity.[22] School banking programs helped to spread the Victorian gospel of thrift by inscribing student

2.2 PHILADELPHIA SAVINGS FUND SOCIETY SCHOOL ACCOUNTS COUNTER, 1920S.
The Philadelphia Savings Fund Society provided a separate counter for school students and stepstools for the youngest among them.
Courtesy of Hagley Museum and Library.

savings bank cards with pithy Poor Richard aphorisms, such as "Take care of the pennies and the dollars will take care of themselves" and "Good principles and good habits are in themselves a fortune."[23]

Even before children encountered school savings banks they were already familiar with these moral injunctions. Children nevertheless regularly flouted them when left to their own devices. Joseph Heller and his brother hid their earnings from clamming and setting crab nets because they knew their affluent, orthodox Jewish parents would make them save the money. They preferred to spend their earnings "frivolously"—"We pissed it away"—on movies, candy, and cigarettes for which they paid a penny a piece instead of buying the entire 6-cent pack.[24] Even when exhorted to save their pennies, one survey indicated, children failed to heed parental advice. A ten-year-old boy confessed, "My father advises me to save [ten cents a day], but I say what's the use? I have all I need." Such flagrant violations of parental directives did not mean that children failed to comprehend adult standards. An eleven-year-old boy admitted that instead of saving his pennies he spent them on "candy and other things which in a way are foolish." Children negotiated the gap between adult and child standards by upholding consumption standards that better suited child culture. Though children spent most of their pennies on candy, the survey found that two-thirds of children drew the line at buying candy from a stand. One child pronounced, "I would go without anything for a year before I would buy at a stand!" Another child plagued by carelessness shared the same resolve: "I never find any money, but I can lose it very often. But I buy at a clean, respectful store!"[25] Such comments suggest that children readily violated some middle-class standards even as they closely adhered to others: the practice of thrift may have fallen by the wayside, but the notion of patronizing reputable shops rather than street peddlers had not.

The attitudes of newsies, bootblacks, scavengers, and other boys of the city streets were even more alarming to progressive-era reformers. As Jane Addams wrote in 1909, "Never before have such numbers of young boys earned money independently of the family life, and felt themselves free to spend it as they choose in the midst of vice deliberately disguised as pleasure."[26] In popular culture and child-saving discourses, children's unimpeded access to spending money inevitably led to a downward spiral of extravagant consumption and immorality (fig. 2.3). Through thrift education school banking advocates hoped to advance a broader agenda of moral reform, which included reducing poor children's access to the city's "dangerous" pleasure zones. Just as Progressive-Era movie reformers sought to control children's spending by mandating movie censorship and prohibiting

2.3 "PLAYING BANK PRESIDENT"
TRADE CARD SERIES: "DINING WITH A
WALL ST. BULL," "ABSCONDING WITH
THE FUNDS," "IN PRISON."
In the Victorian imagination, concerns
about children's access to spending money
merged easily with representations of the
dangers of extravagant consumption.
Courtesy of Hagley Museum and Library.

movie attendance by unaccompanied minors, school banking promoters sought to limit opportunities for children to squander spending money on immoral indulgences. As reformers saw it, working-class children simply could not be trusted to spend their money as they pleased.[27] In this respect, school savings banks were much like the Penny Provident banks favored by Progressive-Era charity workers: an "institutional effort to safeguard and earmark poor people's earnings" for prudent purposes.[28]

In promoting their cause, school bank administrators underscored how safeguarding children's money contributed to healthier morals and healthier bodies. Some boasted of their success in "discouraging foolish purchases of candy, gum and cigarettes" and stemming the "growth of all evil habits," including tobacco use, gambling, and pool playing.[29] As children learned to save by "sacrificing" movies and candy and walking to school instead of taking the bus, program administrators reported seeing the return of "rosy checks, normal weights, and better grades." Solving the problem of sweets was even reputed to quell the delinquent tendencies of preadolescent children "whose mentalities were dwarfed and twisted" by "the candy habit."[30] Parents themselves welcomed such transformations in their children's health and use of leisure. In a survey conducted in 1927, parents of elementary school children in a Minnesota suburb gave school savings banks especially high marks for restricting candy and movie consumption.[31]

Although educators endorsed school savings banks for children of all economic backgrounds, the moral reform efforts of school banking promoters became increasingly intertwined with a social control agenda that targeted poor and immigrant children. Enthusiasm for thrift education, of course, extended to such predominantly middle-class organizations as the Boy Scouts, which required members to open a bank account with at least one dollar in savings before they could be promoted from a "tenderfoot" to a second-class scout.[32] Even middle-class children's magazines echoed the imperatives of thrift education in the schools, enjoining children to save their pennies and resist the temptation to withdraw money from their accounts.[33] But a greater sense of urgency attached to reformers' efforts to reach classes and groups deemed most at risk of becoming a burden to the state.[34] Thrift advocates believed that training in compulsory saving was particularly important for children from "poorer classes . . . who otherwise would be taught only the hand-to-mouth method of earning and spending."[35] Simply put, thrift advocates placed greater faith in the schools than in the family to properly socialize children.

The Philadelphia Savings Fund Society was especially inventive in spreading the gospel of thrift to immigrant and working-class children. During the interwar years, PSFS's service department produced and coached thrift pageants for playgrounds and settlement houses. Children sang thrift songs set to popular tunes, shouted thrift cheers, and listened to speeches laced with the thrift maxims of famous historical figures.[36] The main attraction, however, was a thrift play performed by children for their peers. In one such play, "How Money Grows" (fig. 2.4), children costumed as pennies, nickels, and dimes complain to a girl named Spendthrift that she has misspent them on sweets, movies, and slot machines and deprived them of the opportunity to grow into quarters. At the play's conclusion, a reformed and repentant Spendthrift embraces the producer values that formerly eluded her. "Money," Spendthrift exclaims, "will not grow unless it is planted in a Saving Fund; and even before the first seed is planted the ground must be ploughed by working."[37]

The Philadelphia Savings Fund Society's playground program promoted middle-class ideals of consumption along with the savings habit. Not surprisingly, "How Money Grows" identified squandering money at the movie theater and the penny arcades as particularly noxious vices. In the minds of many middle-class reformers, both entertainment venues were

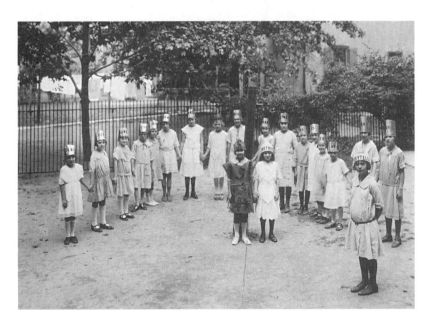

2.4 PHILADELPHIA SAVINGS FUND SOCIETY THRIFT PAGEANT, 1936.
Girls from settlement home perform "How Money Grows," a play in which pennies, nickels, and dimes explain to Spendthrift how they have been misspent and not allowed to grow into quarters.
Courtesy of Hagley Museum and Library.

evocative symbols of mass culture's debasing influence. Other PSFS play narratives taught children that indulging in the ephemeral pleasures of sweets, cheap trinkets, and movies robbed them of opportunities to pursue higher wants and desires. In "The Land of Desire" (fig. 2.5), for example, a boy and girl discover that they can't afford to purchase the prized wares of four spirits—Service, Fame, Learning, and Adventure—because "Want Elves" have stolen their coins and spent them on ice cream cones and movie tickets. Sympathetic to their plight, the "Thrift Fairy" pledges to "keep their coins in his treasure chest and return them safely when they are ready to buy their Hearts' Desire." Only through deferred gratification and disciplined saving, the play moralizes, can children hope to satisfy more enduring, and ultimately more productive, pleasures.[38]

Implicit in such play narratives was the assumption that individual habits of saving and spending rather than systemic inequalities produced

2.5 PHILADELPHIA SAVINGS FUND SOCIETY PLAYGROUND THRIFT PAGEANT, 1924.
With varying degrees of enthusiasm, children perform "The Land of Desire," a play in which spendthrift children learn they must safeguard their coins from the "Want Elves" if they wish to purchase the grander wares of Service, Fame, Learning, and Adventure. Courtesy of Hagley Museum and Library.

class distinctions. Indeed, school banking advocates especially prized thrift education as a means to reduce class antagonisms and promote more hospitable attitudes toward capitalism among immigrants and the laboring poor. That goal resonated powerfully during the 1920s, when labor unrest and the specter of Bolshevism precipitated red scares. As director of the Philadelphia Savings Fund Society's community outreach and school banking programs in the 1920s, Mary Reeves applauded the bank for "gradually proving" that the "line of distinction between Capital and Labor" mattered little because "every individual is a potential capitalist"—"something which only wise living can determine."[39] C. S. Morrison, a physician's wife and club woman who instituted a Girl Scout banking program in Colorado Springs, Colorado, in 1927, similarly delighted in the prospect of using thrift education to Americanize immigrant children and quell labor radicalism. Such training, Morrison argued, would transform second-generation immigrants into thrifty homeowners who assumed "their rightful places in the community, not with the socialistic attitude of the parents, but [as] prosperous, loyal Americans."[40]

With any luck, school banking advocates surmised, children tutored in thrift could in turn become agents of Americanization in their own homes. School banking proponents had long envisioned poor and immigrant children as thrift missionaries, bringing knowledge of passbooks, checks, and deposit slips to parents who themselves lacked banking experience.[41] For parents "too proud to deposit their small savings," children's school accounts might even function as proxy accounts.[42] By the 1920s, reformers with even larger ambitions envisioned school banking as a kind of social worker on a grand scale. Children, some argued, could heighten immigrant confidence in the safety of banking, and through their example, "swell the great number of thrifty American citizens."[43] Through their children's influence, bank-wary immigrants who hid their money in socks and under mattresses could be converted into institutional savers.[44]

Thrift advocates' vision of school banking as an instrument of social control was fraught with ironies. As the targets of reform, some working-class children embraced school banking for reasons its advocates never anticipated. In his recollections of growing up in St. Louis during the late 1920s, Aaron Hotchner described the school savings bank as the only means he had to prevent his erratically employed father from raiding his own meager earnings. "Nobody could get at that money but you," Hotchner recalled. "For me that was very important, because all summer my father had been taking my money, always asking to 'borrow' a dollar for gasoline or carfare, but naturally he never paid any of it back. Once I put it in the bank, I didn't have to 'lend' to him any more."[45] What educators envisioned as a tool to regulate children's spending became in Hotchner's hands a device for combating unwelcome requests for money and seemingly unjust assertions of parental authority.

Thrift advocates' quest to spread the gospel of banking to immigrant and working-class families highlighted another irony.[46] Many immigrants—including Italians, Poles, and Eastern European Jews—saved at rates that surpassed native-born Americans and, in some quarters, were deeply resented for habits of thrift that allegedly "cheapened the American standard of living."[47] Even thrift advocates' own testimony suggests that immigrant parents shared their enthusiasm for thrift education. C. S. Morrison reported that the Italian, Austrian, Bohemian, and Slavic immigrant mining families who enrolled their daughters in the Pike View Coal Mines Girl Scout troop were more interested in thrift training than any other aspect of scouting.[48]

Bankers' own economic self-interest partially explains thrift advocates' zeal for Americanization. School banks would not only promote thrift, after all, but would also promote the use of banks. Bankers plainly acknowledged that school banking was a valuable "advertising medium" that helped to familiarize children with the bank's name and "extend the life of the bank" by creating goodwill among likely future customers.[49] Some may even have seen school banking as an opportunity to cultivate immigrant preferences for American commercial banking institutions over the mutual aid societies and immigrant-run consumer credit institutions they typically relied upon for coping with unforeseen hardships.[50] Even so, most savings banks cast school banking as a community service rather than a profit-making venture, arguing that the costs of administering the program exceeded any gains from increased deposits.[51]

Despite bankers' vehement denials, the charge that school savings programs were a "mere scheme for bank advertising" had merit.[52] In a speech delivered before the National Education Association's 1924 Conference on Thrift, a spokesman for the American Society for Thrift boasted that school savings banks had become sound business practice for the sponsoring banks. While the greatest number of new depositors in Brooklyn's East New York Savings Bank came through adult customer referrals, the second greatest number, the spokesman reported, came from "child depositors who recommend[ed] the bank to their parents and adult relatives."[53] The East New York Savings Bank was hardly passive in soliciting new business, as it published a monthly school newsletter that urged students to "Take This Paper Home to Your Parents." The bank, in fact, sought to make even its student business profitable by awarding monthly prizes worth $2.50, $5.00, and $10.00 to the top three district schools that boasted the largest number of deposits and new accounts.[54]

There was nothing inherently corrupting or even surprising in bankers' moves to promote their economic self-interest along with the practice of thrift. But the growing reliance on contests between classrooms and district schools to promote saving had the effect of subordinating lessons in thrift to a competitive quest for maximum student compliance. These promotional schemes had their roots in World War I, when school banking, at the behest of the Treasury Department's National War Savings Division, was converted into a program for selling Savings Stamps to finance the war effort. As schools rallied children with the patriotic injunction to "save money [so] that we may save lives," the pressure to buy stamps became so intense that students who failed to bring money on stamp day sometimes faced accusations of being pro-German.[55] Despite their overwhelming success in filling the government's coffers, the stamp-selling drives proved much more limited in spreading the gospel of thrift. Much to the dismay of Frank Vanderlip, who headed the National War Savings Division, some wartime schools jettisoned lessons in thrift altogether, preferring to reward children with prizes for their stamp-selling prowess.[56]

During the 1920s educators and thrift advocates sought to move thrift education to the forefront again with the reinstitution of thrift week celebrations and the integration of saving into the curriculum. Some even saw a new urgency for school savings banks as a bulwark against the "vain squandering" and reckless pleasure-seeking that allegedly typified middle-class youth.[57] Adjusting to the temper of the times, PSFS began playing more directly to children's material ambitions by encouraging students to save in order to spend. In a photograph presumably used to promote its school banking program, three proud boy savers, bank books in hand, pose with the purchases their savings afforded: a bicycle, a phonograph, and a subscription to the *Literary Digest*—all testaments to bourgeois striving and manly success (fig. 2.6).[58] For many students, however, lessons in thrift continued to take a back seat to the competitive spirit that prevailed as classrooms and school districts strove to achieve 100 percent compliance. Even more threatening to the Victorian thrift ethic was the return of postwar prosperity and the growing affluence of the middle class. For while the spending habits of the flapper generation strengthened the resolve of some school bank enthusiasts, they also highlighted the irrelevance of compulsory saving to many middle-class children—a group well enough supplied with nickels and dimes not to miss the few they ritually deposited on Bank Day. Gradually, as we shall see, these incongruities gave rise to a new ideal of the savvy child consumer, disciplined not merely to save but to spend wisely in the marketplace.

2.6 PHILADELPHIA SAVINGS FUND SOCIETY PHOTOGRAPH PROMOTING ITS
SCHOOL BANKING PROGRAM, 1925.
Boys proudly posing with their purchases demonstrate the virtue of saving for a
definite purpose. Courtesy of Hagley Museum and Library.

THE ALLOWANCE SOLUTION AND THE
MIDDLE-CLASS CHILD CONSUMER

The allowance idea grew out of the same stew of Progressive-Era reform
ideologies that sought to introduce more system into children's money
training and to restrain the powerful acquisitive instincts that child experts
believed made children incapable of postponing immediate gratification.
"The mark of the child and the savage alike is that each cannot wait," one
allowance proponent explained.[59] Borrowing from G. Stanley Hall's
Darwinian-inspired theory that children recapitulated the history of the
human race in each successive stage of their development, Progressive-Era
reformers tended to view children as primitive versions of adults, who by
nature lacked the civilized restraint that came with training and maturity.[60]

But while children's inability to defer gratification prompted school
banking enthusiasts to endorse compulsory saving, allowance advocates
opted for less draconian measures, recommending a regular but fixed supply of spending money to impart lessons in spending as well as saving.

Though not the first to advocate allowances—as early as 1831 Lydia Maria Child had endorsed allowances to encourage benevolence and fiscal responsibility—Progressives joined a much larger chorus urging reform.[61] Promoted to a largely middle-class readership of women's magazines and parental advice literature, the allowance solution promised to school middle-class children to a different kind of order, making them wise spenders in the vibrant consumer economy and less demanding members of the consumer household.

Historians have viewed children's allowances as a response to children's heightened sentimental value within the middle-class family and as an acknowledgment of their entitlement to a share of its resources.[62] It is important to recognize, however, that children's allowances were as much a critique of the affectionate family as an embodiment of its democratic impulses. As middle-class families became smaller and more child-centered, parents and family experts gave voice to concerns that the child lavished with care and affection might become the tyrannical child—willful, demanding, and unmanageable. Worse still, such attentive childrearing might produce a generation of children who would become selfish, immature adults, lacking in self-direction and inner strength.[63] Allowance proponents sought to discipline parental sentimentality as well as the child spender by replacing parents' haphazard giving of spending money with systematized money training. Caught up in the cultural currents of scientific management that spurred Progressives to rationalize and order their world, allowance advocates believed that lack of system in children's money experiences accounted for their lack of money sense. Too often, Carolyn Benedict Burrell noted, child money "comes from the parental pocketbook in a more or less irregular trickle, rather than in that small but steady stream which develops the child's sense of its value." Absent some "regular system," children would never learn to handle money wisely or value it appropriately. "If given too lavishly," Burrell argued, "it will mean nothing; if doled out too parsimoniously, it will acquire an abnormal value."[64]

In many respects, the allowance solution adapted behaviorist psychology to children's money training problems. Stressing the virtues of regularity and routine over the careless indulgence that typified sentimental parenting, the roots of behaviorist childrearing could be found in L. Emmett Holt's widely disseminated *The Care and Feeding of Infants* (1896), which went through several editions in the early twentieth century. Holt advised mothers to instill healthy habits by adhering to strict schedules of feeding, sleeping, and toileting. Behaviorists urged mothers to resist picking up a crying baby or feeding it on demand, as these responses would only spoil the child and create a demanding little tyrant. Allowance proponents applied the same attention to rationalizing children's economic habits as the advocates of scientific mothering did to rationalizing their physical habits. The rationalist childrearing paradigm became even more dominant during the 1920s and 1930s, when the behaviorist theories of John Broadus Watson and his followers found a popular audience among mothers who attended child-study clubs and who read *Parents' Magazine* and the Children's Bureau's *Infant Care* bulletins.[65]

Convincing parents to replace unsystematic giving with allowances was no easy task. A survey of 630 grammar school children, conducted by a woman's club in 1903, suggests that haphazard giving was the norm. The study found that less than one-third of the children received allowances, while the rest collected money in small sums ranging from a penny to a dime "whenever I ask for it" or "most every day or two."[66] Some parents objected to allowances on grounds that a regular provision of spending money would give their children too much liberty. Before the 1920s such attitudes were especially pronounced in immigrant families, which viewed children's discretionary spending as a threat to the hierarchical basis of family authority.[67] Although wage-earning boys from immigrant families claimed some financial independence, often the only spending money wage-earning daughters enjoyed came from the little they skimmed from their pay envelopes in defiance of parental wishes.[68] By contrast, middle-class parents more commonly rejected allowances as a "stingy" way to treat their children.[69] By its very nature, the companionate family led many parents to equate providing for their children with doling out spending money on demand. Parents invested in meeting their children's needs for emotional satisfaction and individual self-expression often caved in to children's requests. Children, in turn, came to see their fathers in more instrumental terms—as providers of goods and spending money.[70] All too easily, bonds of affection became intertwined with monetary exchange.

During the 1920s and 1930s, allowance advocates partially overcame the sentimental objections to children's allowances by soft-pedaling their behaviorism and stressing their compassion for the child's point of view. One such expert was Angelo Patri, whose newspaper columns and radio broadcasts made him a well-known and widely respected childrearing authority during the 1920s and 1930s.[71] Patri argued that withholding allowances deprived children of valuable experience in money management and unnecessarily prolonged their economic dependency. In order for allowances fulfill their educational mission, Patri recommended that they be generous enough to provide children a small margin over actual needs. Lacking that cushion, allowances "[became] just another narrow and repressive . . . disciplinary measure."[72] Allowance advocates also warned against "too much regulation" of children's spending choices.[73] Parents could achieve better results, allowance boosters contended, if they acted as a tutor instead of a critic, praising the good purchases and overlooking the bad—all the while suggesting ways to spend more economically in the future.[74]

By no means, however, did experts intend to sacrifice parental influence to child autonomy. Child experts calculated that giving children more spending freedom would ultimately mold them into consumers with better tastes. While allowances entrusted children with responsibility for their own spending choices, they also held them accountable for their spending mistakes. As the leading spokesperson for the Child Study Association of America, the vanguard of the parent education movement in the 1920s, Sidonie Gruenberg assured parents that children learned more from their mistakes than from authoritarian pronouncements or "early protection against unwise purchases."[75] In place of advice or admonition, Gruenberg preferred the instructive hand of scientific management and recommended that children be given an account book to keep track of their spending habits and needs. "A stark record of a long succession of ice-cream sodas or short-lived catch-penny toys," Gruenberg argued, may "improve the child's taste or shift his choice of purchases." Eventually, with practice, children learned to "buy daily without regrets."[76]

Allowance advocates' child-centered approach to money training bore the imprint of John Dewey and G. Stanley Hall, who contended that education and childrearing should be molded to the individual child.[77] Indeed, allowance boosters highlighted their superior sensitivity to the child by criticizing habitual saving as an outmoded approach that failed to appreciate child ways of learning. "Saving in response to mother's 'you may be thankful for more money someday' carries no meaning to the small child who has little conception of time beyond today," noted one *Parents' Magazine* contributor. "To him, the bank is a bottomless pit which may never yield back his precious pennies."[78] While young children could be taught to save for a specific purpose, the concept of saving for "remote and vaguely defined needs" generally eluded them until they reached their teens.[79]

In debunking the virtues of habitual saving, allowance advocates questioned both the psychological and moral underpinnings of school banking. School banking's advocacy of compulsory saving took quite literally psychologist Edward Thorndike's contention that constant repetition was essential to habit formation.[80] As allowance advocates saw matters, however, strict adherence to regimen and habit formation could change behavior without actually helping children to internalize self-restraint. Violating a key precept of thrift education, which valorized saving as a virtue in itself, allowance proponents contended that spending practice taught children to exercise self-restraint better than habitual saving. Children learned the value of setting aside money only when they confronted the limits of their allowance. "Saving must . . . come to the child as a means of buying something that costs more than a week's income," Gruenberg argued. "He should learn to save as he learns to value more and more expensive objects, and as he learns to project his desires more and more into the future."[81] The notion that consumer desire itself could discipline the child spender turned conventional wisdom on its head. School banking and toy banks operated on the premise that the savings habit was best nurtured by removing consumer temptation from the equation. The miniature "Bank of America," according to its manufacturer, would *"open automatically only when ten dollars have been deposited."*[82] The toy bank's external mechanisms of control compensated for the absence of discipline in children who had not fully internalized self-restraint.

Paradoxically, the child-centered approach to money training recommended by allowance advocates also invited the child to cross boundaries that had previously sheltered the child from the worries and responsibilities of the adult world. In recounting allowance success stories, allowance proponents often celebrated the knowledge that children acquired about the high cost of living—knowledge that put children in greater sympathy with parents' needs to rein in family spending. Writing at the turn of the century, one father, who expected his preadolescent children to use their allowance for table board, clothing, and other expenses, observed that his children at first could not appreciate "the money value of anything except candy, nuts, cakes." By the end of the year, however, they had grasped the intended lesson. "I've had a hundred and ninety dollars," the son told his father, "and it's all gone but two dollars and twenty-three cents—it costs money, papa, to live, don't it?"[83] Nearly thirty years later, the premier edition of *Parents' Magazine* featured a similar story that about the Thompson twins, Bob and Sally, who came to appreciate "why Mother and Dad keep talking about the 'high cost of living'" and pledged to make more "responsible" choices.[84] To magazine readers the lesson was clear: child-centered means achieved adult-approved ends.

ALLOWANCE MONEY AND FAMILY VALUES

While children's allowances promised to reduce family friction over children's spending, they also raised a series of thorny moral questions concerning the nature of family obligations. Could allowances ease children's resentment of economic dependency without also overinflating their sense of entitlement? Could they teach children the true value of money if parents did not also require children to work? The ideal of a sheltered childhood compounded these moral dilemmas because children's need for spending money preceded their ability to earn. As childrearing authority Benjamin Gruenberg conceded, opportunities for earning were limited "in a world where protection from commercial exploitation is a major concern."[85]

Parents nevertheless contrived a host of ways for children to earn their spending money, including paying them for performing household chores and for bringing home good grades. For many parents, the temptation to use spending money to elicit good behavior proved difficult to resist. Indeed, the sheer scale and variety of such bribery testified to its popularity as a parenting technique. According to a 1926 survey conducted by a Minnesota school thrift organization, parents paid children to eat vegetables, take cod-liver oil, practice music, stay home alone, remain home from a show, come straight home from school, get up early, and stop making noise.[86] Childrearing authorities were aghast. In the eyes of Sidonie Gruenberg, such parenting practices confused "the give-and-take of family life with the buy-and-sell of the market place."[87] Parents' Magazine repeatedly cautioned its readers against using allowance money to reward the performance of duties or to penalize delinquencies.[88] Doing so, contributors admonished, would turn children into "calculating, hard-bargaining adult[s]."[89] By "reduc[ing] the responsibilities of the child to a cash basis," Sidonie Gruenberg argued, parents encouraged the child to bargain over how much should be paid for each good deed or to calculate the next time whether the offense is worth the nickels or dimes that it costs.[90]

By the 1920s and 1930s, debates over the proper use of allowance money focused attention on what many saw as the erosion of boundaries between ethics of the home and the ethics of the marketplace.[91] Historians and critics of consumer culture have argued that the weakening of ideological boundaries between public and private life contributed to the pervasiveness of pecuniary values in the twentieth century.[92] In the minds of allowance advocates, allowance money figured as the dam that could shore up those shaky ideological boundaries. Properly understood as "neither favors nor payments" but rather as an educational and economic entitlement, allowances promised to divest family relationships, at least, of pecuniary values.[93]

Still, the problem of how to link experiences in earning money to lessons in spending was not easily resolved. Allowance advocates concurred that children could not fully appreciate the value of a dollar without ever having earned one, but the ideology of sheltered childhood left children, especially young ones, with few legal and morally unassailable options for earning money.[94] Childrearing authorities proposed that parents pay children only for tasks the family would normally hire someone else to do.[95] In the interest of promoting companionate family relations based on mutuality rather than authoritarian discipline, experts insisted that the child be "free to take the extra job or leave it without needing to apologize or to defend his decision."[96] Otherwise payment for work became "merely a pretext for compelling the child to do work."[97] Besides, allowance advocates contended, earning experiences made more lasting impressions when children saw work not as "a grudged duty" but as a means to fulfill their "ambition for some major purchase."[98] In this formulation, children ultimately came to see the value of work through the refractions of consumer desire.

FAMILY RELATIONS WITHIN THE CONSUMER HOUSEHOLD

During the interwar years, children's spending became an arena for complex negotiations over the proper balance of parental control and children's autonomy. Although family conflicts over spending money were hardly new, sociologists and cultural commentators believed they had grown more intense, thanks in large part to the spending pressures spawned by the new public culture of dating and mass recreation.[99] As that dating culture spread to rural communities in the 1930s, even rural teens, previously a more quiescent group, became interlocked with their parents in "violent, internal" conflict over spending money and the use of the family car.[100] Likewise, working-class families found it more difficult to lay claim to the wages of their wage-earning children without granting sons and daughters a greater share for their own disposition.[101]

Family experts blamed spending money disputes on parents' failure to evolve "new sanctions . . . to fit the new age" and promoted allowances as an aid in modernizing and democratizing the family.[102] The very language child experts used to describe allowances—as the child's "share in the family's 'luxury spending'" or as "a gradually increasing franchise" that grew with the child's age and maturity—underscored their centrality to the modern democratic family ideal.[103] In the minds of child experts, allowances represented a form of both psychological and economic compensation. Envisioned as an economic entitlement, allowances were intended to offset some of the disadvantages that accompanied prolonged dependency. "The youngster who has no regular allowance of pocket money," *Survey* magazine contended, "smarts under a sense of injustice if his request is arbitrarily refused."[104] These resentments, experts warned, could even fuel delinquent behavior if parents failed to expand allowances as children grew into adolescence.[105] In 1934 the White House Conference on Child Health and Protection buttressed such concerns with its finding that adolescents without allowances were more likely to rank low on measurements of "personality adjustment" and "moral habits."[106]

By far the most radical expression of democratized family spending was the family firm—a family round table of sorts that recognized children as "junior partners" and included them in family spending decisions.[107] Home economists and childrearing authorities endorsed frank financial discussions as an important component of family conferences, broadly envisioned as a forum for resolving family disputes and training children in the kind of give-and-take that would later serve them well as citizens of a democracy.[108] The concept of the family firm significantly revised traditional patriarchal arrangements by calling upon fathers to share financial information not only with their wives but also with their children. Patriarchal control of the family purse strings struck family reformers as hopelessly out of step with new cultural ideals that, in historian Robert Griswold's words, valorized the father "as a kindly, nurturing democrat who shared rather than monopolized power."[109] The plea for "financial frankness" among all members of the household, however, stopped well short of a call for full-fledged democracy. Some proposed involving children in discussions of family finances on an occasional basis, as determined by their age and the matter under consideration.[110] Others allowed that children could voice opinions on family expenditures, but reserved the most "voting power" for the family's most able, and presumably most adult, members.[111]

Though the idea of such family conferences had been around since the mid-1920s, the family firm gained more salience during the 1930s, when advocates touted its efficacy as a tool for managing mounting financial disappointments.[112] For many working-class and middle-class families, the Depression dealt a severe blow to expectations of consumer plenitude that had been rising since the 1920s—a decade that saw an enormous proliferation of new consumer goods and services. These expectations became all the more difficult to contend with, historian Winifred Wandersee argues, because the family itself had become less a consuming unit than a collection of individual personalities, each with competing claims on the family's resources.[113] Not surprisingly, childrearing authorities envisioned financial candor as a means to subdue feelings of resentment over limited Depression-era family finances. "The rebellion that some children feel at not being able to have all the money they want," France Frisbie O'Donnell wrote in 1930, "is not likely to be felt by a boy or a girl who has been taken into father's and mother's confidence in financial matters."[114] Likewise, psychiatrist Clare Keith concluded that "the depression . . . need not accentuate" jealous rivalries or resentments so long as parents explained "any deprivations the financial situation requires." Such frank dealings, Keith argued, would, by making children feel valued, in turn motivate them "to help conserve the family income" (fig. 2.7).[115]

The democratic rhetoric that justified children's allowances and the family firm belied the more conservative ends such reforms were intended to serve. Allowances granted children greater spending freedom, but they also compelled children to spend within fixed limits. Though *Parents' Magazine* contributor Marion Canby Dodd seemingly gave her adolescent daughter "complete freedom in the disposition and distribution of [her clothing] allowance," the stipulation that she not ask for more money nor buy anything of which her mother "sincerely disapproved" suggested that adult interests still bounded such freedom.[116] Likewise, while appearing to grant children a greater say, the family firm actually functioned as a form of "democratic social engineering" which allowed parents to secure the desired results by guiding children toward a seemingly spontaneous consensus on appropriate spending limits.

These methods of asserting indirect control through the ostensibly democratic mechanisms of group discussion and group participation were common to other realms of American culture as well during the interwar years. Many important theorists of personnel management, public relations, and progressive education embraced the idea that businesses, teachers, and other leaders could best exercise authority if those they sought to control—students, children, workers, and consumers—were given a stake and a voice in what happened to them.[117] Anticipating the permissiveness that became a hallmark of Dr. Benjamin Spock's enormously influential postwar bestseller *Baby and Child Care*, the new "democratic" model of childrearing constituted a sharp break from the authoritarian discipline of the past but, like Dr. Spock's own theory, was hardly an endorsement of "laissez-faire" parenting.[118] Far from reducing parental influence, disclosing financial information to children often enhanced it by moderating children's demands. Chase Going Woodhouse, who headed the economics division at the United States Bureau of Home Economics in the mid-1920s, observed that children who received allowances and participated in "the family budget council" adopted a more "rational attitude toward the many demands of [their] adolescent group than" children who lacked "these advantages."[119]

These democratic reforms nevertheless constituted real gains in the minds and pocketbooks of many adolescents. Although the statistical data on children's allowances varies, a 1936 survey of 825 children, usefully categorized by class, found that 48 percent of children from professional

By FLORENCE FARISH

PENNY BANK BUDGET

2.7 "Penny Bank Budget," Woman's Home Companion (May 1939).
This illustration for an article advocating family budget councils suggests that children could be taught to moderate their consumer demands in light of other pressing family spending needs.

families and 43 percent of children from semiprofessional and managerial class families received allowances—an impressive increase over the
single-digit percentages that had often prevailed at the turn of the century. Allowances were less common among working-class children, but they
too experienced significant gains, with 28 percent of "semi-skilled" workers and 12 percent of "slightly skilled" workers providing allowances.[120]
Just how much these allowances augmented children's spending funds is
difficult to know, but opinion surveys suggest that many children equated allowances with greater spending freedom. Most of the 400 high school
students who entered Scholastic's "The Kind of Parent I Hope to Be" contest in 1939 favored democratically run households in which children received allowances from early childhood and in which weekly family councils ironed out budgets for each child.[121]

Adolescents, in particular, candidly expressed their yearnings for the financial autonomy that allowances afforded. The sixteen- to eighteen-year-
olds who signed an "Adolescents Want Freedom" manifesto invoked the
new languages of family democracy and psychological adjustment in defending their demands for a clothing allowance and final say in their choice
of apparel. "Many of us who are decidedly anti-social," the teens explained,
"are so only because our parents have not taken care to allow us to dress in
conformity with our social standards and so have let us in for so much
ridicule that we prefer solitude and shun society."[122] Sympathizing with
such adolescent concerns, Gay Head's immensely popular "Boy Dates Girl"
column in Scholastic magazine scripted detailed family dialogues that
showed teens how to win their bids for greater financial autonomy through
negotiation and compromise.[123] This in itself could be viewed as a testament to the triumph of hegemonic discourses that ultimately helped to reconcile children to lower consumer expectations. By the same token, we
should not discount the empowerment children discovered in asserting
their independent claims on the family budget.

Not all children, however, saw allowances as the road to new spending
freedoms. As the sociologists Robert and Helen Lynd reported in their mid-
1920s study of Muncie, Indiana, some high school girls preferred not to
have an allowance, recognizing that "you can get more without one."[124] To
these teenagers, the ostensibly hidden mechanisms of control embedded in
the allowance solution were all too readily apparent.

Children could also prove inventive in appropriating the democratic apparatus of the family firm for their own ends. Such was the case with Frank
Gilbreth Jr. and Ernestine Gilbreth Carey, who described their weekly family council meetings in Cheaper by the Dozen, an autobiographical account
of growing up in the 1920s with the renowned efficiency experts Lillian and

Frank Gilbreth. In such meetings Frank Gilbreth, as father and council chairman, usually controlled the agenda, but on one occasion, the Gilbreth children succeeded in gaining the upper hand. Meeting in advance, the children plotted a scheme to buy a collie, a purchase certain to encounter paternal objections. When the family council convened, the children announced their opposition to the planned purchase of a new violet-colored dining room rug. Noting that they would have to sweep the rug, the children recommended that their mother instead purchase one with a crumb-disguising floral design. They also insisted that only $95 be allotted for the rug's purchase rather than $100, as their mother had planned. The motion carried unanimously. The children then moved and seconded a motion to use the five dollars saved on the rug to buy a collie puppy. Playing to their parents' efficiency-mindedness, the children argued, among other things, that the dog, by eating food scraps, "would save us waste and would save motions for the garbage man." Though their father voted against it and their mother abstained, majority rule prevailed and the Gilbreth children got their dog.[125] If the family firm was merely an expedient arrangement to regulate children's stepped-up demands, clearly it was not an entirely child-proof one.

THE ASCENDANCY OF CONSUMER TRAINING

The democratization of family spending in the 1920s and 1930s marked a significant departure from the thrift education championed in the schools. By asking parents to provide allowances and make children "junior partners of the family firm," child experts were essentially upgrading children from unbridled spendthrifts to budding consumers. Spending money no longer threatened to corrupt children. If doled out regularly and handled systematically, spending money, experts promised, could transform children into wise consumers.

This revaluation of children's spending money highlights an interesting paradox of twentieth-century childhood: at a historical juncture when children's earning power was declining, their economic status and entitlement within the home was rising. What, exactly, drove this reassessment? Some might suspect that the child experts of *Parents' Magazine* were merely doing the bidding of their advertisers, egging parents on in a quest to spread the consumption ethic to every member of the household. Admittedly, child experts sanctioned spending before saving, and, out of necessity, endorsed spending before earning. But rather than view child experts as conspiratorial figures, we would do better to understand how child experts found credence for their convictions in modern psychology as well as old and new traditions of economic thought which associated increased consumption with self-discipline and economic progress.

Childrearing authorities fervently embraced these ideas as they stepped up their attack on excessive thrift during the 1920s and 1930s. They were especially critical of school savings banks for stressing the principles of accumulation over the virtues of wise spending. At best, Sidonie Gruenberg argued, school savings banks gave children "practice in the routine of the simpler banking transactions." But rather than teach children how to use money wisely, she added scornfully, school banks instead "teach thrift as a 'habit' through repeated motions, as if it were possible or desirable to get such a habit."[126] Preferring experiential to rote learning, Gruenberg's disdain for school banking was as much a protest against misplaced educational objectives as it was a critique of pedagogies that sought to instill habits through Taylorized regimentation.

Educators and influential businessmen increasingly found themselves in agreement. Many teachers resented devoting a half hour of valuable class time each week to a program that stressed "mere saving" at the expense of teaching the more valuable principles of wise spending, budgeting, and productive investment.[127] Henry Ford, the automobile maker who advertised "Buy a Ford and Spend the Difference," also voiced skepticism about the value of thrift education. "No successful boy ever saved any money," he told the New York Times in 1928. "They spent it as fast as they got it for things to improve themselves." Saving, Ford advised, was a practice best delayed "until you are forty. It is time enough to save when you can earn more than you can spend wisely. But you will never get to that point by saving."[128] Disenchanted school administrators at one elite private school even took up the cause of promoting allowances as a more effective money training regime. The Tower Hill School requested conferences with parents of children who did not receive an allowance and advised parents of the benefits of "a small allowance for the six-year-old," citing improved school performance and money-handling skills as well as increased initiative and responsibility.[129] So imperative was the need to train future generations of middle-class consumers that some school officials were prepared to substitute one form of compulsion aimed at children for another aimed at parents.

Ironically, it was the very compulsory nature of school banking that drew some of the sharpest criticisms from allowance advocates. Convinced that mandatory saving compromised the educational value of school banking, critics felt that school was not "the place for savings banks. There children are taught obedience, and the lesson taught by saving, if considered compulsory by them, would be followed only when they were under the eye of the teacher."[130] Recalling his own school banking experience, Joseph Heller noted that learning about thrift never really registered on his radar screen: "I wanted a bank account because everybody else had one."[131] Evidence from a questionnaire sent to parents of elementary school children in 1926 also suggests that children's desires to fit in far surpassed their commitment to thrift. Parents often reported that school pride, more than any other factor, motivated their children to save. "The youngest child [a first grader] saves because everyone else does," one parent recounted. "She is not old enough to understand why we save, but she takes great pride in getting 100 per cent." The parent of a second grader thought that school banking taught children more about loyalty to the homeroom than about thrift: "The important thing for the children is to have 100 per cent for their room, and for this reason they always remember their money for the bank."[132] Sponsoring banks compounded such peer pressures to save during the Depression years, as many offered prizes of pencils, writing tablets, thimbles, nursery rhyme booklets, and cash to stimulate competition between classrooms and entire schools.[133]

While children's motivations struck some parents as relatively benign, others perceived them as unwholesome. Sidonie Gruenberg told *Parents' Magazine* readers about children who were driven to pilfer coins from their mother's purse or sell their expensive toys at "ruinous sacrifices in order to make a respectable showing at the school's Thrift Drive."[134] Other children simply rebelled by refusing to deposit any portion of their allowance money on Bank Day. "As they see it," novelist Chester Crowell said of his children, "the school banking system levies a tax, which is part of the cost of their education and therefore properly chargeable to *paterfamilias*. Their own money is for their own use."[135] Crowell's children were hardly unusual: according to a survey of 580 junior and senior high school students, 45 percent of suburban New York City children deposited money that came at least partially from earnings, and another 24 percent deposited part of their allowance money, but the remaining 30 percent deposited money supplied by parents specifically for use on Bank Day.[136] While cynicism among student bankers may not have been as widespread as Crowell intimated, for a substantial group, school banking seems to have done little to foster habits of self-denial.

Far more troubling were concerns that mandatory saving unfairly punished children who could not afford to contribute on Bank Day. Though the overwhelming majority of parents who participated in the 1926 survey approved of school banks, some rigorously opposed them for embarrassing students who either lost their money or lacked the money to make a deposit.[137] For those children, the public ritual of depositing money made

Bank Day a humiliating experience. Noting that school children routinely derided their classmates for "spoiling 100 percent success," one mother gave her fifth-grade daughter "fifty cents a week so she would not be made fun of." Parents also complained that teachers "make the children feel like criminals when they do not bring money," despite the need in many homes for "all the pennies . . . , sometimes even the pennies that the children earn."[138] In a pointed attack on school banking, Chester Crowell decried what he believed was a disturbing pattern in school policies that ranged from making Bank Day compulsory to requiring mothers to sign cards that their children had eaten a hot cereal breakfast. "Beyond doubt," Crowell protested, "[the schools] are becoming a sort of adjunct to the police department, and in their loftier academic services, a delousing plant for the offspring of immigrants."[139]

Although such comments dimmed the prestige of school banking, the Depression itself dealt a much harsher blow. In his autobiographical memoir, Aaron Hotchner recalled losing all the money he had worked "so darn hard all summer for" when the local bank and trust that held the school bank's savings went bust.[140] Other children found their savings accounts drained to pay for basic living expenses when parents lost their jobs or suffered debilitating pay cuts.[141] Although PSFS's *School Bank* magazine touted such withdrawals by "generous little hearts" as proof of the value of school accounts, school banking remained a discredited enterprise in the eyes of many educators.[142] Indeed, the rash of bank failures prompted the National Education Association to denounce bankers as unworthy stewards of children's thrift education.[143] "The banker who was teaching thrift to children a few years ago in a pompous and abstract way," fumed Robert Moore, secretary of the Illinois State Teachers Association, "did not himself understand how to deal with the savings that he lured into his vaults. . . . He was a propagandist, not an educator."[144] Even savings banks that remained solvent found themselves on the defensive. PSFS successfully fended off the board of education's request to provide bond guarantees of student deposits by arguing that any punitive action forbidding PSFS to do school banking might erode public confidence and invite a run on the bank.[145]

In the wake of widespread disenchantment with traditional thrift education, Stuart Chase and other radical voices from the burgeoning consumer movement called for real consumer education in the schools—a curriculum that taught children how to evaluate the merits of consumer products and get the most for their money not just as individual consumers but as members of consumer cooperatives.[146] *Scholastic* magazine endorsed such efforts in a 1935 editorial that urged high school students to arm themselves with a healthy distrust of advertising claims and to organize themselves cooperatively in the pursuit of quality merchandise at reasonable prices.[147] In the end, however, these more radical appeals lost out to the more dominant vision of children's consumer training in the 1930s—one that linked wise consumption with self-improvement and elevated individual taste rather than with the service of collective economic interests.

MONEY TRAINING DURING THE DEPRESSION

The Depression elicited contradictory attitudes toward saving, reviving its importance for some and diminishing its salience for others.[148] Despite his losses, Hotchner continued to be "a very saving type," but countless other children came to view the virtues of thrift and long-range planning with skepticism, if not disdain.[149] One seventeen-year-old girl, having diligently set aside all her Christmas and birthday money for a future purchase, concluded after losing "the savings of a lifetime" that she would have been happier if she "had bought that roadster I wanted last year."[150] In a letter to the *New York Times*, another writer, who claimed membership in the "younger generation," attributed her decision to "never again practice economy" to the "grim example of the thousands of conscientious souls who denied themselves little luxuries and pleasure so that they could 'save their money for an assured future,' and then lost it all anyway." She resolved instead to "obey my impulses and . . . not let any small craving go unsatisfied."[151]

In response to such cynicism, child experts Benjamin and Sidonie Gruenberg conceded that saving was "a form of gamble," but continued to express faith in its value as "an essential part of planning."[152] They might have reminded children of the excessive installment buying that left some destitute after the stock market crash. Indeed, some intellectuals like Stuart Chase, Robert and Helen Lynd, Alfred Bingham, and Carl Zimmerman hoped that the Depression would inspire Americans to reject materialism for simpler pleasures and noncommercialized pursuits.[153] Yet, to a surprising degree during the Depression, child experts became even more committed to the consumer orientation of children's money training. During the 1920s, allowance experts such as Angelo Patri had discouraged borrowing as a violation of "the basic principle" of an allowance—learning to live within a budget.[154] By the 1930s, however, the Gruenbergs had come to appreciate the importance of giving children experience in borrowing and credit. Anticipating that parents would "hesitate to admit children to the benefits of credit," the Gruenbergs reminded parents that the old tradition of discouraging borrowing conflicted with modern practices of buying cars and radios on time-payment plans. Because "our modern business structures are built precisely upon the principle of spending today what we hope to earn next month or next year," they reasoned, children needed "a chance to experience borrowing and lending as well as earning and spending."[155]

This reassessment of children's money training needs did not represent a wholesale rejection of the virtue and value of thrift but a reinterpretation of it. In home economics textbooks and childrearing manuals, the true practice of thrift no longer resided in frugality and saving but in wise spending, efficiency, and consumer education.[156] Instead of teaching children to save for a rainy day, experts advised parents to teach children to save for a purchase that exceeded their current ability to pay. This taught them "to project [their] desires into the future—to forego today's indulgences, to gain a more expensive pleasure, or to anticipate the possibility of a deferred pleasure not yet definitely formulated."[157] In essence, child experts were recasting the virtues of saving in terms of elevated taste and self-improvement. But they were also justifying increased consumption in terms that resonated with puritanical norms of discipline and self-control. "Increased satisfaction through deferred spending—this is the essence of thrift," Thomas Eliot wrote.[158] What they really seemed to endorse was a kind of "calculating hedonism," to borrow sociologist Mike Featherstone's term, which valorized discipline in the pursuit of pleasure.[159]

The notion that consumption could uplift and discipline at the same time had gained currency among intellectuals in the 1910s and 1920s. That these ideas surfaced in the popular advice literature on children's money training in the 1930s suggests just how far mainstream American culture had traveled in embracing consumption as a valued activity. Economist Simon Patten, for example, endorsed the pursuit of luxury as a civilizing process that would refine, discipline, and energize the working class as they worked harder to afford better things.[160] Edwin Seligman's two-volume study *The Economics of Installment Selling* (1927) vindicated the massive expansion of consumer credit that had helped to fuel the rage for installment buying in the 1920s and underwrite middle-class purchases of cars, electric refrigerators, and expensive furniture. Instead of associating consumer debt with improvidence, Seligman suggested that buying on credit merely afforded consumers the opportunity to use goods as they saved for them. In Seligman's view, historian Lendol Calder explains, "buying an automobile was an act of 'saving' just as much as putting the purchase money into a savings account. All that had to be considered was whether the automobile represented a wise investment for the consumer."[161] Saving was still valorized—not for its own sake but as a means to enjoy greater and more productive consumer satisfactions.

Questioning the relevance of traditional concepts of thrift spilled over into a revaluation of consumer desire itself. At the beginning of the century childrearing authorities had stressed the need to curb children's "commercial instincts." By the 1930s, however, spending impulses that had once seemed dangerous and insatiable acquired an aura of benevolence. In place of restrictive measures aimed at restraining consumer desire, experts began to advocate "stimulating" children's desire for socially constructive ends. Reviving older classical liberal appraisals of consumer desire as a goad to industry, Lewis Edwin Theiss recommended such an approach to enhance the child's work ethic.[162] "Particularly helpful is it to arouse in a child some great desire that will necessitate a long-term effort for its gratification—say, the desire for a thirty-dollar bicycle," Theiss wrote in 1936.[163] Child experts gave the same advice to parents who sought guidance for their children's spending problems. Responding to a letter from a parent who complained that her ten-year-old daughter spent all her allowance on "those awful Big Little Books at the five and ten," the expert counseled the parent to call her daughter's "attention to the many other interesting things that are purchasable within the range of her allowance. Sometimes such continuous purchasing of one type of thing arises from just not knowing what else to buy."[164] Instead of restricting children's consumer appetites, experts now recommended that parents stimulate them—though, as this advice suggests, usually in an effort to make children's tastes more like adults'.

Perhaps it should not surprise us that the idea of stimulating desire came to be so attractive during the Depression. As the cure for a flagging economy, the key to a more abundant life, and the guarantor of a reawakened self, desire promised to combat all the enervating effects of the Depression. Best-sellers like Walter Pitkin's *Life Begins at Forty* (1933) and Marjorie Hillis's *Orchids on Your Budget* (1937) urged Americans to get more out of life by living in the moment. Money, Hillis wrote, "should be invested in happiness," as "that drab and old-fashioned virtue," savings, "has never been really enjoyed by anyone except the very penurious and Mr. Coolidge."[165] In the 1930s, success gurus, child experts, and economists alike connected desire with revitalization.[166] Long before the Keynesian revolution of the late 1930s dethroned thrift as the preeminent economic virtue, President Herbert Hoover had directed Americans to help recharge the economy and reduce unemployment by spending instead of saving.[167] During Hoover's tenure, the President's Organization on Unemployment Relief sponsored advertisements instructing consumers that a dollar spent was worth more than a dollar saved in a deflationary economy. One such ad, placed in a 1932 issue of *Boy's Life*, the scouting magazine, conveyed this lesson through a mini-parable about the "Timid Dollar" who hesitated to buy the bargains advertised in the marketplace until it spied another dollar "looking like a dollar-and-a-half, all dressed up in new clothes and carrying a big basket of food." Persuaded to seize the moment, the Timid Dollar took advantage of the "wonderful values" at the marketplace and came home "looking like a dollar-and-a-half, too"—fully revitalized and superior to the "envious Stay-at-home Dollars" who failed to buy when prices were low.[168] Lillian Gilbreth also held out the promise of a revitalized self when she advised *American Girl* readers to budget wisely and spend efficiently so they could not only have more clothes but actually "feel so much better . . . and look happy."[169]

Such positive endorsements of spending did not, of course, receive universal sanction. A 1935 editorial in a Muncie, Indiana, newspaper called for the reinvigoration of the thrift ethic and blamed New Deal ideology for the diminishing importance of thrift in the socialization of children: "Now children are being taught that the less work the better, that one who is without skill has the same right to the fruits of the earth as the man of high intelligence, and that spending for spending's sake alone is a virtue and thrift is a vice."[170] Similarly, a PSFS bank executive championed school banking to counter the "growing lack of independence and the increasing belief that we can lean upon the Government and other agencies for support."[171] Even the most committed thrift advocates, however, found in the rhetoric of spending an indispensable framework for understanding modern economic problems. In a March 1932 issue of the *School Bank* magazine, PSFS's "Bank Lady" devoted an entire column to addressing the query of a junior high school student who wondered why, in light of President Hoover's exhortations to spend, people with bank accounts should not be "forced to draw out their money and spend it." Explaining that the President's gripe was with "hoarders" not bank depositors, the Bank Lady argued that banks were better positioned than ordinary citizens to rejuvenate the economy. After all, banks put depositors' money to work by investing in railroads and buying real estate mortgages and government bonds. Instead of individually spending meager deposits, students could perform a greater public service, the Bank Lady assured, by letting "experienced" bankers "*spend* the money entrusted to them" on real estate investments that would "lift the property depression."[172] Whatever one might say about the Bank Lady's chutzpah in glossing over bankers' recent record of egregious investments, her response illustrates the powerful hold the new spending rhetoric had on the public imagination. Even though PSFS clung to the old verities of thrift education—lessons in self-denial and accumulation still took precedence over lessons in wise spending—it could not completely ignore the shifting cultural terrain (fig. 2.8).[173]

The Miser is a wretched man; he cannot enjoy the gold he hoards

THE THRIFTY MAN

SPENDS CAREFULLY

SAVES THOUHTFULLY

LIVES HAPPILY

Save · DON'T HOARD

THE PHILADELPHIA SAVING FUND SOCIETY

(The oldest Savings Bank in America)

SEVENTH AND WALNUT

Other Offices

1107 MARKET STREET (Temporary Location)

15 SOUTH 52nd STREET	BROAD AND McKEAN STREETS
11th ST. and LEHIGH AVENUE	BROAD AND RUSCOMB STREETS

2.8 PHILADELPHIA SAVINGS FUND SOCIETY ADVERTISEMENT PLACED IN TEN PHILADELPHIA HIGH SCHOOL NEWSPAPERS, FALL 1931.

As Depression-era politicians called upon Americans to help regenerate the economy by spending instead of saving, the Philadelphia Savings Fund Society adjusted its own rhetoric to distinguish virtuous saving from counterproductive hoarding. Courtesy of Hagley Museum and Library.

For the most part, the Depression accelerated and reinforced the legit-imization of consumer spending as a positive social and economic good. Popularizers of modern psychology led the charge in furthering the associ-ation of consumer desire with regeneration and psychic vitality. Worried about the stifling effects of restraint, child experts interpreted rigid con-sumption patterns and excessive thriftiness in children as a sign of a lack-luster imagination or dull personality. During the 1930s, a decade when children's "mental hygiene" and psychological "adjustment" were primary concerns in childrearing discourses, consumer desire became an index of emotional well-being.[174]

The problem of the maladjusted frugal child who rarely spent her al-lowance was especially vexing. Motier Harris Fisher attributed his daughter Anne's "tendency toward miserliness" to a "lack of imagination" and wor-ried that she did not have "more eagerness to live" than her meager spend-ing suggested. To encourage more spending, Fisher replaced his daughter's fixed weekly allowance with a budget plan that required her to submit a list of planned expenditures at the beginning of each week. Although Anne ini-tially relied on her parents to supply ideas, she eventually "discovered," to Fisher's satisfaction, "that spending was as interesting as saving." Increased consumption thus transformed Anne from an unimaginative miser into a spender with a well-adjusted personality, one that better conformed to the broader norms of American consumer society. The same budget plan also suited Fisher's more imaginative son, Timmy, who felt constrained by a fixed allowance. "Given the fertility of Timmy's young mind," Fisher pre-dicted, "his budget is likely to be in a constant state of expansion," but that was precisely what he intended. "Young children's interests wax and wane much more rapidly than those of adults," Fisher explained, "and if one worthy interest is left to die without any expression on the child's part, it is that much definite loss to his general development."[175] Spending denied was a personality denied.

The reappraisal of children's spending also became intertwined with a new "fun morality" that associated healthy psychological adjustment with one's ability to have fun.[176] One minister sanctioned such "fun morality" by giving his four-year-old son three colored piggy banks in which to de-posit his allowance: a pink one called "Church Pig" to hold pennies for the Sunday School collection and "doing good," a blue one named "Business Pig" to collect money for clothes and other personal expenses, and a green pig dubbed "Fun Pig" to store pennies solely for "personal pleasures."[177] The minister's "Fun Pig" gave a moral legitimacy to pleasure-spending that comported well with Protestantism's new emphasis on abundant living as the road to salvation. Succumbing to religious sanctions to let go and live a little, the old trinity of saving, giving, and spending was giving way to a new one of spending, giving, and more spending.[178]

The magnification of sympathy for children's consumer desires during the 1930s also reflected the influence of Freudian psychology. Where previously experts attributed children's spending problems to their insatiable acquisitive instincts, Freudian insights encouraged a more sympathetic view of children's desire for things, seeing it as a reflection of various unconscious needs. The child who spent all her money at the candy store was not an incorrigible spendthrift with a sweet tooth but a child who did not receive enough affection from her parents. A five-year-old who stole money from her seven-year-old brother after being denied an allowance of her own was not cursed with a thief's heart but was consumed by deep-seated feelings of jealousy. Her stealing was less a need for material things than a need for "a type of power which her brother has and she has not."[179] No longer a sign of moral failure, an abundance of consumer desire instead testified to unmet psychological needs. "To the child," psychiatrist Clare Keith explained, "money is merely a symbol of the thing he feels he lacks. . . . When he uses it to buy something, . . . he is attempting to buy for himself the security, the love, of which he feels himself deprived."[180] Allowance money thus not only assisted children's financial education but it assured their psychic security.

The reassessment of the child consumer was one of the most striking outcomes of the shift from thrift education to consumer training. During the first four decades of the twentieth century, the image of the child as an impulsive spendthrift—tolerated by parents and disdained by bankers—gradually gave way to a more hopeful image of the child as a savvy consumer who appreciated the high cost of living and could "buy daily without regrets." Ironically, it was not until the 1930s, a decade not of affluence but of poverty, that the consumer orientation of children's money training most firmly took root. Concerns about psychological adjustment, the rediscovered economic benefits of consumption, "fun morality," and the companionate family ideal all contributed to more benign interpretations of children's spending impulses.

Many children during the Depression were not directly or immediately affected by such ideological transformations. Indeed, Glen Elder's longitudinal study of the depression's impact on family life shows that children who experienced economic hardships developed a conservative financial outlook that lasted long into adulthood. For those children, the depression's most enduring economic lessons underscored the dangers of spending beyond your means.[181] It remains, however, far from clear, as historian Joseph Hawes contends, that the depression "rendered children who grew up under its influence permanently conservative about financial matters."[182] Middle-class children surely also developed outlooks and expectations that facilitated rather than stymied the voluminous consumer spending of the post–World War II years. Yet even this consumer ease did not portend the inevitable rise of a spendthrift nation. Under the allowance regime, middle-class children acquired a managerial ethos befitting the new economic order. They learned not simply new habits of fiscal responsibility but new habits of mental discipline that compelled them to continually imagine and seek better things. In this sense allowance money did not represent the abandonment of producer values but a systematic conjoining of the producer and consumer ethos within the dynamic personality of the savvy child consumer.

CHAPTER 3

Heroes of the New Consumer Age:
Imagining Boy Consumers

IF THE SAVVY CHILD CONSUMER of parents' dreams in the 1920s was a disciplined spender, the savvy child consumer of advertisers' dreams was a master persuader. In popular culture and advertising discourses, no figure better embodied the promise of consumer salesmanship than the white, middle-class American boy. Consider, for example, how a New York talent agency promoted Percy Crosby's famous comic-strip character Skippy as an ideal advertising pitchman in a 1927 issue of the advertising trade journal *Printers' Ink*. Described as "a worthy successor to Huckleberry Finn, Tom Sawyer, and Penrod"—the cunning boy heroes of children's literature—Skippy was not only "wise for his years," the advertisement claimed, but determined to "argue or fight for what he wants. Skippy rarely loses an argument for he knows definitely what he and 'the folks' should have. . . . If Skippy likes your reputable merchandise, . . . so will others and you will profit by having him 'whistle the patter' for you."[1]

To prospective advertisers, Skippy's virtues as an advertising spokesman resided as much in his dynamic boyish charms as they did in his celebrity. For the very traits that made Skippy such a compelling salesman also made him an archetypal American boy: a demanding, influential, and precocious consumer. This image of the American boy became increasingly familiar in the second and third decades of the twentieth century, thanks to the juvenile magazine publishers who promoted him and the advertisers who embraced him as the hero of the new consumer age. Sell the boy, publishers and marketing strategists promised, and you will have at your command a progressive and loyal consumer, eager and able to influence family spending. As an ad placed by *American Boy*, a prominent children's magazine, put it, the boy consumer was nothing short of a "human dynamo—restless, resistless, resourceful. When he wants a thing he gives no one any peace until he gets it."[2]

One might be tempted to view the much-vaunted boy consumer simply as a manifestation of the growing clout and significance of child consumers in the early twentieth century. All child consumers, however, were not equal. Though advertisers targeted both boys and girls, the construct of the demanding, persuasive child consumer was not entirely gender neutral. When admen and children's magazine publishers glorified the progressive appetites and salesmanship of the child consumer, they usually had the manly boy in mind. What made the valorization of the boy consumer so remarkable was its departure from a centuries-long tradition of associating consumption with feminine vices. From the moralists of Greco-Roman times to the republican pamphleteers of the seventeenth and eighteenth centuries, critics of unbridled consumption—what they would have termed luxury—had decried materialistic excess as the mark of effeminate men and lustful women. To be seduced by luxury was, in historian Victoria de Grazia's words, to be overcome by an "out-of-control femininity." Even in the late nineteenth century, when Victorian gender ideology sanctioned women's cultural authority as expert shoppers and arbiters of taste, women remained subject to age-old prejudices that maligned consumer desire. As medical science would have it, the middle-class lady shoplifter was not a thief but a kleptomaniac—weak-willed by nature, narcissistic, ruled by emotions, and incapable of self-control.[3]

Such stereotypes of the woman consumer generated considerable ambivalence among admen toward their predominantly female audience. Recognizing women as the "purchasing agents" of the family, trade journals routinely reported that women accounted for 85 percent of consumer spending. By advertisers' own reckoning, such command over the family purse strings gave women the consumer clout to make or break a product's success with the snap of their pocketbooks. Yet, although awe for women's buying authority sometimes translated into respect for women's consumer sovereignty, it also coexisted with contempt for Mrs. Consumer's fickleness, stupidity, and irrationality. However unfounded, such attitudes helped ease uncertainties many admen felt about their own claims to professional legitimacy and respectability. For despite their college educations and upper middle-class backgrounds, members of this predominantly male profession encountered disapproval from peers and guardians of high culture who criticized advertising for pandering to the vulgar lowbrow tastes and irrationalities of the feminine consuming masses.[4]

Why then, in light of such problematic associations of consumption and femininity, did children's magazine publishers and the advertising trade glorify boys as consumer dynamos? How did the celebrated exuberance of boys' consumer appetites escape association with the allegedly feminine vices of extravagance and frivolousness? Most importantly, how did the architects of mass consumption revise and restore meaning to the conventional gender polarities of work and leisure, breadwinning and consumption, discipline and impulsiveness that masculine consumption threatened to disrupt?

Curiously, although men were targets of advertising and avid consumers of sporting goods, commercialized leisure, clothing, grooming aids, and even crystal, the advertising trade press offered little comment on adult male consumer desire prior to the 1930s.[5] In fact, despite evidence to the contrary, embarrassed automobile marketers and manufacturers, unwilling to concede male interest in "superfluous" features that had little bearing on car performance, clung to traditional gender stereotypes in promoting cars to men and women, sometimes even in the same ad. Thus the Lexington Minute Man Six was advertised to *Sunset* readers as "a man's car in power and speed—and a woman's car because of its luxury, ease of handling, and simplicity of control."[6]

Advertising discourses on the boy consumer resolved the apparent contradictions between consumption and masculine gender identity. Figuring as a kind of bridge between the businessman's allegedly sober rationalism and the irrational extravagances of the archetypal woman consumer, the boy consumer seemed to occupy a liminal space that mediated the transformation from an older producer ethos to a newer consumer ethos. Neither wholly of one or the other, the boy consumer appealed because he wedded the virtues of consumption to the virtues of business. Unlike the feminine consuming masses, in whose hands consumption threatened to spin into hedonism, the boy consumer managed to harmonize the consumer ethos with older ideals of industriousness and disciplined entrepreneurship. He purchased advertised goods to further worthy entrepreneurial ambitions and worked hard to afford them. But if his work ethic preserved traditional notions of bourgeois manhood, other traits made him the embodiment of new ideals of masculinity that accompanied the rise of managerial capitalism. In his passionate enthusiasm, loyalty, and salesmanship, the boy consumer displayed all the hallmarks of the successful corporate personality.[7] Though easily ascribed to youthful enthusiasm, consumer exuberance was made to fit within these new ideologies of manhood. Further, the boy's affinity for technological innovation—his love of cars, wireless, and all things mechanical—made his consuming passions a force of progress. Viewed in this light, the boy consumer's unrestrained embrace of advertised goods could be interpreted as evidence of manly vitality rather than of emasculation.

The boy consumer's appeal suggests, contrary to some interpretations, that advertisers, as purveyors of the new culture of consumption, did not wrestle with their demons simply by pinning hedonistic excesses on women.[8] Rather, they sought to contain the new culture's threatening implications by softening the dichotomies between the producer ethos and the consumer ethos that historians have all too often exaggerated in their portraits of early-twentieth-century consumer culture.[9] As recent scholarship by Jackson Lears and Lendol Calder has suggested, the rise of consumer culture did not invariably lead to a hedonistic ethos, as it created its own rhetoric and mechanisms of self-control.[10] The idealized figure of the boy consumer emerged in advertising discourses as a reassuring emblem of the new consumer age precisely because he showed how consumption could balance the tensions between hedonism and control. Herein lay the psychic rewards of selling the boy consumer. Admen, still not fully convinced of their own legitimacy, cherished the ideal of the boy because he possessed attributes that they most admired in themselves. As one who prized technological innovation and readily adopted the new, the boy seemed to erase the cultural gap that nagged at advertisers in their courtship of Mrs. Consumer. Moreover, as the master salesman who guided family spending, the boy, much like the adman, relished his role as a missionary of progress. In this way, various strands of business ideology—drawn from the worlds of advertising and the modern corporation—helped to forge a new synthesis of consumption and masculine gender identity.

AMERICAN BOY'S CAMPAIGN TO PROMOTE THE BOY CONSUMER

The earliest and most aggressive promoter of the boy consumer was the boys' magazine *American Boy*. Read by well-to-do middle-class boys who ranged in age from nine to nineteen, the magazine aimed to cultivate character and enterprise through its wholesome fiction, articles on ways to make money and things, and features on hobbies and heroes. The magazine's reputation for clean, inspirational reading won it a welcome place in middle-class homes and YMCA reading rooms, where it was embraced as an attractive alternative to the "cheap novels and wild story papers" that progressive-era reformers believed poisoned young minds.[11] Thanks to its popularity among boys and the approval of parents and community leaders, by 1910 *American Boy* boasted subscription sales of 500,000.[12]

Central to *American Boy*'s mission as a character builder was instructing its readers in the virtues and values of advertising. To gain credibility with prospective advertisers, *American Boy* assured firms that its readers learned "a surer and finer appreciation of values—personal and commercial" and were well-schooled in "the underlying principles of advertising."[13] Much as *Good Housekeeping* and *Collier's* had previously done in 1909 and 1910, *American Boy* launched a monthly series of "Advertising Talks" that appeared in its pages from May 1917 through April 1918.[14] These editorials educated boys about the superior value and trustworthiness of advertised goods and helped the magazine cultivate its image as a chummy advisor who guided and shaped the boy market to better serve advertisers.[15]

From the 1910s through the 1920s, the central focus of *American Boy's* ongoing trade press campaign was selling the virtues of the boy consumer himself. In some cases, *American Boy* enticed advertisers with the promise that they could hit "PAY-dirt" advertising to boys, who were prime "paying prospects" for popular products like bicycles (fig. 3.1). A more prominent strategy, however, was to connect the boy's consumer prowess to the child-centeredness of the middle-class companionate family. In *American Boy's* vision, boys commanded the authority of a miniature patriarch within such families. Likening the boy to a "Dictator to the Universe," *American Boy* depicted boys as the center of families in which "*boy* wants, *boy* opinions and *boy* knowledge *go*" (fig. 3.2).[16] Thanks to the special affection middle-class parents held for their sons, boys proved remarkably influential salesmen. "Every boy is an eighth wonder of the world to his parents," *American Boy* reminded advertisers. "They want to follow his interest; they study the magazine he reads; they see the world as he sees it; and they buy the things he wants—not merely because they want the **merchandise** but because they want to **please the boy**."[17]

As if to make sure potential advertisers understood the boy was not milking maternal sentiment alone, the trade press campaign stressed that fathers were especially likely to bend before the boy's demands. According to one ad, "the approval of his boys means more to a man than the approval of anyone else in the world."[18] Other boys' publications concurred. Explaining why "Every Boy Family Is a Center of Buying Energy," the *Boys' Magazine* observed that it was "apt to be rough on father's prestige" if he failed to cater to his boy's consumer demands.[19] Here was a glimpse of the pecuniary underbelly of the companionate family: the breadwinner's fiscal generosity helped to cement bonds of affection that mutuality alone could not seal. Here also was the ultimate assurance of advertising success: who need worry about changing stodgy adult mindsets when courting the boy promised to relax buying resistance from the family breadwinner?

The boy's influence on family spending also owed much to the progressiveness and adaptability of youth. In the newly electrified, motorized, wireless age that gave birth to mass communication and mass transportation, modernist sensibilities reveled in the "here and now" and made a cult

"PAY~dirt"

FROM the thousands of your neighbors there is an important fraction that makes up your list of paying prospects.

In the bicycle trade this fraction consists mostly of boys. To separate these prospects clean from the mass of the population has been a selling problem.

For the bicycle manufacturer and dealer THE AMERICAN BOY magazine has solved this problem. With its tremendous circulation among boys exclusively (more than 500,000 boy readers averaging 15½ to 16 years old) it gets 100% interested attention from your most active customers and prospects. Its advertising columns make the boy want a bicycle *first*. They help the boy to select his bicycle—and a trail of repeat accessories.

THE AMERICAN BOY

"The Biggest, Brightest, Best Magazine for Boys in All the World"

3.1 "PAY-DIRT," 1920.
American Boy's advertisements in advertising trade magazines promised manufacturers a prime consumer audience. Courtesy Ayer Collection.

Dictator to the Universe— the Boy

There never was one like him in the world before. That's what every parent thinks. Naturally in that home *boy* wants, *boy* opinions and *boy* knowledge *go*.

In every family the boy is the *acquisitive* member. With the divine optimism of youth he sees all the good things of life coming his way; he wants a share in the best of everything—and that share is usually a big one.

Every *boy home* is a home of enthusiasm, energy and genuine interest in the progress of the world. From the latest automobile styles to the newest phonograph records; from baseball to army rifles—the boy knows what's going on and he sees that the rest of the family know it, too.

200,000 Boy Homes Reached by

The American Boy

Here are two hundred thousand families interested in *the* boy's magazine *because* the boy is the biggest thing in the world to them. Here are two hundred thousand *boy homes* where dozens of articles are going to be bought only because the boy wants them. Every American Boy home is a home of comfortable living, where money can be found to buy most of the things the boy sets his heart upon.

These boys average 15½ years of age. Their wants are almost a man's wants. And their knowledge stands behind most of the purchases in the home.

THE SPRAGUE PUBLISHING COMPANY
J. COTNER, JR., Secretary-Treasurer, DETROIT, MICH.
H. M. PORTER, Eastern Mgr., 1170 Broadway, NEW YORK

3.2 "DICTATOR TO THE UNIVERSE—THE BOY."
As early as 1912, when this advertisement appeared in the advertising trade journal *Printers' Ink*, *American Boy* touted the boy as an exuberant and influential consumer.

of the new—sensibilities most perfectly embodied in the spirit of youth. As a result, the *Boys' Magazine* boldly claimed, modernity itself had given boy authority more weight than patriarchical authority. Thanks to the rapid pace of change in modern society, one 1912 ad explained, "boy knowledge" had become indispensable. "The boy is the only member of the family with enough **mental agility** to keep pace with the times. He tells father what's what."[20] Manufacturers, weary of resistant adults, could turn to "youth for acceptance—knowing that fellows like Walt and Sam think and talk progress, anticipate it, rush to meet it more than halfway. Youth greases the wheels of progress . . . keeping the oldsters moving forward, well oiled with the spirit of advance."[21]

As such *American Boy* ads implied, boys commanded influence over family spending because of their superior consumer savvy. In one trade press ad, it was the boy, not the mother, who assumed the mantle of family purchasing agent. Boy wonder "Billy Byer" helped solve his mother's dilemma over what brand of cereal to buy when he recommended one regularly advertised in his favorite magazine. Billy's father, exceedingly pleased with his son's interest in learning from advertisements, promptly told his wife "it was right to have [Billy] . . . suggest things we're going to buy."[22] To advertisers who sometimes doubted the woman consumer's savvy, *American Boy* offered a tempting vision of an exuberant boy, schooled in advertising, inspiring Mrs. Consumer on her way to the market.

Promoters of the boy market routinely asserted that deference to the boy consumer was a matter of course within modern, democratic families. "Nowadays," *American Boy* reminded prospective advertisers, "boys are considered more."[23] A series of advertising vignettes featuring sixteen-year-old "Master Billy Byer" underscored the esteem and deference accorded the fact-finding boy consumer. In one such ad Billy's younger sister, recently endowed with a generous handout from Dad, requests her brother's assistance in purchasing a new camera, noting that Mother and Dad had anointed him "the official wise-party on what to buy." The accompanying photograph shows Billy confidently explaining camera features to his awed and grateful sister inside a camera shop. Shot from behind the sales counter, the photo allows us to see only the back of the store salesman, who presumably has been rendered mute—perhaps he too is awed—by Billy's disquisition on the virtues of a particular camera brand.[24]

Much as this particular ad likened the boy's consumer authority to that of an adult male—in this case a seasoned camera store salesman—other *American Boy* ads suggested to prospective advertisers that the boy's consumer authority was equal, perhaps even superior, to his father's, especially in the realm of new technologies like cars, radios, or phonographs.

Advertising photographs of a family conference at the dinner table conveyed the boy's consumer influence in simple, iconographic terms. In one ad, captioned "When Slim Watson talks carburetors his family sits up and takes notice," we see Mother and Dad listening intently and respectfully as young "Slim" offers pointers on what car make to buy (fig. 3.3).[25] In another, all the family members—Mother, Dad, and Sissy Lou—are seated at a round table, except for Billy Byer, who stands behind his father, seeming to guide the discussion over what brand the new family phonograph should be. From the text, we learn that Billy and his father, having both studied *American Boy* advertisements, concur on a phonograph make and prevail over the less-informed consumer votes of Mother and Sissy Lou. Though Billy was a team player in the phonograph's selection—a mirror and reinforcement of patriarchal authority—his position in the photo (standing beside seated family members) visually expressed the boy's dominance in family spending—a fitting pictorial tribute to the consumer mastery of "Master Byer" himself.[26]

American Boy's representation of the family conference as a democracy of consumer equals departed from the more common visual cliché of the family circle that appeared in mainstream mass magazines. Typically, Roland Marchand has shown, children occupied subordinate positions on the floor and the father "retained his stature as the most important and *au courant* family member."[27] The "soft-focus ambience of the family circle" in these consumer advertisements romanticized informal, affectionate family bonds yet "subtly reaffirmed the father's dominant role," blurring the democratic edges of the companionate family.[28] By contrast, the crisp photography of *American Boy*'s trade advertisements hinted not toward the past but toward the modernity of new democratic family arrangements. In *American Boy*'s vision of family democracy, parental opinions easily gave way to boy opinions. The magnitude of boy influence extended from routine household expenditures like breakfast cereal and soap to grander purchases of cars, phonographs, and radios. Even the choice of a private boarding school was no longer father's sole preserve. According to a 1921 ad, in a contest between "Dad's loyalty to his Alma Mater or the preference built up by consistent advertising to the boy in his own magazine . . . the boy's vote often decides."[29]

American Boy no doubt overstated the democratic boundaries of the middle-class companionate family. Indeed, in touting the boy's powers of persuasion, the magazine's trade press campaign sometimes championed boy salesmanship that others might have construed as bratty, spoiled behavior. "When the family sets out for an evening at the movies, son not only tells father and mother *where* to go, but he insists as well that they shall

When Slim Watson talks carburetors
his family sits up and takes notice

The young man at the left of the picture is Slim Watson, none other! He knows a pile about motor-cars and is letting Mother and Dad in on a big earful.

For some time, the head of the family (over there on the right) has been planning to trade in his old car. Like many car-owners, he's in the period of indecision as to which make to buy. Should he trade it in for the same make, an open car or a coupe, one of a different make? Pretty hard to make up his mind. Slim is convincing him that such-and-such a bus is the best buy . . . the one he really ought to have. It isn't the first time that Slim and his Dad have thrashed out the subject, either. Looks as though the youngest of the family were scoring a win at this session!

Slim is just one of the 500,000 up-and-coming near-men who read THE AMERICAN BOY and talk motor-car to their parents. These 500,000 enthusiasts are great boosters for the automobile that has won their respect and confidence. They're your equal in everything but years. Their man-sized opinions are heeded and usually followed by the man who pays the bills. Their wants are man-sized and they usually get what they want.

Enlist the powerful influence of this big army of rooters on your side. Tell them about your motor-car through the advertising columns of THE AMERICAN BOY. It's their favorite publication, and its say-so determines their buying habits. Copy received by January 10th will appear in March.

The American Boy

Detroit   Michigan

3.3 "WHEN SLIM WATSON TALKS CARBURETORS," 1926.

American Boy depicted the middle-class family as a consumer democracy in which boys exercised powerful influence.

Courtesy Ayer Collection.

take his choice. They do—or you don't know the tenacity of a boy's reasoning."[30] Of course, exaggerating the realities of family democracy and deference to boy opinion served a larger purpose. Subscription sales alone would not pay for the fine stories and illustrations the *American Boy* editors commissioned. But a steady supply of advertisers, convinced that the boy market was worthy of their marketing dollars, would.

To gain advertisers' confidence, *American Boy* needed to persuade them that the purchasing power of its mostly high school subscribers was not limited to their spending allowance or meager earnings. Further, the publishers needed to counter common perceptions that juvenile advertising was only of value as a long-term investment in building brand recognition and at best a sales booster of exclusively juvenile products. *American Boy* thus represented itself not just as a valuable juvenile advertising medium but as an upscale class medium. To gain access to the boy was to gain access to prosperous, free-spending families. "'Where there's a boy there's a family'—and in this case a family that pays $1.50 a year" for an *American Boy* subscription enjoyed by all members of the family.[31] By guaranteeing access to families of means, *American Boy* hoped prospective advertisers would come to regard boys as "a direct sales factor"—"When you advertise to them . . . you sell them for today and for tomorrow"—who influenced purchases of boy goods as well as family goods.[32] But even if advertisers were not convinced that boy persuasion was sufficient to close the sale, they could be reassured that their message would be read by other family members who also perused the magazine.[33] The proposition that advertisers could reach multiple consumer constituencies by targeting the boy—not just children, but mothers and fathers as well—meant that the magazine could attract advertising from a wide array of mass marketers. How better to generate revenues than by maintaining a diverse advertising portfolio of toys, cereal, soap, toothpaste, shoes, clothing, sporting goods, automobiles, radios, bicycles, and bicycle tires?[34]

American Boy also enhanced perceptions of the boy's purchasing power by highlighting his role within the "family firm." The concept of the family firm was originally the brainchild of progressive home economists and child experts, who popularized the idea in *Parents' Magazine* and other women's magazines during the 1920s and 1930s. Conceiving the family firm as a sort of round-table conference on family finances, child experts promoted it as a vehicle to teach children the value of money and moderate their consumer demands. But while child experts envisioned a parent-directed family firm that would teach children an appreciation of limits, *American Boy* imagined boys assuming a far more participatory and influential role. As one trade press ad would have it, when it came time to review the ar-

chitects' plan for a new home, the boy "was very much 'in' on the conference—plugging for a certain fire-proof roofing, for floors the gang could
dance on, for an oil-burning furnace (he's been toting ashes in the old
house!)—and a dozen other modern knick knacks and angles."[35] Above all,
American Boy's family firm strategy made clear that the boy was the advertiser's route to deeper family pockets. *American Boy* readers, one ad
claimed, were "man-sized, man-minded fellows" who "are pressing, day after day, in their family buying councils, for the acceptance of progressive
merchandise of every description."[36] Boys need not let a drained allowance
stand in the way of their expansive consumer desires, another ad contended, when they could marshal "the facts for selling-the-family campaigns on
things their allowances can't buy."[37]

Though *American Boy* probably overstated the magnitude of boy influence on family spending, boys' self-conceptions seemed remarkably in sync
with *American Boy*'s laudatory rhetoric. Consider the responses to a 1913
American Boy contest soliciting letters addressed to misguided national advertisers not yet plugging their wares in the magazine. First-prize winner
Berthold Woodhams told Postum Cereal Company that "when you interest the American boy you interest American fathers, mothers, everybody."
Second-prize winner John Prior advised Westinghouse Electric that
"Mother doesn't understand 'machinery,' father's 'busy'; so the handy little electric household appliance isn't ordered by name—unless the family
mechanic, age 15, interferes." Emil Kolar goaded Kellogg Toasted Corn
Flakes to advertise, claiming that a boy "would either buy [the cereal] himself or 'bother' his mother until she would buy it." Wilbur Sterling informed skeptical car manufacturers that the boy's choice "greatly determined" parents' automobile choice.[38] Setting aside the contest committee's
self-serving motives in showcasing such letters, these confident assertions
of boys' consumer prowess and authority reveal the glimmer of reality that
animated *American Boy*'s bold trade press campaign.

The Material and Psychic Rewards of Selling the Boy

Judging by the rapid expansion of space devoted to advertising in *American
Boy, Boy's Life*, and *Youth's Companion* during the 1910s and especially the
1920s, children's magazine publishers had succeeded in awakening advertisers to the lucrative potential of the boy market. In a 1920 study of 72 magazines, *Youth's Companion* and *American Boy* ranked 38th and 43rd respectively in advertising volume, each drawing approximately half a million

dollars in annual advertising revenues—millions shy of the leading wo-men's magazines but more than respected monthly standards like *Atlantic Monthly, Harper's, Physical Culture, Sunset,* and *Scientific American.*[39]

Advertisers were guided in their courtship of the boy consumer by the supposition that the middle-class boy exercised consumer authority not just over family members but over other children as well, especially girls and less affluent boys. If the middle-class boy's privileged status as a dicta-tor of trends made him a miniature patriarch within in his own family, it made him an aristocrat among child consumers. Kodak, for example, ran special advertising contests in *Boys' Life,* the staunchly middle-class scout-ing magazine, on the grounds that Boy Scouts were "the best and liveliest boys in town" and as such sure to set enviable examples for others.[40] Like-wise, *American Boy* touted its well-to-do subscribers as "leaders in their neighborhood—the presidents and treasurers of the little social clubs—the captains of the teams—the most popular men at school—the fellows who stand out as leaders from their boyhood up, and whose opinions carry most weight."[41]

More pronounced was the assumption among advertisers that boys commanded authority over the consumption patterns of girls. Even as ad-vertisers sought the allegiance of both boys and girls, they routinely privi-leged boy culture. For example, when the Streckfus Steamers steamboat company devised an ad campaign to revive interest in steamboat excur-sions, it was entirely keyed to masculine nostalgia—even though the com-pany distributed its advertising booklets to Girl Scouts and Camp Fire Girls as well as Boy Scouts and YMCAs. Boy culture was the highlight when the Streckfus "Mississippi River Steamboat Manual" related dramatic stories of "glamorous deeds," famous steamboat captains, and legendary battles be-tween "daring men" and Indian chiefs along the great river—tales advertis-ers thought would excite the interest of "any red-blooded youth." Like so many advertising efforts, theirs was a campaign to "win back the boy."[42] All too often, catching the girl was but a lazy afterthought in an advertising cul-ture that exalted boy opinion and boy persuasion.

Advertisers, with some justification, judged boys a more responsive au-dience. According to *Printed Salesmanship,* boys comprised 60 percent of children who filled in coupons for premiums offered through advertise-ments.[43] But advertisers concentrated primarily on reaching the boy be-cause they perceived girls to be far more flexible and boys far more rigid in their gender identification. As advertising authority Evalyn Grumbine ob-served, "Girls admire and enjoy boys' books and many boys' activities. Boys, however, do not reciprocate in their feelings about girls' activities."[44] A contributor to *Printers' Ink Monthly* recognized the same lack of reciprocity in girls' and boys' radio preferences, noting that while girls listened to the same radio programs as boys, boys did not pay attention to programs that "hold a feminine audience."[45] Put another way, creators of popular culture expected girls to embrace male heroes as their own, and many girls, having grown accustomed to the denial of female subjectivity, so obliged. As film theorist Laura Mulvey has explained, "for women (from childhood onwards) trans-sex identification is a *habit* that very easily becomes *second Nature*."[46] Such cross-gender identification, however, was not expected of boys and was, if anything, actively discouraged as a potential obstacle to the acquisition of masculinity. In both popular and psychiatric conceptions of boyhood during the early twentieth century, the effeminate boy was maligned as a "homosexual in the making."[47] Advertisers, no less than parents and child psychologists, recognized the importance of preserving gender boundaries between little girls and little boys. By relegating girls to the periphery, or in some cases excluding them altogether, advertisers, historian Ruth Oldenziel has observed, may well have helped "to shore up male identity boundaries in the new world of expanding consumerism precariously coded as female."[48]

Such privileging of boy culture thus served multiple purposes. On the one hand, selling the boy consumer offered numerous material rewards to advertisers, not the least of which was the opportunity to reach multiple consumer constituencies among children and within families. But it was the psychic rewards of selling the boy consumer that made him such a significant cultural phenomenon. To the largely male advertising profession, the boy consumer was an ideal spokesman for the progressive virtues of consumption. As a promoter of the new and improved, the boy consumer mirrored advertisers' own self-image as the engineers of the nation's rising standard of living. Steadfast in his allegiance to modernity, the boy seemed to intuitively grasp that advertising's mission was aligned with progress itself. As *American Boy* noted in its trade press campaign, "The boy today is usually the first to take up the new things, to demand the improvements that have made the American family's standard of living so high."[49] Indeed, the boy consumer's modernity made him the guiding force behind "THE UP-TO-THE-MINUTE FAMILY": "It's almost an obsession with him—to be alert for news of new things, better ways—to see that modern goods and services come up for discussion in the family buying council."[50]

Advertising advocates could point to the boy consumer's modernizing zeal as justification for the trade's claims to professional legitimacy. Since the turn of the twentieth century, advertising partisans had argued that advertising played an essential role in the nation's economy and cultural life. Making the case first in trade journals and then in mass magazines, advertising boosters credited advertising with having made significant contributions to material and cultural progress. Advertising had solved problems of overproduction by stimulating demand and rationalizing distribution, the argument went; it had "elevated" public taste for better things and ways of living by bringing the public "news" of progressive manufacturers; and it had improved the quality and prices of goods by securing outlets for mass-produced, branded goods.[51] "Advertising is **revolutionary**," the J. Walter Thompson agency rhapsodized. "Its tendency is to overturn preconceived notions, to set new ideas spinning through the reader's brain to induce people to do something that they never did before. It is a form of progress, and it **interests only progressive people**."[52]

Despite the advertising trade's confident discourse, lingering doubts about advertising's merits remained. Even as admen distanced themselves from advertising's unsavory past of patent medicine peddlers and snake oil salesmen, caricatures in popular fiction and on the stage continued to stereotype them in unflattering ways. The J. Walter Thompson agency complained in its *News Bulletin* that playwrights and novelists lampooned the adman as "a breezy, cocksure, snap judgment, phrase making individual who is altogether ridiculous from the conservative business viewpoint." Theatergoers recognized him as the fool "who interrupts discussion with snappy inspiration along jazz lines," the *News Bulletin* grumbled. Such slights to admen's expertise magnified their professional insecurities and revived suspicions at J. Walter Thompson that business executives failed to "accept the advertising man as an individual having the same professional or business standards as himself." Desperate to be taken seriously, the ad industry managed to exhibit both defensiveness and an inflated sense of purpose in reasserting its professional legitimacy. Admen, after all, were college graduates, drawn from top universities, far too serious, J. Walter Thompson maintained, to devote "time to thinking up zippy catch phrases or snappy slogans." Rather, they approached "the problem of merchandising and advertising with the same careful and analytical method that a problem of national farming, food distribution, [or] coal distribution . . . would be approached."[53]

Such faith in advertising's value to the nation did not, however, ease all concerns. Though the boy seemed less prone to the vices of Mrs. Consumer, the concept of a masculine consumer identity nevertheless required defense. For all the praise heaped on the boy consumer, his progressive buying habits at times threatened to recall less flattering associations with feminine malleability, extravagance, and vanity—traits advertisers usually reserved for Mrs. Consumer. Take, for example, an *American Boy* trade press ad that applauded the boy consumer for knowing "more about styles

for young men . . . than *Vanity Fair*" or the one that commended his responsiveness to progressive obsolescence: "He buys a new hat every season and a straw hat every summer. . . . He goes out in search of the newest
thing in neck-ties and shirts. And he gets what he wants."[54] Yet, as other
ads implied, fashion-conscious boys were not the victims of progressive
obsolescence but rather the trend-setters who dictated its rapid pace.
"When they crack the whip you jump," *American Boy* cautioned the
trade. "Ask Sam and Andy Stevens what the well-dressed near-man will
wear. They'll tell you. They have the latest dope on shawl collars, bat-
wing ties, patent leathers and pompadours. If they don't like a thing—it's
out" (fig. 3.4).[55]

Advertising boosters unraveled traditional associations of consumption
and femininity by valorizing the masculinity of boy consumers. As one authority on the boy market stressed, advertisements were not addressed to
the "Little Lord Fauntleroy type" but to the manly aspirations of "real
honest-to-goodness back-lot boys who go to school, play and dream
dreams, to say nothing of working at odd jobs once in a while when the
chance offers to pick up a 'couple of bits.'"[56] The reference to Frances
Hodgson Burnett's widely read 1886 novel contrasted the manly boy consumer with the title character, an overprotected prissy who dressed in lace-
collared velvet suits and wore long curls. Exhibiting neither the sartorial excesses nor the aristocratic demeanor that typified little Lord Fauntleroys,
middle-class boy consumers—ones who earned a "couple of bits" now and
then—could not be stigmatized as sissies. A stock figure in early twentieth
century popular culture, the sissy was a recurring foil—a counterpoint to
real manly boys—in Norman Rockwell illustrations that adorned the covers and advertisements of the *Saturday Evening Post*.[57] According to a 1917
ad illustrated by Rockwell, real boys (the "genuine—tree climbing—mar-
ble playing—tousle-headed—made-in-America BOY!") possessed the fashion sense to wear Black Cat hosiery that "the Little Lord Fauntleroys you
read about in storybooks" lacked.[58] In contrasting the sissy's "overtly narcissistic investment" in appearance with the manly boy's casual fashion
aplomb, Rockwell's illustrations suggested that masculine consumerism
and interest in style need not "degenerat[e] into effeminacy."[59]

American Boy's trade press campaign thus drew upon a familiar discourse in popular culture in seeking to desissify the boy consumer. Accordingly, *American Boy* readers were "two-fisted young men whose buying impulse knows no vacation." Instead of deriding boys for their
self-indulgence, the magazine celebrated their expansive consumer desire
as the mark of "near-men" who "buy with a man-sized capacity." Even the
decisive manner in which boys shopped testified to their manliness, anoth-

When they crack the whip you jump

Ask Sam and Andy Stevens what the well-dressed near-man will wear. They'll tell you. They have the latest dope on shawl collars, bat-wing ties, patent leathers and pompadours. If they don't like a thing—it's out.

And, believe it 'cause it's the truth, these chaps are just as much at home on a football field or a basketball floor as at a dance. They wear T-shirts, sweaters, golf hose, plus fours, shorts, longs, blazers —and they have to have 'em! Their shoes and hats and suits are man-sized. They eat like horses. Their appetites are man-sized as are their buying capacities. In short, they're a man's equal in everything but years.

THE AMERICAN BOY is read by 500,000 fellows like Sam and Andy, who average 15½ years of age, 115 pounds on the scales and 5 feet 4 inches tall in their stocking feet. They buy everything you sell to men. They hold man-sized opinions for or against a product. Win them to your side *now* while they are forming the buying habits of a lifetime.

It makes no difference what you make . . . tooth-paste, cameras, radios, automatic pencils, razors . . . these chaps form a big part of your market. Sell to them through the advertising columns of THE AMERICAN BOY, the publication they have made their own. Copy received by December 10th will appear in February.

The American Boy

3.4 "WHEN THEY CRACK THE WHIP YOU JUMP," PRINTERS' INK, 1926.

American Boy depicted the fashion-conscious boy as a trend-setter who was more likely to dictate the pace of progressive obsolescence than fall victim to it.

er *American Boy* ad suggested: "Family marketing is all in the day's work for Reg. When given a grocery order, he isn't backward in asking if he can add on some of his favorite eats. Very often he just brings 'em home anyway, with a 'Gee, but we oughta had some of these long ago!' to back him up." Captioned "Reg Jackson 'brings home the bacon,'" the ad cleverly conflated shopping with breadwinning, as if to root consumption in the more traditional masculine realms of labor and initiative taking.[60]

Perhaps most significant, *American Boy* presented boy consumers as a familiar audience with whom advertisers could readily identify. Advertisers' social and cultural distance from the feminine consuming masses was erased when addressing the boy: "They're your equal in height, weight, buying preferences, intelligence. They're your equal in everything but years."[61] Characterizing boys as decisive, discriminating, and "well-informed buyers," boys' magazines like *American Boy* and *Boys' Life* implicitly contrasted the virtues of the boy consumer with the alleged foolishness and fickleness of the woman consumer.[62] "Snap judgments, with this young army," one ad confided, "are giving way to weighing results. Insatiable in their demands . . . they nevertheless look for values before charging it to Dad or hypothecating next month's allowance."[63]

GENDER IDEOLOGY AND THE LEGITIMATION OF MASCULINE CONSUMER DESIRE

Advertisers could measure the manliness of the boy consumer in part by his difference from the fickle irrationalities of the archetypal woman consumer. But the cultural resonances of the manly boy consumer ran even deeper, for the very traits that made the boy a model consumer—his loyalty, enthusiasm, and decisiveness—also mirrored other contemporary cultural expressions of boyish virtue and manliness. Indeed, gendered discourses of consumption acquired salience and persuasive power precisely because they drew upon ideals of masculinity that reverberated elsewhere in American culture.

During the Progressive Era, a host of social and economic developments led middle-class men to formulate new ideals of manhood that clashed with older Victorian codes of manly self-restraint. For Victorians, a man's character—his ability to control powerful passions, to work hard, and to practice thrifty self-restraint—defined the essence of manliness. Guidebooks presented self-mastery and restraint as both a moral duty and the route to economic independence and material success. Toward the end of the nineteenth century, such ideologies of middle-class manliness, first forged in an era of small-scale, entrepreneurial capitalism, began to lose persuasiveness as managerial capitalism narrowed opportunities for men to achieve dreams of economic independence and ownership. By the 1920s, the autonomous self-made man achieving upward mobility through hard work and ingenuity had been replaced by the corporate team player who subordinated personal autonomy and individuality to company needs. Within the vast corporate bureaucracies that were coming to dominate the economic landscape, only the distant hope of promotion to a coveted position in upper management eased the prospect of lifelong salaried dependence.[64]

Alongside lowered career expectations, middle-class men perceived additional threats to Victorian codes of manliness from the debilitating influences of sedentary work and soft living, the frivolous pleasures of commercial leisure, and the closing of the Western frontier—once an important outlet for manly adventure and self-assertion. For YMCA and Boy Scout leaders, women's dominant influence over boys as teachers in the schools and mothers in the home only amplified the need to reinvigorate middle-class manhood.[65] Edgar M. Robinson, who headed YMCA boys' work, sounded the alarm when he assailed the boy who has been "kept so carefully wrapped in the 'pink cotton wool' of an overindulgent home [that] he is more effeminate than his sister, and his flabby muscles are less flabby than his character."[66]

In their quest for new sources of male power and authority, middle-class men began to embrace new ideologies of "passionate manhood" that valorized decisiveness, bodily fortitude, physical aggression, and a fighting spirit—all "inversions of 'feminized' Victorian civilization."[67] Some men, heeding Teddy Roosevelt's call, took up the "strenuous life," displaying and discovering bold manly vigor in muscular sports like prizefighting, college football, and bodybuilding, in the rugged outdoors, and in the military adventurism sanctioned by United States imperialism. Team sports, YMCA gymnasiums, and scouting provided antidotes to the excessive coddling and passive spectatorship that male character builders believed threatened "robust, manly, self-reliant boyhood."[68] New epithets—"sissy," "pussy-foot," "cold feet," and "stuffed shirt"—scorned "behavior which had once appeared self-possessed and manly but now seemed overcivilized and effeminate."[69] In particular, the words "pussy-foot" and "cold feet" glorified decisive action as a hallmark of vigorous manhood, while deriding hesitancy and paralyzing doubt as signs of weakness.[70]

The single-mindedness and certainty that exemplified ideals of manhood were also evident in the boy consumer's unwavering allegiance to branded goods. A contributor to *Printers' Ink*, lauding the boy consumer's

"passionate loyalty," underscored the martial fervor of the boy's brand devotion: "His heroes are found not only in fiction and the sporting pages,
but in *things*—motor cars, electric refrigerators, radios. And what he ad-
mires he is ready to fight for."[71] Not just ordinary consumers, boys were
"fans," another *Printers' Ink* writer enthused.[72] Such praise for the boy consumer's loyalty and exuberance might have encouraged some advertisers to
regard him as an easy mark. But Progressive-Era discourses on boyish
virtue also allowed advertisers to interpret these traits as manifestations of
manly vitality rather than signs of feminine gullibility and materialistic excess. Where antebellum Americans had sought to restrain boyish energy
and unruliness, Progressives glorified boyhood as a repository of manly
virtues that civilization and feminine influence too often stifled. For many
middle-class men, the path to revitalization lay in recovering the exuberance, spontaneity, and playfulness that reigned freely in boyhood.[73] As historian Anthony Rotundo has argued, "the rising estimation of boyhood began with the growing regard for those childish traits that people considered
more boyish than girlish."[74] Indeed, in the early twentieth century entertainment entrepreneurs successfully capitalized on just this admiration of
boyish play in marketing mass amusements as a childlike world of make-
believe to adult middle-class men.[75]

Progressives' delight in boyish exuberance and their parallel angst over
imperiled masculinity resounded most powerfully in the numerous advertisements for air rifles that filled boys' magazines in the 1910s. Some air rifle makers, echoing Teddy Roosevelt's call for a recovery of the "strenuous
life," spoke to widespread middle-class worries that insufficient outdoor
activity and overfeminized homes were robbing boys of their virility.
Promising to restore manly vigor to pampered middle-class boys, Daisy
Air Rifles claimed that a boy with a rifle was destined to "become a rugged,
strong, bright-eyed boy, full of life and courage, with well-developed muscles and nerves of steel."[76] One Daisy air rifle ad even intimated that rifle
training would fit boys for a reenactment of "Teddy's Charge up San Juan
Hill."[77] King Air Rifles, on the other hand, humorously conveyed the
"boys' side of the air rifle question" in its immensely popular series of
wartime advertisements drawn by cartoonist Claire Briggs.[78] Delighting in
boyish antics, the cartoons expressed boys' yearnings to escape overpro-
tective mothers and the joyless demands of civilized restraint. One cartoon
showed a boy practicing the piano to the discipline of a metronome, while
outside the neighborhood boys marched in a loose soldiers' drill, with their
King air rifles held high. "Do you happen to be a boy?" the ad asked, "A
REAL boy, we mean, with a natural dislike for music lessons, rainy days and
'solitary confinement'?"[79]

Such advertising appeals also played upon Progressive-Era fears that overcivilization was imperiling the white race itself. Progressives from Theodore Roosevelt to psychologist G. Stanley Hall concluded that an infusion of wildness or primitive passions could restore the white man's virility without compromising his claims to embody the best of civilization.[80] It was precisely because of their innate racial superiority, the thinking went, that whites could be strengthened by the primitive rather than debased by it, as Native Americans and African Americans were thought to be.[81] Hall's Darwinian-inspired recapitulation theory, which posited that each successive stage of the child's development repeated the history of the human race, led him to advocate encouraging rather than repressing the primitive qualities that inhered in naturally savage little boys. Reading them bloody frontier stories about Indians, Hall theorized, would allow boys to relive their racial ancestors' savage emotions and thereby "inoculate" them with the primitive strength to guard against weakness and effeminacy when they became civilized adults.[82]

The King Air Rifles advertising campaign suggests just how intertwined cultural fantasies and anxieties about race and masculinity became in the Progressive Era. In one of Briggs' cartoon-style ads, a rifle-deprived boy had to turn down the neighborhood gang's invitation to "play Indian"—a game sure to draw out the "savagery" of real boys—when his matronly mother reminded him that he had not yet "finished shelling those peas and practicing [his] music lessons" (fig. 3.5). Sympathizing with the plight of all boys under maternal command, the ad mocked mothers for failing to grasp boy needs and wants: "Mother must think that shelling peas comes under the head of 'indoor sports.'"[83] The ad not only cleverly dramatized anxieties about curtailed masculinity and the overfeminized home, but it also spoke to the cultural appeal of the savage boy—one echoed in the enormous popularity of Tarzan during the Progressive Era.[84]

While notions of boyish vitality and exuberance provided rifle makers a promising marketing angle for their controversial product, admen also celebrated other boyish traits that more certainly transformed consumption into a manly pursuit: the boy consumer's rationality and technological-mindedness. As one trade press contributor would have it, boys were no-nonsense consumers who, unlike women, responded to "straight selling" rather than emotional appeals or manipulation.[85] If the "reason why" copy that accompanied ads for cars and new technologies was too technical or lengthy for the masses, boys seemed perfectly suited to it. A restless inquirer, the boy, adman Frank Fehlman asserted, was "a sponge seeking facts, more facts, and still more facts. . . . Why, why, why, is the key to his thinking."[86] Further, admen contended, as the mechanic who fixed the family car,

3.5 KING AIR RIFLES ADVERTISEMENT, AMERICAN BOY (MARCH 1917).
Air rifle advertisements tapped into progressive-era fears that overfeminized homes were robbing boys of their virility. Reproduced with permission of Daisy Outdoor Products.*

*See source note on page 284.

electric iron, radio, and washing machine, boys were naturally drawn to technical information and would "read a whole page of 10-pt. type without skipping a word."[87] The boy consumer's affinity for reason-why copy thus transformed his proclivity to consume into a pursuit of knowledge and technological expertise. In so doing, historian Pamela Laird has argued, reason-why copy "gave emotional needs a veneer of rationality."[88]

By constructing boys as technologically conversant consumers, promoters of the boy market safely contained boys' prolific consumer appetites within the masculine realm. Rather than a mark of materialistic excess, the modern boy's desire to possess the latest gear and mechanical equipment—whether it be for sports, home entertainment, or electrical tinkering—was testament to the boy's quest for mastery over new technology and love of progress.[89] Not surprisingly, advertisers' infatuation with the boy consumer coincided with the popularization of wireless experimentation as a boyhood hobby. For middle-class boys, learning to be "handy with tools"—a skill mandated by the Boy Scout manual—and playing with technology were important facets of growing up in the early twentieth century. As radio historian Susan Douglas has written, "If [boys] failed to recognize how the desire for adventure, combat, and the assertion of strength, on the one hand, could be reconciled with the need to prepare for life in the modern world, on the other, popular books and magazines were there to remind them. Everything could be achieved through technical mastery."[90] In the technology-centered world of boy play, consumerism became the means to display mechanical flair, inventiveness, and mastery of technical change—all measures of masculine success.[91]

Boys' own reactions to advertising suggest that they too enjoyed thinking of themselves as technologically conversant consumers and appreciated advertisements that addressed them as such. One adman, observing seven ten-year-old boys comparing three different electric train ads, noted their distinct lack of interest in a full-page color ad with "educational copy devoted to selling the . . . idea of owning a train." The boys, he observed, "had already anticipated all these joys, in a very much keener and more poignant manner than the writer of this ad had got 'over.'" What attracted them instead was a smaller ad jammed with information on "the mechanical perfection of the train" that addressed boys "as though they possessed a knowledge of mechanics."[92] For some boys, the prospect of acquiring technical knowledge, even more than the prospect of acquiring the advertised product itself, contributed immeasurably to the pleasures of ad reading. Recalling his Depression-era boyhood, Charles Jacobson remembered paying a lot of attention to the car advertisements in the *Saturday Evening Post* he thumbed through at the barber shop, not because he fantasized about owning one, but because knowledge of the years and makes of different cars—being able to distinguish the models that had "the best value" from those that merely came with a lot of "useless gewgaws," as he put it—offered a means of gaining prestige among his male peers. Jacobson also studied the bicycle ads, trying to learn which models were "the best," in hopes that he might one day prove himself a more sophisticated consumer than his father, whose gift of a bicycle loaded with superfluous accessories was a source of embarrassment.[93]

These examples suggest how advertising's promise of technical expertise gave boys access to a masculine domain of consumer pleasures and a framework for defining their identity in relation to both peers and family members. Advertisers' most flattering tribute to the boy may have been their equation of his technical mastery with his command of family spending. *American Boy* had long asserted that in the arena of cars and radios grown-ups regularly depended upon boys for guidance in their purchases.[94] By the late 1920s advertisements appearing in boy publications began to echo this vision. Some depicted boys in the role of the brand-conscious consumer savant, instructing mom and dad on what to buy. For example, a 1928 radio battery ad (fig. 3.6) pictured a father returning from the store with the Burgess "Super B" brand his son endorsed. Making the case for boys' superior consumer savvy bluntly, the copy applauded the father for following his son's advice: "It's a wise dad who buys the kind of batteries that his son recommends . . . for the boys of today certainly know their stuff."[95] The accompanying illustration—an etched drawing of a boy greeting and stopping his father at the front door with the question, "Did'ja get the 'SUPER B' I told you about"—underscored the boy's authority by seeming to diminish the father's. Looking every bit the loyal organization man in suit and hat, the package-bearing father appeared to be at his son's beck and call, an errand boy to the boy boss. In a similar vein, a 1927 RCA ad (fig. 3.7), instructing boys to "See that Dad gets the dope on Radiola 20," depicted a Skippy-like boy inside a radio shop pitching the Radiola's virtues to beguiled parents.[96] For boys who read these ads as allegories of boy empowerment—and how could they not?—consumer culture became a realm where they could stage imaginary Oedipal coups, triumphing over fathers as tutors in consumption and master persuaders.

As such ads further suggest, the boy's likeness to the go-getter salesman—indeed, his likeness to admen themselves—was in no small measure responsible for the high esteem in which admen held him. In the popular literature of the 1920s, the salesman emerged as a model of the manly modern businessman. Advertising executive Bruce Barton's 1924 best-seller *The Man Nobody Knows* offered the most ennobling tribute in its portrayal of

Did'ja get the "SUPER B"
I told you about"

It's a wise dad who buys the kind of
batteries that his son recommends....
for the boys of today certainly know
their stuff. For example, they know
that the two Burgess "Super B" Batteries have larger cells than standard
batteries. Naturally, they have more
power and last longer.

Chrome

CHROME is a preserva-
tive that guards power
when your Burgess
"Super B" Battery is not
in use. Extra life and
service are thus added.
It is a patented feature
of the two Burgess
"Super B" Batteries,
which answer practi-
cally all radio set
requirements.

"Super B" No. 22308
A medium size heavy-duty 45-volt battery
designed for general, all around use.

"Super B" No. 21308
The largest size Burgess heavy-duty 45-volt
battery—made especially for heavy-current
consuming sets.

BURGESS BATTERY COMPANY
General Sales Offices: CHICAGO
In Canada: Niagara Falls & Winnipeg

BURGESS "SUPER B" BATTERIES

3.6 BURGESS BATTERIES
ADVERTISEMENT, AMERICAN
BOY (SEPTEMBER 1928).
Advertisers equated the boy's
knowledge of technological
innovation with his command
of family spending. Reproduced
with permission of Dave Prasse, C. F.
Burgess Laboratories, Freeport, IL.
Courtesy Security Pacific Collection,
Los Angeles Public Library.

·See that Dad gets the dope on Radiola 20
—*the best buy in radio today*

RADIO is no fun whatever unless you can tune in just the station you want and tune out the ones you don't want. A fellow has to watch his step on this or he may get stung with a set that can't stand the pace of a lot of stations going at once. But Radiola 20 was made to be specially selective. It's many times as good in this way as the average antenna set. Twenty stations in twenty minutes is no trick at all for Radiola 20 when you have

the dial numbers handy. It's the little giant of radio when it comes to tuning them in sharp as a razor. There are five tubes. And the last

Radiola 20, less equipment . . $78

one is an extra fine power tube. When the words and music come in you'll think the singers or musicians are in the next room. You'll get bands, orchestras, shows, songs, stories, everything, clear as can be — better than on many sets costing twice as much. Just fix it so you and your Dad can hear Radiola 20. The rest will be easy. There's an RCA Authorized Dealer near you. Look him up right away. You'll see this sign.

Buy with confidence   *where you see this sign.*

RADIO CORPORATION
OF AMERICA

RCA~Radiola
MADE · BY · THE · MAKERS · OF · THE · RADIOTRON

NEW YORK · CHICAGO
SAN FRANCISCO

3.7 RCA-RADIOLA ADVERTISEMENT, AMERICAN BOY (JUNE 1927).
In the advertising imagination, the boy's superior consumer savvy made him a masterful salesman. Reproduced with permission of Thomson Consumer Electronics. Courtesy Security Pacific Collection, Los Angeles Public Library.

Jesus Christ as a "magnetic" leader who used his organizational skills, charismatic salesmanship, and business acumen to build "the greatest organization of all." In sharp contrast to the nineteenth-century image of the salesman as a morally suspect "confidence man," twentieth-century discourses cast selling as a productive activity—even a public service—that helped to satisfy wants and stimulate the economy. If masculine virtues seemed missing from the sedentary lives of supervised office workers, they abounded in the salesman's persistence, eagerness to do battle for clients, and enthusiasm. To possess "enthusiasm"—what historian Angel Kwolek-Folland has described as "one of the most frequently used words in the business vocabulary of the early twentieth century"—was to possess a multitude of related and mutually constituting traits: "optimism, persistence, initiative, cheerfulness, and company loyalty." According to Kwolek-Folland, it became "a catch-all word for aggression, competition, and the subversion of self in favor of position and company policy."[97] The figure of the salesman, then, affirmed the presence of masculine virtues even as managerial capitalism rendered him a loyal servant to the modern corporation and eclipsed older ideals of the self-made man.

Much as 1920s business ideology established the virility of corporate salesmen, it also helped to masculinize consumption. When promoters of the boy market celebrated the restless enthusiasm and charismatic salesmanship of the boy, they touted not only his value to prospective advertisers as a consumer but also his masculine credentials as a producer. "Get a boy on your side," one advertising authority promised, "and you have made not merely a sale, but a salesman."[98] In advertising discourses, the boy consumer-salesman assumed the role of a loyal warrior, using advertisers' "data to argue down anybody . . . who dares to disparage" a favored product. Not just a child defending pride of possession, the manly boy, like any worthy salesman, battled on behalf of the firm.[99] The boy even bested the sales professional by virtue of his freedom from professional codes and his trusted position within the family. "He's got it all over your own men in many ways," *American Boy* instructed advertisers. "He's not restricted by sales ethics. He'll paint a gloomy picture of a competitive make your men wouldn't think of painting. And the way he can praise your car would be 'just sales talk' if it came from your agent."[100] Possessing the loyalty of an organization man, the enthusiasm of a sales professional, and the flexible ethics of a fast-talking street peddler, the boy consumer was a formidable amalgamation of virtuoso salesmanship, past and present.

The notion that boys could get away with bold sales talk that professionals would ordinarily avoid only magnified the boy consumer's appeal. Advertisements placed in boy publications played out these fantasies—

shared no doubt by advertisers and boys alike. In them, boys sometimes figured as artful persuaders who would not let a limited spending allowance
stand in the way of oversized consumer ambitions. One such ad suggested
how boys could buy their own home billiards table. A full-page etched
drawing showed a boy, billiard cue in hand, holding out a fee box labeled
"one cent a game," as his father reached into his pocket for change to deposit into the outstretched can before commencing a game of billiards (fig.
3.8). "When the grown-ups want to play," the ad explained, boys who buy
their own table on time-payment plans "require each player to deposit a
cent per game in a small bank or fee box." Some parents might have viewed
the game fee as a brazen display of venality and a corruption of companionate family values, but the advertisement itself applauded the boy consumer's savvy salesmanship in having learned to "play as you pay."[101]
Much like Tom Sawyer, who loafed while gullible companions white-
washed his aunt's fence, the boy consumer relied on entrepreneurial cunning to underwrite consumer desires.

Advertisers who hoped to enlist the boy's dynamic salesmanship
pinned their hopes on winning over the "gang leader," a charismatic
Sawyer-like youth who could sway the consumer loyalties of the neighborhood gang. If advertisers could sell the gang leader, advertising authority
S. C. Lambert reasoned, "the trick is turned, for he is pretty sure to sell the
members of his gang. This may mean five or more sales instead of [just]
one."[102] Advertisers' understanding of gang leaders was partly informed by
conceptions of adolescence, first formulated in the Progressive Era by psychologist G. Stanley Hall, who viewed male adolescence as a pivotal moment of transition in which boys formed gangs and recapitulated the lives
of barbarians. Hall stressed that the gang instinct, if properly channeled,
could be put to constructive ends. Such was the hope, anyway, of character-
building organizations like the Boy Scouts and YMCA, who sought to
shape the gang instinct by ruling through gang leaders. If they could win
the "key boy," character builders surmised, the rest would fall in line.[103]

Much like Scout leaders, advertisers eagerly gambled on the "gang spirit and high-pressure enthusiasm" of the middle-class boy consumer.[104] Numerous advertisements played to boys' desire to be the gang leader by enticing them to start a club organized around a favorite branded good. The
Fisk Bicycle Tire Company, for example, promised special rewards for boys
who formed a Fisk Club of six or more members. Club leaders received a
Fisk club flag, a Fisk signal flag for the signal officer, and Fisk armbands for
each member.[105] Boys who got a "crowd of boys together" for an Auto-
Wheel Coaster Club earned even greater distinction, as they were offered "a
special cap for the Captain" in addition to "FREE caps to all members" and

3.8 BRUNSWICK TABLES ADVERTISEMENT, AMERICAN BOY
(NOVEMBER 1916).

Ads like this taught boys the moral and economic principles of time-payment plans by encouraging them to "play as you pay."

a six-month subscription to the "Auto-Wheel Spokesman."[106] Not to be outdone, U.S. Giant Chain Bicycle Tires promoted its club and tires through spokesman "Joe Fastpeddler," a boy whose last name summoned dual images of athletic prowess and aggressive salesmanship. As president of the fictional Thriftville Boys Bicycle Club, Joe Fastpeddler "issued an order that every member who expects to keep up with the bunch" on the club's bike trips "use U.S. Giant Chains on his wheels."[107]

As such advertisements suggest, clubs honored boys as valiant leaders—captains and presidents—who commanded the respect and consumer loyalties of their peers. Yet even as clubs tied achievement to consumer endeavors—bestowing prizes and honorifics upon boy leaders who purchased advertised goods and inspired peers to follow suit—advertisers subordinated boys' consumer identity to their dominant masculine identity as producers. In going after the gang leader, advertisers believed they were appealing to an entrepreneur ever "on the lookout for new ideas which he can apply to his business."[108] Thus the advertising campaign for Pierce-Arrow coasters defined leadership of a local Coaster Club as the starting point of a successful future as a business executive or professional. From captain of the Coaster Club, the ad promised, it was "an easy step . . . to captain of the baseball team, manager of the football or basketball outfit," and eventual recognition as a leader among men: "It's the boy who develops his genius for leadership that rises to be the bank president, the manager of the big business house, the college professor."[109] At a time of diminishing opportunities for young men at the top of the corporate ladder, the notion that consumer leadership could launch one on the road to upward mobility must have been heartening indeed.

By linking consumer leadership to such career trajectories—all preserves of manly independence—admen suggested new ways in which consumer selfhood could be reconciled with autonomous selfhood. In the new corporate order, the scramble to the top favored team players who cultivated a malleable self and winning personality over solitary strivers who showed dedication through steady work habits. What such organization men often lost in the process, however, was a solid sense of their own identity. Admen were themselves familiar with this dilemma, as they were the ultimate corporate team players, beholden to clients as well as unpredictable consumers. Perhaps feeding their own nostalgic yearnings, admen affirmed that boys could experiment with the new work personality—using their powers of persuasion to promote brand loyalty among their peers—without sacrificing their dreams of becoming a self-reliant professional or business executive. Boys who made personality their capital, admen implied, possessed the kind of dynamic leadership that guaranteed manly independence.

Even so, admen's construction of the boy consumer was fraught with contradictions, for in likening him to a modern salesman admen also likened him to the consummate organization man. A far cry from the independent entrepreneur, the modern salesman was a product of vast transformations in the economy that subordinated the salesman's traditional reliance on initiative and improvisational skills to standardized selling strategies and rationalized sales routes.[110] Such incongruities, however, help account for the boy consumer's appeal: he was simultaneously a part of and apart from the new corporate economy, a symbol of its dynamic salesmanship and an alluring reminder of the autonomy and individualism that no longer reigned supreme.

Depictions of the boy consumer as an aspiring businessman sustained a crucial link between the work ethic and the burgeoning consumer ethos. As the 1920s progressed, however, advertisers began to more openly acknowledge the consumer aspirations that lay at the heart of the boy entrepreneur. This shift was especially notable in advertisements that addressed boys as managers and earners of their own spending money. Initially, most advertisements for earning opportunities addressed boys as entrepreneurs without appealing directly to their consumer desires. Whether it was an ad for fur-trapping supplies, vegetable seeds, or a bike that could speed up a newspaper delivery route, boys were first and foremost businessmen striving to earn their own way. One bicycle manufacturer, for example, told boys that with a bike they could make "twice as much money" selling newspapers "in half the time," and liberate themselves from having "to keep asking Dad for money."[111] Not merely a mode of transportation, the bike became a vehicle for instilling traditional producer values: "With a bike he can deliver newspapers and parcels . . . run errands and carry messages . . . all of which give him an early and sound training in good business habits, thrift and independence."[112]

The purchase of a bike, though itself an act of consumption, served the boy's entrepreneurial drives rather than his dreams of acquiring more consumer goods through augmented earnings. *American Boy* endorsed this view in its own editorials on the virtues of advertising. The magazine's editors recommended careful study of advertisements not just because boys would learn to spend more intelligently but so they might "discover business opportunities" and acquire "an understanding of business" and advertising practices essential to their future success.[113] Even as the magazine's editors promoted consumption, they distanced boys from its more threatening, potentially emasculating, implications. Becoming absorbed in the advertisers' world of consumer abundance was an exercise in business preparation, not an act of self-indulgence. To underscore the point, in 1922 *American Boy* published a seven-month serial by Edward Edson Lee about the adventures of "Advertising Andy," a plucky teen who rapidly advances from delivery boy to advertising manager by convincing the proprietor of Landers General Store to use advertising and put some "jazz" into stodgy merchandising. Dreaming of becoming the advertising manager of a big company one day, Andy spends evenings studying advertising books, an endeavor endorsed by a traveling salesman who tells Andy, "You can't make a mistake by learning all you can. . . . Pretty nearly every business has its advertising problem."[114] As the serial unfolds, the salesman's words reverberate with wisdom, as Andy discovers that nearly every business problem has its advertising solution.[115]

By the mid-1920s, the relationship between work and consumption had begun to shift somewhat in advertisements for money-making opportunities. Where previously consumption had been lauded as an investment in capital—the means to further business aspirations—now consumer aspirations became the goad to industry. Accordingly, advertisers began speaking to boys not just as entrepreneurs in the making but as unfulfilled spenders. Picturing an enticing array of sporting goods floating in black space, Ferry's Purebred Seeds Company framed boys' quest for spending money in explicitly material terms: "The stores are full of just what you want—cameras, swimming suits, fishing tackle, baseball equipment, running shoes, tennis racquets and camping shoes. Why waste time merely wishing for them when there is a fine way to earn money to buy them?" (fig. 3.9).[116] Another Ferry's ad, illustrated with a drawing of fields sprouting baseball bats and trees laden with baseballs, linked the cultivation of nature's abundance to the satisfaction of consumer desire.[117]

Several factors account for advertisers' willingness to appeal more overtly to boys' consumer appetites. First, advertisers could reassure themselves, as they often did in the trade press, that consumer desire stimulated the work ethic. Perhaps more important, though, the change in focus reflected advertisers' new assessment of boy culture in the 1920s. Through both observation and rudimentary market research, advertisers discerned a more pronounced consumer orientation in boys who grew up during the Jazz Age.[118] Indeed, as advertisers adapted their campaigns to the desires of their audience, the boy consumer began to look more like a shallow materialist than a disciplined entrepreneur. Consider the contest held by Ferry's Purebred Seeds Company in 1928 for the best letter on "Why I Plant a Garden." The contest announcement had suggested as possible answers "helping out the home-table" or "competing with . . . a neighbor" for the best

Vegetables will pay for them

THE stores are full of just what you want — cameras, swimming suits, fishing tackle, baseball equipment, running shoes, tennis racquets and camping outfits.

Why waste time merely wishing for them when there is a fine way to earn money to buy them? A garden planted early will produce vegetables which you can easily sell to your neighbors. You'll be surprised what a demand there is for fine, fresh vegetables such as peas, beets, lettuce, string beans, limas, radishes, green corn and tomatoes.

The thing to do now is to plan your garden. You'll be greatly helped if you let us send you Ferry's Seed Annual. It is packed with just the advice you want about seeds. Tells when and how to plant them—when you can expect the harvest—the size and color of the different varieties of vegetables. It also tells the importance of purebred seeds, the only kind that ever go into Ferry seed packets. Unless you plant purebred seeds, you run the risk of being disappointed in your garden results.

Ferry's purebred Seeds come from ideal parent plants. After harvesting them we test these seeds in our experimental gardens to determine that they are true to type. When you buy Ferry's purebred Seeds, you can always be sure that they are *clean, fresh* and *tested*.

Choose your seeds now "at the store around the corner," from the Ferry Box. Also fill in the coupon below and send it to us so you can get your copy of Ferry's Seed Annual. D. M. Ferry & Co., Detroit, Mich.; San Francisco, Cal.; Windsor, Ont.

FERRY'S purebred SEEDS

D. M. FERRY & CO.
Detroit, Mich.

I want to have a garden this year.
Please send me Ferry's Seed Annual.

Name

Street

City

3.9 FERRY'S SEEDS ADVERTISEMENT, AMERICAN BOY (MARCH 1926).

By the mid-1920s, advertisements for business opportunities appealed to boys' consumer ambitions more overtly than they had in the past.

Printed by permission of Ferry-Morse Seed Company.

produce, but their subsequent advertising campaign in 1929 and 1930 reflected an entirely different set of motives, presumably based on boys' contest responses. Boys' entrepreneurial ambitions were informed less by a sense of family duty or friendly rivalry than by bold materialism.[119] "Put a rake into the soil in your own backyard and pull out Money," baited one ad.[120] Vegetable gardening, boys were told, could yield "plus fours for the afternoon's golf game, a tuxedo for the evening's affair; a radio set; plenty of cash in the pocket—or full equipment for baseball and hockey."[121]

The boy audience juvenile advertisers imagined bore a remarkable similarity to Ted Babbitt, George Babbitt's son in Sinclair Lewis's satirical 1922 novel about the spread of pecuniary values. A manly boy to be sure, Ted was "a natural mechanic" and an inveterate "tinkerer of machines."[122] He was also a fashionable dresser—"proudest of all was his [Fancy Vest] waistcoat, saved for, begged for, plotted for"—whose vast consumer desires outstripped the intensity of his work ethic.[123] Having no use for the impractical "old junk" and "camembert" taught in high school, Ted collected clippings of advertisements for correspondence-courses like the one that "bore the rousing headline: 'Money! Money!! Money!!!' "[124] Intrigued that the promise of "BIG money" demanded minimal expenditure of time and study, Ted amassed a collection of "fifty or sixty" such ads.[125] Though he eventually headed off to college, Ted's flirtation with correspondence school underscored the shifting calculus of work: no longer an end in itself, work was not so much the measure of the man as it was the handmaiden of consumer ambition.

By the close of the 1920s, both consumer ambition and entrepreneurial drive expressed the virtues of the modern businessman. The consumer-savvy businessman, reflected in the idealized figure of the boy consumer, signaled the emergence of a new emblem of masculinity befitting the age of mass consumption. In overturning less flattering associations of consumption with feminine excess, the boy consumer both advanced and reflected the positive revaluation of consumption during the early twentieth century. In one sense, the glorification of the boy consumer is a measure of the profound anxieties that attended the growth of modern consumer society. Advertisers, never fully convinced of their own legitimacy, admired boys for the flattering reflection they projected back onto their own cultural mission. Through the figure of the virile boy consumer, advertisers could refashion consumer desire to suit their own masculine self-image as producers and champions of modernity. As a progressive buyer who valued technological innovation, the boy consumer seemed in perfect sync with advertisers' self-proclaimed crusade to raise the American standard of living. Uniting consumer desire with entrepreneurial ambition, the boy consumer offered proof that the consumer ethic need not under-cut the work ethic. But in another sense, the glorification of the boy con-sumer suggests that anxieties over the growth of consumer society were beginning to fade. Consumption had become a manly virtue—not a sign of effeminacy or childlike dependency, but a legitimate, even productive, activity within the masculine domain.

CHAPTER 4

Athletic Girls and Beauty Queens:
Imagining the Peer-Conscious Adolescent Consumer

DURING THE LATE 1920S, Keds' juvenile advertising campaign un-
veiled a new archetypal consumer—the peer-conscious adolescent girl—
that surfaced with increasing frequency in the advertising pages of *American Girl*, *Everygirl's*, and *Scholastic*, the national high school weekly. The
peer-conscious teen had not always occupied such a prominent place in the
advertising imagination. Earlier in the decade, Keds ads focused on the
Athletic Girl—an energetic, physically adroit sportswoman, who, like the
reigning women tennis champions, sought comfortable yet durable shoes
that could withstand the rigors of tough competition.[1] Working from the
assumption that "boys and girls follow the lead of champions in sports and
sport equipment," J. Walter Thompson, the ad agency that handled the
Keds account, promoted Keds as "the shoe of the champions."[2] By the
spring of 1927, however, the Keds campaign had taken a new turn. The once
self-assured Athletic Girl of advertisers' imaginations was now beset by insecurity and concerns about her appearance. In her stead was a peer-
conscious consumer, whose sports shoes helped cultivate the "womanly
beauty" essential to social success. Underscoring the importance of "bodily poise and grace of carriage," the new series of Keds ads warned girls that
choosing the right athletic shoe could determine their fate at the "College
Prom of a few years from now, your debut, dances and teas" (fig. 4.1).[3] Victory on the court, it seemed, had taken a backseat to victory in the competitive games of dating and peer approval.

J. Walter Thompson's shift in advertising strategies made perfect sense
in the face of rising high school attendance rates in the 1920s and 1930s. For
the first time in American history, teenagers of all social classes were spending more time in the company of their peers than with adults. Poised to exploit such trends, advertisers for a diverse array of goods—cereal, health
drinks, soap, musical instruments, and sewing machines—began following
a similar peer-conscious cultural script. Many ads read like adolescent ver-

4.1 Keds advertisements in January 1927 (left) and November 1927 (right) issues of American Girl. Advertisers' former emphasis on athletic competition gave way to a new focus on winning peer approval, a shift evident in the copy as well as in the literal erasure of rival basketball players from the advertising illustration. Reproduced with permission of The Keds Corporation.

sions of the ubiquitous advertising fables historian Roland Marchand has dubbed "Parables of the First Impression," reminding juvenile readers that they, too, were susceptible to the impersonal judgment and surveillance of the high school crowd.[4] Impression management had become as essential in the peer-oriented world of the American high school as it already was in the bureaucratic world of the modern corporation.

The move to peer-conscious advertising also spoke to changing conceptions of adolescent girlhood that paralleled broader changes in twentieth-century gender ideology. As women gained access to the public world of politics, higher education, and the workplace, advertising and popular culture in the twenties and thirties often narrowed and subverted the liberating implications of those new gender freedoms. Mass marketers, beauty experts, and filmmakers such as Cecil B. DeMille may have celebrated women's emancipation from Victorianism, but they ultimately helped to anchor normative femininity ever more firmly to a consumerized and sexualized private sphere.[5] "Ironically," historian Kathy Peiss writes of early-twentieth-century beauty advertising, "a period that began with cosmetics signaling women's freedom and individuality ended in binding feminine identity to manufactured beauty, self-portrayal to acts of consumption."[6]

Juvenile advertisers' courtship of adolescent girls proved just as paradoxical, suggesting how changes and contradictions in gender ideology transcended boundaries of age. When advertisers imagined the popular girl, they often lionized the Athletic Girl—a fitting poster child for the emancipations enjoyed by the New Woman. Yet as much as juvenile advertising valorized the athletic girl's liberation from Victorian notions of feminine fragility and dependency, it also worked at deeper levels to encourage a conformist, peer-directed sense of self and to equate beauty with feminine accomplishment. Most striking is the way beauty culture discourses suffused juvenile advertising even though the products promoted, such as cereal and shoes, had little to do with cosmetics or personal grooming.

These tensions between new gender freedoms and new gender restraints complicated adolescent girls' struggles with peer approval and personal identity in ways that seem both foreign and strikingly familiar to twenty-first-century readers. Juvenile advertisers and a new breed of advice columnists—the adult advisor to high-school age youth—stepped in to help teens mediate the meanings, conflicts, and experiences of adolescence. In guiding adolescent girls through the trials of high school peer culture, advertisers and advice columnists were also helping teens navigate the transition from a Victorian cultural order to a modern, consumerist one. Much of their advice challenged the Victorian emphasis on inner virtue and in the process reinforced the very peer consciousness that drove adolescent girls to seek their counsel. But Victorian notions of character and feminine self-sacrifice did not wholly disappear, as advertisers and advice columnists also struggled to temper the perceived consumer excesses of girls, especially when the Depression threw class distinctions into sharper relief. In popular culture discourses, the peer-conscious adolescent girl thus figured as both an ideal and a problem to be solved.

ADOLESCENT GIRLHOOD AND THE BEAUTY IMPERATIVE

In the 1920s and 1930s, adolescent readers of *American Girl* and *Everygirl's* magazines became familiar with a stock figure in juvenile advertisements: the peppy, athletic modern girl. Invariably, advertisers contended, the modern girls most envied were active, athletic, acne-free, and glowing with vitality. Consider, for example, the "popular girl" featured in a 1926 advertisement who, to the great fortune of her social life, had made Shredded Wheat a daily habit: "Always In Demand. Bright eyes, clear complexion, abounding health and happiness—that's personality! Active, athletic, smart and attractive. . . . Irresistible with the poise that physical fitness assures."[7] As counterparts to the New Woman, such modern girls exuded the confidence and energetic enthusiasm befitting a post–Victorian age. Rejecting the retiring diffidence expected of their Victorian predecessors, modern girls instead embraced new models of girlhood that celebrated physical fitness, outdoor activity, and adventure-seeking.[8]

Modern girls, however, faced new restraints along with new gender freedoms as the body increasingly came to be viewed as "the ultimate expression of the self."[9] This trend began in the 1920s, historian Joan Brumberg argues, when "movies, magazines, and department stores . . . all gave primacy to a woman's visual image." As a result, Brumberg contends, "even young teenagers . . . began to worry about their appearance in ways that required increased attention to their bodies."[10] Some teenage girls, fearing that unflattering clothes and overweight bodies would make them social pariahs, embraced the task of bodily improvement with the hope of creating "a new image . . . that would win popularity and status at school."[11]

Juvenile advertising validated and encouraged this preoccupation by continually casting the body as an image-making machine.[12] In the mid-1920s, when new advertising channels for reaching preteen and adolescent girls first emerged in *American Girl* and *Everygirl's*—published by the Girl Scouts and the Camp Fire Girls, respectively—advertisers celebrated the adolescent body as an emblem of progress and generational identity. A 1926 series of Postum advertisements, for example, dramatized the modern girl's advances over her grandmother's generation. In grandmother's day, one ad informed its readers, "the young miss of the 'seventies was better fitted for sitting and knitting than for any real exercise." Hampered by a delicate constitution and a bathing costume weighted down by yards of fabric, grandmother usually "sank in four feet of water" only to be "borne tenderly to the beach, where she swooned in complete exhaustion." Not so the modern girl of today: "*You* go into the water to swim—to strike out on your own."[13] Like Postum, Cantilever Shoe ads hailed the dawn of a new era in which girls knew the joys of "basketball, tennis, field sports, hockey, hikes, camping, Girl Scout life" and were no longer hindered by the "petticoats, stiffened collars, armor-like corsets . . . [and] narrow pointed shoes" of their mothers' generation (fig. 4.2).[14]

There was a class dimension to this portrait of modern adolescent girl-hood, as the vitality and unpretentious middle-class virtues of the athletic girl were sometimes contrasted with the affectations of effete, high-society sophisticates. Promoted especially to Girl Scouts and Camp Fire Girls—groups that prized sports and outdoor physical activities—Cantilever Shoes distinguished their wearers not only from older generations but from their contemporaries as well.[15] As one ad claimed, Cantilever's "boyish" oxfords and "modish" pumps made the Camp Fire Girl, with her tireless "free-swinging, natural stride," an object of envy and admiration. Boldly headlined "The Camp Fire Girl in Town," the advertisement featured a drawing of two high-society girls, dressed in fur-lined coats and high heels, who couldn't take their eyes off the confident but casually attired Camp Fire Girl walking down the boulevard in her low-heeled oxfords. Seemingly unimpressed by the constraining hyper-femininity of their economic betters, the "*regular* girls" who wore Cantilevers set their own style, making graceful athleticism a fashion statement in its own right.[16]

In many respects, the Postum and Cantilever advertisements, like the Keds sports champion ads of the mid-twenties, paid tribute to new models of energetic, publicly active womanhood that gained favor in the wake of the 1920 suffrage victory and the newfound celebrity of women athletes. Athletic opportunities for women had been increasing since the 1890s, when girls and women—no longer confined to tennis, badminton, and croquet—began taking up basketball, rowing, canoeing, golf, swimming, cycling, and some track and field.[17] But it was not until the 1920s that accomplished women athletes gained the stature of popular culture icons. A decade of enormous growth in women's sports, the 1920s produced tennis champions Helen Wills and Suzanne Lenglen; Olympian Gertrude Ederle, the sixth person to swim the English Channel; and Sybil Bauer, the twenty-

4.2 CANTILEVER SHOE ADVERTISEMENT, EVERYGIRL'S (MAY 1925).
Advertisers appealed to adolescents' sense of their own generational distinctiveness and applauded their spirited defiance of Victorian notions of feminine fragility and dependence.

year-old swimmer who broke the world (men's) record in the backstroke. All, according to historian Susan Cahn, "became overnight sensations, second only to movie stars in national fame."[18] Celebrity athletes in turn emboldened sports-loving girls and young women, who "took to the playing fields" in school yards, cities, and towns across the country.[19] An emblem of the modern virtues associated with the "New Woman," the Athletic Girl celebrated in sports journalism and juvenile advertising helped to promote new conceptions of feminine abilities and aspirations that defied Victorian notions of feminine fragility and dependency.

Advertisers played to these new cultural ideals of womanhood, telling girls not only that their lives were more fulfilling than their grandmothers' but that investing in the body could help them lay claim to new freedoms and adventures. Body consciousness, however, also implied adherence to changing cultural ideals of girlhood that often narrowed the scope of feminine aspirations and feminine achievement. Paralleling the ebbing of feminist energies in the late 1920s and 1930s, admakers began promoting peer acceptance and beauty rather than athletic performance as the ultimate rewards of bodily discipline.

Though new to the field of juvenile advertising, beauty appeals had been prominent in women's advertising since at least 1916, when Woodbury's Soap debuted its landmark "A-Skin-You-Love-to-Touch" campaign. Favoring emotional over utilitarian appeals—a hallmark of the new modern advertising sensibility—Woodbury's and the many imitators who followed promised to enhance not only women's physical appearance but their romantic prospects as well.[20] By the late 1920s, women's magazines dedicated some 20 percent of ad space to advertisements for cosmetics and skin-care regimes.[21] Exploiting anxieties over male approval, such ads continually bombarded women with reminders that in the "beauty contest" of life romantic success came to those who observed the "duty" to be beautiful.[22]

Despite the ubiquity of such beauty appeals, there was nothing inevitable about their rising dominance in juvenile magazines like *Everygirl's* and *American Girl*. For one, the readership of these magazines, ranging in age from ten to seventeen, included preteen subscribers who in all likelihood were not yet as susceptible to the demands of peer approval or as self-conscious about their appearance. Early-twentieth-century girlhood remained for many a period in which conformity to traditional gender expectations temporarily took a back seat to the enjoyment of physical activity and the outdoors.[23] Even an ostensibly conservative organization like the Girl Scouts—with its homemaker, seamstress, and laundress merit badges—recognized girls' yearning for boyish freedoms and adventures. In fact, the cross-gendered appeal of the Girl Scouts proved essential to its early success.

By inviting girls to participate in conventionally male pursuits like camping and hiking, the Girl Scouts attracted a sizable girl audience that otherwise "might have rejected yet another cooking and sewing club."[24]

Not unreasonably, then, advertisers might have played more aggressively to girls' longings to participate in a tomboyish world of risk and adventure. Paeans to tomboyism, however, became the exception not the rule by the late 1920s.[25] Most advertisers addressed girls as peer-conscious teens who wanted to be *sought* by the boys, not one of the boys. Instead of valorizing the Athletic Girl's triumph over Victorianism, Postum now dramatized how bodily neglect created obstacles to popularity and heterosexual appeal. Lack of physical vitality was precisely why Virginia found herself without an invitation to Ruth and Alan's upcoming house-party. Noting that Virginia was "always having headaches" and copping out "when anyone suggests a hike or something else a little strenuous," Alan insisted that they "count Virginia out" (fig. 4.3).[26] In subsequent ads, physical beauty mattered even more than physical stamina in the quest for peer approval. Invariably, a thirty-day trial of Postum dramatically transformed lackluster girls into effervescent beauties. Sally North, once an unmemorable blonde, became a "radiant" belle chosen by her college classmates to be the May Day Queen of Beauty.[27] Corrine Marvin's girlfriends marveled with envy over how she had "changed herself from a muddy-complexioned, indifferent-looking girl into a stunning beauty" courted by Broadway producers.[28]

Teens who read the chatty, almost catty dialogue of the Postum ads could have seen the advertising scripts either as a ridiculous parody of teen culture or as confirmation of their worst suspicions. In either case, the ads served to remind girls that physical appearance not only determined social standing but also supplied ample fodder for gossip. In a typical Postum vignette, Vere and Jinny bemoan the dreaded prospect—"HORRORS!" Vere exclaims—of having to find a date for Edith, who was coming into town to attend a dance the next evening. Jinny holds out little hope: "'Nobody'll take her. . . . Of course she's clever, and she dances well. But she's so dull and colorless that she just doesn't register.'"[29] While adolescent girls might be reassured that Postum worked its magic on Edith, sparing her the fate of being a social pariah, such ads must have also confirmed nagging insecurities: in the looks-obsessed world of peer culture, judgmental gazes abounded from near and afar. And while the ultimate goal may have been to make oneself more dateworthy, girls learned that the female gaze—the scrutiny of female peers—was often the most unforgiving.[30]

Advertisers' vision of adolescent vulnerability to peer scrutiny bore remarkable similarities to their vision of mass urban society as an impersonal social landscape in which traditional markers of identity—kinship ties,

"Shall we invite Virginia?"

"WE SIMPLY *must* decide this morning which boys and girls we want for our house-party next month," said Ruth. "Here's the list I've made. See what you think of it."

Alan, her brother, read the list over. "Fine!" he said. "But you need another girl!"

Ruth nodded. "That's exactly what I wanted to talk over with you, Alan—the question of a fourth girl. Shall we invite Virginia?"

Alan sat up suddenly as if a bee had stung him. "We shall *not*, if I have anything to say about it!" he exclaimed. "Virginia's a nice girl, all right, but what good would she be on our kind of a house-party? She's always having headaches and when anyone suggests a hike or something else a little strenuous she usually says, 'Oh, let's not do that—I really don't feel like it today!' If we have her, Ruth, she'll spoil everybody's fun!"

"I guess you're right," said Ruth, regretfully.

© 1926, P. C. Co.

Postum is one of the Post Health Products, which include also Grape-Nuts, Post Toasties (Double-thick Corn Flakes), Post's Bran Flakes and Post's Bran Chocolate. Your grocer sells Postum in two forms. Instant Postum, made in the cup by adding boiling water, is one of the easiest drinks in the world to prepare. Postum Cereal is also easy to make, but should be boiled 20 minutes.

mention EVERYGIRL'S when writing advertisers

"Of course I'm right!" said Alan. "Count Virginia out—we'll pick another girl!"

Every girl wants to be "counted in" on all the good times her crowd has. It's too bad that some girls, like Virginia, neglect health. They sit up too late at night. They don't get enough fresh air and exercise. They eat unwholesome food. And, perhaps worst of all, they have formed the habit of drinking tea and coffee—drinks which contain caffein! Caffein is a drug stimulant—dangerous to health. But you need a hot mealtime drink. Use healthful Postum!

Postum is a delicious drink, made of whole wheat and bran, roasted. Instant Postum, made with hot (not boiled) milk instead of the usual boiling water, is especially popular with healthy, vigorous girls and boys. We'd like you to try it for thirty days, just to prove to yourself how wholesome and nourishing a hot drink can be. Your grocer has Postum—or, if you wish, we will send you one week's supply, free. Just fill out the coupon below—and mail it today!

MAIL THIS COUPON NOW!

P.—E.G. 3-26

POSTUM CEREAL CO., Inc., Battle Creek, Mich.
I want to make a thirty-day test of Postum. Please send me, without cost or obligation, one week's supply of

INSTANT POSTUM . . . . ☐ *Check*
(prepared instantly in the cup) *which you*
POSTUM CEREAL . . . . . ☐ *prefer*
(prepared by boiling)

Name

Street

City_____State

In Canada, address CANADIAN POSTUM CEREAL CO., Ltd.
45 Front Street East, Toronto 2, Ontario

4.3 POSTUM ADVERTISEMENT, EVERYGIRL'S (MARCH 1926). Juvenile advertisers exacerbated adolescent anxieties about peer approval even as they offered purchasable solutions to problems of peer acceptance. Reproduced with permission of KF Holdings. POSTUM® is a registered trademark of KF Holdings. Courtesy Security Pacific Collection, Los Angeles Public Library.

character, religion, and community allegiance—carried less weight than external appearances.[31] Whether negotiating the relatively anonymous worlds of the big city, the big corporation, or the large public high school, one could never be sure what minor and superficial considerations might matter to casual acquaintances. As teen advice columnist Hazel Rawson Cades noted, "competition is so keen and . . . the world moves so fast that we can't afford not to sell ourselves on sight. . . . People who pass us on the street can't know that we're clever and charming unless we look it."[32]

The Postum vignettes translated the scrutiny of strangers into the gossipy gab sessions of teen acquaintances, scripting new parables of impression management that exploited adolescent insecurities and self-consciousness. These parables taught girls that attention to fitness and diet yielded an enhanced appearance and more marketable self, while bodily neglect assured unpopularity and glum dating prospects. Evidence from the diaries of adolescent girls suggests that such parables must have resonated with considerable force and credibility. According to Joan Brumberg, the diaries of Yvonne Blue and Helen Laprovitz, both high school students in the 1920s, revealed an obsessive concern with physical appearance, peer approval, and the image they projected to the world. Having internalized the messages of popular culture, Yvonne, Brumberg writes, "became acutely self-conscious about both her body and her personality and this led to bouts of self-scrutiny that were prolonged and painful." Already by age fifteen, Yvonne was keeping "lists of which students and teachers like her, which didn't, and why."[33] Diaries also suggest that the practice of self-scrutiny easily slid into critical assessments of female friends, who perhaps applied makeup with too heavy a hand. Even high school yearbooks evidenced the growing centrality of dieting and body shape to teenage girls with the tradition of senior girls who facetiously "willed" their "slender figure" to younger classmates.[34]

Adolescent concerns with physical appearance were certainly not the wholesale invention of consumer culture. Adolescent girls in the nineteenth century, for example, exhibited great concern over skin blemishes and took pains to hide them under bangs, making the hairdo a fashionable emblem of generational identity.[35] Nevertheless, Victorians held the adolescent preoccupation with good looks in check because they prized moral character and spirituality over physical beauty. Shunning cosmetic artifice, Victorian beauty discourses contended that moral virtue was the only beautifier women and girls required.[36] In the early twentieth century, however, the rise of the movies, mass-market advertising, and celebrity culture fostered a new, more external orientation to beauty.[37] Girls learned about the malleability of personal image from movie stars like Mary Pickford and

Gloria Swanson, who often changed their appearance for new dramatic roles and openly celebrated the possibility of personal reinvention as cosmetics spokeswomen.[38] "Close-up" camera work in movies and advertising photography encouraged greater self-scrutiny, but the drawings that appeared more frequently in juvenile advertisements also taught girls new ways of looking. Indeed, some admakers theorized that drawings sold fantasies more effectively than photographs because, as one advertising executive explained, "people do not want to see themselves in terms of reality."[39] The highly slenderized and impossibly long-legged girls that juvenile admakers typically drew were easily two or three dress sizes smaller than the real adolescent girls who appeared in advertising photographs. This streamlined modernist aesthetic may well have fostered greater emotional investment in achieving the slim figures that adolescent girls admired (fig. 4.4).

Even sports culture did not escape the beauty imperative in the 1920s. Suzanne Lenglen's stunning athletic ability made her a tennis champion, but it was her beauty and sexual allure that transformed her into a popular culture icon.[40] Lauded as much for their physical beauty as their physical prowess, female athletes actually helped advertisers appeal to diverse girl audiences for whom body consciousness meant different things. A 1928 Postum ad told how Mollie, a second-rate basketball player in high school, earned a spot on the college five by drinking Instant Postum and adopting Postum's health rules. Though impressed by her athletic accomplishments, Mollie's friends, themselves not "particularly anxious to play basketball," were far more envious of her "radiant complexion, shining eyes and hair."[41] Appealing to athletic aspirants as well as the nonathletically inclined, beautified athletes like Mollie proved compelling commercial icons precisely because they were pliable symbols of feminine achievement, open to multivalent readings.

Adolescent girls increasingly found themselves enmeshed in a narcissistic world of self-surveillance, as adult advice columnists joined advertisers in promoting a new beauty culture. Teen beauty columns emerged in *American Girl*, *Everygirl's*, the *Ladies' Home Journal*, and *Woman's Home Companion*, which regularly publicized upcoming highlights of its "Twelve-to-Twenty Talks" column in the Camp Fire Girls magazine.[42] Magazine reader surveys suggest that many girls sought the advice such columns offered. *American Girl*'s 1926 "What-I-Wish-in-My-Magazine Contest" revealed a strong interest in articles about clothes, dating etiquette, and "being good looking," prompting the creation of a new column expressly devoted to these issues.[43] The revamped Girl Scout magazine mirrored similar adjustments made to the scouting program in the interest of

What "*happened*" to Ruth

JUST after Easter vacation, three excited girls gathered in Polly Newman's room. There was so much to tell—everyone talked, nobody listened.

"— the most wonderful time!"

"— and Mother said —"

"What *I* want to know is—what's happened to Ruth Bishop?" It was Polly's voice that rose above the rest and brought comparative quiet to the room. "She certainly looks different," she went on. "Remember how pale and —well, sort of unattractive she used to be? You never could get her to do anything, either, because she was always tired out or 'run down'. And *now* she's going to try out for the tennis team!"

Ruth's way to beauty and vitality

If Ruth Bishop had heard the comment, she might have laughed softly to herself. For nothing had "happened"—she herself had achieved the change. Not only with the "tonics" we all know about—outdoor exercise, plenty of sleep, and nourishing food—but with a special "good looks" program all her own. Postum made with milk. This delicious hot mealtime drink supplies materials for strength and

Postum is one of the Post Food Products, which include also Grape-Nuts, Post Toasties, Post's Bran Flakes, and Post's Bran Chocolate. Your grocer sells Postum in two forms. Instant Postum, made in the cup by adding boiling water, is one of the easiest drinks in the world to prepare. Postum Cereal is also easy to make, but should be boiled 20 minutes.

vim and vitality as well as good looks!

Postum is made of whole wheat and bran, roasted. Combined with hot (not boiled) milk, Instant Postum makes an ideal drink for young folks. The fine flavor of Postum makes it popular everywhere—even with those who don't care for plain milk. And it leaves no place in the diet for tea or coffee. These drinks contain caffein—a harmful drug.

Make Ruth's test—send for Beauty Booklet

Ruth proved to herself the benefits of drinking Postum made with hot milk. After making a thirty-day test, she and her friends noticed a real difference. Make this test for yourself and see what Postum made with milk will do for *you*. Thousands of girls and boys have made the test . . . they keep right on drinking Postum!

A week's supply of Postum, and a fascinating booklet on beauty will be sent you free. Fill out the coupon now.

© 1929, P. Co., Inc.

MAIL THE COUPON NOW!

POSTUM COMPANY, Inc., Battle Creek, Mich.   P.—A. G. 4-29
Please send me, without cost or obligation, your booklet, "The Garden Where Good Looks Grow," and a week's supply of Instant Postum.

Name_____

Street_____

City_____State_____
Fill in completely—print name and address

In Canada, address CANADIAN POSTUM COMPANY LTD.
812 Metropolitan Bldg., Toronto 2, Ontario

4.4 POSTUM

ADVERTISEMENT, AMERICAN

GIRL (APRIL 1929).

In choosing to use drawings rather than photographs of adolescent girls, juvenile advertisers promoted a streamlined modernist aesthetic that bore little resemblance to girls' actual bodies.

reducing membership turnover in the 1920s. Sensing that the allure of mass commercial recreation was draining their ranks, Girl Scout leaders began to replace the organization's previous "social feminist . . . emphasis on public health, scientific housekeeping and pioneering . . . with more traditionally girl-centered activities" that focused attention on good grooming and personal health.[44] Far from being foisted upon them, the addition of beauty columns may well have reflected adolescent girls' desire to make juvenile magazines more like women's magazines and the beauty column–laden tabloids and movie magazines, which they read in far greater numbers.[45]

Adolescent girls may have gotten more than they bargained for when they sought beauty advice, for columnists raised the stakes in the quest for good looks in ways that exacerbated self-consciousness about physical appearance. "There was a time when good looks was neither so common nor in such demand," Hazel Rawson Cades explained in her inaugural column. "But, Twelve-to-Twenties, those days are past. Being good-looking is no longer option. . . . There is no place in the world for women who are not." Adolescent self-consciousness certainly could not have been eased by Cades' assertion that "the bar" for acceptable beauty standards had been raised: "Where once you could get through on C, now you're ashamed to take less than B+; if you don't believe it, look around you and see how many girls are ranking A, with ease."[46] Elizabeth Woodward, editor of the *Ladies' Home Journal*'s "Sub-Deb" column, offered little more than cold comfort in commiserating with girls' struggles to be beautiful, noting that "any lad teethed on Garbo, Dietrich and Lamarr adds high."[47]

In justifying the new beauty imperatives, advice columnists explicitly challenged Victorian precepts that defined beauty in terms of internal qualities such as moral character, spirituality, and health. "It's positively disgraceful nowadays to sit back with a sigh and think that, after all, 'Beauty is only skin deep,' then meditate complacently on our good moral characters," Grace Hallock informed *American Girl* readers.[48] Some advice columnists even conceived of self-beautification as its own form of good works. "Girls who make themselves as good-looking as possible," Cades opined, "contribute in large measure to the happiness of the world, just as gardeners and house builders and interior decorators and builders of bridges and beautiful ships do."[49] Sadly, even as such beauty discourses preserved the link between beauty and virtue, they shifted the locus of girls' virtue from the interior to the exterior self.

Beauty may have become a feminine duty, but advice columnists insisted it was within everyone's reach.[50] Cades promised that "Any girl can be good looking"—a motto column promoters believed would compel girls who "never felt that way before . . . to prick up their ears and make that line come true."[51] Simply stated, beauty was an achievement open to all who put forth the effort. Healthy habits, good grooming, and wise consumption mattered far more than the unique blessings of family genetics. "Good looks is not something that one is born with or misses," Cades insisted. "Good looks is something that you *get*."[52] Advertisers adopted the same democratic rhetoric, promising results not just for beauty queens but for girls who simply wanted to look their best.[53] Beauty became something one worked at and trained for, much like an athletic event or a forensics tournament, as Postum suggested when it advised adolescent girls to practice "beauty-building" health habits and begin "training right away" for better looks.[54]

The notion that beauty could be *acquired* meshed nicely with other consumer metaphors advice columnists used to champion the pursuit of beauty. Grace Hallock, for example, proposed that girls approach good looks as a budgeting problem that any savvy consumer could solve. "Every girl has an allowance of good points just as she has a certain amount of pocket money," Hallock wrote. The challenge was learning "to make our allowance go as far as we can."[55] To become a successful beauty budgeter, girls first had to take inventory of their beauty assets and liabilities, carefully examining their face and figure for flaws that could be minimized and improved upon. Such advice encouraged a level of self-scrutiny that would have appalled Victorians as excessively vain. To Hallock's way of thinking, however, monitoring one's looks was a hard-hearted managerial exercise— one that demanded a blunt appraisal of strengths and weaknesses. *Scholastic* magazine's serialized 1939 "Boy Dates Girl" column even sanctioned such beauty budgeting as the path to heterosexual success. In a vignette tellingly entitled "First Aid," the chubby and dateless Angela "Tubby" Adams compiles a rather impressive list of liabilities—pimply faced, overweight, colorless, flyaway hair, "squeaky voice"—in her quest to "buckl[e] down, tak[e] inventory, and build up [her] stock where it was weakest."[56]

Such advice traded on older discourses deeply rooted in Protestant religious traditions that prized self-examination as the route to self-improvement. Beauty experts, however, shifted the focus of self-improvement from concerns with inner character and spiritual salvation to concerns with external appearances and impression management.[57] By their lights, the importance of relentless self-scrutiny could not be underestimated. "Many a chance of a job," Cades warned teen readers, "has been lost by way of a soiled glove or an inexpertly applied lipstick."[58] Girls who thought talent and intelligence outweighed good looks in the marketplace of jobs and dates had better think again. They need only consider the words of the famous educator Cades quoted in her column—"I would rather that a girl should go out into the world knowing how to comb her hair than wearing a Phi Beta Kappa key"—or the admonition of a successful businessman—"There's no place in my office for the girl who isn't smart enough to know how much appearance counts."

The visual rhetoric of Cades' inaugural column—its illustration of two young women gazing into opposite sides of a table mirror—also trumpeted the virtue of self-scrutiny. In the picture, one young woman—an unkempt adolescent with straggly hair and unruly shoulder straps peaking out from her dress—holds a partially eaten apple, while the other—a vision of sleek, polished modernity—grasps a powder puff instead. The duckling pictured behind the former and the swan behind the latter complete the visual narrative, linking Hans Christian Anderson's renowned fable of becoming to the transformative powers of good grooming and self-scrutiny.[59] The decorative frieze adorning Cades' column was at once fitting and richly ironic: relishing stories of magical transformation, modern beauty culturists refashioned Anderson's fable about the follies of judging external appearances into a parable for the new consumer age.

CONSUMER CULTURE AND HIGH SCHOOL PEER SOCIETY

Juvenile advertisers' own fables of becoming gained persuasive power partly from the congenial editorial environments that supported them. Having raised the beauty bar, advice columnists helped to cultivate a looks-conscious audience primed for purchasable solutions to problems of personal appearance and peer acceptance. Though advertisers eagerly exploited teen insecurities and conformist impulses for economic gain, they did not single-handedly create them. Rather, advertisers mirrored and amplified an emerging social reality: teenagers, like the college students who formed the vanguard of the much-vaunted and defamed twenties youth culture, were becoming full-fledged members of a distinctive peer society, with its own norms and hierarchies.

A variety of social and economic trends increased the salience of peer-group socialization in the early twentieth century. Chief among them was the widening segregation of adult and child leisure, fueled by the spread of mass commercial recreation and teens' greater access to automobiles.[60] More important still was the dramatic expansion of high school attendance during the 1920s and 1930s—a demographic shift that prompted one advertising authority to herald the dawn of "the Billion Dollar High School Market" in a 1930 issue of *Advertising and Selling*.[61] Throughout much of the nineteenth century, only a small elite—those preparing for college and professional schools—had gone to high school.[62] At the century's end, a minuscule six percent of the nation's youth were graduating from American high schools.[63] Those meager percentages rose dramatically during the first three decades of the twentieth century, thanks to compulsory education laws, which raised the age limit for school attendance; child labor laws, which forced more working-class youths into the schools; and the rising corporate demand for high school graduates to staff the new economy's expanding white-collar sector. As a result of such legal and economic changes, high school attendance rates climbed to nearly 60 percent by the early 1930s.[64] Diminished job opportunities for young people during the Depression swelled enrollments even higher by the decade's end, when attendance reached almost 80 percent.[65]

Upon entering high school, many teens found themselves immersed in a new and sometimes perplexing social pecking order. Large urban high schools could feel especially intimidating and impersonal, as students often lived in widely separated neighborhoods and therefore had less contact with one another outside of class.[66] As teens quickly discovered, popularity hinged on observing new codes of conduct and developing new styles of self-presentation that conformed to peer expectations. Without stylish clothing, sociologists Robert and Helen Lynd reported in their mid-1920s study of Muncie, Indiana, adolescent girls faced dim dating prospects and certain exclusion from the handful of select sororities that, though officially banned, continued to persist on larger high school campuses under the guise of social clubs.[67] Boys lacking fashionable attire, access to the family car, or the athletic prowess to win a coveted spot on the high school football or basketball team also found themselves relegated to the social sidelines.[68] While *Middletown* may have exaggerated the extent to which teens succumbed to the consumerist pressures and ideals of high school peer culture, the Lynds' widely read study popularized the idea that America's young ranked among the nation's most materialistic and appearance-conscious members.

Although sociological evidence suggested that adolescence was an intensely peer-centered period for both boys and girls, comparatively few advertisers explicitly addressed adolescent boys as appearance-conscious, peer-oriented consumers even though *American Boy* beckoned prospective advertisers to do precisely that. In a 1917 advertising trade press advertisement entitled "The CONSUMER HATCHES," *American Boy* linked the boy's consumer awakening to the adolescent boy's sexual awakening and growing interest in impressing girls. "There comes a day in every boy's life when he voluntarily scrubs his face until it glows and makes his first call on a girl.

That day marks the beginning of his identity as a consumer. He grows particular about the cut of his suit and coat, the style of his hat and collar, the quality of his hose and shoes."[69] Despite such arguments, only a few advertisers took *American Boy*'s bait. Stacomb Hair Cream asserted that the boys at "the center of a crowd" had surmounted the anonymity of high school by embracing a "hard, cold fact—that in the game called Life what counts is *appearance*."[70] Makers of musical instruments wove the popularity appeal into their advertising pitches, promising that the boy who learned to play the harmonica or saxophone would be "the most sought for fellow in his crowd."[71]

More tellingly, however, the very same companies that aggressively courted adolescent girls as appearance-conscious consumers seemed less concerned with helping boys create a physically beautiful exterior than with helping them realize a more conventionally masculine form of achievement: victory through competitive struggle. Postum's "good looks" regimen for date-hunting girls was thus a "training" program for wannabe male athletes, one that promised to bring "honor and glory" to boys who made the team and won the race.[72] While Keds shoes offered girls the hope of acquiring charm and popularity, they offered boys the hope of acquiring the magic "footwork" that transformed a fourth-string fullback, once jeered off the field, into a beloved all-American finalist who played on "one of the finest college teams in the country!"[73] Perhaps because popularity and heterosexual success were implied rewards of athletic distinction, Postum and Keds did not feel compelled to underscore such points. Rather, such ads echoed narratives of male metamorphosis well known to any boy familiar with the stories of Theodore Roosevelt, bodybuilder Charles Atlas, strongman Eugene Sandow, and physical-culture promoter Bernarr Macfadden, all of whom had transformed their frail and sometimes sickly bodies into admirable, even enviable, models of manly vigor.[74] In early-twentieth-century popular culture, stories about remaking the male body still fit comfortably within older Victorian paradigms of the inner-directed, self-made man. They offered testament to "a man's ability to make his way in the world against all adversaries, strictly on his own merits."[75]

Themes of peer adjustment were less prominent in boy advertising partly because peer-mindedness challenged older notions of male autonomy. Further, boys who displayed too strong an interest in self-beautification might be mistaken for sissies.[76] Besides, even without more overt references to heterosexual success, advertisers were confident that their fables of triumph over lethargy and physical weakness would hit their mark. As advertising authority Frank Fehlman commented, the boy "can be sold any food in the world if you can promise him a better body, capable of helping him win something." A boy, he noted, will undertake anything that will make him a "sure winner."[77] Fehlman had good reason to be confident. Many high school boys, sociologist W. Ryland Boorman discovered, "spend a lot of time daydreaming or imagining themselves becoming champions" and covet "high standing as an athlete . . . more than any other honor."[78]

While dreams of enhanced heterosexual appeal no doubt accompanied many adolescent dreams of athletic distinction, advertisers did not stress the issue until the depths of the Depression. Perhaps advertisers, like com- posers of romantic swing songs, sensed that adolescent boys were ripe for messages about triumphs of love, which in the midst of the Depression seemed easier to achieve than more materialistic forms of success.[79] But while swing music romanticized love, advertising transformed it into yet another competitive struggle. Athletic prowess alone could no longer guar- antee victory on the dating field. Even a star athlete—the school's "idol on the 'diamond'"—proved a "dud at dances . . . *until he learned how to stop* '*B.O.*,'" a Lifebuoy Soap ad observed (fig. 4.5).[80] Likewise, acne-plagued Ted, the school's star baseball player, almost lost election to student presi- dent because the girls would not vote for him—that is, until he used Fleis- chmann's Yeast to clear his complexion.[81] If even star athletes could fall from social grace, no boy could afford to risk his popularity with a bad case of body odor or acne.

Depression-era advertising broke new ground in acknowledging the painful self-consciousness that afflicted adolescent boys in their quest for heterosexual appeal, none better than Fleischmann's Yeast comic-strip style ads, which explained how reclusive, unhappy boys triumphed over pimples and became popular. Their faces blighted by large dots, the Fleischmann's Yeast boys suffered through dateless weekends, were turned down for the prom, and sometimes swore off dates, parties, and dances altogether out of sheer embarrassment.[82] Not only socially withdrawn, they were also prone to excessive self-scrutiny—a habit that itself called their masculinity into question.[83] Invariably, Fleischmann's Yeast rehabilitated the acne-plagued boy's tattered masculinity by putting him "back on the social register lists again!" and into the good graces of fawning female admirers.[84]

While the Depression eased advertisers' reluctance to address adoles- cent boys as appearance-conscious consumers, advertisers needed little convincing of the peer-orientation of adolescent girls. Many worked from the assumption that girls, like their mothers, were motivated by narcissism and an instinctive "feminine urge" to "Keep Up Appearances." Writing in a J. Walter Thompson agency newsletter, Margaret Weishaar argued that childhood conditioning made girls more sensitive to matters of appear- ance. "From the day her mother first rolls up her hair in rag curlers,"

Star athlete, but a dud at dances

...until he learned how to stop "B.O."

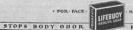

LIFEBUOY

4.5 LIFEBUOY ADVERTISEMENT, AMERICAN BOY (JUNE 1932). By the 1930s, juvenile advertisers increasingly regarded boys, too, as peer-conscious consumers. Reproduced with permission of Cheesebrough-Pond's, Inc. Courtesy Security Pacific Collection, Los Angeles Public Library.

Weishaar theorized, the girl "gets the idea that she can and must constantly *improve herself.*" The boy, in contrast, "takes for granted the dreary fact that beyond wearing well-tailored suits he can do little to improve his appearance. He can win distinction by what he does!"[85]

Advertisers presented their products as the solution to the teenage girl's pressing concerns with peer approval and image control. Household goods advertisers stressed the cultivation of domestic virtues as the route to popularity. Fels-Naptha Soap, for example, vowed that the "girl whose home has a bright, cheerfully inviting veranda" cleaned with its product was "likely to be one of 'the crowd's' most popular hostesses."[86] Such ads buttressed the recipe for popularity favored by *Everygirl's* advice columnist Aunt Cherry, who argued that the "gracious and clever hostess, who creates fun for her companions is almost invariably sought after."[87] Others, like Kellogg's All-Bran, revived older health-reform discourses that stressed careful living, a positive mental attitude, physical fitness, and "regular elimination" as the basis of a vivacious personality that easily attracted friends and male admirers."[88]

Advertisers' portraits of the popular girl celebrated the joys of exploring new gender freedoms through extracurricular school activities and dating. In Keds advertisements, popular girls invariably led "busy," overcommitted lives—a sure sign that they had surmounted the dreaded anonymity of high school. Not only did Peggy never miss a party, one ad proclaimed, but she had a "full schedule at school," including dramatics, tennis, and playing "guard on her class basketball team."[89] In another Keds ad, three "men" and two "girls" speed in their car toward Betty's "to stir up an impromptu party" at the home of their favorite hostess.[90] Significantly, none of the joy-riding party seekers appear attached as dates, as one girl has her arm encircled around the other girl, raising the delicious possibility that three prospective beaus are simultaneously pursuing Betty—a decidedly enviable prospect in the competitive "rating-and-dating" system that thrived on college and high school campuses throughout the 1930s.

In the newly emerging public culture of dating, popularity was measured by the frequency and variety of dates one commanded. Especially during the Depression, when many postponed marriage because they could not afford a home of their own, young people valued dating less as a means of choosing a lifelong mate than of securing their social standing. Maintaining the facade of popularity proved particularly important for women because men preferred to date women whom other men also desired. As a result, women college students studiously fostered impressions of desirability by being seen with the most popular men—the ones that "rated"— by turning down last-minute invitations, and by never being caught on the dance floor without a dizzying array of partners.[91] These dating conventions filtered down to the high school, where some female students, eager to avoid humiliation at school dances, actively campaigned for "the elimination of stags and the establishment of fixed-partner dates."[92] Keds acknowledged the competitive nature of the new dating culture in narrating the story of Mary Wheeler's transformation "from wallflower to butterfly in *one short summer*" (fig. 4.6). Having taken up sports, Mary, who previously "went to girls' parties mostly," now frequently "turned up at parties," where she was showered with male attention.[93] The accompanying illustration of a suave young man "cutting in" on Mary's handsome date made her transformation all the more compelling.

The Keds' campaign pushed advertisers' role as trusted teen advisors one step further when it launched Nancy Dell's Corner "for girls who want to be popular" in October 1930.[94] Appearing in *American Girl* and *Everygirl's* magazines, Nancy Dell's Corner answered girls' letters in the fashion of an advice-to-the-lovelorn column—a technique that capitalized on teen interest in such magazine features.[95] Only a small photograph of Keds shoes and a short concluding paragraph plugging the virtues of Keds reminded adolescent girls that they were reading an advertisement (fig. 4.7). Premised on the notion that "every girl *should* be popular" and "that very nearly every girl *can* be popular," Nancy Dell's column borrowed the democratic rhetoric of beauty experts but articulated a basis for popularity much less focused on good looks.[96] Promoting participation in sports as the single most important thing girls could do to become popular, Nancy Dell reassured plain Janes that "many girls who are not the least bit good looking . . . are . . . invited to all the parties because they are the 'alive' members in any group." Such glowing vitality was its own "form of good looks" and the reason why girls who lacked conventional beauty were nevertheless often "the center of the group."

At first blush, Dell's column seemed to subvert the counsel of teen beauty culturists. Yet even as Dell downplayed the importance of "handsome" features, she reminded her readers that attractive "sports costumes" outfitted with Keds went "a long way towards solving that question of good looks."[97] Far more insidious, however, was Dell's insistence that what ultimately determined a girl's heterosexual appeal was not her athleticism but her sports-*mindedness*. Time and again, Dell informed her readers that sports offered "an interesting topic of conversation . . . and . . . an easy, informal way of making new friends."[98] Dell encouraged girls to train hard in sports, since the better players were more in demand, but she did not promote athletics as an arena of female achievement.[99] Rather, Dell endorsed athleticism as a means of grooming girls for heterosexual success. Citing a

From wallflower
to butterfly
in one short summer

Mary Wheeler was just a very usual sort of girl. Nice enough—even rather pretty—but really *not* very exciting.

She went to girls' parties mostly, except for an occasional dance to which her brother would take her when his girl was away. And those never were much fun—she rarely danced even half the dances.

But, rather quickly last summer, a change came over Mary. When she turned up at parties (which she did, with increasing frequency), she was gay and sparkling. And the men began gathering about her and showing her a wonderful time.

Nobody asked Mary what had happened. And perhaps even Mary herself wasn't fully aware that the *sports* she had just that summer taken up so seriously were responsible for her new vivacity and charm.

A fresh, clear complexion; assurance; energy; a gay, happy, normal frame of mind—these are some of the things sports will give you.

So go in for them—*regularly*. And be sure you wear the right clothes. Loose, roomy, sleeveless frocks for tennis; well-cut shorts or bloomers for basketball and hockey; and for every sport—proper shoes.

For, in sports, footwork is all-important. It means poise, sureness, speed.

Keds are built especially to help you excel in sports—all kinds of sports. They are pliable, so your feet have perfect freedom. They are porous, so there is plenty of breathing space. And they're designed so as to give the foot snug, firm protection.

You'll find Keds at all the best shoe dealers' from $1 to $4 a pair. Ask for Keds by name. They are not Keds unless the name "Keds" is on the shoe.

United States (US) Rubber Company

Keds "Minerva"

This smart oxford at the left comes in white with colored trimming. The athletic shoe at the right comes in suntan trimmed with tan or in white trimmed with black or colors to match gym uniforms.

Keds "Suntan Juno"

4.6 KEDS ADVERTISEMENT, EVERYGIRL'S (MAY 1930). Juvenile advertisers taught adolescent girls how to improve their heterosexual appeal and rate high in the competitive game of dating. Reproduced with permission of The Keds Corporation. Courtesy Security Pacific Collection, Los Angeles Public Library.

Nancy Dell's corner for girls who want to be popular

Dear Miss Dell: Please write to me and tell me how I may become popular. I have been living in this city only a short time and know very few people. I am attending high school, where I see many attractive girls and boys. How may I become better acquainted with them? S. P.

Dear S. P.: I know how lonely you must feel at times with a strange group and away from all your old friends. And you sound like a girl who should be very popular! . . . Of course it takes a little time to become fully acquainted with a new group, but here is one way. Why not go in for sports? They offer a splendid way to make friends. On the sports field it is easier to get over the newness of introductions than it is anywhere else; and there's a matchless feeling of good-fellowship there, too. Try taking part in your school games—I'm sure there are happy times ahead for you!

I've quoted S. P.'s letter and my answer because I want every one of you to share my conviction that sports can do a very great deal to make you popular. So, as I told S. P. above, go in for sports! Work at them. And be sure you dress properly for them—in loose, com-

comfortable well-fitting clothes and Keds. Keds are the smartest sports shoes ever designed. Did you know that the members of the Davis Cup Teams have worn Keds in the international matches, both here and abroad? Keds are designed with all kinds of different soles and reinforcements to help you with the footwork that is so important in all sports.

I hope you'll go right away and see the new 1931 Keds styles and colors. Please take my advice and rely on these wonderful shoes to help you become expert at sports; and on sports to help you become popular. And then write and tell me what a nice time you're having!

Nancy Dell

1790 Broadway, New York City
Dept. KK-31

United States Rubber Company

REG. U. S. PAT. OFF.

The Shoe of Champions

The name "Keds" is stamped on all genuine Keds. Look for the name and be sure. Keds at $1, $1.25, $1.75 and up to $4. The more you pay the more you get—but full value whatever you spend.

Keds "Diana"—This athletic Keds style laces clear to the toe and is especially good for gym work.

Keds "Juno"—The lace-to-toe Keds above come with colored trimming that harmonizes well with gymnasium uniforms.

4.7 KEDS ADVERTISEMENT, AMERICAN GIRL (MARCH 1931).
Juvenile advertisers capitalized on girls' preoccupation with peer approval by mimicking the narrative styles of advice-to-the-lovelorn columnists. Reproduced with permission of The Keds Corporation.

recent survey of young bachelors, Dell reported that "**what they like best in a girl is *naturalness*.** Men liked girls who are good comrades . . . ready for any sort of wholesome fun." Girls who participated in sports, Dell asserted, could expect romance to blossom with a boy who shared their enthusiasm for tennis, golf, or basketball.[100]

Like so much of thirties dating advice, Dell's was inherently contradictory. Although ostensibly rewarded for their "naturalness," girls, in reality, learned to follow certain codes of self-presentation—in essence to hide their true selves—if they were to make themselves dateworthy. Ideologies of love and romance encouraged young women to define their sexual subjectivity not on their own terms but in the service of men.[101] Overly assertive women who veered from the prescribed intellectual passivity seemed particularly threatening in light of heightened Depression-era anxieties over the viability of male breadwinning. Not surprisingly, by Dell's lights, becoming sports-minded required girls to limit the arts of conversation to topics that were fun but not intellectually demanding. As Dell advised the bookwormish girl who longed to join the "popular crowd," "**Books are interesting but they don't afford half the chance for laughing, noisy argument that a 'net ball' or a tricky basket shot does.**"[102] Contemporary dating etiquette, however, frowned even on pronounced displays of sports-mindedness at sporting events, no doubt leaving some teens in a quandary over whether to open their mouth or keep it shut. Girls should certainly bone up on sports, *Scholastic* magazine's advice columnist Gay Head offered, but not become so expert or brash that they "take on the air of a hard-boiled sports critic. . . . An intelligent silence with an occasional leading comment to indicate a passing knowledge of the game is much to be desired."[103]

Warnings like these about the dangers of an assertive feminine intelligence suffused Depression-era popular culture. Postum's thirty-day "beauty course," one ad proclaimed, transformed Jean from a studious girl, who could never sustain a boy's interest, into a fit exerciser. Jean's reward for spending less time in the library and more in the gym was high praise from the sought-after captain of the football team: "Jean, you're always studying hard—and now I believe you're taking a course in *good looks*! And you certainly get A-plus!"[104] Such ads reinforced negative attitudes toward female academic achievement that abounded in the advice literature of the thirties, a decade when many viewed intelligent and capable women as potential competitors in a limited job market and threats to male dominance in the workplace.[105] In her *Personality Book for Girls*, Mary Brockman counseled teens that boys preferred girls who knew when to sit back and look interested over those who talked too much or appeared too wise.[106] Some adolescent boys seemed just as eager to shore up male dominance at a time when masculinity was in deep crisis. Writing in the "Student Forum" of *Scholastic* magazine, Charles Sords, a Pittsburgh high school student, complained about "girls who may know *just a bit* more than their escorts, and continually remind them of that fact *in public*. This is very embarrassing to said escort, because all men (and boys) like people to believe that they know everything there is to be known! You'd better think that over, some of you brainy (?) girls."[107] By endorsing such views, juvenile advertisers circumscribed the new gender freedoms enjoyed by peer-conscious female adolescents.

MANAGING THE CONSUMER EXCESSES OF THE PEER-CONSCIOUS ADOLESCENT GIRL

In popular culture and childrearing discourses, the peer-conscious adolescent girl alternately figured as a social ideal and a problem to be solved. According to popular wisdom, the adolescent girl was forever given to outspending her allowance, waging extravagant demands on the family clothes budget, and taking fashion and makeup to extremes in a bungled attempt to imitate glamorous movie stars.[108] Advertisers and advice columnists undoubtedly contributed to those very excesses, for by awakening teens to the possibilities of personal reinvention, they also fueled the fires of self-doubt and insecurity that propelled consumer experimentation.

More contradictory still were the efforts of such teen advisors to reconcile other-directed consumer selfhood with older notions of self-sacrificing femininity. As many teenage girls discovered, pleasing others involved a complex negotiation of seemingly conflicting priorities and moral dictates. Teen advisors, after all, instructed girls to abandon old gender constraints when they played on the athletic field but to respect them when they played the dating field. They urged girls to scrutinize their appearance and inventory their flaws yet not succumb to vanity or obsess over their looks. They validated girls' sense of economic entitlement yet urged them to be more respectful of their dates' wallets and honor economic obligations to their families before themselves. Such contradictory messages undergirded the turbulence and turmoil of adolescent girlhood.[109]

Even in the prosperous 1920s, juvenile advertisers and advice columnists implicitly recognized how heavily class background, family income, and the prejudices of schoolmates weighed upon girls in their quest for peer approval. The rising cost of active participation in high school social life—including tickets to movies and athletic games, club dues, dance fees, and party clothes—not only increased the spending requirements of teens but raised the stakes of income inequality.[110] In an article originally published in *Vanity Fair*, "genius-IQ" teenager Elizabeth Benson shared with *Everygirl's* readers her dismay at parents' failure to understand the importance of spending money to girls' standing within adolescent peer society. "There are a myriad little social distinctions in any set of people," Benson wrote, "and the 'society' of childhood has rules as important and as complex as those of society. There are circles within circles in school society, and a girl can feel social ostracism as keenly as her mother . . . if she does not 'treat' the 'crowd,' when her turn comes . . . [and] entertain them in accordance with their rigid standards."[111] Faced with fewer opportunities for earning money, adolescent girls from varied social and economic backgrounds were primed for advice which could teach them how to harness scarce parental resources and cope with a class-conscious peer culture.

Advertisers eagerly fulfilled that role, giving voice to a variety of class- and age-based economic resentments. Some, like the *Woman's Home Companion* Pin Money Club and the Girls' Club of the *Ladies' Home Journal*, publicized opportunities to make money by selling magazine subscriptions, a dignified form of child labor considered appropriate for girls. While similar money-earning clubs for boys presented subscription sales as a form of business training, girls' clubs conceived of earning as a way to pad allowances spread thin by the demanding social schedule and fashion needs of adolescent girls. "Maybe," a Girls' Club ad suggested, "you're like Emma F., who 'outgrows' her allowance now and then," and finds that "'a day never passes but what an extra quarter or fifty cents is needed for something."[112] Thanks to such pin-money clubs, girls who previously had to make do "with a small weekly allowance" no longer had to deny themselves the pleasures of nice clothes, silk stockings, and commercial recreation enjoyed by their economic betters.[113]

Even as money-earning clubs acknowledged the inadequacy of girls' spending allowances, they reinforced popular cultural stereotypes of girls as slaves to their own boundless consumer desires.[114] Girls had to be taught to overcome their spendthrift ways. By turns sympathetic and scolding, the Pin Money Club urged girls to exercise more fiscal responsibility and stop pestering their parents for more spending money. "You're woman enough already to know that Dad has given you as much money this week as he can, that to ask for more will only bring the worry-wrinkles to his eyes, because he hates to say 'no' to you."[115] Only when girls stopped requesting reprieves from spending restrictions could they truly vanquish economic dependence. Mary Daw did just that when she used her club earnings to purchase a more expensive party dress than her mother was prepared to buy: "I've never seen Mother so astonished. Father was proud of me too."[116]

Pin-money clubs promised just the sort of moral transformation child experts expected when parents entrusted adolescents with responsibility for earning part of their own spending money: a child who invested spending decisions with greater pride and forethought. A similar narrative of moral transformation shaped juvenile advertisements for sewing machines, which stressed that economizing was sometimes the shortest route to bountiful consumption. Offered the choice of a sewing machine or an expensive dress that would bust her clothing budget, one teen surprised her father by opting for the Singer Electric, calculating that, for the same price as the single ready-made dress, she could have material for more pretty dresses "than I ever dreamed of having this season."[117] By showing how consumer plenitude could be reconciled with consumer economy, Singer addressed a sore spot for many working-class and less affluent middle-class adolescent girls: a paucity of attractive clothes for school days and social activities. Unable to match the sartorial standards of their more affluent peers, some working-class youths in Muncie dropped out of school to avoid embarrassment and the anguish of social exclusion.[118] Handmade clothes, however, carried their own stigma, and girls who wore them had to contend with the patronizing attitudes of better-off schoolmates. There was no deeper insult, testified one Muncie high school graduate, than being told how "nice" your party dress looked, for "if your mother makes a dress at home people always come up to you and say, 'How ni-ice you look! Isn't it pretty!' and you know they're condescending."[119]

Singer's case for homemade clothes became more compelling during the Depression, when economic dislocation exacerbated class distinctions. While social competition had always been present at Muncie's Central High School, the Depression aggravated tensions to the point where some students preferred to take the side entrance than face the front "steps crowded with richer students looking you over."[120] Feelings of social exclusion were so pronounced among poorer youth that many parents lobbied for the creation of a separate South Side high school to spare their children from competitive consumption. Some girls withdrew from school altogether.[121] Nevertheless, the pressures of competitive clothing persisted among Muncie youth and, not surprisingly, sales of Singer sewing machines rose. By 1933, the shame surrounding homemade clothes had sufficiently eroded in Muncie that the home economics class staged its fashion show in February, to allow enough time for commencement dresses to be completed in senior sewing classes.[122] Singer advertisements further destigmatized home-made clothes by revealing that the secret behind every well-dressed girl was not always money or a well-employed father but simply the willingness to take classes at the Singer Sewing School.[123]

Depression-era popular culture valorized self-reliant adolescent girls who refused to wallow in their economic woes but instead found creative solutions to unfortunate circumstances. By contrast, the self-pitying, down-on-her-luck teen was a singularly unbecoming figure. "Who's snobbish now?" Gay Head pointedly asked girls who felt "ashamed of [their] family and home. . . . Is it because Margaret Jourdain's family has a two-car garage, a grand piano, and silken gowns? Are these things worth more to you than character, honesty, and congeniality?"[124] Girls equipped with the proper outlook and a heavy dose of self-reliance, Depression advertisements suggested, could take charge of their economic destiny and put their economic woes behind them. The sole, sad-faced girl who marched in a Girl Scout parade without a uniform had only herself to blame, one advertisement claimed (fig. 4.8). "SHE *COULD* HAVE BEEN HAPPY TOO!" blared the headline, had she only made the effort to collect labels from cans of Libby's Evaporated Milk, labels that could be exchanged for uniforms and camping equipment.[125] Girls could once again become full participants in peer society, the ad promised, without even "spending a dime"—a clear play on the Depression-era lament, "Oh Brother, can you spare a dime?"[126]

Some might be tempted to view advertisers' encouragement of self-reliance in girls in liberating terms. After all, insisting that girls earn their own way valorized a measure of economic autonomy usually associated with masculine virtue. But in Depression-era popular culture self-reliance also resonated with more conservative gender discourses. The ideology of feminine self-sacrifice was very much at work during the Depression, when girls, far more than boys, were expected to temper their consumer desires and adopt a cooperative spirit in heeding limits on family spending.[127] Perhaps, Gay Head suggested, if girls spent less money trying to match their economic betters, "Mother could have a new hat, Dad a new car, and the living room a new sofa."[128]

For the sake of preserving friendships, *American Girl* urged girls to maintain a happy disposition—even when short finances brought misery. "When Bob or Bill or Irene or Mary comes to call, don't put on a long face and tell them your troubles. . . . It shows poor taste and it's boring to listen to." Honoring the more ennobling virtues of feminine self-sacrifice meant girls had to learn to mask negative emotions and suffer in private. The advice to keep a lid on one's emotions was informed as much by older ideals of feminine self-sacrifice as by new ideals of personality that, as historian Peter Stearns has written, "involved adjusting appropriately to signals from the outside world and maintaining enough emotional control to do this consistently."[129] To this end, *American Girl* invited girls who wanted to vent their fiscal frustrations without committing a social faux pas to write

4.8 LIBBY'S ADVERTISEMENT, AMERICAN GIRL (OCTOBER 1933).

In Depression-era popular culture, the self-pitying, down-on-her-luck teenage girl was a singularly unbecoming figure. Reproduced with permission of Nestle USA, Inc.

"Betty Brooks" for consolation and advice on how to acquire cash and equipment by selling *American Girl* magazine subscriptions.[130]

Undoubtedly, the pressures on girls to bear their misery with a cheerful smile made teens all the more anxious to seek insights that would help them cope with class snobbery and feelings of inadequacy. Though Depression-era teens were perhaps no more prone to excessive self-scrutiny than their twenties predecessors, they were armed with a new psychological vocabulary and a propensity to see "inferiority complexes" behind their struggles with peer adjustment. Growing impatient with such self-diagnoses, *Everygirl's* Aunt Cherry chided girls for "getting a bit morbid about complexes," adding that analysts would soon be working overtime "to cure us of *complex* complexes, if we don't look out." Her own solution to girls' self-esteem dilemmas—"a lot of fresh air and plenty of work"—reflected the new tenor in Depression-era advice.[131] While twenties advice had sanctioned consumer culture's emphasis on external appearances, thirties advice columnists tempered the excesses of the Jazz Age by reminding readers that the "sturdier virtues," as Aunt Cherry called them, still had their place in forming and extending peer relationships.[132]

Advice columnists comforted those who felt "outclassed" and outspent by highlighting, and sometimes even mocking, teens' consumer vices with a vigor unseen in the twenties. Aunt Cherry took on the very mentality—the inordinate other-directedness—that made quick, purchasable solutions to image problems so irresistible to teens. "I thought the 'how to be popular' letters had stopped coming, but during the past month they began again. . . . It is really pathetic. . . . Get the aid of the specialists when possible, but DON'T THINK ABOUT IT ALL THE TIME!"[133] Advice columnists also pilloried class snobbery. Indeed, Gay Head's immense popularity among Depression-era teens owed at least something to her sympathy for the economic underdogs in adolescent peer culture. In a column encouraging teens to "Be Yourself," Head sided with poorer teens against their more affluent classmates who "place ownership of things and material wealth ahead of cultural qualities . . . They are superficial buzz-buzzes, and will sting you with their tongue if you give them half a chance."[134]

Though Gay Head earned plaudits from both sexes for her accurate representations of adolescent foibles, the economic underdogs who most often won her sympathy were boys.[135] Whether stood up for a richer date or drained of their spending money, boys routinely found themselves on the losing end of girls' expectations of a good date. Viewing feminine dependence on "Romeo's pocketbook" as an "outmoded custom," Gay Head urged girls to consider the dutch treat and be more respectful of their date's wallets. If girls suspected "a precarious financial situation," they should offer to pay their own way to a football game and for the eats afterward.[136] Head's message was clear: dateworthy girls subordinated their own sense of economic entitlement to a nobler ethic of feminine self-sacrifice. Girls did not always welcome such advice. "You may consider this a mid-Victorian attitude in a modern age," a Montana teen responded to Head, "but all of the girls in our class . . . feel that if we are good enough to be invited out, our escort should feel that we are good enough to spend some money on. If he cannot afford to take us out, we would just as soon go somewhere not as expensive or not go at all."[137] Boys protested in kind. DeWitt Porter, a Ft. Wayne high school student, complained bitterly that "certain girls in every crowd" not only failed to heed Head's advice but "live[d] up to the title of 'small time gold digger.'"[138]

Boys' objections to the high cost of dating were certainly not new to the 1930s. Burdensome dating expenses in the mid-1920s had left one beleaguered Muncie youth longing for the days of courting on the "davenport at home" when you could "have a date . . . without making a big hole in a five-dollar bill."[139] During the thirties, when jobs and spending money were even harder to come by, a backlash against "gold diggers" and class-conscious snobs ensued. A stock character in *Amos 'n' Andy* radio skits and romantic comedies screened in movie theaters, the gold digger became the focal point for a host of male economic anxieties sparked by the Great Depression.[140] Gay Head ably captured male resentment of female incursions on limited resources in the dialogue she attributed to boys. One "Boy Dates Girl" column, featuring the musings of several boys on the girl of their dreams, defined the ideal date as a girl who, among other things, "knows how to reconcile appetites to pocketbooks." As the jam session concluded, the boys vowed revenge against girls who stood them up for a richer date with "a better car," promising to boycott girls who practiced such "date discrimination."[141] A new form of consumer retribution, the dating boycott would force girls to scale back their demands on boys' spending money.

The fault lines of the adolescent "gender wars" extended from conflict over dating expectations to conflict over the rules of good grooming—another arena in which girls allegedly were prone to consumer excess. Topping the list of boys' pet peeves, according to Gay Head, were the foibles of looks-obsessed girls who continually monitored their appearance in the mirror and fell victim to the "Great Evils of the Cosmetic System: high-fever cheeks, prize-fighter eyes, plaster-of-Paris noses, greasy lips, gory fingernails and overdoses of loud-smelling perfume."[142] From girls' perspective, the consumer inadequacies of boys matched, if not surpassed, the consumer excesses of girls. Acting as a translator of girl opinion, Gay Head advised boys to "add longer home working hours on personal appearance."[143] "*How Dare*

You," Gay Head admonished, "think that toothbrushes and toothpaste are just something you read about? 50,000 ads can't be wrong."[144] In Head's characterization of the adolescent female point of view, boys' appearance deficits amounted to a deficit of consumer consciousness. As the reigning queens of rigorous self-scrutiny, adolescent girls seemed to think a little more male narcissism might go a long way.

Adolescent girls, however, may not have been as quick to vouch for advertisers as Gay Head supposed. Even as they emptied their wallets to purchase alluring new brands of cosmetics and personal grooming aids, teenage girls, historian Kelly Schrum has shown, often "retained a sense of humor about [advertising's] extravagant claims."[145] Beth Twiggar was an old hand when it came to mocking advertisers' tales of magical self-transformation in various diary entries: "Exit Halitosis! I spilled a bottle of listerine all over myself. The results will be immediate!"[146] Indeed, adolescent skepticism of advertising can be seen as one dimension of a self-conscious teenage identity: a proclamation that they were no longer "foolish innocents."[147] Such consumer cynicism could also be found in the *Whatsit*, a widely read miniature children's tabloid from the late thirties. Written by adults from a kids' point of view, the *Whatsit*'s Lovelorn Column mercilessly satirized advertisers' obsession with health and beauty as the solution to problems of romance and popularity. In one such column, "Eunice Person" complained that she used "Bobo soap, Blisterine Tonsit gargle and Deteriodent Toothpaste" and diligently read "the ads for new products like these," but nevertheless remained a "wallflower" at parties. Stumped and nearly certain that Eunice was a "hopeless case," the love counselor invited readers' help and suggested that Eunice "learn to play the zither"—a reference to the ubiquitous ads that touted musical ability as the road to popularity.[148] In another issue, Madame Jo, a fictitious Hollywood beauty advisor, lampooned advertisers and beauty experts who defined a people-pleasing external appearance as the key to social success. "Just like any business," Madame Jo advised, "Charm is based on figures. Are you too fat? Well, then you will have to get thin! Are you too thin? You must do everything to get fat!"[149]

Gay Head's own qualified defense of advertising underscored the very real appeal of such parodies. "You can laugh at 'avoid offending' and 'what your best friend won't tell you,' but unless you form the sensible habit of using a deodorant, you needn't wonder why he never came back."[150] Adolescent consumer skeptics could deny the authority of individual advertising claims, but only at their own peril could they deny the authority of their peers. Head's commentary captured the essence of adolescents' ambivalent relationship with consumer culture. However much they smirked at advertisers' exaggerated promises and melodramatic narratives, few could dispute one truth advertisers spoke: the quest for peer approval had become a defining feature of adolescents' own struggles with self-identity. Consumer culture proved such a potent force because it supplied adolescents, never quite certain of their own identity, with new ways to satisfy fantasies of personal reinvention.

In imagining adolescents as peer-conscious consumers, advertisers were thus coming to grips with a profound shift in the nature and experience of early-twentieth-century adolescence. The transition from childhood to adult responsibility no longer involved simply adjusting to the norms and expectations of adulthood. As high school enrollments ballooned and adolescents began spending more time in the company of their peers, the central dilemma of adolescence had come to center on adjusting to the norms, expectations, and hierarchies of age-based peers.

CHAPTER 5

Revitalizing the American Home:
Playrooms, Parenting, and the Middle-Class
Child Consumer

AS MIDDLE-CLASS ADOLESCENTS became more deeply enmeshed in the enchantments of consumer culture and commercialized recreation, parents and child experts grew ever more anxious about the erosion of family values and the growth of an autonomous youth culture. Now that teens were spending more time in the company of peers and most of their leisure in unsupervised activities outside the home—going on dates, attending movies, and motoring—traditional modes of family authority seemed to be losing sway over social and sexual mores.[1] In a 1927 study of girl life in America, Henriette Walter sounded a familiar lament about the shrinking influence of the family as a guardian of middle-class values. Complaining that commercialized recreation had usurped home entertainment, Walker observed that the home was "rapidly becoming merely the place . . . where we sleep and perhaps eat, but do little else." Just as the nineteenth century had removed work from the home, Walker argued, the twentieth century was "doing the same . . . to its play, and breaking down the ties which have held the home together."[2] Adding play to the list of family functions lost to the public sphere, Walker gave voice to fears that the modern family was in crisis. Though rising divorce rates, relaxed sexual mores, and expanding opportunities for women outside the home contributed to such fears, Walker's complaint addressed the equally troubling concern that parents were losing control over their sons and daughters to an autonomous youth culture and the public world of mass recreations.

Historians have analyzed how these perceptions of "crisis" in the family spurred efforts to revitalize the domestic sphere and modernize family relations. Under the assault of rising divorce rates, a revolution in morals and manners, changing sex roles, and recalcitrant youths, the Victorian family gave way to one that was more democratic and less formal. Rejecting hierarchical relationships bound by duty, the modern family instead enshrined romance, sexual fulfillment, and companionship as the defining characteristics of marital success. Relationships between parents and children also became more democratic, as children gained more freedom from parental control and fathers assumed new roles as playmates to their children. In place of the old controls, family experts looked to affection—the nurturance of the emotional needs of each family member—as the new basis for solidifying the family. "Shorn of its traditional educational and productive functions, the stability of [the modern family]," Steven Mintz and Susan Kellogg have written, came to hinge "on the tenuous basis of affection, compatibility, and mutual interest."[3]

This chapter makes explicit what historians have only hinted at: during the early twentieth century play itself became essential to stabilizing and buttressing the emerging companionate family ideal. A number of changes dating back to the turn of the century contributed to this rethinking of the role of play in the companionate family. Middle-class families had grown smaller, but so, too, had their houses and backyards, reducing the space allotted for children's play. No longer the primary center of leisure pursuits for women and children, the home now competed with a broadening array of recreational choices offered by commercial establishments. As the gulf between child and adult leisure widened, many parents and middle-class reformers interpreted children's attraction to the movies, amusement parks, and other commercial playworlds as a threat to family values, parental authority, and middle-class aesthetics. Movie palaces, filmmakers, and vaudeville theaters eventually accommodated such concerns by adopting decency codes that made public recreation "safe" for middle-class consumption.[4] But as Elaine Tyler May has written, Progressive reformers also sought to counter the temptations of mass culture by "incorporating some of the new leisure ethic into domestic life itself."[5]

During the decades between 1910 and 1940, family experts and childrearing authorities promoted a new vision of children's play that promised to restore the primacy of family ties and combat the allures of mass recreation. Writing in child-study journals and popular women's magazines, some of these experts were university-trained psychologists, sociologists, or educators, but others were semiprofessionals or critics who, perceiving a receptive audience, simply offered their advice for the taking. These authorities envisioned play as a positive force in children's lives—not simply as a diversion to keep children healthy and out of mischief, as in the Victorian conception of play, but as an essential aid in children's mental and physical development. As many child experts proposed, the true "work of childhood" was play itself. Play provided a wholesome outlet for children's self-expression and channeled their youthful energies along the proper path of development. It was "serious business" indeed.[6]

During the interwar years, anxieties about children's attraction to mass recreation and an autonomous youth culture provided an inescapable context for selling and interpreting the merits of children's play in a revitalized domestic sphere. Although psychological theories propounding the virtues of play informed these domestic reforms, the new understandings of play also acquired salience and persuasive power because they were tied to the promises and perils of consumer society. Rather than reject commercial culture outright, child experts exhorted parents to embrace its ethos of salesmanship and enticement in constructing a wholesome alternative playworld within the home. Together with interior designers, child experts advised parents how to transform frumpy homes into enticing play sites equipped with playrooms, backyard swing sets, and educational toys which stimulated the imagination. Play with the "right" kinds of toys in the "right" kinds of settings, experts believed, would help elevate children's taste for edifying amusements and inoculate them against the passive spectatorship that made them vulnerable to the attractions of mass culture. Just as critically, parents could make the home more inviting by forsaking harsh discipline for understanding companionship. Play thus acquired a vital role in reclaiming the authority of the companionate family, promising not only to remake the complacent "movie-mad" child into a respectable middle-class consumer, but also to reinvigorate parent-child relationships.

BATTLING THE ALLURES OF MASS CULTURE

When child experts embraced playrooms and educational toys as antidotes to the allures of mass culture during the interwar years, they both revised and drew upon long-standing middle-class cultural discourses that valorized edifying, purposive play in the private sphere over the debasing amusements of the public sphere. In the early nineteenth century, Victorian etiquette manuals advised readers to use leisure to improve oneself or acquire knowledge rather than waste it in idle or corrupting pursuits.[7] Riddled with do's and don'ts, such manuals warned women and children to shun bawdy, masculine public amusements such as minstrel shows, circuses, and dance halls in favor of the more genteel domestic pastimes of piano playing, singing, arts and crafts, and Bible reading.[8] Children's attraction to the new mass-commercial recreations that emerged at the turn of the twentieth century deeply troubled Progressive reformers, who saw the sensual and sensational appeals of amusement parks, penny arcades, public dance halls, and nickelodeons as a corruption of children's playtime and a perversion of play itself. These entertainments were threatening not only because they asked audiences to surrender self-control and forsake edification for mere amusement, but also because their immense popularity persuaded the guardians of middle-class morality that they were "losing control over . . . the lower classes and even over their own young."[9]

Eager to rescue children's play from commercial interests, Progressive reformers launched a "play movement" to create public playgrounds and community recreation centers that could supplant the debasing influence of mass-commercial recreations. Through supervised play activities specifically geared to the child's stage of development, reformers hoped to nurture children's moral and physical development and strengthen habits of self-control and cooperation deemed essential for living in an interdependent, industrialized democracy. Although Progressives shared Victorians' disdain for purposeless play, they were also far more enamored of the playful, instinctive side of human nature. Jane Addams, in fact, exhibited great sympathy for children's "insatiable desire for play" and faulted the modern city's lack of wholesome play outlets for the rise in working-class juvenile delinquency. Rather than seeking to suppress children's play instincts, play theorists like psychologist G. Stanley Hall and Luther Gullick, who helped found the Playground Association of America in 1906 and the Camp Fire Girls in 1914, sought to optimize them for society's advantage. Hall's "recapitulation" theory, which suggested that children repeated the biological evolution of the human race in passing through various stages of development, established the intellectual rationale for a series of prescriptive play activities, each a prerequisite for the development of more advanced social and physical skills. If guided through the approved progression—learning first from imitative play, then competitive play, and later cooperative play—children would develop the leadership skills, habits of social cooperation, and creativity essential for their future success.[10] By the same token, dire consequences would result if children's play instincts were frustrated through suppression or corrupted by the dangerous temptations of mass culture.

During the interwar years, the mission to improve children's play continued to be intertwined with a critique of mass culture, but the locus of progressive reform energies shifted from the public sphere of municipal playgrounds and mass commercial amusements to the private sphere of the family and the home. Admittedly, the impulse for censorship remained strong among traditional moralists; pressure from the Legion of Decency and other religious organizations who joined Catholics in boycotting the film industry during the Depression finally compelled Hollywood studios to adopt a more stringent production code in 1934.[11] But now that large numbers of middle-class children had joined their working-class counterparts at the movies, there was also a nagging sense among family experts and childrearing authorities that regulation of amusements and of children's access to them only went so far in solving the problem. The real problem lay much closer to home.

Echoing the earlier sentiments of Jane Addams, many interpreted the success of commercial recreation as a rebuke to the home, the schools, and the community for failing to recognize children's needs for companionship and adventure. Ethel Puffer Howes, for example, suggested to parents that an uninspiring home life may be at fault if "your children have developed no engrossing, self-activating occupation" or "just mope around," settling on the movies for lack of anything better to do.[12] Nursery school educator Elizabeth Cleveland put the case more bluntly. Unlike parents and social agencies, she wrote in *Parents' Magazine*, the "commercial interests" understood well "how to provide the thrill that youth craves, how to tempt the instinct that loves to play with fire, how to satisfy the burning desire to appear sophisticated."[13] The 1932 White House Conference on Child Health and Protection concurred, conceding that commercial recreation centers like the movie theater, dance hall, and roadhouse had done a better job of quenching children's thirst for adventure. "Commercial recreation," the conference committee on delinquency reported, "has been most conscious of conditions and trends in modern life, and the most alert to profit from the things which appeal to children."[14]

If mass culture receded in relative importance as the target of reform, it nonetheless remained a crucial focal point of disenchantment with the hedonism and superficial values that middle-class children seemed to embrace. Child experts and play reformers blamed commercial amusements for producing and reinforcing a host of personality defects typically associated with the culture of the Jazz Age. Critical of the shallowness that mass culture promoted, Girl Scout leader and physical education specialist Agnes Wayman argued that too much passive recreation gave children the impression that buying could substitute for actual life and experience.[15] Other commentators viewed children's habits of mindless consumption as the outgrowth of a fast-paced, technology-driven society that deprived children of opportunities for true relaxation or creative pursuits. Lacking time to cultivate their own tastes or develop "an intelligent appreciation of things and affairs and books," modern children, Ruth Frankel lamented, eventually became adults who "turn . . . complacently to bridge and golf, movies and radio, gossip and endless rushing from one amusement to the next."[16] Equally contemptuous of this flighty "jazz-age" personality, Ruth Danehower Wilson mourned that overstimulated children, sapped of their initiative, were growing into "the young person of the restless, always-on-the-go but accomplishing-nothing type."[17]

These critiques of mass culture's artificial and passive pleasures inspired child experts and reformers of various stripes to insist on children's need for a refuge from them. Nursery school educator Elizabeth Cleveland urged parents to limit movie viewing to once every two or three weeks and to co-operate with schools in cultivating their children's taste for "finer forms of recreation" such as reading, Shakespearean theater and other drama, clas-sical music, and art appreciation. "Once [children] have learned to appre-ciate the best," Cleveland contended, "they are safe from the inferior."[18] Likewise, interwar proponents of summer camps, historian Leslie Paris writes, envisioned camp life as "an antidote to modernity's cheap thrills" and "that dread modern disease—'spectatoritis.'" Through carefully super-vised recreation and outdoor exercise in rural settings, summer camps promised to awaken the creativity and wholesome energies of the city's "pitiful sophisticates," as one camp director referred to his young charges.[19]

The very kinds of craft-oriented and educational play in which campers took part mirrored the active play child experts envisioned in the revital-ized home—one equipped with a playroom and backyard playground. While prepared to concede that home activities could never completely re-place outside amusements, child experts believed that improving the play spaces and playthings within the home could make them less appealing. "The child who is busy with many things—who has a work-bench in the cellar or a ping-pong table for rainy days, who is interested in photography or puppets or stamp collecting," Josette Frank wrote, "is far less likely to find 'going to the movies' the only way of spending a free afternoon."[20] Similarly, PTA mother Mrs. Robert E. Simon recommended that children spend less time at the movies or listening to the radio and the victrola and more time at home working on "creative music, writing, painting, and handicraft." Children so engaged, Simon argued, would be less tempted to spend their time, as so many children did, "haphazardly following the line of least resistance."[21] Middle-class parents and child experts readily ac-knowledged popular culture's seductive appeals, but they also expressed a new determination to teach children how to resist them.

CHILDREN'S PLAYROOMS AND THE REVALUATION OF PLAY

Parents had long been encouraged to provide their children with playthings and the space in which to use them, but interwar childrearing authorities raised the stakes of failing to do so. By not giving children a room of their own and the creative toys to cultivate skills and hobbies, Zilpha Carruthers Franklin asserted, parents ran the risk of turning "children adrift in a world of movies and street excitement," presumably unprepared to resist their demoralizing effects.[22]

Critical commentary on the lack of play space in modern homes was not entirely new to the 1920s and 1930s. As far back as the turn of the century, writers in popular women's magazines had complained that modern homes lacked sufficient play space for the educational and developmental needs of the child. In the smaller, modern home, playrooms had vanished along with the parlor, and the cozy attics that had once occupied children on rainy afternoons had been converted into servants' quarters or storage space. The results for the child, critics complained, were disastrous. In an 1898 article on the child's place in the home, nursery school teacher Katherine Beebe criticized modern homes for requiring children to "live too much and too soon in the adult world." Surely, Beebe argued, "children would lead a much more wholesome and childlike life" in a playroom rather than "listening to the proceedings of the last meeting of the Women's Club, the gossip of the neighborhood, or the discussion of their own talents, achievements, ailments, and shortcomings." Although Beebe's suggestion that children needed protection from mother's world of gossip and social acquaintances gave a new twist to the Victorian concept of worldly corruption, the idea of a sanctuary in the home where children "could remain secure and sequestered from the dangers of the adult world" was an old one, originating in the 1830s with the emergence of nurseries.[23] Beebe's ultimate goal, however, was distinctly modern in recognizing that children needed not just protection but the "space and freedom" to realize the full "physical, mental, and ethical results of play."[24]

During the early years of the twentieth century, Progressives like Beebe applauded the playroom's benefits to both the children and the adults of the household. Reflecting their penchant for order and efficiency, Progressives seemed equally enamored both with the playroom as a space that satisfied children's developmental needs for unthwarted play and with the prospect of a noiseless, clutter-free home.[25] Suitable play spaces, they observed, reduced household friction by allowing children to do what came naturally without fearing parental reproach for disorderly conduct. No longer a "household pest" but a "proprietor," the child with a playroom, Helen Bennett claimed, "soon understands the annoyance he causes grown folks when he encroaches upon their domain, for he well knows how they encroach upon his."[26] By giving children a place for their toys, the playroom also freed mothers from having to "pick up" after their children.

Bringing peace and freedom to the entire family, not only did the playroom liberate the child from incessant requests to be quiet and keep out of the way, but it provided mothers deserved "relief from eternal disorder."[27]

By the mid-1920s, however, the notion of the playroom as a barrier between the children and adults of the household gave way to a more exclusively child-centered vision of the room's purpose. If the sequestered Victorian nursery had isolated children to protect their innocence and adult privacy, the modern playroom now did so to allow children free reign to express their selfish impulses and explore their desires.[28] Child experts vigorously promoted playrooms as an essential requirement for growing children, whose healthy development and psychological adjustment depended on access to stimulating environments and playthings. Reflecting Freudian psychology's criticism of undue repression, the playroom advanced modern childrearing practices that advocated self-expression and freedom over rigid conditioning of child behavior.[29] Experts depicted the playroom as an integral feature of a home, where, as Emma Kidd Hulbert put it, "restrictions are few" and "don't is a word seldom heard." In contrast to delicately furnished bedrooms, where "play must be restricted and 'Don't' is written large over the door," Hulbert explained, the playroom allowed children to indulge whatever "delightful thing [their] imagination may dictate."[30] The playroom, so envisioned, gave spatial expression to the idea that "Free, 'unbossed' play is the most serious business of the child"—a childrearing principle so important that a 1918 international conference on childhood enshrined it in their "New Bill of Rights of Childhood."[31]

Teaching parents just how to create the ideal playroom became the mission of popular magazines such as *Parents' Magazine* and *Garden and Home Builder*. They advised their predominantly middle- and upper middle-class readership that a well-designed playroom privileged child-directed play and exploration over adult tastes and standards. Playroom authorities recommended that parents outfit the rooms with sturdy, simple furnishings that could withstand messes and rambunctious play. Disdaining fussy decor, Marian Bachrach urged parents to furnish the playroom to suit children's tastes. "Too often," she complained, "this 'children's room' is theirs in name only. . . . With the blind egotism of adults we have carried our own likes and dislikes into the very place from which we pretended to exclude them." As Bachrach saw it, the tastes of children and adults were so divergent that a playroom modeled after children's likes might strike parents as "drab or bare." Instead of the "nursery wallpapers and permanent pictures," which "show the grown-up finger in the pie," a real playroom, she argued, would have walls that could "withstand the frequent onslaught of thumb-tacks."[32] Ethel Reeve admonished mothers accustomed to decorating in subtle shades that in the playroom it was "fitting to key the palette high" and use the bright, primary colors children preferred.[33] D. D. Hutchison's "honest-to-goodness playroom" also shunned "grown-up" decorations and furnishings. There children could chalk games onto a patternless, black linoleum floor, draw on the blackboard, or study the maps that decorated the walls (fig. 5.1).[34]

In some respects, child-centered playrooms mirrored broader trends in early-twentieth-century interior decoration. As prim parlors gave way to informal living rooms styled to capture the home owner's personality, interior decoration, historian Karen Halttunen writes, shifted "emphasis from the Victorian concern with the moral self and its improvement to a modern concern with personal temperament and its self-expression."[35] The new orientation in design comported well with modern psychology's injunction to stimulate rather than repress children's play instincts and undoubtedly amplified designers' sensitivity to children's color preferences and needs for self-expression. Even so, playroom promoters did not completely abandon the older Victorian notion that objects and well-designed home interiors "contributed to the moral improvement of those who lived

5.1 PLAYROOM FEATURED IN ARTS AND DECORATION (DECEMBER 1931). Designed for a well-to-do boy, this brightly colored playroom featured blue linoleum floors, light yellow walls, gender-specific toys, and uncluttered space in which to play.

[in and] among them."[36] Envisioned as an arena for active play, the playroom directed children's play toward wholesome pursuits and, eventually, experts hoped, molded them into respectable middle-class consumers who preferred creative endeavors to passive recreations.

With this aim in mind, many designers criticized elaborately decorated playrooms as antithetical to the room's purpose. Marian Bachrach preferred an empty, unfurnished room that invited children to "mould it in the direction of [their] changing wants" to "elaborate surroundings," which, she argued, "discourage original effort and set up the too familiar refrain of 'Buy me.'" In Bachrach's vision, the ideal playroom was "not really a room at all, but the spirit that can live in a room. . . . It is a room capable of being a stage one day and a shoe-shining parlor the next. In it one can publish a newspaper, build a boat, or merely contemplate one's toes in the sun."[37] Penelope Baldwin also cautioned parents to "guard against over enthusiasm" when furnishing the playroom, advising them to leave plenty of open floor space for games, and to keep costumes on hand for "dressing up as pirates, Indians, fairies, and all the other characters so dear to the hearts of childhood."[38]

The anticonsumerist sentiments reflected in such advice were not universally shared. Some playroom boosters—blurring the line separating wholesome play environments from overly luxurious or vulgar ones—could not resist the opportunity to inculcate middle-class standards of taste through the room's decor. Ethel Reeve believed the risks of exposing children's impressionable tastes to cheap furnishings so great that she pitied families who could not afford special equipment for the playroom. "Many a man has grown fond of some frightful cast-off," Reeve noted, "merely because it was an intimate associate of his childhood. It is a shock to learn that he has been harboring a viper in the matter of taste for years and he usually persists in liking it anyway . . . for the damage is by that time irreparable." Reeve advised parents to "discard things which are too flagrantly bad" rather than allow them to shape the "unformed taste of their children."[39] Dorothy Gladys Spicer also set a high premium on the quality of the playroom's decor. "The pictures a child sees," Spicer argued, "mold his taste just as inevitably as the thoughts he thinks, the books he reads, and the games he plays."[40]

The toys and creative equipment that stocked the playroom were, of course, at least as important as the room's design and decor. According to child experts, educational toys were themselves considerable aids in the battle against passive spectatorship. Stressing the importance of toys that stimulated creative activity, experts preferred toys with multiple play possibilities to mechanical toys and other eye-catching novelties that involved the child as "merely a spectator."[41] They instead recommended a "well-rounded play plan" that included outdoor and indoor toys, dramatic toys, and creative material like clay, paste, and scissors.[42] Toy expert Minetta Sammis Leonard reminded parents that while there was a place for toys that brought momentary pleasure, they were not as valuable as toys that "hold the interest longer and encourage creative effort."[43]

Toy retailers and toy companies embraced the themes of play reformers in their own promotions. Echoing reformers' calls for well-rounded play plans, the *Dry Goods Reporter* urged retailers to classify toys by their specific educational benefit, indicating whether the toy was designed to stimulate learning, develop muscles and motor skills, foster good dispositions, or promote moral and spiritual growth. Declaring its sympathy with "national movements in child welfare work and Americanization," the trade journal explained that "a toy without a play outline is only a temporary relief to the mother."[44] Toy makers, capitalizing on parental anguish over children's attraction to potentially corrupting outside amusements, advertised their products as the surest way to keep children absorbed in wholesome play. "You, being a wise parent," a catalog for Buddy "L" dump trucks and machinery noted, "want to satisfy the boy's urge to be doing" and "keep him . . . off the street."[45]

Though perhaps too big for the average playroom, home billiard tables also promised to combat the appeal of "outside allurements" by making the home environment more attractive to straying adolescents. The home billiard table, the advertiser assured, was "How Present-Day Parents Keep the Hat-Rack Filled."[46] Eastman Kodak's children's movie projector, easy enough for a seven-year-old to operate, promised to bring the "great thrill[s]" children had come to expect from the movie palace into the privacy and security of the playroom, while still giving parents the chance to reassert control over their children's movie consumption. Any parent willing to fork over the fee for a Kodatoy movie projector and a miniature theater with "silvered" screen in the early 1930s—dealers reported a Kodatoy Christmas "landslide" in 1930—was not likely to object to the film fare available in the Kodaplay movie catalog. Would it be Charlie Chaplin, Felix the Cat, famous athletes, travel adventures in strange lands, westerns, airplane flights, or perhaps even battle scenes (fig. 5.2)?[47]

Whether modestly furnished or elaborately supplied, the modern playroom was a costly venture, requiring extra space in the home, special equipment, and judiciously selected playthings. Child experts tried to make allowances for families who lacked an extra room or an attic or basement that could be converted into a playroom (fig. 5.3). Even small apartment dwellers, *Mother's Own Book* suggested, could create a "Peter Pan House"

THRILLS
ADVENTURE
COMEDY

...In this New EASTMAN Movie Projector that children run themselves

KODATOY
A MOVIE PROJECTOR FOR CHILDREN

PLAYROOM movies give children a great thrill. They're entertaining. Instructive. And such a barrel of fun for boys and girls of all ages.

Kodatoy is amazingly simple . . . entirely safe. Yet it's an efficient movie projector—made by Eastman, the world's largest maker of home movie equipment. A seven-year-old child can easily run it.

There's a whole catalog of Kodaplay movie films to choose from. Airplane flights, Felix the Cat. Battle scenes. Sports. Westerns. Charlie Chaplin, and other famous comedians. Travel wonders. Adventure. All moderately priced; 30 cents, 60 cents, 90 cents per reel.

Kodatoy uses 16 mm. safety film—100-foot reels or less. It has a powerful projection lens and three-blade shutter. Framing is automatic. You'll be surprised at the bright, clear quality of the movies it shows and the steady, flickerless projection.

Complete outfit—Kodatoy, miniature theatre with "silvered" screen, and two empty 100-foot metal reels—costs but $12. Motor drive unit available as an accessory. Price, $6.50.

Any leading Kodak dealer, toy or department store will demonstrate Kodatoy for you. Take the children along, too, and let them see for themselves how easy it is to operate Kodatoy—and what fun.

Fill out and mail the coupon below for interesting descriptive folder giving you full details about this practical playroom projector.

Eastman Kodak Company, Rochester, N. Y.
Please send me FREE without obligation the folder describing Kodatoy.

Name _____
Street _____
City _____

S. E. P. 3-7

5.2 KODATOY MOVIE PROJECTOR ADVERTISEMENT, SATURDAY EVENING POST (MARCH 7, 1931). Eastman Kodak promoted its Kodatoy projector as a wholesome addition to the playroom. Reproduced with permission of Eastman Kodak Company.

by employing a five-foot screen to cordon off a section of a room for children's exclusive play use.[48] But even that advice would have been impractical for many poor and working-class families, for whom budgets were tight and space came at a premium. Experts defended the expense as a worthy price to pay for the benefits of healthy child development and a happy home life. In their view, failure to provide children with the proper accoutrements of play was not only "tragic" for the child but a lost opportunity to cement family friendship and loyalty.[49] Such guilt-inspiring appeals reminded parents that play was directed at a definite end: producing a cultured child, with good taste, the capacity for self-directed play, and a refined appetite for edifying forms of entertainment. So long as children were armed with such middlebrow appetites, the excesses of the Jazz Age could not harm them.

Parents' Magazine (originally called *Children: The Magazine for Parents*) dramatized this association of childhood play with wholesome living in a 1926 cartoon captioned "We don't view with alarm this tendency on the

5.3 "A Child's Play Shelf," featured in Ladies' Home Journal (March 1919).

Though far from the playroom ideal, a play shelf, play boosters argued, could wholesomely occupy children who lived in houses and apartments with limited space.

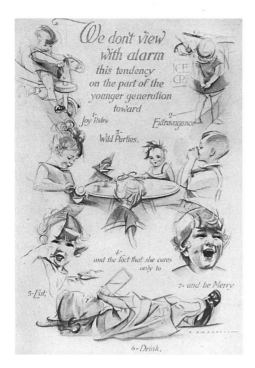

5.4 DRAWING IN CHILDREN:
THE MAGAZINE FOR
PARENTS (NOVEMBER 1926).
This portrait of an innocent
"youth culture" offered a reassuring contrast to the hedonism
of the flapper generation.

part of the younger generation toward Joy Rides, Extravagance, Wild Parties, and the fact that she cares only to Eat, Drink, and be Merry." Instead
of depicting the social lives of adolescent flappers, the cartoon showed
cherubic toddlers riding a rocking horse, purchasing an ice cream cone, enjoying a tea party, eating breakfast, drinking from a bottle, and laughing.
While some parents may have read the cartoon simply as an homage to
childhood innocence and playfulness, others may have interpreted its opti-
mistic portrait of an innocent "youth culture" as reassurance that children's
hedonistic impulses could indeed find wholesome outlets (fig. 5.4).[50]

PLAY IDEOLOGY AND PERMISSIVE PARENTING

Child experts championed play not only as a vital tool of child socialization
but also as a new basis for exercising parental authority within the companionate family. As experts saw it, the revitalized home required revitalized parents who themselves were infused with the spirit of play. If parents
wanted to restore the primacy of family ties and battle the allures of commercialized leisure, they would have to abandon their old-fashioned authoritarian ways for more fun-loving interactions with their children.

A wide range of family experts during the 1920s and 1930s advanced new conceptions of motherhood and fatherhood that promised to revitalize the domestic sphere. *Parents' Magazine*, founded in 1926, headed the charge. Proclaiming itself a leader of the "better parenthood movement," the magazine promised to bring its middle- and upper middle-class readers the latest scientific findings about childrearing. Convinced that good parenting required expert guidance, *Parents' Magazine* assembled an editorial board and group of advisory editors that read like a who's who in the fields of child study and child welfare. Included among its luminary advisors were juvenile court judges, professors of sociology and psychology, home economists, and health and hygiene educators. Often, however, the magazine's best-received articles were not written by experts. As publisher George Hecht recalled in 1972, the magazine could often "'get better and more useful articles' from 'just average mothers' who were 'intelligent' and 'who had successful experiences with their own children.'"[51]

It was not enough just to read experts' advice. *Parents' Magazine* also urged readers to join child-study clubs and follow the study program included in each monthly issue. In the view of child-study experts Benjamin C. Gruenberg and Sidonie Gruenberg, enrollment in such groups was a matter of urgent necessity. Because parents and children had fewer and briefer contacts, the Gruenbergs argued, parents had "no minutes to spare for blundering or agonizing."[52] Interest in learning about childrearing during the interwar years was intense, especially among middle-class mothers and fathers. According to a national survey of 3,000 American families in the early 1930s, 91 percent of mothers and 65 percent of fathers from the professional class read childrearing advice in newspapers and magazines, while 35 percent of mothers and 12 percent of fathers from the lower rungs of the working class reported doing so.[53]

The increasing importance of expert advice may have made some parents more confident in their abilities but it also magnified the significance of parental blunders. Blamed for everything from the movie-mad child to the rise in juvenile delinquency, parents were faulted for being too absorbed in their own selfish recreational pursuits to be good companions to their children, for failing to provide opportunities for play in the home, and for lacking sufficient training for the scientific demands of parenthood.[54] Experts leveled especially harsh criticism against mothers who failed to make the home an inviting place. Attributing the breakdown of family ties to lax standards of domesticity, Lillian Wald, president of New York City's Henry Street Settlement, noted that the "small, congested, and too often unlovely rooms of the majority of our home-makers frustrate the high purpose of the home and send its members out for pleasure and

interest and . . . 'self-expression.'"[55] Equally mindful of domesticity's higher purpose, *Parents' Magazine* editor Clara Savage Littledale reminded her
middle-class readers that "delinquent and problem children" were not
produced by "tenement houses alone."[56]

Even as experts raised the stakes of domesticity, however, they also expressed contempt for mothers who discharged their homemaking duties
with too much zeal. As bad as the uninspired homemaker was the stuffy
mother who appeared too concerned with maintaining household order.
One anonymous expert, answering the letter of a concerned parent, attributed the reluctance of a twelve-year-old girl to entertain friends at home to
the mother's failure to relate well with children. "The mother, although she
means to be hospitable, may be too good a housekeeper to make children
with their noise and confusion really at home. Or she may be so critical of
their manners and social status that she sets up adult barriers against happy normal play."[57] Charged with the tasks of beautifying the home and
managing it scientifically, the ideal homemaker was now also expected to
accommodate and foster the spirit of play.

Fathers, too, drew censure and rebuke for failing to inject play into relationships with their children. Cataloguing a host of grievances against
them, Frank Lee Wright asserted that too many fathers had become "impatient, unsympathetic, indifferent, stubborn, intolerant and tyrannical."
The ideal father, Wright scolded, should be a friend and "an enjoyable
companion" to his children rather than "a policeman."[58] Business
metaphors underscored the kind of personal transformation fathers were
now expected to undergo. "In business, if a man can get on a 'friendly-
kidding' basis with a customer, he counts it a gain. With his children as well
he should not hesitate to cultivate this friendly attitude of give-and-take,"
a compendium of parental advice explained.[59] In business and family life
alike what counted was a winning personality. Entrusted with new duties as
buddies and playmates to their children, fathers acquired increasing cultural significance in the 1920s and 1930s, Robert Griswold has shown, as domestic life came to center around nurturing personal growth, fostering psychological adjustment, and satisfying emotional needs.[60]

Such conceptions of middle-class motherhood and fatherhood reflected the conviction that parental authority was more effectively exercised
through play and friendship than through obedience and discipline. Experts characterized the new and improved parent as an up-to-date, understanding friend. No longer an "old fusspot" who obsessed over discipline
and responsibility, the modern parent related to children on an equal basis,
learned their slang, and adapted to their world.[61] Weaver Pangburn,
spokesman for the Playground and Recreation Association of America,

heaped praise on the modern "American Daddy" who entered into the play life of his children. "He remembers that he was once a boy himself, and as he romps and plays with his own boys and girls, he, for the time being, becomes a boy again."[62] Such connection in play, experts contended, was the key to closing the gap of misunderstanding between parents and children. Peggy Pond Church urged parents to stay young at heart. Be more interesting to your children, she commanded. Forget about responsibility. Retain a sense of wonder and imagination. In short, become Peter Pan. Such a carefree frame of mind, Church told parents, was the key to recovering the play spirit within themselves and fostering it in their children.[63] The Gruenbergs also urged parents to "grow along with their children." Surely, they argued, "an intelligent adolescent who discovers that her mother has made no advance over the slogans and proverbs and reasoning that served for an older sister" would lose respect for her mother. As Sidonie Gruenberg saw it, modern parents should cultivate "friendly and human relations with [their] children" rather than setting themselves "up as minor deities, stern and exacting, to be obeyed and feared."[64]

Competition between the home and the public world of commercial amusements provided a major impetus for such revisions of parenting ideals. Particularly striking is the way experts employed metaphors of "salesmanship" and enticement to illuminate the challenges and goals of modern parenting. Nursery school educator Elizabeth Cleveland urged parents to give family fun some "attractiveness, instead of a wishy-washy, negative, colorless ideal of deadly, dull goodness. . . . if our stimulation is to compete with Satan's . . . we must provide legitimate thrills." Like other child-study experts, Cleveland believed that children's desire for romantic adventure, risk, and self-expression could be transferred to constructive activities such as competitive games and athletics, scouting, manual work, and even household chores. Her aim was to "make a game of every day living," no matter what the activity. Legitimate thrills, she believed, could be had as easily from word games and surprise treats as from a competition between dish-washing teams to set the record for the quickest cleaning.[65] Although Cleveland seemed to appreciate children's desires for adventure, one wonders how her prescription for manual work, household chores, and competitive dish-washing could possibly have competed against the thrills of the movie theater and other public amusements.

Despite its obvious naïveté, Cleveland's vision was taken even further by self-anointed expert Happy Goldsmith, who drew a stronger analogy between parenting and salesmanship. He advised parents that they could retain some influence over their children if they abandoned destructive discipline for the strategies of persuasion that advertisers had perfected. The "competition which exists between the corner store and the home for the patronage of the youthful public," Goldsmith observed, "is just about putting the average parent out of business." Unless parents learned the principles of good salesmanship, Goldsmith warned, the "wholesome foods . . . of the home shop" would waste away. Goldsmith recommended that parents make spinach irresistible by telling their children that celebrities enjoyed spinach or by naming spinach dishes after their idols. "Why not 'Babe Ruth's Home Plate,'" Goldsmith advised *Parents' Magazine* readers, "or 'Mary Pickford's Beauty Compound'?" Goldsmith also urged parents to learn their children's slang and laugh at their jokes, just as the clerk in the corner store did. "That's why the boys and girls trade there," Goldsmith explained. "Probably a genius at child psychology," the clerk listened to children and treated them as his friend.[66]

Parents' Magazine thought Clifford "Happy" Goldsmith's diagnosis of parental inadequacies and prescription for reform sufficiently insightful that they reprinted it in a special compendium of important childrearing essays.[67] Goldsmith's proposal to adapt business psychology to home problems, however, underscores an irony of parental attempts to combat the attractions of commercial amusements. Preserving distinctions between wholesome consumption and commercialized distractions often entailed further blurring of the boundaries between them. The strategies of the advertiser or the movie promoter became the strategies of the parent, each attempting to "make a game out of every day living." But still there was a critical difference. Parents wanted children to thrill to the adventure of spinach, dishwashing, and family word games, not the more sensual appeals of movies, candy, and penny arcades. Disguising their authority in the colorful garb of consumer culture, parents were simply adopting new "commercial" means to achieve the old ends of family harmony and wholesome living.

Goldsmith's advocacy of parental salesmanship also suggests a more complex relationship between modern advertising and changing ideals of parenting. Roland Marchand has persuasively demonstrated how advertisers crafted merchandising strategies around child-guidance theories that recommended subtle psychological manipulation of children's natural impulses in place of strict discipline. Tapping into the swelling "child consciousness" of the 1920s, advertisers exploited contemporary childrearing theories, often exaggerating their dictates, to sell a variety of goods.[68] Advertising did not simply reflect or distort these new models of child management, however. Evolving amid a growing recognition of the commercial world's success in attracting children, the childrearing advice popularized in *Parents' Magazine* seems to have taken some of its cues from advertising's own models of social influence. This historical context suggests that there existed a symbiotic relationship between advertising and contemporary childrearing theories, one in which the two discourses continually influenced and reshaped each other.

Despite their affinities, advertisers and child experts often employed similar means to achieve quite different ends. While advertisers promoted a vision of family democracy that privileged children's consumer desires, child experts envisioned an enlightened family democracy that retained a fair degree of parental control. As their efforts to reinvigorate home life suggest, progressive rhetoric about the virtues of unthwarted play and family fun often belied more conservative goals. A case in point involves the home-play campaigns launched by the Playground and Recreation Association of America [PRAA] in the 1920s. Designed to foster a "bond of sympathy and comradeship" between parents and children, these campaigns asked parents to devote at least three hours a week to playing with their children. Local merchants joined in the effort by displaying equipment and supplies for home play in store windows. Gimbel department store, working in cooperation with the PRAA, invited children (accompanied by their parents) to try out their model city and suburban backyard playgrounds, equipped with slides, sandboxes, sand toys, and a gym with swings, rings, and a trapeze.[69] In a radio address for Better Homes in America, a national nonprofit organization that built and displayed model homes under the auspices of the U.S. Department of Commerce in the 1920s and 1930s, PRAA spokesman Weaver Pangburn suggested how play could be enlisted in the service of parental authority. If the play spirit prevailed, Pangburn promised, it would "illuminate all the activities of the home, including the dish washing, making the beds, and picking things up."[70] Charles Gates, a social scientist, made the ultimate goal of family companionship more explicit: "Only by . . . genuine sympathy with the child can [parents] hope to control the child."[71]

These conservative impulses help explain the popularity of the backyard playground movement in the 1920s and 1930s. Building on the Progressive-Era movement to establish public playgrounds, recreation reformers now set their sites on the middle-class family in promoting backyard playgrounds as a way to tie children's play to the safety of the home. "The child with a backyard playground," Natt Noyes Dodge wrote, "develops the habit of contentment at home. Home becomes the center of his life, not merely a place to eat, and sleep, and have his ears washed."[72] Such assurances addressed a number of parental anxieties about the dangers of street play amid car traffic and unwholesome social influences.[73] James Ford, executive director of Better Homes in America, advocated backyards to spare children "the physical and social risk of playing on the street" un-supervised.[74] Using veiled language that betrayed fears of race and class mixing in public play spaces, reformers praised the backyard for providing privacy, a "safe and interesting retreat for after school fun," and the oppor-tunity for children to associate with their own friends. As Florence Fitch saw it, the home with a backyard playground was a place where there pre-vailed such a strong "spirit of goodwill and mutual interest" that "children will not go to a public playground because they prefer to have their friends in their own yard."[75]

Many parents took the advice to equip their homes with children's play in mind quite seriously. "By the early 1930s, 46 percent of professional par-ents had backyard swings (as compared to nearly a quarter of lower-working-class parents), while 58 percent of the professionals and 17 percent of the manual laborers had sandboxes."[76] Parents were also persuaded that play could cement family ties and strengthen parental authority. Middle-town mothers from the business class often attributed their parenting suc-cess to their willingness to devote more of their leisure to their children. "I certainly have a harder job than my mother; everything today tends to weaken the parents' influence," one mother confessed. "But we do it by spending time with our children. I've always been a pal with my daughter, and my husband spends a lot of time with the boy. We all go to basketball games together and to the State Fair in the summer." A working-class mother with two teenage boys in Middletown also identified play as the crux of successful modern parenting. "I just can't afford to grow old. . . . I put on roller skates with the boys and pass a football with them. In the evenings we play cards and on Sundays we go to ball games. My mother back East thinks it's scandalous, but I tell her I don't think anything very bad can happen to boys when they're there with father and mother."[77]

Experts also hoped to strengthen the authority of the home and family by involving all family members, particularly children, in homemaking. Some proposed giving children "a voice in arranging the family program of social activities, and even in rearranging the furniture and decorations of the home to suit their own tastes and uses."[78] Pauline Duff, an interior dec-orator who wrote numerous columns for *Parents' Magazine* on the "Whole-Family House," recommended that family members give a Christ-mas gift to the house, so that each would have "a happy sense of participa-tion in homemaking."[79] By giving children a stake in the home's physical appearance, childrearing experts hoped to make the home a magnet for children's leisure.

Florence Fitch believed that children's participation in homemaking was essential to the "well-ordered home." The best homes, she argued, were places "where sons and daughters take as keen interest as their parents in the selection and arrangement of home furnishings, and the greatest pride in seeing the mother becomingly dressed."[80] Fitch's comments indicate yet another way in which experts held mothers to a demanding standard for creating an enticing home environment. Beauty columnist Hazel Rawson Cades even suggested that mothers who honored their duty to be beautiful enhanced their parental authority. "Whatever you may think about the frivolity of exterior decoration," Cades counseled, "you've got to realize that nowadays it counts" if you want "to keep your husband interested or your children believing you're as clever as they'd like to think you are."[81] The notion of family involvement in homemaking also elevated the importance of what historian Margaret Marsh has called "masculine domesticity."[82] In addition to their roles as playmates, fathers were now encouraged to take part in shopping and home decoration. Some even recommended that boys study home economics so that they, too, would know how to "maintain a happy and successful home."[83]

Although the 1930s presented new obstacles to the enjoyment of a happy home life, some play experts saw in the Depression an opportunity to reinvigorate family ties through simpler pleasures and pastimes.[84] "The biggest benefit the new leisure can confer on you," advertising executive Ernest Elmo Calkins told *Parents' Magazine* readers, "is the opportunity to become acquainted with your children." Calkins promoted play with children as a rewarding and rejuvenating "hobby" for adults. "The average child," Calkins wrote, "is far more original, unhackneyed, interesting than the average grown-up . . . [who] has been beaten into the stereotyped pattern by our mechanical standardized civilization."[85] *Parents' Magazine* design consultant Helen Sprackling also championed play with children to restore the Depression-weary spirits of parents: "Matching wits against the younger generation in a good stiff game of checkers or putting one over on them in ping-pong, helps to clear the mind for tomorrow's struggles and aids digestion."[86] During the 1930s, the family rec room or family playroom gave spatial expression to hopes that "the family that plays together stays together."[87] Helen Sprackling proposed a new room "dedicated to the sole purpose of family fun" where "old and young alike may happily meet and become one in spirit." Equipped with a movie projector, dart board, ping-pong table, games tables, and a blackboard to keep score, Sprackling's family playroom contained the excitement of the public movie theater and pool house within the walls of the revitalized home.[88] Activities that had once threatened to spawn an autonomous youth culture now promised to unite adult and child leisure in a private, domestic setting.

In planning such rooms, however, designers also recognized the limits of family togetherness. The "Parents' Magazine Rec Room," designed by university experts in collaboration with Marshall Fields department store, provided space for both solitary and social uses of leisure.[89] Perhaps fearing that home play might become as standardized as commercialized leisure, the Gruenbergs criticized compulsory family fun that failed to consider individual preferences. Instead they envisioned the home as a democratic playground where family members could pursue their "own interests under conditions of affection, approbation, and recognition." In homes that lacked mutual respect, they argued, the radio, the car, and other play equipment that promised to unite families became sources of discord.[90] The well-planned rec room, however, seemed to embody family expert Ernest Burgess's seminal conception of the family as "a unity of interacting personalities," one that successfully accommodated the needs of each family member for fulfillment and satisfaction.[91]

Experts often turned to consumer culture for assistance in balancing the needs for individual happiness with the demands of family togetherness. Toy expert Charlotte Ross Mochrie's Christmas gift tips for children between eight and sixteen recognized the delicate compromise between freedom and control within the revitalized home. Among other gifts, she recommended a telephone with a cord long enough to "stretch from the house to the garage or to a neighbor's house," imagining that it would spur "the organization of a boys' club" that communicated by private wire.[92] Like the playroom and the family rec room, the long-corded telephone promised children their own space while keeping them tied, sometimes literally, to the home.

In the 1920s and 1930s, middle-class parents, educators, and childrearing experts struggled to reclaim the authority of the family and redefine its mission amid the growing popularity of public commercial amusements. Parents tried to combat the allure of these new amusements by becoming understanding companions and creating an enticing home-play environment. Equipped with playrooms, stimulating playthings, and backyard play areas, the revitalized home sought to remake the complacent child consumer into a model consumer-citizen capable of discriminating among better sorts of entertainment.

Such efforts to revitalize the middle-class family were fraught with ironies. Child experts sought to contain popular culture's threat to family unity and middle-class aesthetics by mimicking its strategies of enticement. In so doing, they blurred the distinction between domestic and commercial space even as they tried to assert the authority of the former over the latter.

Some have seen in the new interest in educational toys and developmental-ly appropriate play an "anticonsumerist" quest to shore up the domestic sphere against the encroachments of "the indulgent and promiscuous world of consumerism."[93] But, setting aside child experts' antipathy toward flashy toys and passive recreation, it is difficult to detect much hostility to consumerism in their infatuation with enticement and salesmanship as a means of modernizing parenting—to say nothing of their interest in ex-pensive backyard swing sets. For all their pragmatic accommodations of the market, however, experts naively underestimated the appeal of mass cul-ture, proposing wholesome alternatives that often seemed a pale reflection of the real thing. One wonders how many children schooled in the delights of mass culture were so easily distracted from the glummer realities of household chores with fun and games. Even the revitalized companionate family could not displace the countervailing effects of peer-group social-ization and rebellious self-seeking that drew some children to the public world of commercial amusements.

In some cases, the childrearing regime prescribed by experts may have unwittingly fueled the very problem experts sought to solve. Critic Ruth Frankel complained that childrearing advice compelled too many parents to cram their children's lives full of cultural activities. As a result, Frankel argued, "the modern child, with his days set into a patterned program, goes docilely from one prescribed class to another, takes up art and music and French and dancing . . . until there is hardly a minute left." Eventual-ly, Frankel observed, such overstimulated children became jaded and turned "desperately to the corner movie in an effort to escape ennui."[94] As Frankel saw it, the culturally enriched child and the movie-mad child were often one and the same. More confounding still, as we shall see, many would discover in the 1930s that play was at best a tenuous basis for exer-cising parental authority in the face of aggressive radio advertising appeals to children.

Radio Clubs and the Consolidaton of Children's Consumer Culture During the Great Depression

WHEN THE CREAM OF WHEAT COMPANY launched its H.C.B. Club for children in 1928, it offered mothers a "simple plan" guaranteed to arouse their child's interest in "correct breakfast habits." At no extra charge, the Cream of Wheat Company would send children shiny badges, brightly colored wall charts, and gold stars to document their progress toward good health. For the pièce de résistance, Cream of Wheat would reveal the secret meaning of the club's initials to members who achieved a perfect record of weekly cereal consumption. Promoted in women's magazines with endorsements from leading child authorities, the H.C.B. Club promised mothers a more satisfying and effective method of getting children to eat a nutritional breakfast than scolding, punishment, or tiresome wheedling. Appealing to the child's sense of fun while solving common childrearing problems, the club idea won legions of fans among parents and children alike.

By the early 1930s, however, the parental romance with the club concept had begun to sour. As advertisers took to the airwaves, clubs became the marketing arm of children's radio serials that were broadcast during the late afternoon and early evening hours. Tantalizing children with offers of secret decoding devices, membership badges, and other special premiums in exchange for proofs of purchase, radio clubs like Ovaltine's Little Orphan Annie's Secret Circle and Post Toastie's Inspector Post Junior Detective Corps gained widespread popularity among nine- to twelve-year-olds.[1] Much to advertisers' delight, membership in children's radio clubs soared into the millions, a stratospheric increase over the thousands who had joined the H.C.B. Club before the advent of children's radio advertising. To the dismay of many parents, however, radio clubs encouraged children to ceaselessly lobby for goods valued for their prize-winning box top. Worse still, radio clubs seemed to cement children's loyalty to programs that many parents believed exerted an unwholesome influence on children's morality and psychological well-being.

These shifts in both the perception and formulation of children's clubs illustrate several important dynamics and tensions in the making of children's consumer culture. In courting the child consumer, mass marketers straddled two distinct consumer constituencies—parents and children—ultimately hoping to win over children without sacrificing parental goodwill. Initially, the children's club marketing formula fused child enticement and parental appeal by transforming consumption itself into a game. Offering charts that monitored progress toward good health and stars that rewarded good behavior, advertisers fashioned children's clubs as a modern parenting tool that could help manage childrearing problems, instill good habits, and restore harmonious family relationships. Advertisers sanctified their marketing ploy with the imprimatur of modern science, hailing new theories of psychological development that stressed play as part of learning and development. In doing so, advertisers successfully merged parental needs and children's play into a winning marketing strategy.

With the advent of children's radio programs in the 1930s, however, clubs became more peer-oriented in their appeal and less tied to middle-class parents' notions of taste, wholesome consumption, or even good behavior. Though advertisers did not push anything resembling an oppositional children's culture—they still strove to win parental cooperation, if not goodwill—children's enthusiasm for club memberships and premiums was largely influenced by their identification with radio heroes and "blood-and-thunder" story lines. Advertisers increased parental ire the more closely they linked children's clubs to other forms of children's popular culture and the more aggressively they pushed repeat purchases as a prerequisite for children's participation. Parental irritation and protest, however, did little to dent the success of children's radio clubs as a marketing strategy. In forging a more distinctive children's consumer culture, advertisers gambled that irritated parents would give in to the incessant demands of their children.

 Conventional histories of children's marketing have mostly focused on how advertisers exploit children's gullibility and shape them into obedient consumers. In this formulation children's culture is "produced for and urged upon children" rather than something children themselves give meaning to or have a hand in creating.[2] Admittedly, advertisers exercise a powerful role in shaping children's consumer culture. Their control, however, is not complete, for the competing and complementary agendas of parents, child experts, and children themselves also contribute to the development of children's culture. As recent works in cultural studies and cultural anthropology remind us, consumer goods are not merely "distant impersonal" creations of mass marketers and mass producers. Rather they

acquire their full cultural value when consumers invest them with meanings that reflect their own needs and experiences.[3] Not simply the product of advertisers' machinations, children's consumer culture can be more profitably understood "as the site of contested and contradictory attempts to define the child."[4]

This chapter analyzes how changing conceptions of parental authority and childhood dependency, as well as traditional discourses of childhood innocence, coalesced and collided over the creation of corporate-sponsored children's clubs. The appeal of commercial children's clubs and conflict over them, I argue, rested upon their potential both to stabilize and to erase boundaries of childhood dependency. Middle-class parents embraced children's clubs that helped them to manage and direct their children's yearnings for independence into wholesome channels. Parents became decidedly less enthusiastic for club memberships and premiums as advertisers transformed consumer culture into a zone of empowerment that offered children both real and imaginary ways to cross the boundaries of dependency.

Children's radio clubs became an alternative play universe in which children could contemplate and adopt—and sometimes challenge—adult notions of what it meant to be a child and to become a man, a woman, or a good citizen. Children used the clubs to create a world of their own—a fantasy world of secret club passwords and messages where children became masters of their destiny and adults could not trespass. Although corporate needs and interests structured this play universe—demanding ever greater purchases to participate in its pleasures—it would be a mistake to characterize children simply as the hapless victims of advertisers' efforts to boost sales and build brand loyalty. As well shall see, the experience of joining radio clubs also taught children powerful lessons in consumer disappointment—lessons that sometimes provoked mockery of exaggerated advertising claims and inspired resistance to advertisers' cultural authority.

THE H.C.B. CLUB AD CAMPAIGN: HARMONIZING PARENTAL AND CHILD APPEALS

At J. Walter Thompson Company, the advertising agency that handled the Cream of Wheat account, the genesis for the H.C.B. Club advertising campaign was the realization that boosting cereal sales called for a new kind of "selling inventiveness." Writing in the company *News Bulletin*, advertising executive Harold Wengler set forth the rationale for the campaign. The advertiser's challenge, he argued, was not convincing the public at large of the product's merit. "Mother, the family doctor, teacher, in fact practically everybody, agree that a hot cereal will do Little Gormley lots of good," he wrote. Rather, the advertiser's challenge was convincing Little Gormley himself. "The creative advertiser," Wengler declared, was "the one that decides that Little Gormley is the market" and builds the "whole selling edifice . . . on interpreting his cereal in terms of things that pique his imagination, that thrill him, that move him."[5]

J. Walter Thompson's H.C.B. campaign, somewhat surprisingly, did not appeal directly to the child. Rather the campaign sought to sell mothers on the virtues of motivating and manipulating the child. As Cream of Wheat's H.C.B. Club campaign unfolded in the pages of women's magazines, advertisements addressed mothers as an intelligent audience well versed in the health merits of hot cereal but misguided in the ways of motivating children.[6] Too often, the ads observed, mothers unwittingly fostered resistance by urging children to eat their cereal because it was good for them. "It's just human nature for these irresponsible youngsters to balk a bit whenever they hear 'because it's good for you,'" one advertisement noted.[7] Being "too earnest at the breakfast table"—sometimes even allowing "anxiety to creep into their voices"—was counterproductive.[8] Still more detrimental was the "fatal mistake" of scolding or insisting that children "must" eat their cereal as a "matter of stern duty."[9]

Enlisting the expert guidance of several distinguished childrearing authorities, the Cream of Wheat ads promised to help mothers reinvent their parenting style and succeed where traditional mothering had failed. Nearly every month, the two-year-long campaign showcased a different child expert, each pictured in a cameo inset alongside a plug for his or her most recent book.[10] Notwithstanding the ad campaign's rotating panoply of child experts, the advice always remained the same: mothers could best help their children form lasting habits by appealing to their sense of play. As we have seen in chapter 5, by the mid-1920s, child experts writing in popular middle-class venues like *Parents' Magazine* had come to view play not only as an important avenue of child learning but also as a new basis for exercising parental authority. In keeping with this view, Cream of Wheat advertisements represented grade-school children as "little adventurers," "little scamps," and "little fun-lovers" whose high spirits needed to be channeled and redirected rather than dampened or constrained.[11] A Cream of Wheat advertisement headlined "'Rules 'n' regulations' . . . *now turned into play*" adroitly encapsulated the permissive turn in childrearing advice.[12]

In promoting such advice, Cream of Wheat extended an invitation to mothers to join the growing parenting vanguard, which had left the old customs behind. As Dr. Douglas A. Thom proclaimed, "Today many parents are appealing to children's love of games and of achievement to *lead* them—instead of *pushing* them in the old way."[13] Dr. Thom's emphasis on leading rather than pushing underscored a central psychological principle of the experts' new science of fun: the key to instilling sound habits was getting children to want to do what parents wanted them to do without being aware of the parental voice of authority. "Once children *want* to do a particular thing," Gladys Huntington Bevans advised, "then the thing almost does itself."[14]

Experts' sympathetic attitudes toward children's play stemmed in part from the conviction that "true influence" was achieved in the hidden realms of psychological manipulation. Much like the emerging theories of "democratic social engineering" then gaining influence in professional personnel management, new ideals of parental authority strove to "engineer consensus" through indirect suggestion rather than authoritarian coercion.[15] According to advertisers and child experts, mothers could achieve this kind of covert influence by cloaking their authority in the guise of play and relating to children on their own terms. To underscore the point, Cream of Wheat advertisements upheld professional clowns and Tom Sawyer, who "made whitewashing seem the one pleasantest thing in all the world to do," as model play engineers whom mothers should emulate (fig. 6.1).[16] Implicit in these advertisements was the message that mothers could gain more influence over children if they blurred the lines of parental authority and adopted the carefree, playful mindset of a clown or a cunning child. Such strategies created the illusion of child autonomy even as they preserved traditional boundaries of childhood dependency. Children could believe they were the agents of their own destiny, having consumed the breakfast cereal of their "choice," while parents gained assurance that they were protecting children from bad habits and poor health.[17]

The H.C.B. Club's brand of child appeal, with its gold stars and wall charts to document children's breakfast "achievements" (fig. 6.2), proved irresistible to mothers, if not their children. By November 1928, eleven months into the campaign, Cream of Wheat could boast that 90,000 mothers had enrolled children in the club. Letters from grateful moms, included in the ads as sidebars, vouched for the club's effectiveness in reinvigorating child appetites and eliminating the need for coaxing.[18] Some mothers even reported that the club had transformed children into zealous health missionaries. "When the club materials came," Mrs. J. C. R. wrote, "my little Jane hung the posters on the wall and said to her little brother, 'Now, Jimmy, see that you do your work.'"[19] A bossy older sister to be sure, Jane, her mother could proudly claim, had nevertheless internalized the voice of parental authority.

As some mothers would soon discover, however, the effort to disguise parental authority in the garb of child enticement sometimes inadvertently

6.1 CREAM OF WHEAT ADVERTISEMENT, DELINEATOR (MAY 1929).
Child experts' endorsements of Cream of Wheat's club plan "to turn routine into play" put modern childrearing theories in the service of mass marketing strategies.
Reproduced with permission of KF Holdings. CREAM OF WHEAT® is a registered trademark of KF Holdings.

Sky Blue! Hop Scotch! This little girl never misses. One secret of her skill and strength is a *hot* cereal breakfast every morning — *Cream of Wheat.*

6.2 CREAM OF WHEAT WALL CHART.

This wall chart boasts the perfect record achieved by one child enrolled in Cream of Wheat's H.C.B. Club. Reproduced with permission of KF Holdings. CREAM OF WHEAT® is a registered trademark of KF Holdings. Courtesy Warshaw Collection.

led to the surrender of parental control. The dawn of radio clubs in the 1930s ushered in a new breed of children's clubs, many of which turned the new parenting paradigms on their head, converting the child into the master persuader and the parent into the object of psychological manipulation. With the rise of children's radio clubs, advertisers expanded and systematized their earlier quest to tap children's powers of persuasion and created new opportunities within children's popular culture for demanding child consumers to ply their craft.

CHILDREN'S RADIO CLUBS

When advertisers began courting children over the airwaves in the 1930s, the club formula underwent a number of changes. Clubs still awarded badges and tied membership to consumption of the advertiser's product. But now a club just wasn't a club without the additional offer of a secret decoding device or some other prize premium that admitted children into the inner circle of their favorite radio heroes and heroines. Children who owned such devices could view themselves as invisible partners in the radio adventures of Little Orphan Annie, Jack Armstrong, or Buck Rogers, equipped to foil the plots of greedy gangsters, evil criminals, or intergalactic villains. Radio's other major revision to the club formula was that advertisers now addressed their sales pitch directly to children. Instead of teaching mothers how to sell their kids on cereal, they now taught children how to sell their mothers. Though radio advertisers sometimes instructed children to call their mothers into the room for the commercial announcement, more often than not the advertisement was geared for child ears.

The revamped club formula worked wonders. Memberships soared to heights that amazed even the most hopeful advertisers. In 1934 Wrigley's Lone Wolf Tribe Club boasted more than 700,000 members, all fans of the short-lived radio serial of the same title.[20] Advertisers also successfully adapted the premium-based club formula to print advertising, using serialized comic-strip advertisements that mimicked the adventure-narrative style of children's radio programs. Within the first four months of Post Toasties' 1932 comic-strip ad campaign, more than half a million children had enrolled in the Inspector Post Junior Detective Corps, with an additional half million joining over the course of the following year.[21]

Not surprisingly, the onslaught of child joiners paid handsome dividends. The Junket Company boosted sales of its milk drink mix by 500 percent when it abandoned its health-oriented advertisements in juvenile magazines and began promoting "Prizes for Everybody" who joined the

Jolly Junketeers Club.[22] "In one winter season with *Uncle Don*," *Time* reported, "I.V.C. Vitamin Pearls, a capsuled vitamin, increased its sales 125% with little other advertising."[23] Even more impressive profit margins were enjoyed by an advertiser whose $70, 861 investment in children's radio advertising ballooned annual sales by half a million dollars.[24] Advertising authorities hailed such successes as testimony to their skillful manipulation of child nature. Referring to children as "inveterate collectors" and "natural joiners," some hoped that children's fervent associationalism could bring an end to what one commentator in a 1931 issue of *Sales Management* called the "Year of Thin Nickels."[25]

The widespread popularity of clubs owed much to the allure of acquiring a "free" premium during economic hard times. A 1934 survey of children's memberships in radio clubs found that middle-class and lower middle-class children were more likely to join than more affluent children, perhaps because the latter, already blessed with an abundance of toys, had less use for advertisers' premiums.[26] Indeed, some children, strictly materialists, joined clubs merely for the "free" prize. As advertising professionals understood all too well, emulation of peers also proved a powerful motive for seeking club premiums.[27] In a 1937 interview with advertising authority Evalyn Grumbine, eight-year-old Donnie confided that his interest in acquiring premiums was purely conformist: "Some of my playmates had them and I heard about them over the radio." Ten-year-old Jean, on the other hand, sent for decoder pins, an initial ring, and a birthstone ring because "no one else had them yet and I wanted to be the first one to have them."[28] Program sponsors, eager to stimulate prompt and large responses to premium offers, routinely exploited children's desires to be the envy of the neighborhood. "If you hurry," prodded the announcer for *Howie Wing*, "you can be among the first in your neighborhood to be a member—and wear those regulation Corps Wings of glistening chromium that every member gets!" Some children discovered that being the first to own a decoding device paid handsome social dividends. As Little Orphan Annie fan John V. Cody recalled, "When I received my pin, all the gang would be over at my house to learn what was coming up with our little heroine. I was a real big shot and would make a big show of decoding the 'exceedingly difficult' code." Though Cody's improved social standing ultimately proved a fleeting accomplishment—"Suffice to say, others later received the pin, and my big shot status soon evaporated"—Cody nevertheless enjoyed his moment in the sun.[29]

The glories of peer adulation and the more mundane satisfactions of peer acceptance were only some of the psychic rewards that club membership offered. Clubs also quenched children's yearnings for recognition and autonomy that the adult world seldom acknowledged. In Jean Shepherd's semiautobiographical novel about Depression-era boyhood in a small industrial midwestern town, the protagonist, seven-year-old Ralphie Parker, experienced such payoffs when he received his long-awaited membership card for the Little Orphan Annie Secret Circle. Signed by Little Orphan Annie and countersigned by radio announcer Pierre Andre, the membership card signified a moment of arrival: "BE IT KNOWN TO ALL AND SUNDRY THAT MR. RALPH WESLEY PARKER IS HEREBY APPOINTED A MEMBER OF THE LITTLE ORPHAN ANNIE SECRET CIRCLE AND IS ENTITLED TO ALL THE HONORS AND BENEFITS ACCRUING THERETO." Addressed as "*Mister* Parker," something "they hardly ever even called my Old Man," Ralphie acquired status previously reserved for men of reputation and importance.[30] As Ralphie and countless other children learned, membership conferred privilege and honor, benefits ardently prized by children who often felt powerless in the face of adult authority.

Clubs provided even deeper compensations for childhood dependency. Associating the joys of club membership with the joys of being "in the know," radio clubs supplied children with secret passwords, mysterious hand signals, and cryptic messages—the building blocks of an autonomous children's culture. Children who sent off for the Little Orphan Annie Super Decoder Pin to decipher the radio program's secret messages also received the Secret Club Book which divulged the club's secret password and door knock.[31] Members of Wrigley's Lone Wolf Tribe learned the club's secret sign of greeting as well as Indian picture writing and sign language—communication forms probably valued less for their dubious multicultural authenticity than for their immunity to adult comprehension. Lone Wolf Tribe members also cultivated an autonomous child-world by violating adult norms of monetary exchange. Instead of cash and coins, they used wampum (Wrigley Chewing Gum wrappers) to purchase "genuine Indian arrowheads" and other articles of "Indian craftsmanship" listed in the club's "tribe book."[32]

For many children, radio clubs functioned as a distinct kids' world that needed to be zealously guarded against those who would betray its secrets or dishonor its obligations. Taking their responsibilities as club members quite seriously, children took umbrage at peers who violated codes of club secrecy and proved themselves disloyal consumers. According to a 1939 *Saturday Evening Post* article, much of the *Lone Ranger*'s mail came "from children angrily declaring that a certain member [was] not eating the sponsor's bread or [had] revealed the code (read A for B, B for C, and so on)." In ways that perhaps even advertisers failed to anticipate, some children seemed to have made brand loyalty and protection of club secrecy factors in their peer code of ethics. Indeed, radio's fantasy world of secret codes

and cryptic messages proved so alluring that some parents confronted unforeseen obstacles when they attempted to access their kids' secret world.
Such was the case with the father of one Lone Ranger fan, who was forced
to wire the radio station for the code when his son sent him a letter "so important that he did not dare trust it to the mails uncoded."[33]

Advertisers sustained the allure of being "in the know" by making secret decoding devices and other club premiums essential for full participation in the exploits of children's favorite radio heroes and heroines. Fans of
Jolly Bill and Jane who had consumed enough Cream of Wheat to earn the
club's map of the moon could track the wanderings of Uncle Bill and his
companions as they trekked across the Lunera, from the Sawtooth Moun-
tains to the evil Bolta's Palace. The show's announcer also informed loyal
listeners that they could have a hand in assuring a happy resolution to the
episode's cliff-hanger ending if they were lucky enough to possess the club's
good luck scarab pin. With an army of scarab-rubbing *Jolly Bill and Jane* listeners behind them, Uncle Bill, Jane, and Professor Ver Blotz were sure to
be rescued from the depraved clutches of Johnny Foo and Bolta.[34]

By linking premiums to plot lines, sponsors gave children a greater
stake in club membership, spurring them to acquire the extra proofs of
purchase needed to enjoy a more interactive radio experience. This strategy of enticement further blurred the lines between commercials and programming, which were never very fixed to begin with, since sponsors rather
than networks created the radio programs. Nevertheless, putting the entertainment value of the sponsor's message on par with the show itself helped
to structure how children experienced and gave meaning to radio. As Joan
Waller recalled of her Depression-era childhood, "Missing a commercial
proved almost as much a disappointment as missing a moment of the action itself. I enjoyed sending for the advertised products, especially those,
like the decoder ring, which became part of the story." Joan's husband,
Robert Waller, who grew up on a tenant farm during the Depression and
was "too poor to send off for a decoder ring," never won admission to the
ranks of those "in the know." Instead he made do with his own version of
interactivity: "I frequently copied the clues about the next program in
hopes of breaking the code. I do not recall any successes, but it was fun trying," he recalled.[35]

The interactive nature of children's clubs, in fact, allowed children to
conceive of themselves as powerbrokers in a world of mystery and in-
trigue, where their own ingenuity and know-how could win the day. Children could transform their ordinary lives into high adventure when they
collaborated with the likes of spunky, self-reliant Little Orphan Annie or
teen hero Jack Armstrong in vanquishing evildoers. As members of Post

Toasties' Inspector Post Junior Detective Corps, children could pride themselves on their savvy and daring in mastering the secrets of courageous crime fighters. For just two box tops, the club awarded children a shiny detective badge along with a book of unsolved cases that revealed the club's "secret codes and mysterious signs." Fashioned after the popular comic-strip hero Dick Tracy, Post Toasties' 1932 comic-strip ads, placed in various farm journals, tracked Inspector Post and his junior detective aides, Tom and Nancy, as they thwarted nefarious art thieves, counterfeiters, and revolutionaries bent on overthrowing foreign governments. In the serialized comic-strip ads, Tom and Nancy were not merely detectives in training, but clever assistants who used their newfound knowledge of mysterious signals and secret codes—knowledge available only to club members—to help Inspector Post solve cases.[36]

Children also found pleasures in club membership that bore little relationship to the radio programs themselves and that even advertisers seemed not to anticipate. As Selma Heller recalled of her school days in Los Angeles, owning a decoder ring or a wristband decoding dial provided children with a new surreptitious means of exchanging gossip and other classified communications with school chums. Enjoying a more interactive radio experience was less important than simply being able to pass coded notes in class that, if intercepted, the teacher could not possibly decipher. Children, so inspired, may have done more to sell club memberships to classmates than advertisers' own heavy-handed promotions, since children could not communicate with each other unless their friends also owned a decoding device. Fortunately for teachers, the fad wore off within a matter of weeks, as children discovered that communicating secrets in Pig Latin was far more efficient than laboriously decoding encrypted messages.[37]

Children who enrolled in radio clubs thus belonged to a world where kid know-how not only triumphed over evildoers, but where kids, not schoolteachers and parents, held the upper hand. Clubs offered children a way to become masters of their own destiny at a stage in life when they regularly confronted the limits of their dependence. It was a dreamworld that would have pleased Horace Wade, a precocious twelve-year-old novelist turned ad copy writer who in a 1920 issue of *Printers' Ink Monthly* had advised ad men to "come down off your high horse" and speak to boys' fantasies of "getting the best of it—fighting against great odds." Boys, Wade insisted, were "dreamers" not utilitarians. They cared little "what a thing costs—just so long as it can be used in making [their] dreams come true."[38] In the child's world, consumer passion was ignited by the promise of magical self-transformation. Promised bulging biceps and superlative strength that could defeat the school bully, eight-year-old Andrew insisted that his mother purchase Cocomalt, despite her vain suggestions that ordinary, less expensive cocoa could supply as much pep.[39]

In many respects, children's radio clubs were a part of broader trends then transforming the American toy industry. Indeed, children's clubs helped to organize and extend an emerging playworld of children's fantasy toys. As historian Gary Cross has argued, the rise of fantasy toys during the 1930s paralleled the growth of a national entertainment industry and culture of celebrities, drawing inspiration from children's comic-book heroes and radio idols.[40] During the Depression, licensed character toys based on children's celebrities—Mickey Mouse, Charlie McCarthy, Shirley Temple, and Superman—helped to revitalize toy sales at a time when many toy companies were struggling for survival.[41] Much like the secret decoder rings, detective paraphernalia, and intergalactic adventure gear offered by commercial children's clubs, these licensed character toys, Cross writes, "invited the young into a 'secret garden' of imagination where they could be free from the constraints of the adult world."[42]

Within this imaginary world of play, children discovered new opportunities for self-expression and gender-based play. Toys and premiums based on radio characters gave shape to children's play, supplying kid role models to emulate and story lines to revamp and reenact. As Cross argues, "By possessing a celebrity toy the child owned a bit of the spunk, charm, power, or even good luck of the character."[43] A Depression-era favorite, Little Orphan Annie held particular appeal as a heroic figure who "prevail[ed] over the poverty and insecurity that many children of the Depression knew all too well."[44] And as a spunky girl adventurer, Little Orphan Annie inspired legions of girl fans to become Ovaltine-drinking members of the radio program's secret society, making it the only children's club to enjoy more girls than boys among its ranks.[45]

Other sponsors' concerted but apparently ineffectual efforts to enlist more girls in clubs suggest that girls may have resisted clubs or simply not bothered to tune into programs that did not nurture their fantasies of girl heroism. Kellogg's, for example, bent over backward to make girls feel welcome in *Howie Wing*'s Cadet Air Corps. Urging girls to "get in on the fun," *Howie Wing*'s announcer reminded girls that women flyers and airline stewardesses had proved women's rightful place in aviation. Commercial announcements even featured guest spots by a licensed girl pilot, a United Airlines stewardess, and the champion woman racing pilot, Louise Thadden—each testifying that Kellogg's Corn Flakes had given them the energy and mental alertness essential to their aviation success.[46] Yet the repeated prodding suggests that such feminist appeals may have been insufficient to overcome story lines that featured the only female character on the show in the role of Howie Wing's supportive sidekick, not as a gutsy adventurer in her own right. A 1936 study of children's radio programs concluded as much, advising advertisers that "it might be profitable to add programs directed especially at the girl audience."[47] Advertisers' token efforts to appeal to girls' own fantasies suggest that advertising authorities were at best only halfheartedly beginning to revise traditional assumptions that girls would automatically embrace male heroes as their own.

Radio narratives and club premiums provided boys a more fertile field for imaginative play and self-expression. Though girls were always welcome to "join in on the fun," radio shows offered up teen heroes like the All-American high school student Jack Armstrong, the aviator Howie Wing, and the preadolescent rancher Bobby Benson as models of boy courage and boy heroism. Children's clubs also validated boys' yearnings for real-world achievement and daring adventure, erasing demoralizing boundaries of dependency. Not just kids' stuff, *Howie Wing*'s Cadet Aviation Corps was a *"real aviation club"* that included leading airmen like Jimmie Mattern, the famous transoceanic flyer, and Jack Knight, senior pilot of United Airlines, as august members. Cadet Aviation Corps premiums promised admission into an authentic world of airmen, offering "regulation Corps Wings of glistening chromium—the kind *real* flyers wear!"[48] The popular *Jimmie Allen* radio serial, recounting the "hair-raising" international airplane adventures of an adolescent telegraph messenger, spawned Jimmie Allen Clubs that delivered even more spectacular rewards of authentication to its two million members. Open to boys who made seven visits to Skelly or Richfield gasoline stations, the clubs awarded a certificate and monogrammed pilot's wristlet to boys who passed an exam covering material in a flying instruction manual. Thousands of club members also enjoyed the opportunity to display their own model airplanes, built with parts that participating gasoline stations sold at cost, in the model plane competition at local "Jimmie Allen" air meets.[49]

Children's clubs allowed boys to vacillate between the worlds of fantasy play and adult achievement, testing boundaries of dependency as they explored new roles and emulated new heroes. As a Buck Rogers Solar Scout, boys could create their own twenty-fifth-century space adventures using space helmets, repeller ray rings, lite-blaster flashlights, and other club premiums as play props.[50] They could join the ranks of Melvis Purvis's Junior G-Man Corps (fig. 6.3), learning from "America's No. 1 G-Man" the secret methods that resulted in the capture of such notorious criminals as Dillinger, "Pretty Boy" Floyd, and "Baby Face" Nelson. With an official Junior G-Man fingerprint set, they were sure to uncover sinister criminal activities closer to home.[51] Post Toasties' comic-strip advertisements featuring the daring

6.3 Post Toasties advertisement, Country Gentleman (September 1936).

Post Toasties promoted membership in its Junior G-Man Corps by using cartoon-style ads that mimicked popular children's radio serials. Reproduced with permission of KF Holdings. POST TOASTIES® is a registered trademark of KF Holdings.

exploits of Melvin Purvis actively encouraged such play by printing queries from junior Secret Operators who wanted to know how to trail suspects and distinguish a real clue from a fake one. Post Toasties gave these queries the appearance of authenticity by including an actual photograph of six scheming boys from Long Island who had formed a Squad of Secret Operators.[52]

Refusing to make light of child ambitions, commercial children's clubs validated children's aspirations to have a hand in righting wrongs and setting the world on a steadier, more just course—aspirations that the turbulent world of the Great Depression intensified. For some children, no doubt, the satisfactions of imagining oneself an ace G-Man or an intergalactic superhero provided compensations for the sense of security, order, and justice that the Depression had disrupted. These courageous defenders of right against wrong proved especially appealing at a time when the authority of jobless fathers was diminishing and children might have yearned for heroic father substitutes.[53] They also provided a stark contrast to other cultural representations of battered manhood that filled the airwaves during the 1930s. Anxieties over the threatened collapse of traditional male authority figured prominently in popular radio comedies, such as the *Jack Benny Show, Amos 'n' Andy,* the *Burns and Allen Show*, and Eddie Cantor's *Chase and Sanborn Hour*, where male leads were often the butts of jokes.[54] Within this cultural context of deflated masculinity, the male heroes of children's popular culture offered an enticing alternative vision of masculine heroism.

Children's radio clubs thus spoke to a range of child ambitions and uncertainties in a changing world. Children could embrace clubs as vehicles of their magical self-transformation, using them to realize in fantasy dreams of becoming an aviator or a self-reliant kid adventurer, of battling schoolyard enemies with the power and finesse of a twenty-fifth-century space adventurer, or of outsmarting them with the savvy of a crack detective. Even if Depression-era children could not vanquish economic uncertainty in real life, children's radio clubs empowered them to become masters of their own destiny in the imaginary realm of play. Commercial clubs provided children an *alternative* play universe—one in which they figured as powerful actors rather than impotent dependents. It was not, however, an *oppositional* play universe that fundamentally challenged respect for adult authority, traditional gender roles, and adult notions of success. Granted, children could use clubs to create a secret kids' world that adults could neither understand nor control. But these clubs also upheld adults like G-Man Melvin Purvis, the kindly Uncle Don, and renowned airmen and airwomen as role models worthy of emulation. Indeed, G-Men and ace flyers also figured prominently in the pantheon of adult celebrity idols.[55]

More profoundly still, commercial children's clubs enmeshed children in a world of goods that bonded their allegiance to consumerism and the material plenty that capitalism produced. If children's clubs provided a temporary escape from some of capitalism's hardships, they also provided sanctuary for some of its more egregious consumerist excesses.

RADIO CLUBS UNDER FIRE

Though enormously popular with children, radio clubs came under fire from child experts, mother's groups, and PTAs. Baffled by their appeal but unable to resist children's demands, many parents became reluctant, if not resentful, accomplices in advertisers' schemes to boost sales of cereal and milk drinks. Behind this parental complicity, however, lay a deep reservoir of misgivings about radio's effects on children and advertising's manipulation of young, impressionable minds. Writing in women's magazines and the popular press, a wide range of child experts and cultural commentators gave voice to these misgivings, by turns soothing and aggravating parental anxieties.

Much of the debate over children's radio clubs was framed by traditional discourses of childhood innocence. As has long been the case, adults often interpret the promises and perils of new mass media technologies in light of their impact on society's most vulnerable members. Since the late eighteenth and early nineteenth centuries, Western culture has viewed children as pliable innocents who could be molded for the better or the worse by the adults and the cultural environment that surrounded them. By the turn of the twentieth century, the introduction of new forms of mass entertainment like movies, amusement parks, and penny arcades magnified concerns about the wider culture's influences on children and the family's diminishing capacity to shield children from it. What made radio's arrival particularly troubling to some was that the home itself had now become host to some of the wider culture's most pernicious elements.[56]

Many greeted the advent of children's radio broadcasts with a strenuous round of protests. The new medium, they argued, was weakening children's morals, giving children nightmares, and distracting them from their studies. Calling radio a "curse upon your children's minds," Worthington Gibson bemoaned the endless cacophony of wailing police sirens, rattling machine guns, exploding hand grenades, and shrieking gun victims that had invaded children's radio hours. Now a daily ritual, radio, Gibson lamented, was "cultivating our children's morals—with blood and thunder effects."[57] Parents and child experts were as troubled by juvenile radio's crime-laden plot lines as they were by the mind-numbing fixation with which children listened. Children's serials, the National Education Association journal complained, "have acquired a powerful and pernicious hold on the interests of the children. Little boys and girls sit with their ears glued against the radio, their eyes bulging with excitement or filled with tears, their faces flushed, their hearts thumping."[58] As if it were not bad enough that radio was treating children to "four hours of lessons on the art of crime and higher skulduggery," parents griped, it was also teaching them bad grammar and bad language.[59] Most disheartening of all, surveys of children's radio preferences discovered that children's favorites were the very programs parents liked least. Reporting the results of one such survey, *The Nation* quipped, "If any mother has any faith remaining in the better nature of children it should be completely wiped out."[60] Radio, it appeared, was tainting not only childhood but the myth of its innocence.

Children's advertising only amplified parental resentment of children's radio. Even some commentators in the advertising trade press chided overzealous radio advertisers for their short-sightedness in antagonizing parents, noting that the primary aim of juvenile advertising was to gain parents' patronage and buying power.[61] As critics saw matters, advertisers abused their position by preying upon children's gullibility and "suggestible" minds. According to the authors of a study on the psychology of radio, children were simply "unable to see through the implausible claims of advertisers . . . The child is easily 'sold' to a product, and . . . believes in it with all his heart, just as he believes in any fairy tale."[62] Making matters worse, radio pronouncements seemed all the more authoritative because children believed the "spoken word . . . more devoutly" than the written word.[63]

As criticism of children's radio advertising mounted, the Child Study Association of America added the weight of its moral authority to the debate. In November 1934, the child welfare organization formally condemned juvenile radio programs for misleading their immature listeners with the lure of "absolutely free" prizes in exchange for box tops, wrappers, or other evidence of purchase.[64] The association's protest—later joined by the letter writing campaigns of PTAs, mothers' groups, and better grammar leagues—came at a time when consumer agitation against all kinds of advertising, but especially broadcast advertising, was growing more intense.[65] Historian Susan Smulyan has noted that public disappointment with radio advertising deepened during the early 1930s, as it became apparent that "the radio industry had broken its promise" to advertise indirectly "and instead had moved to more direct 'spots' and more advertising-supported sponsored shows."[66] In the 1920s early radio promoters had envisioned broadcast advertising as "unobtrusive publicity," involving nothing more than the simple airing of the sponsor's name.[67] Some promoters even spoke glowingly of "how radio magically allowed the advertiser to become a guest in a consumer's home," taking care not to offend with "the slightest attempt at direct advertising."[68] Thanks to financial constraints and the complexity of producing radio shows, however, broadcasters began ceding greater control to advertising agencies, which increasingly assumed responsibility for programming. In fact, according to Smulyan, "By the early 1930s 'virtually all sponsored network programs were developed and produced by advertising agencies.'"[69] To many minds, advertisers now more closely resembled unwelcome pests than well-mannered guests in the American home.

The seamless boundary between advertising and the shows themselves was evident in radio comedy for adults as well as for children, but the disjuncture between the promise of "unobtrusive publicity" and the reality of full-blown commercialism seemed especially egregious in children's radio.[70] Even tamer children's fare offended some sensibilities with its incessant sales talk. Though free of crime narratives, *Uncle Don*, grumbled one disgruntled parent, "is driving parents almost to distraction with the monotony of [club] procedure and tiresome plugs. I timed him one evening giving eleven minutes to the alleged virtues of Hormel soup, one of his four sponsors."[71] Considering a total air time of just thirty minutes, *Uncle Don*'s shameless generosity with its commercial allotment did not merely blur the lines between commercials and programming but nearly obliterated them. The absence of such distinctions was apparent to another outraged parent, Mrs. William H. Corwith, who complained in a letter to the *Ladies' Home Journal* that children's radio idols too often functioned as mouthpieces for the advertiser. It was bad enough that the programs themselves were poor quality, but worse still, she wrote, that "characters in their parts insist that children must eat the product advertised or they will never be big and strong."[72]

As Corwith's comments suggest, critics of children's radio perceived advertisers not simply as mass manipulators but as bullies who browbeat children into buying their products. Noting that his son suffered pangs of guilt after listening to *Little Orphan Annie*, Arthur Mann complained that advertisers intimidated child listeners by "hinting that they have no right to tune in on a program unless they purchase the product of the sponsor."[73] Mothers also criticized advertisers for making children fear that their favorite program would go off the air if they failed to buy the sponsor's product.[74]

What most irritated parents and child experts about children's radio advertising, however, was its attempt to revise the balance of power between the generations. They particularly resented radio advertising for teaching children "how to argue with their parents." Take, for instance, the pitch radio idol Jack Armstrong made for Wheaties in an attempt to break down long-standing parental preferences for hot cereal: "If your father and mother tell you that you must eat warm breakfast food to keep your bodies warm, just tell them that they don't shovel hot coals on the fire to keep the house warm." Radio critic Thomas Henry was willing to concede the point, "but most parents," he added, "prefer the dietary advice of their family physicians to that of the saintly Jack Armstrong."[75]

For some children, of course, no amount of pleading could soften parental resistance. Joseph Heller could never persuade his mother to purchase Wheaties, because the cereal, as he recalled being told, lacked rabbinical approval.[76] Mothers who lacked such definitive fallback positions faced greater challenges as the gatekeepers charged with controlling commercial culture's influence over children's desires for kitschy premiums and pricey cereals. The Child Study Association of America, in fact, calculated that an irresolute mother who purchased all of the prize-winning box tops would increase the family's grocery bill by at least two dollars a week.[77] A study of mothers' reactions to radio club advertising found that those who disapproved, about 40 percent of those surveyed, were especially resentful of advertising's usurpation of their buying authority and consumer judgment. Regarding themselves the best arbiter of product merit, these mothers believed that they, not children, should determine family purchases.[78]

Angry parents, not surprisingly, were sometimes not as responsive as advertisers hoped. Inspector Post's Junior Detective Corps, for example, was forced midstream to revise its qualifications for advancement within the club from Lieutenant to Sergeant. Issuing a "SPECIAL NOTICE TO ALL P. J. D. C. OPERATIVES," Post Toasties announced in a 1932 advertisement that it was now requiring only four box tops instead of ten to reach the exalted rank of Sergeant. Perhaps calculating that children lost interest when gratification was too-long deferred, they concluded that the promise of quicker promotion supplied children with a new incentive and a new justification for nagging their mother to purchase more cereal. "Now that it is easier to become a Sergeant or a Lieutenant, ask your mother to buy Post Toasties regularly," the advertisement counseled. But should their mothers fail them, a sidebar featuring "Post's Junior Detective News" suggested some other methods children might use to acquire box tops. Who could miss the heavy-handed hint when the ad reported on a Washington State squad that was charging Post Toasties' box tops for admission to their theatrical shows?[79]

Post Toasties' revision of its promotion requirements, coming at the depths of the Depression in 1932, tells us something about how Depression-era economics forced advertisers to temper their bloated expectations of children's prowess as selling agents. But the need to revamp club regulations also signaled a deeper flaw in the club marketing formula. As a 1936 study revealed, while radio club advertising was enormously successful in securing one-time purchases, it was much less so "in holding customers" after the first purchase. This may have suggested, as the study's author contended, that children were urging mothers to buy the product for the premium rather than the product itself.[80] Finding it a "nuisance" to purchase products their children wanted only for the prize, many mothers, as another survey discovered, fortified their resolve and refused to buy more.[81] But the decline of repeat purchases also may have betrayed a more serious problem for advertisers' cherished marketing formula: the slackening of child interest in the radio clubs themselves. For as we shall see, children's radio clubs were not only teaching children lessons in the virtues of competitive consumption. They were also teaching them lessons in consumer disappointment.

CONSUMER DISAPPOINTMENT AND THE ULTIMATE KIDS' WORLD

As studies of radio advertising's effectiveness suggested, advertisers' success in attracting large numbers of children to clubs and contests was not always matched by their success in sustaining consumerism's enchantment. By the late 1930s, after two decades of experimentation, advertisers began to take stock of their failures and accomplishments in the juvenile field. Most sobering perhaps was a new awareness of children's consumer disappointment and of the limits of their consumer pliancy. In a stern warning to her colleagues, advertising authority Evalyn Grumbine cautioned advertisers to be mindful of children's consumer savvy. Children, particularly those over eight, she argued, were already accustomed to shopping and resented premiums that neither lived up to advertisers' glowing promises nor measured up to their own standards. By Grumbine's lights, children were neither the gullible creatures of advertisers' fantasies nor the obedient innocents of parents' dreams. "Children today are not easily fooled," Grumbine noted. "They go to the store for their mother and also shop for themselves and as a result have their own ideas of values and what is worth . . . their own or their parents' money."[82]

Children encountered numerous disappointments in their quest to realize consumerism's magical promises of happiness and fulfillment. Working-class children may well have resented being thrown into a world where consumption became a competitive endeavor. To sustain children's interest, many radio clubs encouraged children to work for progressive ranks, titles, or degrees. Although any child who joined the Pops Pirate Club could become a Third Mate just for sending a letter, actual purchases of Pops Cereal were required to climb through the ranks. For ten proofs of purchase, children could rise to Second Mate and acquire a rubber dagger; twenty more got them a red bandanna pirate headpiece and a First Mate button. The rank of Captain and a gold button were bestowed on those who amassed fifty additional proofs of purchase.[83] Such goads to competitive consumption taught children a number of lessons about living in an American capitalist culture. By linking status to a child's consumer prowess, advertisers drove home what must have been a bitter lesson to many children of the Depression: purchasing power buys rank. Children who lacked the family resources to purchase any, let alone multiple, box tops or package wrappers faced exclusion or had to content themselves with simply being admitted to the club. But, as advertisers implied, social and economic striving demanded discontentment with an undistinguished place among the rank and file.[84]

Some advertisers tried to remove the sting of consumer inadequacy by wrapping competitive consumption in the guise of altruism. American Molasses Company's 1931 advertising campaign on *Uncle Don*, for example, promised to remedy the unemployment situation if children worked together for a collective goal. Uncle Don told his audience of a half-million children that they could "Help Someone's Daddy Get a Job" by eating as much molasses as they could and getting their parents and friends to use it. For every 5,000 labels children sent in, the American Molasses Company promised to add one man to its employment rolls.[85] Through their exertions on behalf of unemployed breadwinners, children could help transform consumption from an act of self-indulgence into an instrument for social change.

The example of *Uncle Don*'s "benevolent" campaign aside, advertisers more typically encouraged children to associate greater consumption with status and achievement. Indeed, sponsors often used closing commercials to stimulate a frenzy of competitive consumption, egging children on with promises of better prizes and more social prestige. "By this time," goaded the *Buck Rogers* announcer, "every A-1 Solar Scout should own at least two pieces of the swell 25th-Century equipment shown in the secret handbook. And the more the better."[86] At the close of subsequent *Buck Rogers* episodes, the announcer pushed even harder, reminding members of the Buck Rogers Solar Scouts to keep working toward their "promotion to Space Ship Commander," as they would be entitled to "swell trick badges" plus "a lot of special equipment that other Solar Scouts aren't allowed to use."[87]

Such premiums, however, rarely lived up to their promise. The ultimate betrayal of children's consumer innocence was the realization that they had been conned. Like so many other Depression-era children, such was the misfortune of Ralphie Parker, the seven-year-old protagonist of Jean Shepherd's semiautobiographical remembrances of Depression-era childhood. Ralphie believed he had stumbled on a wonderful find, when walking home through his favorite alley one day, he discovered an empty Ovaltine can with its aluminum inner seal still intact. A treasure among trash, the aluminum seal supplied the proof of purchase Ralphie needed to obtain a Little Orphan Annie Secret Decoder Pin. No longer would he have to sit idly by at the show's conclusion when the radio announcer called out a long series of numbers that revealed yet another secret message from Little Orphan Annie. No longer would he be left in the dark while, as Ralphie put it, other "kids were getting the real truth from Orphan Annie." Anticipating the joy of being in the know, Ralphie anxiously awaited the arrival of his prize in the mail. Three weeks later, after what seemed an interminable wait, the gold plastic decoder pin and card signifying his membership in the Little Orphan Annie Secret Circle arrived. Gripped by excitement, Ralphie frantically decoded Little Orphan Annie's message, letter by letter, word by word. Enthusiasm quickly turned to disappointment, however, when Ralphie realized that the message he had just deciphered was nothing but a "crummy commercial!": B-E S-U-R-E T-O D-R-I-N-K O-V-A-L-T-I-N-E.[88]

As Ralphie Parker's bitter realization testified, advertisers' glowing promises were not always fulfilled. Indeed, such lessons in consumer disappointment became an increasingly familiar experience for Depression-era children, if not a childhood rite of passage. Some adults, recalling their Depression-era childhoods, still remember the unbearably lengthy delays they suffered while awaiting the arrival of their special premium. "After one had been able to persuade one's parents to part with a very scarce quarter and had devoured enough cereal to get the required number of box tops," Roger Rollin recalled, "the wait—what seemed like months, but which more than likely was only weeks—was agonizing."[89] Jean Shepherd's character Ralphie Parker vividly captured the trauma children endured when he compared waiting three weeks for his prize to "being asked to build the Pyramids singlehanded, using the #3 Erector set, the one without the motor."[90] Such sentiments, though not as colorfully expressed, were widely shared. In interviews that Evalyn Grumbine conducted in 1937, children candidly declared their dismay. Eleven-year-old Eugene confessed that he "got all up in the air" about his three-week wait for the Orphan Annie mug and the Wheaties' Shirley Temple cream pitcher.[91] Five-year-old Patsy recalled going downstairs every day to meet the mailman only to learn that her ring had not yet arrived. She complained bitterly to her mother "that the people were naughty to keep me waiting so long."[92] Similar thoughts occurred to eight-year-old Donnie, whose four-week wait for an initial ring led him to conclude scornfully that "they were lazy at that office."[93]

The chintziness of some premiums was also a major source of disillusionment. Ten-year-old Jean complained that she could not read the numbers on her decoder pin and that the premiums which cost an additional outlay of ten cents "weren't worth the money."[94] When Vivienne Jacobson's Dick Tracy crime-buster ring arrived, she quickly realized that the mirror attachment—the device that allowed the ring wearer to see behind without turning around—barely functioned. Her hopes of becoming a crime-solving heroine in Chester, South Carolina, were quickly dashed.[95] Although Eugene was satisfied with his Orphan Annie mug, he admitted being "disappointed with the identification tag—they said it showed the number on the inside—but when I got it I found that the number was simply on the back. Their description didn't fit with my idea of what it was."[96] Some children were spared such dissatisfaction because they were never able to save enough box tops to win a prize. As one child acknowledged, "I used to save Wheaties box tops but" got tired of saving and "just forgot about them."[97]

Perhaps it was the cumulative toll of such hard lessons in consumer disappointment that paved the way for children's enthusiastic reception of the *Whatsit*, a miniature newspaper with a readership that reached close to four million children. The *Whatsit* began in 1935 as a tie-in with *The Land of the Whatsit*, a radio program that revolved around the adventures of Billy and Betty White, two fictitious kid reporters who publish an amateur newspaper on their press in the family barn. Children could read the fruits of Billy and Betty's labors in a four-page insert that appeared in the monthly *True Story* magazine, a confessional-style tabloid that attracted a working-class audience. The four-page *Whasit* was also distributed in select cities by Sheffield Farms Milk Company, the radio show's sponsor, and by Safeway grocery stores.[98]

Promoted as a newspaper "By children for children," the *Whatsit* solicited contributions from children and filled its pages with their prize poems, jokes, cartoons, and drawings. The rest of the tabloid was devoted to columns by Billy and Betty White and announcements of contests. Numbering about twenty per issue, *Whatsit* contests rewarded children for their cleverness rather than their brand consciousness. *Whatsit* readers could win dollar prizes for solving brain-teasers, drawing cartoons, submitting funny jokes, or writing the neatest and most complete translations of Pig Latin, Double Dutch, Cambodian Cipher, or some other kid language. The shot at a dollar prize and the chance to share in the creation of their own newspaper proved irresistible. During the peak period after each edition, children submitted an average of 5,000 letters a day.[99]

The *Whatsit* owed much of its popularity to its contest prizes. Initially, more than half of its prizes were merchandise like roller skates, footballs, sweaters, bicycles, books, and pencil sets. But when *Whatsit* editor and publisher Charles Morris discovered that the best returns came from the offer of "crisp new $1 bills," the newspaper dramatically scaled back its offer of merchandise. Behind children's marked preference for dollar-bill prizes was a mounting legacy of consumer suspicion and disappointment. "Obviously," Morris remarked, "children discount the value of merchandise prizes; they are afraid they will be shoddy. Perhaps they have been disappointed, on former occasions, with cheap premiums and low-grade merchandise prizes, and they prefer not to take chances" (fig. 6.4).[100]

Children's preference for the dollar-bill prize also reflected their yearnings for autonomy. They could spend a dollar as they pleased—a small fortune to a poor or working-class child growing up during the Depression—but would be compelled to save or hand over a grander sum of five dollars or one hundred dollars. The *Whatsit*'s own research affirmed the popularity of the dollar bill over any other prize. In a contest that asked children to draw pictures of their favorite prize, promising "What you draw is what you get," not a single child drew a five-dollar or a ten-dollar bill. Children who did not want one-dollar bills drew pictures of bicycles, typewriters, roller skates, and books. However much children liked prizes, what they really wanted, it seemed, was the purchasing power to make their own choices in the marketplace. As one adman put it, children's prize preferences showed "a shrewd and practical turn of mind."[101]

The appeal of the *Whatsit*, however, was as much cultural as it was material. A Depression-era precursor to *Mad* magazine, the *Whatsit* routinely mocked adult pretensions and stuffiness. Subtle notes of rebellion sprang from its pages, as the unaffected, common-sense rationality of kid knowledge was contrasted with the pomposity and decorous preachiness of adult rules and regulations. Observing that proverbs, being "made up by fuddled-duddedly old professors," often made no sense, the *Whatsit* sponsored a contest in hopes of generating "some fresh, new vibrant proverbs made *by* children *for* children." If, as adults say, "*It's never too late to mend*," the editors wondered, why mend now? The proverb "*Children should be seen and not heard*," was "so foolish" that the editors agreed not to "insult the intelligence of our readers with an explanation." As a modernized al-

True Story Magazine's National

WHATSIT

BILLY WHITE
Boys' Editor

| JULY | *We Print All The News We Like* | RSVP-FINAL |

BETTY WHITE
Girls' Editor

LEARN HOW TO EAT AND ENJOY IT

BRAND NEW DIET IDEA EVEN MAKES IT FUN TO EAT SPINACH

By BILLY WHITE

Five $1 Prizes

Eating used to be a very simple thing. You just sat down and put into your mouth whatever you found in front of you. That's the way it used to be. But now experts have come along and changed everything. Experts, as you know, are people who make things complicated. The Whatsit is against experts. We're in favor of making things simple.

Since experts have been advising us on our diet, eating is a problem in arithmetic.

We didn't realize how bad the situation was until we met our Congressman, the Hon. J. Tewksbury Watson, who had just come back from Washington after having tried to dispose of the surplus problem in Congress.

Congressman Watson is a big man who usually can dispose of any surplus single handed. However when we saw him he looked almost as thin as a rail.

He told us the reason was that he had consulted an expert on the subject of food, but then he'd forgotten his multiplication tables and couldn't figure out his calories and proteins and carbohydrates and so forth. So he just had to stop eating.

Practically every other Congressman is in the same fix, his Honor, Mr. Watson, informs us. An epidemic of food experts is threatening to wreck the nation by ruining the dispositions of our lawmakers.

So we've decided to do something about it. All that's needed is a simple system of eating which doesn't require arithmetic or physics to figure out. A system that will enable Congressman Watson to eat again. A system that will enable every boy and girl to march bravely up to any soda fountain and order a triple combination double dip sundae with cream instead of a triple bromide.

We've got it, too! Our system is still in the experimental stage but it sounds awfully good. We call it: *The Whatsit Color Diet.*

It's really the simplest thing on earth. It's the simplest diet

invented since Christopher Columbus started the hard boiled egg fad.

All you do to follow *The Whatsit Color Diet* is to choose your foods according to their color. Eat as many different colors as possible.

Here's a sample Whatsit Diet meal: tomato juice (red); lettuce (green); steak (brown); corn (yellow); prunes (black); and milk (white).

See how simple it is? And how delicious? All you have to do is be sure you have as many colors as possible, every meal. Never mind the taste, the color is what counts!

YOU try figuring out a meal that combines as many colors as possible. Then send it in to us. We'll make you a charter member of The Whatsit Dietitian Association. But more important, we're also giving *Five $1 Prizes* for the five most colorful menus we receive.

IT PAYS TO TUNE IN ON THIS PROGRAM

Five $1 Prizes

Below is a list of the radio stations on which Billy and Betty appear at 5:30 in the afternoon, every day from Monday to Friday. On the left are the call letters of the stations; on the right are the cities where the stations are located. Can you match 'em up correctly? Five $1 prizes for the neatest correct lists.

WEAF	Boston
KYW	Buffalo
WTIC	Hartford
WNAC	New York
WBEN	Pittsburgh
WCAE	Philadelphia

JUST SCIENTIFIKAL NOT NONSENSIKAL

By ASPARAGUS SMITH

Diss yere Cullah Diet dat my respeckted Chief, Billy White, am tryin' am all wet.

He says to eat as many diffrunt cullahs as possible for every meal. F'rinstance Ah figahs accordin' to his system mah ideal lunch would be beets (red), horse radish (white), huckleberries (blue) and mustard (yellow). Ah asks you, does that make sens', or does it ain't. De answer am "No."

His objick am to simplificate dis eatin' business but all he is doin' am complificatin' it.

Dere ain' no way he can get 'roun' de fac' dat dere am certain substances we's got to have in our diet. F'rinstance you needs starch in yo' diet. Don't ask me how Ah knows, cause' as scientifikal editor ob dis publication, Ah knows!

Now how is you gwan to find out ifen yo' lunch's got starch in it by de Cullah Diet. You ain't!

But me and you, we tests it. You puts a few drops ob iodine in yo' glass ob watah. Den you takes a little ob de food what you suspects hez starch in it an' mashes it up in a nudder glass wid some watah in it. Den you pours de two together. Pwesto, it all turns de pwetties' blue you eber see, pwovin de pwesence ob starch. If de solution don't turn blue den you know you ain' got no starch.

Try dis on bread or 'taters an' see de results ob science.

JUST TEST YOUR WIT ON THIS POETIC BIT

Five $1 Prizes

The five neatest and completest answers to the questions at the bottom of this poem each win one dollar. It's not a poetry examination, so don't get scared. Besides all the questions are answered in the poem.

Montezuma met a Puma
Going to the fair.
Said Montezuma to the Puma,
"Your coat I'd like to wear."
Thereupon replied the Puma,
"Your impudence, I swear,
Despite the rump of your huma,
Is more than I can bear."
Montezuma and the Puma
Walked on thru the rye

Montezuma made the Puma
Into apple pie
Invitation to the nation—
Every one delighted.
Rose a ruma that the Puma
Was a bit too lean,
And Montezuma sole consuma—
The nation thought him mean!
Montezuma heard the ruma
Shouting "Pie-dish, it is *my* dish!
Kings can do no wrong!"
Exclamation of the nation.
Every one excited;
Indignation, perturbation—
They'd been grossly slighted!

Consternation! Degradation!
Feeling running high—
So Montezuma joined the Puma
In the apple pie!

Author's Note:

I'm no fussa, I'm no fuma,
And I hate to pull a bluma,
So I hope that you will dooma
Answer to this test, and booma
What trend for nonsense huma.
If you send it promptly tooma,
You've a chance to win Mazuma.

EXAMINATION

1. What did Montezuma meet?
2. What did he demand of his new friend? Was the demand granted?
3. Why was the throng displeased with Motezuma?
4. Do you approve combining "do me a" into one word "Dooma".

WEATHER

Here is the latest Weather Reports as worked out by Asparagus Smith at our private observatory atop the Whatsit World's Fair Building.

DOGGY WEATHER

P'ups it will, p'ups it won't

TRUE STORY MAGAZINE'S NATIONAL WHATSIT MEANS DOLLARS AND FUN FOR EVERYONE

6.4 FRONT PAGE OF WHATSIT TABLOID (JULY 1939).

The *Whatsit*, promoted as a newspaper by and for children, won over skeptical child consumers by offering dollar-bill contest prizes instead of premiums of dubious value.

ternative, the editors suggested *"Don't throw your mouth into gear before your brain is turning over."*[102] Another contest, rebuffing the "learned heads" who "spend their lives looking for complicated stuff to study and write about," offered five one-dollar prizes for the best hundred-word letters answering some simple but important problems: "Who killed Cock Robin? How slow is molasses? How crazy is a loon? How hard are nails? What kind of life did Reilly live? How snug is a bug in a rug? How high is up? How quick is a flash?"[103]

The *Whatsit*'s brand of humor exhibited a kinship with much of the absurdities that typified Depression-decade humor. According to historian Lawrence Levine, a number of factors made this era "one of the most creative periods of humor in our history. The distrust of institutions, the sense that the world no longer worked as it was supposed to, that the old verities and certainties no longer held sway, was expressed in one of the decade's most ubiquitous forms of humor: the humor of irrationality." From the Marx Brothers and Abbott and Costello to Ogden Nash and Mae West, the "thirties assault on American truisms," Levine has written, "took place on all levels of humor." In no small measure, then, the *Whatsit*'s propensity to toy with old maxims—much as Ogden Nash had when he proclaimed "A penny saved is—impossible"—reflected the cultural sensibilities of the decade.[104]

What made the *Whatsit*'s own humor of the absurd so appealing to children was the way it managed to mock adult pretensions while simultaneously poking fun at children's foibles. Though the tabloid curried favor by adopting the kid point of view, the *Whatsit* was not above launching its own crusades to eliminate bad habits. Instead of preaching goodness, however, the *Whatsit* invited children to examine their failings and establish their own parameters of appropriate behavior. Avoiding any hint of condescension, the *Whatsit* addressed children not as unsocialized charges in need of refinement but as well-intentioned strivers who, if entrusted with the opportunity, could police themselves. In an editorial that at once ridiculed and sanctioned the gospel of Dale Carnegie and other such success missionaries, Billy White claimed that the best way to "win friends and be president" was to avoid any display of "annoying habits" like fingernail biting, knuckle cracking, gum clicking, talking in movies, and reading over people's shoulders. The *Whatsit* offered five one-dollar prizes to children who composed the best list of "*other* annoying habits that are keeping you or some of your friends from the popularity necessary to be Chief Executive."[105]

In another crusade Billy and Betty White sounded the alarm as "Dopey Fever" spread laziness among thousands of boys and girls who had adopted Walt Disney's seventh dwarf as their mentor. Admitting that Dopey fever had swept their staff, too, the *Whatsit* editors pondered the best cures for laziness: "Will spanking help? If so, what kind? Or cold showers? Or castor oil? Or chocolate sodas?" This quandary prompted yet another contest in which the *Whatsit* asked children for "the benefit of your experience" and offered five one-dollar prizes to children who came up with the "most interesting" cures to laziness.[106] Here was a tantalizing chance not just to win a buck but to sound off on techniques of parental discipline that ranged from Victorian authoritarianism to positive reinforcement. From its parody of Dale Carnegie, the high priest of personal salesmanship, to its humorous take on divergent strategies on parental persuasion, the *Whatsit* seemed to be holding up the ostensibly hidden adult practices of manipulation to the light of child scrutiny.

The *Whatsit*'s dedication to advancing to the kid point of view even extended to creating its own Whatsit Fashions. Drawings and cartoons submitted by *Whatsit* readers inspired a whole line of dresses, raincoats, pajamas, hats, gloves, handkerchiefs—even draperies, wallpapers, and Christmas cards.[107] These fashions were sold under the Whatsit trademark in stores throughout the country, including Bloomingdale's, Filene's, Bullock's, and the Emporium. Some fabric designs were patterned after "Dijevers"—pronounced as a contraction of "Did-you-ever"—a *Whatsit* word game that made puns from noun-verb reversals. One child, for example, illustrated "Dijever see a Vegetable Shop?" with a picture of an anthropomorphized carrot with leafy hair and a purse in hand. Another child's "Dijever see a Spelling Bee?" depicted bees surrounded by letters of the alphabet. Other Whatsit fashions grew out of drawing contests that asked readers to design wallpaper for their rooms and fabrics for their clothes. Their fanciful sketches were then refined by trained artists and adapted to textile designs that became known in trade circles as Bacon and Eggs, Hobby Horse, Jumping Rope, Hat Band, Ball and Jacks, and Tic Tac Toe. As a critic attending the 1936 Wallpaper Exposition in New York commented, Whatsit patterns "made many of the designs (by adults) look extremely old-fashioned" (fig. 6.5).[108]

Ultimately, the *Whatsit* could be enjoyed as both a celebration and a mockery of children's consumer culture. The *Whatsit* was the ultimate kids' world—one that privileged child creativity and child aspirations without demanding a single proof of purchase. Unlike the manipulative advertisers whose prized decoding devices revealed only another crummy commercial, the *Whatsit* supplied children with the know-how to create their own secret messages. It taught them the mysteries of Pig Latin, Cambodian Cipher, and Double Dutch—kid languages that adults could not possibly decipher—and the secrets of invisible letter writing. (Letters written with

6.5 WHATSIT CHILDREN'S FASHIONS
SOLD AT BLOOMINGDALE'S (1936).
Drawings by *Whatsit* readers, adapted to textile designs by trained artists, inspired a line of fashions sold at major department stores. Below, girls model *Whatsit* dresses at a Bloomingdale's children's fashion show in New York, 1936. Ad reproduced with permission of Bloomingdale's.

lemon juice, the *Whatsit* instructed, could be read by holding the paper over a hot light bulb.)

The *Whatsit* seemed to grasp what made consumer culture seem alternately miraculous and ridiculous. For the correct solution to a simple *Whatsit* word game, children could collect a prize of ten buttons for ten different Whatsit clubs, including the Whatsit Mystery League, the Whatsit Secret Code Society, the Whatsit Movie Fans Club, and the Whatsit Sleuths Club. The buttons were the be all and end all of club membership, as none of the Whatsit clubs conducted any activities, acknowledged ranks, or required observance of any rules and regulations. Some children, perhaps those who could never save up the requisite proofs of purchase for membership, could see the Whatsit clubs as a sarcastic parody of an advertising fad run amok. The working-class children who read the *Whatsit* insert in their mother's copy of *True Story* may have embraced the Whatsit clubs as an expression of class rebellion against an advertising culture that nurtured the exclusionary competitive consumption of their wealthier age cohorts. For other children, the buttons may have represented all that was really necessary—a way of signaling to their peers that they, too, enjoyed the honors and recognition that membership bestowed. It was a motive the *Whatsit* editors understood all too well: "If you don't belong to any clubs now, and even if you do," the *Whatsit* proclaimed, "you're going to be proud to wear these big, colorful, significant buttons, each bearing the official insignia and colors of a different club" (fig. 6.6).[109]

As the *Whatsit* parodies suggest, children's acculturation to consumer culture's glowing promises meant that they were also becoming familiar with its empty promises. Not surprisingly, parents and child experts welcomed these early stirrings of consumer cynicism. Arthur Mann's previous alarm over children's radio diminished when he began to observe more and more children growing skeptical of advertisers' claims. "The children realized gradually," he claimed, "that they were being victimized, and used as a tool to purchase an article that could not, or at least did not, build its demand in the open market on merit alone."[110] Mothers surveyed by the Child Study Association revealed that older children in some families had become critical of children's programs which contained "obvious sales talks" and questioned their accuracy.[111] Mothers and child experts increasingly embraced such findings as comforting evidence that radio clubs and "blood-and-thunder" programs were nothing more than a passing fancy. Radio clubs, it seemed, had taught children an important lesson about the age-based hierarchies of an advertising culture that was especially willing to con children. Children's loss of consumer gullibility thus constituted a rite of passage of sorts into the upper echelons of the consumer pecking order.

FACE THE WORLD BOLDLY IN WHATSIT CLUB BUTTONS

6.6 CARTOON IN WHATSIT (NOVEMBER 1937).
The *Whatsit* mocked advertising strategies that rewarded children's brand loyalty with special club memberships, but sympathized with children's yearnings to belong.

Complaints that radio corrupted childhood innocence receded in the face of new arguments that clubs fulfilled children's developmental needs for "substitute experiences and adventure."[112] Even the very excesses that had so disturbed parents could bring consolation. "In the course of time," Josette Frank reassured *Parents' Magazine* readers, "we will find, if we are patient, that many of the programs bring their own immunity."[113] By 1945, attitudes toward radio clubs had softened to such an extent that one could even say the tide of expert opinion had turned in advertisers' favor. What advertiser would not be pleased by the Child Study Association's recommendation that parents learn to cope with "the annoyance" of children's desires for advertising premiums on the grounds that "such things stir youngsters to activity and participation, both of which are wholesome and desirable"?[114]

Such accommodations of children's consumerism suggest how new parenting paradigms and developmental psychology helped to legitimate children's marketing. By viewing children's consumer excesses and "lowbrow" tastes as a passing fancy or developmental stage, parents and experts found a way, at least temporarily, to come to terms with the destabilizing potential of children's consumer culture. In this light, children's enthusiasm for club premiums constituted a developmental stage rather than a threat to traditional boundaries of dependency. Even so, such sympathetic attitudes toward the child—and by extension the advertiser—did not seem to fully appreciate the deeper yearnings for rebellion against adult constraints and childhood dependency that children's consumer culture often satisfied. Nor, in judging children's quest for prizes a wholesome activity, did experts concern themselves with how children served advertisers self-interests. In accommodating the child, parents and experts had further erased boundaries that formerly divided the family from the marketplace.

BY THE END OF THE DEPRESSION, the child consumer, so eagerly courted over the airwaves, had become a familiar subject of commentary in women's magazines, parenting guidebooks, and the advertising trade press. Complaints about the commercial excesses of broadcast advertisers persisted, perhaps becoming even more inflamed during the television age, but the ideological groundwork had already been laid during the interwar years for widespread acceptance of children's consumption. National advertisers, of course, were not unequivocally triumphant. Parents and child experts sought to temper the mass market's influence and bend it to their own ends, while some child consumers became dubious of the mass market's enchantments. Far more striking than these subtle contestations, however, is how marketing strategies converged with permissive childrearing philosophies, new theories of psychological adjustment, and transformations in the national political economy in the early twentieth century that legitimized children's consumption.

This outcome was by no means inevitable. Children's socialization as consumers in the early twentieth century was first and foremost a battle over how to educate and organize children's desires. To a disparate set of commentators, children seemed to possess boundless consumer appetites that led them to yield quickly before temptation. But while there was much agreement on children's lust for consumer goods, there was little consensus over how to channel their desires. Advertisers and children's magazine publishers trained children to recognize brand names and encouraged them to lobby their parents for consumer goods. Parents, educators, and child experts, on the other hand, devised their own programs of money training and moral reform to regulate children's stepped-up consumer demands. Even so, as traditional thrift education lost favor to allowances among childrearing authorities, efforts to moderate children's consumer desires were accompanied by a new recognition of children's entitlement to make their own spending decisions and spending mistakes as they learned better ways of money management.

Although the new consumer training could sometimes dovetail with advertisers' goals of mobilizing children's consumer desires, there was still a profound difference in emphasis. Advertisers aimed to instill brand consciousness, while middle-class parents and child experts sought to enhance children's consciousness of taste and financial limitations. The savvy child consumer of advertisers' dreams was a master persuader, whose careful study of advertisements and devotion to the "new and improved" continually modernized family purchasing. The savvy child consumer of parental fantasies was a disciplined budgeter with a taste for better, more expensive goods that could be had only by spending wisely and saving strategically. As a contested emblem of modernity, the child consumer embodied competing ideals of progressive spending: one rooted in "the cult of the new," the other grounded in the managerial ethos.[1]

To a great extent, however, the idealized figure of the boy consumer resolved the tensions between these competing visions. His magical blend of consumer desire and entrepreneurial cunning made him a reassuring emblem of the new consumer age: the consumer ethos and the producer ethos, it seemed, were not mutually exclusive. But even the boy consumer did not dispose of all the tensions between the family and the market. Children's own material ambitions often conflicted with the varied efforts to manage their consumer behavior. They sometimes used the new instruments of money training in ways that expanded their autonomy and subtly subverted efforts to control them. A poor child like Aaron Hotchner used the school savings bank to protect earnings that would have otherwise fallen into the hands of his father. Middle-class and affluent children refused to use their own allowance money to make deposits on Bank Day, insisting that parents supply them with additional funds to meet a mandatory school requirement. Children like the Gilbreths who participated in family buying councils used the collective weight of the kids' vote to advance their own spending agenda and upset what parents thought were predetermined outcomes.

Children's socialization as consumers also created a slightly different tug-of-war between the commercial world and the middle-class home that intensified during the 1920s and 1930s. At stake in this conflict was nothing less than the allegiance of the new child consumer. Child experts and parents responded with alarm as middle-class children increasingly gravitated toward the thrilling new urban culture of movie palaces, amusement parks, and penny arcades and spent more time in the company of their peers. Yet rather than reject commercial culture outright, parents and child experts embraced its ethos of salesmanship and enticement in constructing a wholesome alternative playworld within the home. A home equipped with a playroom, backyard swing set, and educational toys would not only cultivate the child's imagination and taste for edifying pursuits, but, with any luck, inoculate children against the attractions of mass culture.

In actuality, however, the new ideology of play made the boundaries between family values and commercial values that much harder to detect. The supreme irony of consumer culture was that it thrived in an atmosphere in which Americans were trying to save the family from the vulgarities of the commercial marketplace. The new companionate family fought to preserve its position as the primary arena of personal fulfillment and happiness by absorbing the ideological imperatives of consumer capitalism. What began as a tug-of-war between the family and the commercial world often dissolved into an uneasy alliance. Just as parents imported aspects of commercial culture into the home, advertisers cleverly incorporated critiques of mass culture into their messages. In *American Boy* magazine, makers of home billiard tables promised to teach straying adolescents "the love of home . . . and *clean companions*," while radio manufacturers promised to restore the home as the center of family recreations.[2] Parents periodically revived the jeremiad tradition decrying commercial excess when advertisers overstepped their bounds in appealing to children's autonomy, but as these advertisements suggest, advertisers and parents alike were increasingly content to embrace the best consumer culture had to offer in order to combat its worst excesses.

Advertisers' indebtedness to play ideology as a sales strategy went beyond these not-so-subtle attempts to exploit parental anxieties. Much like the child experts who contributed articles to *Parents Magazine*, advertisers used play to dramatize a new way of exercising authority in modern democratic families. Sometimes singing literally from the same advertising page, advertisers and child experts taught mothers to instill good habits through play rather than restraint and routine. Like consumer culture itself, the new theories of child management promised results to parents who disguised their authority in play and privileged the child's way of learning. Good parenting, like good salesmanship, relied on enticement and psychological manipulation rather than excessive coaxing or coercion.

For all of its supposed virtues, however, disguised authority was also more open to misappropriation and negotiation. Mothers could support their child's interest in joining a juvenile club that promised to reduce family friction over teaching children habits of healthy eating and proper hygiene. But what children sought from such clubs seemed to have little to do with such lofty maternal ambitions. Armed with secret passwords, decoding devices, and mysterious languages impervious to adult comprehension, children discovered that the privileges of club membership gave them an authority all their own. Instead of buttressing parental authority, juvenile clubs merely reinforced children's autonomy within the companionate family and augmented their ability to pressure parents to buy a winning supply of box tops. Parents who embraced juvenile clubs often belatedly discovered that the authority such clubs disguised was not their own but that of consumer culture itself.

In the second half of the twentieth century, parents found themselves even more often on the losing side of the battle to control children's attraction to consumer culture. During the postwar years, the spread of affluence and permissive childrearing gave children greater economic power, while the advent of television gave advertisers new means to reach children en masse. Despite some initial doubts about television's viability as an advertising medium, advertisers enthusiastically took to the airwaves once they became convinced that popular programs like the *Howdy Doody Show* and the *Mickey Mouse Club* could deliver a captivated audience.[3] Radio and magazines, however, remained the favored venue in the mid-1950s for reaching the typical teenager, who on average spent $555 annually on such goods as records, cosmetics, and training bras.[4]

In the last two decades of the twentieth century, the barriers between children and the market all but disappeared. Not only did children's media consumption become more difficult to monitor in families with both parents in the workforce—now the American norm—but parental restraints became more difficult to enforce. Parental acquiescence, of course, also contributed to the commercialization of childhood. Advertisers' work is certainly made easier when children enjoy personal televisions and computers with Internet access in their own private bedrooms. Still, the most vigilant parents can at best exercise limited control over children's exposure to commercial messages. Even in public schools, a morning viewing of the Channel 1 news service exposes children to a daily dose of commercials along with news of current events. Indeed, what began as a marriage of convenience between underfunded public schools and advertisers in the 1920s has grown into a virtually irresistible collaboration, thanks to the antitax movement of the past quarter-century and voters' reluctance to approve school bond measures. Cash-strapped public schools welcome the additional revenues—an exclusive contract with a soda companies can net millions, while a restricted arrangement with a computer company can yield a new supply of "free" computers. In return for their largesse, corporations are rewarded with an advertising venue that reaches masses of children far more cheaply than television.[5]

Like their early-twentieth-century predecessors, contemporary school advertisers produce posters, booklets, magazines, videos, and other "sponsored educational materials" that purport to be "strictly educational" but, as *Consumer Reports* has observed, often relay "biased or incomplete information" that "favors the company or its economic agenda."[6] That self-serving corporate messages bear the imprimatur of the public schools makes them all the more galling. Consider, for example, Laguna Beach school district's brochure of school lunch menus—the "Monthly Munch"—a colorful glossy in which plain and peanut M&Ms issue the perversely ironic directive: "It's plain nutty if you don't eat healthy."[7] As a measure of "just how far the tentacles of consumerism extend into the space of childhood," lessons in brand consciousness now even occur under the auspices of cultural enrichment programs for children. At the Kidspace Children's Museum, a hands-on discovery museum in Pasadena, California, that exposes children to the arts, sciences, and humanities, children can "shop" and play store in a kids-sized grocery store equipped with Trader Joe's labeled products, miniature Trader Joe's push carts, Trader Joe's smocks, and a cash register.[8]

In their quest to tap the salesmanship and spending power of child consumers, advertisers have added some new spices to old recipes for marketing success. While the Junior Store inducted children of the 1920s into the world of shopping and branded goods, the Barbie doll, with her endless array of fashion accessories, allowed legions of postwar girls to act out their shopping fantasies and rehearse the joys of carefree consumption. More recently, MasterCard joined forces with Mattel to introduce Cool Shoppin' Barbie, the first doll to come with her own toy credit card (a MasterCard tie-in), a cash register, a talking scanner programmed to say only "credit approved," and a cardboard MasterCard for the child—all provided, of course, with a view to cultivating future MasterCard customers. Complaints from consumer credit counseling services and some beleaguered parents that the doll encouraged irresponsible spending failed to dissuade most holiday shoppers, who made Cool Shoppin' Barbie a top seller in 1997.[9] MasterCard's Barbie tie-in was hardly a new marketing innovation. Like so many fast food chains that use movie-inspired toys to simultaneously boost hamburger sales and publicize new releases, MasterCard's strategy harkened back to the Great Depression, when toymakers revitalized sagging sales by creating licensed character toys that revolved around children's celebrity idols such as Mickey Mouse, Shirley Temple, Buck Rogers, and Superman.[10]

Television advertisers have also built on the practice, first perfected on radio, of weaving product endorsements into children's entertainment programming and making those product purchases central to children's enjoyment of the program. Just as possessing a secret decoding device had allowed children to become active participants in the unfolding drama of their favorite radio serial, a popular 1950s animated TV show, *Winky Dink and You,* went to new extremes "by making the program completely dependent upon the product it advertised." With the purchase of a special kit of rub-off crayons and a plastic "magic window" that covered the TV, children could draw in scenery or features on the cartoon characters' faces to help complete story lines.[11] When a 1974 FTC ban on such practices was lifted a decade later, advertisers flooded the airwaves again with toy-based television programs like the *Smurfs, Strawberry Shortcake,* and *He-Man*— a marketing ploy the toy industry cynically defended by asserting that children needed preformulated story lines to help them play.[12]

Much like their early-twentieth-century predecessors, contemporary marketers judge the effectiveness of children's advertising by the so-called nag factor—the aim being to maximize the nag until the parental gatekeeper yields. But where earlier advertisers were more cautious about upsetting the balance of power within the family—winning parental goodwill, after all, was the goal of winning juvenile goodwill—late-twentieth-century advertisers have pushed the limits of those boundaries more aggressively. The promises of self-improvement and edification that appeased previous generations of parents have given way to a children's advertising culture in which hedonism, antiauthoritarianism, and kid power reign supreme. Today's kids, as Ellen Seiter puts it, are "sold separately," with appeals designed more to amp the nag factor than to placate the parental gatekeeper.[13] In fact, marketers of popular products like "Toxic High" stickers and the Garbage Pail Kids have learned that children's enjoyment of toys that parents consider inappropriate can dramatically increase their sales potential.[14]

To acknowledge contemporary marketers' greater investment in creating a distinct children's fantasy culture, however, is not to romanticize the early twentieth century as some utopian moment in children's consumer culture. Far from it. The Pokemon fad of the 1990s, in fact, can be viewed as a direct descendant of the children's radio clubs of the 1930s. Just as the promise of special premiums from Little Orphan Annie and Jack Armstrong got children to pester their parents for more Cocomalt or Wheaties, the Pokemon craze led children to pester their parents for the precious trading cards that would help them capture all 150 Pokemons, the mythical "pocket monster" creatures featured in the popular animated kids' television show and video game. While in each case clever market tie-ins with radio idols or popular television shows provided the building blocks for the craze, the appeal of joining a distinct kids' world, impervious to adult comprehension, fueled the fad. Radio club members decoded secret messages to which only their peers were privy, while Pokemon traders became experts in a whole separate world of Pokemon lore, memorizing the names, special fighting skills, and point values of each Pokemon.[15]

In the decades since the 1950s, this privileging of children's culture has contributed to greater age segmentation within the children's market. The often fuzzy distinctions between teenagers and children that typified advertising in the interwar years have evolved into clearly delineated categories ranging from toddlers to kids to 'tweens to teens. Recent research showing that children as young as two can recognize brands has persuaded marketers to set their sights on yet another cohort—the under-two set, a group that marketers previously targeted through moms.[16] Marketers also expend much more time and money gathering data about their various child audiences. Information formerly gleaned from contest data, children's advertising testimonials, and a smattering of personal interviews now comes to advertising agencies through the more scientific channels of surveys and focus groups. Companies like Levi Strauss, Dupont, and Mars pay teens for their views on what's cool. Likewise, the consulting firm Youth Intelligence relies on teens to sort the resonant commercials from those that miss the mark.[17] Marketers even host slumber parties to learn what makes nine- to twelve-year-old girls spend.[18] Indeed, the most striking change from the advertising culture of the interwar years is that marketers now recognize girls as cultural trendsetters with their own distinctive tastes and interests.[19] It's no longer sufficient to highlight boy interests and boy heroes and expect that the girls will follow.

During the 1990s marketers found more deceitful means to glean information about children's tastes and preferences by requiring them to provide critical personal data (including name, sex, age, email address, favorite television show, and musical group) before they entered certain Web sites. In exchange, Web sites offered children prizes, even cash, with the promise of more if children filled out other surveys. The most devious Web sites profited again by selling such valuable market research data to other companies. In response to indignant parents and media watch groups, the FTC instituted new guidelines in 1998 under the Children's Online Privacy Act that made it illegal to solicit personal information from preteens online without parental permission. Nevertheless, children's advertisers still hold high hopes that children's attraction to the Internet will make the virtual mall as popular a teen hangout as the neighborhood shopping mall. Indeed, e-commerce is doing its best to make that a reality by issuing e-wallets—a kind of virtual credit card that allows kids to make purchases online with money their parents have set aside in a special account.[20] While it is possible that parents envision e-wallets much like allowances—as an expedient means to limit children's spending to a fixed sum—the spending freedom that e-wallets afford also suggests that some parents have few qualms about conceding control over children's spending choices.

Advertisers may employ new means to reach children on a grander scale, but their primary motives for courting children have changed little. Children's advertising remains, in their eyes, a worthy investment for cultivating brand loyalty and a reliable avenue for reaching parental pocketbooks. The proceedings at the third annual Advertising and Promoting to Kids Conference, held in September 2000, offer a case in point. Participants could attend sessions on "Building Brand Recognition" and "The Fine Art of Nagging," confident that mastery of such techniques would yield impressive—and immediate—results.[21]

As one 1999 study reported, children's powers of persuasion influence approximately $188 billion of household purchases each year.[22] Advertisers, of course, also have their eye on children's expanding discretionary funds. In 1999 the typical weekly allowance for thirteen- to fifteen-year-olds, according to the Rand Youth Poll, ranged from $30.50 to $34.25, with girls receiving on average $3.00–$4.00 more than boys. Supplementary earnings typically doubled the weekly yield for teenage boys and girls. Though younger children, aged ten–twelve, only received a modest $5.00–$6.00 boost to their weekly income from earnings, allowances on average swelled their weekly take by an additional $21.00–$22.00.[23] According to one 1996 estimate, allowances accounted for more than a third of the $89 billion in spending money at children's disposal.[24] Children's collective consumer clout is weighty indeed.

Despite the dramatic growth in the scope and scale of children's consumption, what is ultimately most noteworthy is how much the dialogue surrounding children's encounters with consumer culture continues to resonate with early-twentieth-century discourses. Much like their predecessors, contemporary advertisers attribute children's inclusion in family spending decisions to their superior technological know-how; in many households, marketing specialists note, the computer-savvy child assumes the authority of a respected consultant on family purchases.[25]

Equally resonant today is the image of the greedy child consumer so familiar to readers of turn-of-the century magazines. That image abounds in contemporary parenting television programs that offer tips on how to manage the "'gimme' syndrome," but is perhaps most memorably enshrined in *Charlie and the Chocolate Factory*, Roald Dahl's cautionary tale about the dangers of excessive desire.[26] In both the popular 1964 novel and the 1971 film, a parade of stock child characters—the gluttonous chocoholic, the spoiled brat, and the demanding tyrant—meet terrible, though ultimately curable, fates thanks to their own consumer excesses and their equally blameworthy overindulgent parents.

Echoes from the early twentieth century can also be heard in contemporary commentaries lamenting the demise of childhood as a period of economic innocence. If children's greed is cause for moralizing, however, their precociousness seems to elicit humored tolerance. A 1995 cartoon editorializing on the sinking value of the dollar, for example, pictured a boy rejecting his father's handout of dollar bills with the retort, "If it's all the same to you, I'd prefer to have that in Yen."[27] Like the fabled kid pitchmen in turn-of-the-century ads for Cream of Wheat and Wool Soap, the precocious child consumer also remains an iconic advertising spokesperson. In television ads for E.A. Kids, Ethan Allen's line of scaled-down grown-up furniture, a little boy seated in a wooden chair, his feet not quite touching the floor, announces "I've always been drawn to the simplicity of Shaker design," while a little girl bouncing on her bed exclaims, "It's really the comforter that pulls the whole room together."[28] Whether Ethan Allen's young sophisticates are truly expressing their own opinions or just what their parents hope they might be, advertisers clearly recognize the precocious child consumer as a defining emblem of modern childhood.

The parents who raise and live with these precocious consumers face many of the same dilemmas that vexed middle-class parents three-quarters of a century ago: whether to tie children's allowances to chores or good behavior, how to interest children in creative, culturally elevated endeavors rather than ready-made commercial entertainments, how to lower children's expectations of consumer abundance, and how to reassert parental control without overtly squelching children's consuming pleasures. Much as earlier generations sought to temper children's consumer excesses by stimulating their imagination with creative in-home play, middle-class parents in more than one hundred United States cities have joined "simplicity circles" in hopes that children will learn to find as much pleasure in the "intangible stuff" as they do in a trip to the mall or the toy store. As part of this "antispoiling movement," one Silver Springs, Maryland, mother— fed up with the birthday extravaganzas she staged for her own preschoolers—now requests on party invitations that guests only give art supplies.[29] Many interwar childrearing authorities would surely have concurred with her strategy to make creative play an alluring alternative to a commercial culture run amok.

In the eyes of child experts, educators, and many parents, raising children's financial literacy remains the best means to control their precocious consumer appetites. Indeed, the case for allowances has changed surprisingly little since the Great Depression. Although a few dissenting parents believe that allowances merely "promote materialism and consumerism," the dominant consensus among childrearing authorities is that children with allowances develop character and more regular habits of saving, while children without a steady supply of funds only master how to manipulate family breadwinners.[30] Though an educational tool in theory, children's allowances more often than not function solely as an economic entitlement—an indication perhaps that children owe their spending power more to the tenets of family democracy than to concerns about inculcating wise spending.

Even more impressive evidence of the triumph of consumerism can be seen in the postwar transformation of school savings bank programs. In place of the old emphasis on saving as a virtue in itself, many school bank programs made lessons in "consumership" their primary mission. A teacher's manual written for the Minneapolis school district by the Farmers and Mechanics Savings Bank in 1947 pronounced "wise spending" the "most important component" of thrift education. Echoing the "fun morality" that informed allowance advocacy during the interwar years, the teacher's manual insisted that "saving is better taught if the fun of spending later is emphasized rather than the dire results of not saving."[31] Pamphlets written for Minneapolis high school students similarly stressed the joys of saving with a definite spending goal in mind.[32] While the new emphasis on consumership may have helped account for the revival of interest in elementary school banking programs during the 1950s and 1960s, it appeared insufficient to sustain student interest at the junior and senior high school levels, where participation rates fell dramatically.[33] In teaching children to be money wise, school savings banks may have even contributed their own demise in the 1970s, when the 5.5 percent interest offered by savings banks seemed a poor bargain compared to the 15 percent interest awarded by money market funds.[34]

If the celebratory figure of the savvy child consumer makes it more difficult to imagine children as economic innocents, the rhetoric of childhood innocence nevertheless remains the polemical framework of choice among those who voice resistance to excessive commercialism. Politicians routinely invoke children's innocence when they criticize media companies and advertising firms for deliberately promoting violent products and films to children. So, too, do psychologists when they express concerns about advertising's intrusions on children's psyches. In 2000 a group of alarmed psychologists, characterizing the "enormous onslaught" of children's advertising as "the largest single psychological project ever undertaken," took their colleagues to task for using their talents "to promote and assist the commercial exploitation and manipulation of children." At the urging of many of its members, the American Psychological Association formed a committee to examine the ethics of using "psychological techniques to assist corporate marketing and advertising to children."[35]

Ultimately, however, these invocations of childhood innocence and proposals for limited external controls do little to rein in a capitalist culture resistant to infringements on free markets and commercial free speech. Indeed savvy child consumers themselves have discovered avenues of resistance only within the parameters of consumerism itself. One of these avenues is *Zillions*, a magazine for kids, published by Consumer Reports, that teaches children the basics of product testing and comparative shopping. For many child fans of *Mad* magazine, a publication beloved for its parodies of advertisements, outsmarting the advertisers was not nearly as satisfying as mocking their foolish pretensions. Children have also turned consumerism into a language of protest, marketing their own anticorporate sentiments through self-styled Internet zines and fashions. In their hands, the products of capitalist culture supply the means to ridicule that culture. Two students at Greenbrier High School in Evans, Georgia, for example, expressed their objection to using students in an in-school promotion of Coca-Cola by wearing Pepsi T-shirts on "Coke in Education Day"—an action that resulted in their suspension.[36] In becoming walking advertisements themselves, however, the students also illustrate the limits of consumerism as a language of protest. All too often, such critiques of consumer culture amount to little more than a celebration of consumers' entitlement to do their own thing—itself a foundational premise of late-twentieth-century consumerist ideology. And this is perhaps the lasting lesson that children both today and in the early twentieth century have learned about the enchantments and false promises of consumer culture: fashioning the self through consumerism can be as limiting as it is liberating.

NOTES

INTRODUCTION

1. William Leach, "Child-World in the Promised Land," in James Gilbert et al., eds., *The Mythmaking Frame of Mind: Social Imagination and American Culture* (Belmont, Calif.: Wadsworth, 1993), 209–238; David Nasaw, *Children of the City: At Work and at Play* (New York: Anchor Press/Doubleday, 1985); David Nasaw, "Children and Commercial Culture: Moving Pictures in the Early Twentieth Century," in Elliott West and Paula Petrik, eds., *Small Worlds: Children and Adolescents in America, 1850–1950* (Lawrence, Kans.: University of Kansas Press, 1992), 14–25.

2. Important exceptions are Miriam Formanek-Brunell, *Made to Play House: Dolls and the Commercialization of American Girlhood, 1830–1930* (New Haven: Yale University Press, 1993); Gary Cross, *Kids' Stuff: Toys and the Changing World of American Childhood* (Cambridge: Harvard University Press, 1997); and Leach, "Child-World in the Promised Land," which nicely encapsulates arguments that also appear in his *Land of Desire: Merchants, Power, and the Rise of a New American Culture* (New York: Pantheon, 1993). Significantly, the most sophisticated work has centered on dolls, toys, and department stores but has not explored just how broad the phenomenon of children's consumption was.

3. An extensive literature examining conceptions of childhood developed after the publication of Philippe Ariès's seminal work, *Centuries of Childhood: A Social History of Family Life,* trans. Robert Baldick (New York: Knopf, 1962). Some excellent cultural histories that investigate how adult anxieties inform constructions of childhood include Karin Calvert, *Children in the House: The Material Culture of Early Childhood, 1600–1900* (Boston: Northeastern University Press, 1992); Ann Lombard, *Making Manhood: Growing Up Male in Colonial New England* (Cambridge, Mass.: Harvard University Press, 2003).

4. Lizabeth Cohen, *A Consumers' Republic: The Politics of Mass Consumption in Postwar America* (New York: Knopf, 2003), 7.

5. Leach, *Land of Desire*; Elaine Abelson, *When Ladies Go A-Thieving: Middle-Class Shoplifters in the Victorian Department Store* (New York: Oxford Uni-

versity Press, 1989); Daniel Horowitz, *The Morality of Spending: Attitudes toward the Consumer Society in America, 1875–1940* (Baltimore: The Johns Hopkins University Press, 1985); T. J. Jackson Lears, "From Salvation to Self-Realization: Advertising and the Therapeutic Roots of the Consumer Culture, 1880–1930," in Richard Wightman Fox and T. J. Jackson Lears, eds., *The Culture of Consumption: Critical Essays in American History, 1880–1980* (New York: Pantheon, 1983), 1–38. For an insightful analysis of tensions between husbands and wives over consumer credit in England, see Erika Diane Rappaport, *Shopping for Pleasure: Women in the Making of London's West End* (Princeton: Princeton University Press, 2000), 48–73.

6. Viviana Zelizer, *Pricing the Priceless Child: The Changing Social Value of Children* (New York: Basic Books, 1985), 3.

7. Carolyn Benedict Burrell, "The Child and Its World," *Harper's Bazaar* 33 (November 3, 1900), 1721. For a discussion of the notion of children as redeemers, see Bernard Wishy, *The Child and the Republic: The Dawn of Modern American Child Nurture* (Philadelphia: University of Pennsylvania Press, 1968), 1, 79.

8. Stuart Ewen, *Captains of Consciousness: Advertising and the Social Roots of the Consumer Culture* (New York: McGraw-Hill, 1976).

9. Susan Strasser, *Satisfaction Guaranteed: The Making of the American Mass Market* (New York: Pantheon, 1989); Richard Tedlow, *New and Improved: The Story of Mass Marketing in America* (New York: Basic Books, 1990).

10. Leach, *Land of Desire;* Leigh Eric Schmidt, *Consumer Rites: The Buying and Selling of American Holidays* (Princeton: Princeton University Press, 1995).

11. Zelizer, *Pricing the Priceless Child*, 6.

12. Elaine Tyler May, *Great Expectations: Marriage and Divorce in Post-Victorian America* (Chicago: University of Chicago Press, 1980); Stephen Mintz and Susan Kellogg, *Domestic Revolutions: A Social History of American Family Life* (New York: Free Press, 1988), 107–131.

13. Lynn Spigel, *Make Room for TV: Television and the Family Ideal in Postwar America* (Chicago: University of Chicago Press, 1992), 12–26.

14. Paula Baker, "The Domestication of Politics: Women and American Political Society, 1780–1920," in Linda Gordon, ed., *Women, the State, and Welfare* (Madison: University of Wisconsin Press, 1990), 55–91; Nancy Cott, *The Grounding of Modern Feminism* (New Haven: Yale University Press, 1987).

15. Spigel, *Make Room for TV*, chapter 4.

16. Christopher Lasch, *Haven in a Heartless World: The Family Besieged* (New York: Basic Books, 1977).

17. Peter Stearns, "Historical Perspectives on Twentieth-Century American Childhood," in William Koops and Michael Zuckerman, eds., *Beyond the Century of the Child: Cultural History and Developmental Psychology* (Philadelphia: University of Pennsylvania Press, 2003), 96–111; Gary Cross, *The Cute and the Cool: Wondrous Innocence and Modern American Children's Culture* (New York: Oxford University Press, 2004), chapter 3.

18. Lendol Calder, *Financing the American Dream: A Cultural History of Consumer Credit* (Princeton: Princeton University Press, 1999); Jackson Lears, *Fables of Abundance: A Cultural History of Advertising in America* (New York: Basic Books, 1994).

19. Abelson, *When Ladies Go A-Thieving*; Victoria de Grazia, ed., *The Sex of Things: Gender and Consumption in Historical Perspective* (Berkeley: University of California Press, 1996); Roland Marchand, *Advertising the American Dream: Making Way for Modernity, 1920–1940* (Berkeley: University of California Press, 1986), 66–72, 84–87; John Sekora, *Luxury: The Concept in Western Thought* (Baltimore: Johns Hopkins University Press, 1977).

20. Margaret Finnegan, *Selling Suffrage: Consumer Culture and Votes for Women* (New York: Columbia University Press, 1999); Regina Blaszczyk, *Imagining Consumers: Design and Innovation from Wedgwood to Corning* (Baltimore: Johns Hopkins University Press, 2000).

21. Woody Register, *The Kid of Coney Island: Fred Thompson and the Rise of / American Amusements* (New York: Oxford University Press, 2001), 15.

22. The quoted material comes from Leslie Paris, "Children's Nature: Summer Camps in New York State, 1919–1941" (Ph.D. diss., University of Michigan, 2000), 11. Paris also makes a similar point.

23. Stephen Kline, *Out of the Garden: Toys, TV, and Children's Culture in the Age of Marketing* (London: Verso, 1993) is a more conventional model. For some works that give more consideration to the meanings children attached to consumption, see Formanek-Brunell, *Made to Play House*; Allison James, "Confections, Concoctions, and Conceptions," in Henry Jenkins, ed., *The Children's Culture Reader* (New York: New York University Press, 1998), 394–405; Ellen Seiter, *Sold Separately: Parents and Children in Consumer Culture* (New Brunswick, N.J.: Rutgers University Press, 1993); Georganne Scheiner, "The Deanna Durbin Devotees: Fan Clubs and Spectatorship," in Joe Austin and Michael Nevin Willard, eds., *Generations of Youth: Youth Cultures and History in Twentieth-Century America* (New York: New York University Press, 1998), 81–94.

 Scholars have often been content to determine meaning by uncovering the hidden ideological function of a popular culture text. Best exemplified by the Frankfurt School, this work assumes a passive, unreflective audience and ignores how audiences themselves become involved in the making of cultural meaning. Max Horkheimer and Theodor Adorno, *The Dialectic of the Enlightenment* (New York: Herder and Herder, 1972) is a classic example of an approach more concerned with assessing the effects of popular culture than its appeals. My own work has been informed by scholarly literature on audience reception and the communicative capacity of goods, especially Lawrence Levine, "The Folklore of Industrial Society: Popular Culture and Its Audiences," *American Historical Review* 97 (December 1992): 1369–1399; Mary Douglas and Baron Isherwood, *The*

World of Goods (New York: Basic Books, 1979); Grant McCracken, *Culture and Consumption: New Approaches to the Symbolic Character of Consumer Goods and Activities* (Bloomington: Indiana University Press, 1988); and Stuart Hall, "Encoding/Decoding," in Stuart Hall et al., eds., *Culture, Media, Language* (London: Hutchinson, 1980), 128–138.

1: "BIG SALES FROM LITTLE FOLKS"

1. Advertisement, *Printers' Ink* 94 (January 20, 1916), 72.
2. "Magazine-Reading Families," *News Letter* 10 (September 1, 1928), 1, Newsletter Collection, Main Series, box 4, JWT Archives.
3. The 50,000 figure comes from Margaret Finnegan, *Selling Suffrage: Consumer Culture and Votes for Women* (New York: Columbia University Press, 1999), 157, 166. According to Finnegan, publishing experts repeatedly informed the managers of the *Woman's Journal* that the suffrage periodical could not attract national advertisers until its circulation reached 50,000. *Everygirl's*, the Camp Fire Girls' magazine, also saw the 50,000 figure as a benchmark for acquiring more advertising, and urged its 30,000 readers in a 1929 editorial to solicit more subscriptions. See "A Heart to Heart Talk with Every Camp Fire Girl," *Everygirl's* 16 (January 1929), inside front cover.
4. Theodore Peterson, *Magazines in the Twentieth Century*, 2nd ed. (Urbana: University of Illinois Press, 1964), 171.
5. Gary Cross, *Kids' Stuff: Toys and the Changing World of American Childhood* (Cambridge: Harvard University Press, 1997); Stephen Kline, *Out of the Garden: Toys, TV, and Children's Culture in the Age of Marketing* (New York: Verso, 1993); Richard Tedlow, *New and Improved: The Story of Mass Marketing in America* (New York: Basic Books, 1990). Susan Strasser acknowledges that children were "special targets for promotional materials" but does not focus on children's advertising in *Satisfaction Guaranteed: The Making of the American Mass Market* (New York: Pantheon, 1989), 166–167. Liz Cohen sees market segmentation as a post–World War II phenomenon, but market segmentation by age was already developing two decades earlier. See Lizabeth Cohen, *A Consumers' Republic: The Politics of Mass Consumption in Postwar America* (New York: Knopf, 2003), 292–344.
6. Kline, *Out of the Garden*, 63, 74, 164–165, 167.
7. Stuart Ewen, for example, represents children's advertising as an attempt to transfer authority from fathers to the corporation, in *Captains of Consciousness: Advertising and the Social Roots of the Consumer Culture* (New York: McGraw-Hill, 1976). William Leach argues that "the total effect of all the enticements [American merchants] created for children was to create . . . an alliance" between children and the stores "that had the potential to subvert the decision-making authority of parents" in "Child-World in the Promised Land," in James Gilbert et al., eds., *The Mythmaking Frame of Mind: Social Imagination and American Culture* (Belmont, Calif.: Wadsworth, 1993), 226.

Ellen Seiter views advertisers' promotion of a distinct children's culture, rooted in hedonistic, antiauthoritarian values, as a late-twentieth-century phenomenon in *Sold Separately: Parents and Children in Consumer Culture* (New Brunswick, N.J.: Rutgers University Press, 1993).

8. J. H. Plumb, "The New World of Children," in Neil Kendrick et al., eds., *The Birth of a Consumer Society: The Commercialization of Eighteenth-Century England* (Bloomington: Indiana University Press, 1982). Plumb argues that eighteenth-century middle-class English parents spent lavish sums on children's books, clothing, educational games, and toys.

9. Ellen Garvey, *The Adman in the Parlor: Magazines and the Gendering of Consumer Culture, 1880s to 1910s* (New York: Oxford University Press, 1996), 19; Strasser, *Satisfaction Guaranteed*, 164–166.

10. Richard Ohmann, *Selling Culture: Magazines, Markets, and Class at the Turn of the Century* (New York: Verso, 1996), 201.

11. Magnetized Food Company trade card, 1882, quoted in Robert Jay, *The Trade Card in Nineteenth-Century America* (Columbia: University of Missouri Press, 1987), 91.

12. James C. Clark, "An Advertising Veteran Applies the Lessons of 77 Years to Today," *Printers' Ink Monthly* 17 (December 1928), 37, 137. For examples of advertising jingle books, see *Little Bo-Peep and Other Jingles* and *Rock a Bye Baby and Other Rhymes*, both published by Clark's O. N. T. Spool Cotton, ca. 1883, and Corticelli thread company's *A Parody on the House that Jack Built* (St. Louis: Times Printing House, 1882), Children box 4, Warshaw Collection.

13. Jay, *Trade Card*, 95–96.

14. *Fairy Tales*, second series (Chicago: The N. K. Fairbanks Company, 1898); *Fairy Tales*, third series (Chicago: The N. K. Fairbanks Company, 1903), Soap box 2, Warshaw Collection.

15. *The Little Red Book*, 1896, Children box 2, Warshaw Collection.

16. For more on gender and scrapbook making, see Garvey, *Adman in the Parlor*, 16–17, 26, 42–44.

17. Shirley Teresa Wajda, "Collecting," in Miriam Forman-Brunell, ed., *Girlhood in America: An Encyclopedia* (Santa Barbara: ABC-CLIO, 2001), 135.

18. This story is recounted in Garvey, *Adman in the Parlor*, 28. For additional details on Arbuckle Coffee's trade card series, see Jay, *Trade Card*, 93.

19. Walter Dill Scott, *The Psychology of Advertising: A Simple Exposition of the Principles of Psychology in Their Relation to Successful Advertising* (Boston: Small, Maynard, and Company, 1913), 82–83. For an extended discussion of early-twentieth-century theorists of advertising, see Patricia Johnston, *Real Fantasies: Edward Steichen's Advertising Photography* (Berkeley: University of California Press, 1997), 93–97; and Garvey, *Adman in the Parlor*, 52–55.

20. *The J.W.T. Book: A Series of Talks on Advertising* (New York: J. Walter Thompson Co., 1909), Company Publications, box 5, JWT Archives; Wal-

ter Dill Scott, *The Theory and Practice of Advertising: A Simple Exposition of the Principles of Psychology in Their Relation to Successful Advertising* (Boston: Small, Maynard, and Company, 1908), 42–43.

21. Garvey, *Adman in the Parlor*, 53.

22. For a discussion of turn-of-the-century advertisements that used testimonials, see Ohmann, *Selling Culture*, 187–191.

23. For some examples, see Mennen's baby powder trade card advertisement, n.d., "Children's Bathing" folder, Children box 3, Warshaw Collection; Clinton Safety Pins advertisement, *J. Walter Thompson Co. Advertising, 1897*, J. Walter Thompson Company Publications, box 3, JWT Archives; Ivorine trade card, n.d., "Children at Play" folder, Children box 3, Warshaw Collection; H-O cereal trade card, n.d., Cereal box 1, Warshaw Collection; "Mother's Dream," Post Toasties trade card, n.d., Cereal box 2, Warshaw Collection; Wool Soap advertisement, *The Thompson Blue Book on Advertising, 1904–1905*, J. Walter Thompson Company Publications, box 4, JWT Archives.

24. Kline, *Out of the Garden*, 52–53; Jay, *Trade Card*, 93–94.

25. Advertisement, 1906, Cereal box 1, Warshaw Collection.

26. Advertisement, ca. 1909, *The Thompson Blue Book on Advertising, 1909–1910*, J. Walter Thompson Company Publications, box 5, JWT Archives.

27. Viviana Zelizer coined the phrase "economically 'worthless' but emotionally 'priceless'" in *Pricing the Priceless Child: The Changing Social Value of Children* (New York: Basic Books, 1985), 3; David Macleod, *The Age of the Child: Children in America, 1890–1920* (New York: Twayne, 1998), 25.

28. Zelizer, *Pricing the Priceless Child*; Henry Jenkins, "Introduction: Childhood Innocence and Other Modern Myths," in Henry Jenkins, ed., *The Children's Culture Reader* (New York: New York University Press, 1998), 19–20.

29. "A Busy Day," advertising poster, 1896, Soap box 7, Warshaw Collection; a full-color poster version is located in folder 1, box 187, Warshaw Collection.

30. Cream of Wheat advertisement, 1907, Cereal box 1, Warshaw Collection; Shredded Wheat trade card, 1911, Cereal box 2, Warshaw Collection; Shredded Wheat pamphlet, 1910, Cereal box 2, Warshaw Collection; Pettijohn's advertisement, n.d., box 7, series 1, Ayer Collection.

31. Advertisement, February 1913, *McCall's*, Chewing Gum box 1, Warshaw Collection.

32. Advertisement, 1902, box 11, series 1, Ayer Collection.

33. Advertisement, ca. 1906, *The Thompson Blue Book on Advertising, 1906–1907*, J. Walter Thompson Company Publications, box 4, JWT Archives.

34. The concept of children as "redeemers" is elaborated in Bernard Wishy, *The Child and the Republic: The Dawn of Modern American Child Nurture*

(Philadelphia: University of Pennsylvania Press, 1968), 85–93. The phrase "moral precocity" appears in David I. Macleod, *The Age of the Child: Children in America, 1890–1920* (New York: Twayne, 1998), 23. Karin Calvert also discusses the Victorian reverence for childhood innocence in *Children in the House: The Material Culture of Early Childhood, 1600–1900* (Boston: Northeastern University Press, 1992), 106–109. For more on how changing notions of childhood were implicated in children's literature, see Gail Schmunk Murray, *American Children's Literature and the Construction of Childhood* (New York: Twayne, 1998), 51–81.

35. Quoted in Macleod, *Age of the Child*, 23.
36. T. J. Jackson Lears, *No Place of Grace: Antimodernism and the Transformation of American Culture, 1880–1920* (New York: Pantheon, 1981), 144–149.
37. A Shredded Wheat ad, for example, sympathetically defended a boy's clandestine late-night hunt for a snack of Shredded Wheat Whole Biscuits, explaining that the "Desire for Natural Food is Natural." The real sinners, the ad claimed, were mothers who "pervert [children's] tastes by the use of unnatural food." See advertisement, n.d., box 11, series 1, Ayer Collection.
38. Korn-Kinks advertising postcards, 1907, Cereal box 1, Warshaw Collection.
39. Garvey, *Adman in the Parlor*, chapter 2.
40. Advertisement, *The Thompson Blue Book on Advertising*, 1909, 308, Company Publications, box 5, JWT Archives.
41. Advertisement, *The Thompson Blue Book on Advertising*, 307.
42. "A Course in Advertising FOR BOYS AND YOUNG MEN," advertising proof sheet, 1917, box 197, series 1, Ayer Collection.
43. *Special Curtis Edition of News Bulletin* 78 (14 May 1921), 6, J. Walter Thompson Company Newsletter Collection, Main Series, JWT Archives.
44. William Leach, *Land of Desire: Merchants, Power, and the Rise of a New American Culture* (New York: Pantheon, 1993), 85–87.
45. Hugh E. Agnew, "A Seasonal Market Taken During the War Is Made Continuous," *Printers' Ink* 113 (December 2, 1920), 94.
46. R. L. Burdick, "Dodging Father's Objections in Advertising to Sons," *Printers' Ink* 113 (December 30, 1920), 77.
47. "What the Coupon Brings," *Printed Salesmanship* 48 (February 1927), 515, 516.
48. "Talking to the Younger Generation in Its Own Language," *The Printing Art* 43 (August 1924), 530.
49. *New Bulletin* 89A (August 21, 1922), 6, Newsletter Collection, Main Series, June 10–October 16, 1922, box 2, JWT Archives.
50. Margaret A. Bartlett, "A Mother Tells of the Advertising That Appeals to Her Children," *Printers' Ink* 117 (November 17, 1921), 132; John Allen Murphy, "The Miniature Product—How and Why It Is Marketed," *Printers' Ink Monthly* 6 (February 1923), 21.
51. *The Girls' Companion* advertisement, *Printers' Ink* 117 (November 10, 1921), 131; *American Girl* advertisement, *Advertising Age* 1 (June 14, 1930), 10.

52. "Building the Sales Message for Young People," *Printed Salesmanship* 51 (August 1928), 520.

53. Robert S. Lynd, "The People as Consumers," in *Recent Social Trends in the United States: Report of the President's Research Committee on Social Trends* (New York: McGraw-Hill Book Company, 1932), 866.

54. Quoted in E. Evalyn Grumbine, *Reaching Juvenile Markets: How to Advertise, Sell, and Merchandise Through Boys and Girls* (New York: McGraw-Hill Book Company, Inc., 1938), 358.

55. *Annual Report of the Business Division*, Girl Scouts USA, 1930, 36. The annual report also noted that the largest manufacturer of rubber footwear (undoubtedly Keds), though initially "dubious" about advertising in *American Girl*, experienced "outstanding" results.

56. Quoted in Grumbine, *Reaching Juvenile Markets*, 358.

57. Grumbine, *Reaching Juvenile Markets*, 359–360.

58. "Ten Minutes with the Boss," *The Kodak Salesman* 6 (April 1920), 13, Ellis Collection.

59. "Follow Each Camera with a Letter," *The Kodak Salesman* 10 (December 1924), 11, Ellis Collection.

60. "What the Coupon Brings," 515.

61. Quoted in Grumbine, *Reaching Juvenile Markets*, 355–356.

62. Robert S. Lynd and Helen Merrell Lynd, *Middletown in Transition: A Study in Cultural Conflict* (New York: Harcourt, Brace, and World, Inc., 1937), 170–171.

63. Paul Fass, *The Damned and the Beautiful: American Youth in the 1920s* (New York: Oxford University Press, 1977), 59–60.

64. Fass, *The Damned and the Beautiful*, 63–64, 90.

65. Fass, *The Damned and the Beautiful*, 89–118; Steven Mintz and Susan Kellogg, *Domestic Revolutions: A Social History of American Family Life* (New York: Free Press, 1988), xx, 107–132; Robert Griswold, *Fatherhood in America: A History* (New York: Basic Books, 1993), 88–118.

66. Fass, *The Damned and the Beautiful*, 88–89.

67. Robert S. Lynd and Helen Merrell Lynd, *Middletown: A Study in American Culture* (New York: Harcourt, Brace, and World, Inc., 1929), 144–145. According to the Lynds, high school boys and girls ranked "respecting children's opinions" second only to "spending time with children" as a desired quality in fathers. Boys and girls rated "respecting children's opinions" fourth and fifth in importance, respectively, as a desired trait in mothers, perhaps owing to the fact that fathers were typically responsible for discipline and laying down the family rules.

68. Fass, *The Damned and the Beautiful*, 88–89, 217–218; Lynd, "The People as Consumers," 866.

69. "How Marshall Field & Co. Cater to the Coming Generation," *Printers' Ink* 110 (February 5, 1920), 159.

70. Charles G. Muller, "Don't Overlook the Sons and Daughters of Mr. and Mrs. Consumer," *Printers' Ink* 155 (May 21, 1931), 57.
71. "Impressing the Junior Market," *Printers' Ink Monthly* 26 (June 1933), 49–50.
72. "Advertising to the Child to Reach the Parents," *Printers' Ink* 165 (October 12, 1933), 70.
73. "More Profit on Kodatoys: Give Children's Projector Prominent Place on Your Holiday Program," *The Kodak Salesman* 17 (November 1931), 12, Ellis Collection.
74. Advertisement, *Printers' Ink* 137 (October 7, 1926), 32.
75. C. B. Larrabee, "Selling Little Bill to Get at the Old Man," *Printers' Ink Monthly* 13 (November 1926), 30.
76. Grumbine, *Reaching Juvenile Markets*, 11–12; W. L. Bruns, "Changing Appeal from Parent to Child Broadens Market," *Printers' Ink Monthly* 13 (October 1926), 70.
77. "What the Coupon Brings," 521.
78. Advertisement, *Printers' Ink Monthly* 36 (February 1938), 96.
79. Bartlett, "A Mother Tells," 129.
80. Lynd and Lynd, *Middletown in Transition*, 290–291.
81. James True, "How National Advertisers Reach Farm Girls and Boys: Working Through the Department of Agriculture to Reach Members of '4-H' Clubs," *Printers' Ink Monthly* 13 (August 1926), 41–42, 106, 108.
82. Advertising proof sheet, May 2, 1927, microfilm reel #26, JWT Archives.
83. Advertisement, *Everygirl's* 14 (October 1926), 27.
84. Advertisement, *American Girl* 11 (July 1928), 33.
85. Advertisement, *American Girl* 11 (July 1928), 39.
86. "When father was a boy—," advertising proof sheet, 1920, box 198, Ayer Collection.
87. "For Youngsters Over and Under Twelve," *The Kodak Salesman* 16 (April 1930), 16, 18, Ellis Collection.
88. "The Party is Over and the Presents are at Work," *The Kodak Salesman* 16 (June 1930), 4, 10–11, Ellis Collection.
89. Thomas Frank, *The Conquest of Cool: Business Culture, Counterculture, and the Rise of Hip Consumerism* (Chicago: University of Chicago Press, 1997), 118.
90. Ray Giles, "Making Youth the Bull's-Eye of the Advertising Target," *Printers' Ink* 120 (September 14, 1922), 57.
91. Giles, "Making Youth the Bull's-Eye," 58, 60.
92. "Talking to the Younger Generation," 529.
93. Grumbine, *Reaching Juvenile Markets*, 45. Noting children's fascination with streamlined design in toy airplanes and toy cars and the influence of youth in family decisions, General Motors' own Consumer Research department urged GM not to lag behind in adopting modern designs for its

own cars. See Roland Marchand, "Customer Research as Public Relations: General Motors in the 1930s," in Susan Strasser, Charles McGovern, and Matthias Judt, eds., *Getting and Spending: European and American Consumer Societies in the Twentieth Century* (Washington, D.C.: German Historical Institute, and New York: Cambridge University Press, 1998), 95.

94. Giles, "Making Youth the Bull's-Eye," 58.

95. Giles, "Making Youth the Bull's-Eye," 57, 60.

96. "Talking to the Younger Generation," 531.

97. George Lipsitz, "The Meaning of Memory: Family, Class, and Ethnicity in Early Network Television Programs," *Cultural Anthropology* 1 (November 1986): 355–387.

98. Grumbine, *Reaching Juvenile Markets*, ix; Bartlett, "A Mother Tells," 132. Grumbine attributed the success of children's advertising to children's "natural instincts"—"their enthusiasm, their loyalty, their responsiveness to anything that interests them." Bartlett described children as naturally "quick observers, rapid memorizers," and as perpetually "on the lookout for something of interest to them."

99. "Building the Sales Message," 518.

100. Advertisement, *Printers' Ink* 133 (December 12, 1925), 85.

101. Uthai Vincent Wilcox, "Arousing the Interest of Children," *Inland Printer* 77 (August 1926), 722.

102. "What the Coupon Brings," 517.

103. Peterson, *Magazines in the Twentieth Century*, 18, 27, 69–71.

104. For interesting discussions of such advertising boosterism in magazines aimed at adults, see Pamela Laird, *Advertising Progress: American Business and the Rise of Consumer Marketing* (Baltimore: Johns Hopkins University Press, 1998), 351–354; Garvey, *Adman in the Parlor*, 166–171.

105. "A Course in Advertising FOR BOYS AND YOUNG MEN," advertising proof sheet, 1917, box 197, series 1, Ayer Collection.

106. "Why We Carry Advertising: Advertising Talk No. 3," *American Boy* 18 (July 1917), 18.

107. "The Advertising in THE AMERICAN BOY: Advertising Talk No. 10," *American Boy* 19 (February 1918), 26.

108. "Why Read Advertisements?: Advertising Talk No. 4," *American Boy* 18 (August 1917), 24.

109. "Why Buy Advertised Goods?: Advertising Talk No. 5," *American Boy* 18 (September 1917), 24.

110. "Advertising Must Be Honest: Advertising Talk No. 8," *American Boy* 19 (December 1917), 26.

111. Jackson Lears, *Fables of Abundance: A Cultural History of Advertising in America* (New York: Basic Books, 1994), 201–204.

112. "Why Buy Advertised Goods?" 24.

113. "Trademarks: Advertising Talk No. 7," *American Boy* 19 (November 1917), 24.

114. "Advertising Reduces the Selling Price: Advertising Talk No. 6," *American Boy* 18 (October 1917), 24.

115. "Advertising Fundamentals," *Scholastic* 13 (October 6, 1928), 26.

116. Barton, Durstine, and Osborn, Inc., "The Value of Advertising to Business," *Scholastic* 13 (November 17, 1928), 25.

117. "In the Morning Mail," *American Boy* 30 (August 1929), 26.

118. "Well, of All Things!" *American Girl* 12 (October 1929), 7.

119. "Well, of All Things!" 7.

120. "In the Morning Mail," *American Boy* 30 (September 1929), 64.

121. "Show Windows of the World," *American Boy* 104 (March 1930), 65; "Our Advertising," *American Boy* 104 (April 1930), 69; "You and Co.," *American Boy* 105 (January 1931), 47; "When the Easiest Way is the Best Way . . . ," *American Boy* 110 (January 1936), 49; "Step a Little Closer, Folks!" *American Boy* 111 (January 1937), 33.

122. "You and Co.," 47. For more on Depression-era corporate public relations campaigns, see Roland Marchand, *Creating the Corporate Soul: The Rise of Public Relations and Corporate Imagery in American Big Business* (Berkeley: University of California Press, 1998), 202–248.

123. "Step a Little Closer, Folks!" 33.

124. For examples, see advertisements for Venus sanitary napkins in *American Girl* 20 (October 1937), 33, and *American Girl* 21 (December 1938), 37, and see advertisements for Hood gym shoes in *American Girl* 14 (October 1931), 40, and *American Boy* 111 (May 1937), 51.

125. Garvey, *Adman in the Parlor*, 55–69.

126. Advertisement, *Printers' Ink* 169 (October 25, 1934), 66.

127. Helen Ferris, "Will Every Subscriber Help Me Make Our Magazine Better by Answering These Questions?" *American Girl* 8 (June 1925), 45–46.

128. A. L. Townsend, "Creating Novelties in Sample for Children," *Printers' Ink* 118 (March 23, 1922), 81.

129. *News Letter* 45 (September 18, 1924), 6, Newsletter Collection, Main Series, box 2, JWT Archives.

130. "What the Coupon Brings," 518.

131. "Impressing the Junior Market," 49–50.

132. "Building the Sales Message," 518; "What the Coupon Brings," 518. A woman who specialized in writing children's stories earned over $50,000 preparing fairy-story–like ad copy in 1927.

133. "What the Coupon Brings," 517–518.

134. Hanford's Balsam produced *The Noah's Ark Primer* (New York: G. C. Hanford Manufacturing, 1913), Children box 4, Warshaw Collection.

135. Bartlett, "A Mother Tells," 132; Larrabee, "Selling Little Bill," 31.

136. "Nursery Rhymes to Sell Ice-Cream to Children," *Printer's Ink* 116 (August 18, 1921), 36.

137. *Money for the kiddies, Health for everyone*, Shredded Wheat Co., 1929, Cereal box 2, Warshaw Collection.

138. Garvey, *Adman in the Parlor*, 57.
139. Advertisement, *American Boy* 104 (November 1930), back cover.
140. "Talking to the Younger Generation," 533.
141. "Advertising Direct to School Children," *Printers' Ink Monthly* 14 (May 1927), 84.
142. Myron H. Watrous, "How Shredded Wheat Uses School Chart to Build Future Sales," *Printers' Ink Monthly* 6 (May 1923), 112.
143. John Allen Murphy, "How Advertisers Are Getting Schools to Use Their Literature," *Advertising and Selling* 8 (April 6, 1927), 23, 86–87.
144. "Jingle Book Helps Describe Varieties of Skookums," *Printers' Ink* 143 (May 31, 1928), 137–140; Henry Penn, "Reaching Parents Through a Contest for School Children," *Printers' Ink* 154 (February 12, 1931), 41–42.
145. For more on the "imperial rhetoric" of soap advertising campaigns, see Lears, *Fables of Abundance*, 163–164.
146. A. R. Hahn, "Procter & Gamble Lends Romance to the Wash Bowl," *Sales Management* 13 (November 16, 1927), 931–932.
147. Murphy, "How Advertisers Are Getting Schools," 88.
148. Murphy, "How Advertisers Are Getting Schools," 23.
149. Watrous, "How Shredded Wheat Uses School Chart," 113.
150. Murphy, "How Advertisers Are Getting Schools," 86, 88.
151. Grumbine, *Reaching Juvenile Markets*, 258–259.
152. Advertisement, *Printers' Ink* 141 (November 24, 1927), 183; advertisement, *Printers' Ink* 145 (November 8, 1928), 181.
153. Murphy, "How Advertisers Are Getting Schools," 86–88.
154. Advertisement, *Printers' Ink* 113 (October 7, 1920), 147; advertisement, *Printers' Ink* 117 (November 17, 1921), 79; advertisement, *Printers' Ink* 117 (November 24, 1921), 61.
155. Cream of Wheat proof sheet for ad placed in the *Normal Instructor*, December 13, 1927, microfilm reel #5, JWT Archives.
156. Murphy, "How Advertisers Are Getting Schools," 86–88.
157. Cream of Wheat proof sheet for ad placed in the *Normal Instructor*, October 24, 1927, microfilm reel #5, JWT Archives.
158. Joseph Hawes, *Children Between the Wars: American Childhood, 1920–1940*, (New York: Twayne, 1997), 66–67.
159. Advertisements promoting the Cream of Wheat school plan appeared in the *Saturday Evening Post, Woman's Home Companion, Ladies' Home Journal, Good Housekeeping, Pictorial Review, Delineator*, and *McCall's* from 1926 through 1928.
160. Cream of Wheat explicitly touted PTA cooperation in a May 1926 ad placed in *Good Housekeeping*: microfilm reel #5, JWT Archives.
161. Cream of Wheat proof sheet for newspaper ad, January 20, 1928, microfilm reel #5, JWT Archives.
162. Murphy, "How Advertisers Are Getting Schools," 23.
163. Dewey H. Palmer and Frederick J. Schlink, "Education and the Con-

sumer," *Annals of the American Academy of Political and Social Science* 173 (May 1934), 192.

164. Lynd and Lynd, *Middletown*, 196.

165. Palmer and Schlink, "Education and the Consumer," 188.

166. Larrabee, "Selling Little Bill," 156; "Advertising Direct to School Children," 84; Grumbine, *Reaching Juvenile Markets*, 261.

167. Murphy, "How Advertisers Are Getting Schools," 86. In the absence of opportunities to mold consumer habits through the behaviorist approach used on children, Lever Brother's adult campaign strategy, by contrast, made a virtue of Lifebuoy's odor, adopting the slogan "The Odor Tells You Why" to tout the soap's antiseptic properties. See "Partial List of J. Walter Thompson Company Clients," JWT Archives Information Center Records, box 1, Case Studies, Partial List of JWT Co. Clients, 1920s.

168. E. Evalyn Grumbine, "Age Groups of Children," *Printers' Ink Monthly* 30 (April 1935), 38.

169. C. B. Larrabee in forward to Grumbine, *Reaching Juvenile Markets*, xv.

170. Burdick, "Dodging Father's Objections," 77.

171. Howard Henderson, "Behind the Doorbell," *New Bulletin* 101 (August 1923), 5, Newsletter Collection, JWT Archives.

172. Henderson, "Behind the Doorbell," 6.

173. Kline, *Out of the Garden*, 179; Seiter, *Sold Separately*, 115–128.

174. Advertisement, *American Boy* 18 (December 1916), 25.

175. Advertisement, *American Girl* 13 (April 1930), 50.

176. Children's Advertising Review Unit, *Self-Regulatory Guidelines for Children's Advertising*, 4th ed. (Council of Better Business Bureaus, Inc., 1991), 4.

177. Advertisement, *American Boy* 17 (May 1916), 7.

178. Advertisement, *American Boy* 106 (December 1932), 30.

179. Advertisement, *Child Life* 8 (May 1929), 208.

180. Advertisement, *Child Life* 8 (June 1929), 272.

181. Stephen Kline contends that advertising guidelines that eschewed urging children to make requests to their parents proved "superfluous . . . because marketers had already realized children needed no instruction on the tactics of getting what they wanted"; see Kline, *Out of the Garden*, 184.

182. Griswold, *Fatherhood in America*, 135.

183. Advertisement, *Child Life* 8 (April 1929), 150; advertisement, *Child Life* 9 (April 1930), 144.

184. American Flyer Trains catalog, 1932, 2, Toys box 1, Warshaw Collection.

185. Advertisement, *American Boy* 22 (November 1920), 61.

186. "Talking to the Younger Generation," 531.

187. Advertisement, *American Boy* 16 (December 1914), 48; advertisement, *American Boy* 25 (May 1925), 31; advertisement, *American Boy* 29 (November 1927), 61.

188. For fuller discussion of new ideals of fatherhood, see Griswold, *Fatherhood in America*, 88–118.

189. Advertisement, *American Boy* 23 (November 1921), 40.

190. American Flyer Trains catalog, 1933, back cover, Toys box 1, Warshaw Collection.

191. Lionel Electric Trains catalog, 1932, 3, Toys box 2, Warshaw Collection.

192. "Advertise Children's Vehicles in Child Life," advertising proof sheet, 1922, box 457, series 1, Ayer Collection.

193. *Child Life* advertising proof sheet, April 26, 1932, placed in *Toy World*, microfilm reel #26, JWT Archives.

194. Robert Ramsey, "Planning Direct Advertising to Appeal to Children and Through Them to Their Parents," *The Inland Printer* 71 (June 1923), 385.

195. Bruns, "Changing Appeal from Parent to Child," 71.

196. Ellen Seiter, "Children's Desires/Mother's Dilemmas: The Social Contexts of Consumption," in *Children's Culture Reader*, 301–308; Marchand, *Advertising the American Dream: Making Way for Modernity, 1920–1940* (Berkeley: University of California Press, 1985), 172; Ruth Schwartz Cowan, "The 'Industrial Revolution' in the Home: Household Technology and Social Change in the 20th Century," *Technology and Culture* 17 (1976): 1–23.

197. Advertisement, *American Girl* 10 (June 1927), 41.

198. B. J. Duncan, "Capturing the Home Citadel Through the Nursery," *Printer's Ink Monthly* 25 (October 1932), 36; "Stories for the Children Win Good Will," *Gas Age* 65 (March 29, 1930), 452; "Stories for Children as Good-Will Copy," *Printer's Ink* 149 (December 19, 1929), 80.

2. FROM THRIFT EDUCATION TO CONSUMER TRAINING

1.   David Nasaw, *Children of the City: At Work and at Play* (Garden City, N.Y.: Anchor, 1985), 115–118.

2.   William Leach, "Child World in the Promised Land," in James Gilbert et al., eds., *The Mythmaking Frame of Mind: Social Imagination and American Culture* (Belmont, Calif: Wadsworth, 1993), 209–238; William Leach, *Land of Desire: Merchants, Power, and the Rise of a New American Culture* (New York: Pantheon, 1993); Miriam Formanek-Brunell, *Made to Play House: Dolls and the Commercialization of American Girlhood, 1830–1930* (New Haven: Yale University Press, 1993).

3.   Carolyn Benedict Burrell, "The Child and Its World," *Harper's Bazaar* 33 (November 3, 1900), 1721.

4.   "Money Sense in Children," *Child-Study Monthly* 5 (April 1900), 473.

5.   "Children's Sense of Money," *Child-Study Monthly* 3 (May 1897), 58.

6.   Sophia Yarnall, "Between Princes and Paupers," *Hygeia* 11 (August 1933), 718–721.

7.   For an interesting and insightful discussion of the allowance debate, see Viviana Zelizer, *Pricing the Priceless Child: The Changing Social Value of Children* (New York: Basic, 1985), 103–110.

8.   For an overview of the history of school banking, see Agnes Martin, "A

School for Thrift," *The School Bank* 6 (May 1937), 1–7, box 46, PSFS Archives.

9.   David M. Tucker, *The Decline of Thrift in America: Our Cultural Shift from Saving to Spending* (New York: Praeger, 1991), 67.

10. Martin, "A School for Thrift," 5; Mary B. Reeves, "Service Departments as Advertising Mediums," address before the Eastern District Conference Savings Bank Division, American Bankers Association, Boston, Mass., March 13, 1925, box 45, PSFS Archives.

11. E. Evalyn Grumbine, *Reaching Juvenile Markets: How to Advertise, Sell, and Merchandise Through Boys and Girls* (New York: McGraw-Hill, 1938), 363.

12. David Nasaw, *Schooled to Order: A Social History of Schooling in the United States* (New York: Oxford University Press, 1979), 100; Joel Spring, *Education and the Rise of the Corporate State* (Boston: Beacon, 1972); Marvin Lazerson, *Origins of the Urban School: Public Education in Massachusetts, 1870–1915* (Cambridge: Harvard University Press, 1971); Paul Violas, *The Training of the Urban Working Class: A History of Twentieth Century American Education* (Chicago: Rand McNally, 1978). For an excellent review of this literature, see Ronald D. Cohen, "Child-Saving and Progressivism, 1885–1915," in Joseph M. Hawes and N. Ray Hiner, eds., *American Childhood: A Research Guide and Historical Handbook* (Westport, Conn.: Greenwood, 1985), 283–285.

13. Andrew Price, "Teaching Thrift as a Branch of Public Instruction," *Education* 37 (October 1916), 117, 120; Sara Louisa Oberholtzer, "School Savings Banks," *Annals of the American Academy of Political and Social Science* 3 (July 1892), 22, 28; J. H. Thiry, "School Savings Banks in the United States," *Proceedings of the International Congress of Education of the World's Columbian Exposition, Chicago, July 25–28, 1893* (New York: National Education Association of the United States, 1895), 286–287; "Penny Savings Banks in Schools," *Child-Study Monthly* 4 (May 1898), 54–55. The phrase "alarming increase" comes from Thiry.

14. Cohen, "Child-Saving and Progressivism," 273–309; Lawrence Cremin, *The Transformation of the School: Progressivism in American Education, 1876–1957* (New York: Knopf, 1961), 85–89; Lary May, *Screening Out the Past: The Birth of Mass Culture and the Motion Picture Industry* (Chicago: University of Chicago Press, 1980); Richard Hofstadter, *The Age of Reform: From Bryan to F.D.R.* (New York: Vintage, 1955).

15. Waldon Fawcett, "A School Savings Bank," *St. Nicholas* 30 (September 1903), 1020.

16. Oberholtzer, "School Savings Banks," 24; Tucker, *Decline of Thrift*, 66–67.

17. Letter from manager of Philadelphia Savings Fund Society Industrial and School Department to Fred Staker, March 9, 1937, Requests for School Savings Information, 1937–1959 file folder, box 44, PSFS Archive.

18. Oberholtzer, "School Savings Banks," 23–24.

19. Selma Heller, interview by author, September 8, 2001; Bernice Davidow, interview by author, September 8, 2001.

20. "The School-Bank in Action," *Literary Digest* 51 (October 30, 1915), 970.

21. Fawcett, "A School Savings Bank," 1021.

22. Lendol Calder, *Financing the American Dream: A Cultural History of Consumer Credit* (Princeton: Princeton University Press, 1999), 74–108.

23. Oberholtzer, "School Savings Banks," 24.

24. Joseph Heller, interview by author, September 9, 2001.

25. Agnes Bailey Ormsbee, "How Children Spend Their Money," *Harper's Bazaar* 37 (July 1903), 682.

26. Jane Addams, *The Spirit of Youth and the City Streets* (New York: Macmillan, 1909), 5–6.

27. David Nasaw, "Children and Commercial Culture: Moving Pictures in the Early Twentieth Century," in Elliott West and Paula Petrik, eds., *Small Worlds: Children and Adolescents in America, 1850–1950* (Lawrence, Kans.: University Press of Kansas, 1992), 15, 17.

28. Viviana Zelizer, *The Social Meaning of Money: Pin Money, Paychecks, Poor Relief, and Other Currencies* (New York: Basic, 1994), 140.

29. "To Save Pennies," *Child-Study Monthly* 4 (December 1898), 324–325; "School Children's Savings Banks," *Child-Study Monthly* 4 (April 1899), 580; Price, "Teaching Thrift," 119–120.

30. Mrs. C. S. Morrison, attachment to letter to the Board of Directors of the American Bankers Association, June 1, 1927, 5, 8, 11, Thrift Encouragement, 1923–1929 file, Coolidge Papers.

31. Robert E. Scott, "The School Savings Bank," *Elementary School Journal* 27 (June 1927), 777. Approximately 87 percent answered affirmatively that earning money for bank deposits had helped "solve [their child's] proper use of leisure time." Another 85 percent concurred that their children had "refrained voluntarily from spending money for candy" to save for their school bank accounts. Somewhat fewer, 75 percent, noticed "improvement in [their] child's health from eating less candy."

32. "Boy Scouts as a Market," *Printers' Ink* 87 (June 4, 1914), 74.

33. See, for example, "Friendly Talks with the Editor," *American Boy* 18 (May 1917), 3; "Friendly Talks with the Editor," *American Boy* 18 (July 1917), 3; "Friendly Talks with the Editor," *American Boy* 22 (August 1921), 3; "A Thrift Machine," *American Girl* 5 (June 1922), 24.

34. Price, "Teaching Thrift," 120.

35. Helen B. Seymour, "Money Matters with Young People," *Outlook* 48 (September 23, 1893), 553.

36. "Thrift Education for Playgrounds," ca. 1920s. Playground narrations, plays, and scripts file folder, box 45, PSFS Archive.

37. "How Money Grows," ca. 1920s. Playground narrations, plays, and scripts file folder, box 45, PSFS Archive.

38. "The Land of Desire," ca. 1920s. Playground narrations, plays, and scripts file folder, box 45, PSFS Archive.

39. Mary B. Reeves, "Women at the World Court of Economy," 10–11, school savings reference material file folder, box 45, PSFS Archive.

40. Morrison, letter to American Bankers Association, 3.

41. Price, "Teaching Thrift," 118–119; "The School-Bank in Action," 967; Oberholtzer, "School Savings Banks," 25.

42. Price, "Teaching Thrift," 119.

43. Dorothy W. Harrington, "Boy Bankers Teach Thrift," *Outlook* 36 (February 13, 1924), 283–285.

44. Charity workers promoted postal savings banks in an effort to counter such immigrant savings habits. See Zelizer, *Social Meaning of Money*, 140–141.

45. A. E. Hotchner, *King of the Hill* (New York: Harper and Row, 1972), 85–86.

46. This point suggests how school banking, like many other reforms, ultimately reveals more about the reformers than the objects of reform. For some examples of scholarship that challenges the social control thesis, see Linda Gordon, *Heroes of Their Own Lives: The Politics and History of Family Violence, Boston, 1880–1960* (New York: Viking Penguin, 1988); Roy Rosenzweig, *Eight Hours for What We Will: Workers and Leisure in an Industrial City, 1870–1920* (New York: Cambridge University Press, 1983).

47. Tucker, *Decline of Thrift*, 108–111; Daniel Horowitz, *The Morality of Spending: Attitudes Toward the Consumer Society in America, 1875–1940* (Baltimore: Johns Hopkins University Press, 1985; Chicago: Ivan R. Dee, Publisher, 1992), 116.

48. Morrison, letter to American Bankers Association, 6.

49. Mary B. Reeves, "Service Departments as Advertising Mediums," address before the Eastern District Conference Savings Bank Division, American Bankers Association, Boston, Mass., March 13, 1925, 1–6, box 45, PSFS Archive.

50. David Beito, *From Mutual Aid to the Welfare State: Fraternal Societies and Social Services, 1890–1967* (Chapel Hill: University of North Carolina Press, 2000); Calder, *Financing the American Dream*, chapter 1.

51. "School Savings and Schools at War," forum sponsored by the savings division of the American Bankers Association, the Waldorf-Astoria, New York, N.Y., September 13, 1943, miscellaneous pamphlets file folder, box 46, PSFS Archive.

52. Leo Day Woodworth, "New Data on School Saving," *Journal of National Education* 12 (June 1923), 234; "Reports: School Savings Banking in the United States," *School and Society* 24 (October 16, 1926), 493.

53. H. R. Daniel, "School Savings-Bank Systems," National Conference on Thrift Education, June 27–28, 1924 (Washington, D.C.: National Education Association, Committee on Thrift Education, 1924), Coolidge Papers.

54. *School Savings Bank Monitor* 4 (March 1924), Thrift Encouragement, 1923–1929 file, Coolidge Papers.

55. Tucker, *Decline of Thrift*, 88–89, quote on page 88; Arvie Eldred, "Conservation of Resources—School Savings Banks and Thrift Education," *Addresses and Proceedings* 56 (New York: National Education Association of the United States, 1918), 644–649; Jonathan Cox and Paul W. Terry, "The Colonial Hill School Savings Banks Plan," *Elementary School Journal* 17 (June 1917), 741.

56. Tucker, *Decline of Thrift*, 91, 93–94.

57. Russell Curtis Grimshaw, "Is the School Bank Worth While?" *Educational Review* 73 (March 1927), 161–167.

58. Photograph, 1925, box 16, Pictorial Collection, PSFS Archive.

59. Helen Louise Johnson, "The Training of Children in the Spending of Money," *Journal of Home Economics* 7 (April 1915), 205.

60. For more on G. Stanley Hall, see Dorothy Ross, *G. Stanley Hall: The Psychologist as Prophet* (Chicago: University of Chicago Press, 1972); Joseph Kett, *Rites of Passage: Adolescence in America, 1790 to the Present* (New York: Basic Books, 1977); Julia Grant, *Raising Baby by the Book: The Education of American Mothers* (New Haven: Yale University Press, 1998), 36–37.

61. Lydia Maria Child, "Management During the Teens," *The Mother's Book*, 1831, in Carolyn L. Karcher, ed., *A Lydia Maria Child Reader* (Durham: Duke University Press, 1997), 113–114.

62. Zelizer, *Pricing the Priceless Child*, 104–105, 108.

63. Paula Fass, *The Damned and the Beautiful: American Youth in the 1920s* (New York: Oxford University Press, 1977), 102–103.

64. Burrell, "The Child and Its World," 1721.

65. For more on behaviorism and the rationalist paradigm, see Grant, *Raising Baby by the Book*, 41–45, 139–145. For discussions of scientific motherhood, see Steven Mintz and Susan Kellogg, *Domestic Revolutions: A Social History of American Family Life* (New York: Free Press, 1982), 121–122; Susan Strasser, *Never Done: A History of American Housework* (New York: Pantheon, 1982), 234–240; Robert Griswold, *Fatherhood in America: A History* (New York: Basic Books, 1993), 32–33.

66. Ormsbee, "How Children Spend Their Money," 682.

67. Nasaw, *Children of the City*, 130–131.

68. Kathy Peiss, *Cheap Amusements: Working Women and Leisure in Turn-of-the-Century New York* (Philadelphia: Temple University Press, 1986), 68; Elizabeth Ewen, "City Lights: Immigrant Women and the Rise of the Movies," *Signs* 5 (1980), 56; Nasaw, *Children of the City*, 133.

69. Angelo Patri, "Your Child's Allowance: Spending-Money as an Aid to Character-Building," *The Delineator* 102 (January 1923), 3.

70. Griswold, *Fatherhood in America*, 135–138.

71. For more on Patri, see Griswold, *Fatherhood in America*, 108–115, 119–120,

122–123; Joseph Hawes, *Children Between the Wars: American Childhood, 1920–1940* (New York: Twayne, 1997), 81–82.

72. Patri, "Your Child's Allowance," 3. Allowance advocates typically advised giving children a small sum as soon as they learned that "a penny has buying power" and gradually increasing the amount with the child's age and judgment to cover more and more personal necessities from clothes to amusements. See Frances Frisbee O'Donnell, "Every Child Needs an Allowance," *Parents' Magazine* 5 (March 1930), 19.

73. Sidonie Matsner Gruenberg, "Children and Money," *Federation of Child Study Bulletin* 1 (January 1924), 3.

74. Elizabeth J. Reisner, "When Money Makes a Difference," *Parents' Magazine* 12 (January 1937), 62; Patri, "Your Child's Allowance," 3; Mrs. L. M. P., "The Family's Money: Are You Teaching Your Children How to Spend?" *American Magazine* 95 (January 1923), 144; The Child Study Association of America, eds., *Parents Questions* (New York: Harper and Brothers Publishers, 1936), 245–246.

75. Gruenberg, "Children and Money," 3.

76. Sidonie Matsner Gruenberg, "Money: Training Children in Its Use," *Children: The Magazine for Parents* 2 (March 1927), 10.

77. Grant, *Raising Baby by the Book*, 43; Cremin, *Transformation of the School*, 101–105, 115–126.

78. Mabel Rollins, "Learning to Spend and Save," *Parents' Magazine* 10 (December 1935), 26.

79. Benjamin C. Gruenberg and Sidonie Matsner Gruenberg, "Teaching Children the Use of Money," *Parents' Magazine* 6 (December 1931), 48, 50.

80. Grant, *Raising Baby by the Book*, 44.

81. Gruenberg, "Money," 10. Saving up for purchases also encouraged children to take better care of the playthings they purchased for themselves. As one mother told *Parents' Magazine*, toys in their household didn't get lost or broken as often once her two little girls started buying them out of their own allowance. See "Everyday Problems and How Parents Meet Them," *Parents' Magazine* 4 (October 1929), 28.

82. Advertisement, *American Boy* 17 (October 1916), 41. Self-registering toy banks that operated on this principle were quite common in the 1910s and 1920s. See American Wholesale Corporation catalog, Toys box 1, Warshaw Collection; advertisement, *Child Life* 7 (December 1928), 729.

83. E. Kimber, "Children's Money Sense," *Child-Study Monthly* 3 (June–July 1897), 102.

84. "The Thompson Twins Talk It Over," *Children: The Magazine for Parents* 1 (November 1926), 34.

85. Benjamin C. Gruenberg, "Pennies from Heaven," *Child Study* 14 (March 1937), 165.

86. Scott, "School Savings Bank," 774–776; "How Children Earn Money," *Journal of Home Economics* 26 (January 1934), 28–29.

87. Gruenberg, "Money," 11.
88. Gruenberg, "Money," 9, 11; O'Donnell, "Every Child Needs an Allowance," 40; Mary Robbins, "Learning to Spend and Save," *Parents' Magazine* 10 (December 1935), 26, 72.
89. Robbins, "Learning to Spend and Save," 26, 72.
90. Gruenberg, "Children and Money," 3.
91. For an interesting discussion of this issue, see Zelizer, *Pricing the Priceless Child*, 106–109.
92. See particularly Christopher Lasch, *Haven in a Heartless World: The Family Besieged* (New York: Basic Books, 1977), xvii. For more on the primacy of pecuniary values in twentieth-century American culture, see Leach, *Land of Desire*.
93. Gruenberg, "Money," 9.
94. For more on debates over child labor, see Zelizer, *Pricing the Priceless Child* and Viviana Zelizer, "From Useful to Useless: Moral Conflict over Child Labor," in Henry Jenkins, ed., *The Children's Culture Reader* (New York: New York University Press, 1998), 89–90.
95. Thomas D. Eliot, "Money and the Child's Own Standard of Living," *Journal of Home Economics* 24 (January 1932), 4; Gruenberg, "Pennies from Heaven," 165.
96. Gruenberg, "Pennies from Heaven," 165.
97. Gruenberg, "Children and Money," 3.
98. Eliot, "Money and the Child's Own Standard of Living," 4.
99. Robert S. Lynd and Helen Merrell Lynd, *Middletown: A Study in American Culture* (New York: Harcourt, Brace, and World, Inc., 1929), 141. According to the Lynds, 37 percent of high school boys and 29 percent of girls indicated that "spending money" was a source of family conflict.
100. Earl H. Bell, "The Family: Age Group Conflict and Our Changing Culture," *Social Forces* 12 (December 1933), 238–239.
101. Susan Porter Benson, "Gender, Generation, and Consumption in the United States: Working-Class Families in the Interwar Period," in Susan Strasser, Charles McGovern, and Matthias Jundt, eds., *Getting and Spending: European and American Consumer Societies in the Twentieth Century* (Washington, D.C.: German Historical Institute; New York: Cambridge University Press, 1998), 223–240.
102. Bell, "Age Group Conflict and Our Changing Culture," 243.
103. Child Study Association, *Parents Questions*, 245; Sidonie Matsner Gruenberg, "The Child's Own Money," *Child Study* 9 (May 1932), 254; Gruenberg, "Children and Money," 2; Eliot, "Money and the Child's Own Standard of Living," 4.
104. "Learning About Money," *Survey* 63 (October 15, 1929), 88.
105. Gruenberg, "Money," 11; Gruenberg, "The Child's Own Money," 258.
106. White House Conference on Child Health and Protection, *The Adolescent in the Family* (New York: D. Appleton-Century Company, 1934), 229, 230,

279, 293. The conference's study of 1,736 urban white boys and girls found that only 5 percent of poorly adjusted boys and 8 percent of poorly adjusted girls received allowances, while a mere 11 percent of boys with weak morals and 5 percent of girls with weak morals did so. Another conference study of adolescent boys in Chicago found that predelinquent boys were more likely to earn their spending money and less likely to receive allowances than nondelinquent middle-class boys. Although the study attributed delinquent tendencies to work that brought boys into contact with undesirable elements, the researchers also intimated that allowances would go a long way toward reducing delinquency.

107. Mabel Rollins, "Sharing the Budget with the Children," *Good Housekeeping* 82 (March 1926), 216–217.

108. Eva Morse, "Family Conferences," in *Parents' Magazine*, eds., *The Mother's Encyclopedia* (New York: Reynal and Hitchcock, 1934), 269–276.

109. Griswold, *Fatherhood in America*, 99; Benjamin R. Andrews, "Family Finances," *Child Study* 9 (May 1932), 261–262.

110. Benjamin R. Andrews, "Every Family Needs a Budget," *Parents' Magazine* 6 (March 1931), 20.

111. Chase Going Woodhouse, "How to Live Happily on Your Income," *Children: The Magazine for Parents* 4 (January 1929), 44.

112. For examples of such advocacy in the mid-1920s, see Rollins, "Sharing the Budget," 216; Gruenberg, "Children and Money," 3.

113. Winifred Wandersee, "Families Face the Great Depression," in Joseph Hawes and Elizabeth Nybakken, eds., *American Families: A Research Guide and Historical Handbook* (New York: Greenwood, 1991), 129.

114. O'Donnell, "Every Child Needs an Allowance," 40; Motier Harris Fisher, "Are Allowances Really Practical?" *Parents' Magazine* 12 (April 1937), 88.

115. Clare Keith, as told to Sara J. Wardel, "Children Never Steal," *Parents' Magazine* 10 (January 1935), 46.

116. Marion Canby Dodd, "A Girl and Her Money," *Woman's Home Companion* 62 (March 1935), 15.

117. For a discussion of democratic social engineering, see William Graebner, *The Engineering of Consent: Democracy and Authority in Twentieth-Century America* (Madison: University of Wisconsin Press, 1987).

118. For more on Dr. Spock, democratic social engineering, and the interwar intellectual influences on his childrearing theories, see Graebner, *Engineering of Consent*, chapter 6; William Graebner, "The Unstable World of Benjamin Spock: Social Engineering in a Democratic Culture, 1917–1950," *Journal of American History* 67 (December 1980): 612–629.

119. Woodhouse, "How to Live Happily," 44. The Bureau of Home Economics was part of the U.S. Department of Agriculture.

120. White House Conference on Child Health and Protection, *The Young Child in the Home: A Survey of Three Thousand American Families* (New York: D. Appleton-Century Company, 1936), 207. According to the study,

23 percent of children from class III families (major clerical workers, skilled mechanics, and retail businessmen) received allowances, compared to 18 percent of farm children and 8 percent of children whose fathers worked as day laborers. An 1896 survey of 2,000 California boys and girls found that 7 percent of girls and 10 percent of boys received allowances. See David Macleod, *The Age of the Child: Children in America, 1890–1920* (New York: Twayne, 1998), 114.

Unfortunately, the available statistics on children's allowances are sometimes contradictory. *Scholastic*'s survey of 4,091 American high school students found that roughly one-third received allowances. See "Results of Scholastic Student Opinion Poll—3," *Scholastic* 34 (April 15, 1939), 30; "Brother Can You Spare the Time?" *Scholastic* 34 (April 15, 1939), 31. A much smaller *Scholastic* survey of 259 boys, published in February 1930, yielded more dramatic results, with 56 percent receiving allowances that averaged $9.43 a month—figures undoubtedly skewed by the small sample size, the gender of the allowance recipients, and the exuberance of the stock market in the late 1920s. See Ray Giles, "Catching Up with the Billion Dollar High School Market," *Advertising & Selling* 14 (February 19, 1930), 56. A 1931 survey of 634 pupils in Rochester, New York, and Brookline, Massachusetts, reported that 57 percent had allowances, suggesting that the results from *Scholastic*'s earlier survey may not be atypical for middle-class children. See White House Conference on Child Health and Protection, *The Home and the Child* (New York: The Century Co., 1931), 132. In the mid-1920s, the Lynds found that 17 percent of Muncie boys and 21 percent of Muncie girls received allowances—percentages that may be lower owing to aggregated data. See Lynd and Lynd, *Middletown*, 142.

121. George Lawton, "The Kind of Parent I Hope to Be: Results of the Prize Contest in 'Problems of Living,'" *Scholastic* 35 (November 20, 1939), 3–4.

122. "Adolescents Want Freedom," in *The Mother's Encyclopedia*, 38–42. For more on the importance of psychological adjustment in the 1930s, an era Warren Susman has dubbed "the age of Alfred Adler," see Warren Susman, "Culture and Commitment," in *Culture as History: The Transformation of American Society in the Twentieth Century* (New York: Pantheon, 1984), 200–201.

123. See, for example, Gay Head, "Boy Dates Girl: Bagby and Son," *Scholastic* 35 (October 2, 1939), 33; Gay Head, "Boy Dates Girl: One Girl's Family," *Scholastic* 37 (November 25, 1940), 39–40; Gay Head, "Boy Dates Girl: A Bag of Tricks," *Scholastic* 37 (December 2, 1940), 32; Gay Head, "Boy Dates Girl: A New Leaf," *Scholastic* 37 (January 8, 1940), 36–37.

124. Lynd and Lynd, *Middletown*, 142 n. 20.

125. Frank B. Gilbreth Jr. and Ernestine Gilbreth Carey, *Cheaper by the Dozen* (New York: Thomas Y. Crowell Company, 1948), 37–42.

126. Gruenberg, "The Child's Own Money," 257.

127. Olive M. Jones, "Wise Spending as a Teacher Sees It," National Conference on Thrift Education, June 27–28, 1924, 51–55, Coolidge Papers; "Learning About Money," *Survey* 63 (October 15, 1929), 88; "Using Money as a School Experience," *Child Study* 9 (May 1932), 269.

128. Henry Ford, quoted in "Do School Banks Teach Thrift?" *Scholastic* 18 (March 7, 1931), 25; Tucker, *Decline of Thrift*, 96–97.

129. "Using Money as a School Experience," 269.

130. Kimber, "Children's Money Sense," 102.

131. Joseph Heller, interview by author, September 9, 2001.

132. Scott, "School Savings Bank," 781, 782, 785.

133. Grumbine, *Reaching Juvenile Markets*, 365–366, 371, 373.

134. Gruenberg, "Money," 10.

135. Chester T. Crowell, "Bank Day," *American Mercury* 20 (May 1930), 90.

136. White House Conference, *The Home and the Child*, 135.

137. Scott, "School Savings Bank," 778. The survey reported that 98 percent of parents approved of school banks.

138. Scott, "School Savings Bank," 779, 780.

139. Crowell, "Bank Day," 93.

140. Hotchner, *King of the Hill*, 86. In a noble gesture Superintendent Henry J. Gerling of St. Louis, where Hotchner resided, pledged $25,000 of his own money to launch a campaign to reimburse school children who suffered losses. See E. A. Krug, *The American High School* (Madison: University of Wisconsin Press, 1972), 203.

141. Grumbine, *Reaching Juvenile Markets*, 372.

142. *The School Bank* 4 (Christmas 1934), 2, box 46, PSFS Archive.

143. Tucker, *Decline of Thrift*, 123.

144. Robert C. Moore, quoted in Krug, *American High School*, 205.

145. Letter from Edward Merchant, Philadelphia Board of Public Education, March 7, 1932, official correspondence re: procedures, 1932–1946 file folder, box 44, PSFS Archive; letter from Pennsylvania State Secretary of Banking to Hon. James Rule, State Superintendent of Public Instruction, March 16, 1932, official correspondence re: procedures, 1932–1946 file folder, box 44, PSFS Archive.

146. Tucker, *Decline of Thrift*, 123–25; Stuart Chase, "The Story of Toad Lane," *Scholastic* 26 (February 9, 1935), 15, 20; E. J. Lever, "Consumer Clubs in America," *Scholastic* 26 (February 9, 1935), 17. For more on Stuart Chase and the consumer movement, see Jackson Lears, *Fables of Abundance: A Cultural History of Advertising in America* (New York: Basic Books, 1994), 239–242; Charles McGovern, "Consumption and Citizenship in the United States," in *Getting and Spending*, 50–54. Ruth Brindze wrote a monthly "Getting Your Money's Worth" column for *Scholastic* that began October 9, 1939.

147. "Learning How to Consume: An Editorial," *Scholastic* 26 (February 9, 1935), 1.

148. Lawrence Levine, "American Culture and the Great Depression," in *The Unpredictable Past: Explorations in American Cultural History* (New York: Oxford University Press, 1993), 221–223; Robert S. Lynd and Helen Merrell Lynd, *Middletown in Transition: A Study in Cultural Conflict* (New York: Harcourt, Brace, and World, Inc., 1937), 478–479.

149. Hotchner, *King of the Hill*, 86.

150. Quoted in Sidonie Matsner Gruenberg and Benjamin C. Gruenberg, *Parents, Children, and Money: Learning to Spend, Save, and Earn* (New York: Viking Press, 1933), 93–94.

151. Quoted in Gruenberg and Gruenberg, *Parents, Children, and Money*, 94.

152. Gruenberg and Gruenberg, *Parents, Children, and Money*, 95.

153. For a discussion of how various intellectuals responded to the Depression, see Horowitz, *Morality of Spending*, 153–155, 158–165.

154. Patri, "Your Child's Allowance," 3.

155. Gruenberg and Gruenberg, "Teaching Children the Use of Money," 50; Benjamin C. Gruenberg and Sidonie Matsner Gruenberg, "The Parent Faces a New World," *Parents' Magazine* 6 (October 1931), 23.

156. Tucker, *Decline of Thrift*, 116–177.

157. Gruenberg, "Pennies from Heaven," 165.

158. Eliot, "Money and the Child's Own Standard of Living," 3.

159. Mike Featherstone, "The Body in Consumer Culture," *Theory, Culture, and Society* 1 (September 1982): 18. Featherstone uses the term "calculating hedonism" to describe the tensions between hedonism and discipline in consumer culture's promotion of body maintenance regimes.

160. For a fuller exposition of Simon Patten's ideas, see Lears, *Fables of Abundance*, 113–177; Leach, *Land of Desire*, 231–244.

161. Calder, *Financing the American Dream*, quoted at 252, 203–204, 238–261.

162. For more on classical liberal views of consumption, see Joyce Appleby, "Ideology and Theory: The Tension Between Political and Economic Liberalism in Seventeenth-Century England," *American Historical Review* 81 (June 1976): 499–515.

163. Lewis Edwin Theiss, "Children, Too, Should Learn to Prepare for a Rainy Day," *American Home* 16 (July 1936), 47.

164. "Parents Questions and Discussion," *Child Study* 14 (March 1937), 175.

165. Quoted in Levine, "American Culture and the Great Depression," 223.

166. For an informative discussion of economists' and consumer advocates' theories of underconsumption and their impact on policymaking during the Depression, see Meg Jacobs, "The Politics of Purchasing Power: Political Economy, Consumption Politics, and State-Building, 1909–1959" (Ph.D. diss., University of Virginia, 1998), chapters 2–3.

167. For more on the impact of Keynes and the arguments of underconsumptionists, see Alan Brinkley, "The New Deal and the Idea of the State," in Steven Fraser and Gary Gerstle, eds., *The Rise and Fall of the New Deal Order, 1930–1980* (Princeton: Princeton University Press, 1989), 85–121.

168. Advertisement, *Boy's Life* 22 (February 1932), 4.

169. Lillian Gilbreth, "The Young Budgeter," *American Girl* 16 (January 1933), 11.

170. Lynd and Lynd, *Middletown in Transition*, 478.

171. Letter from I. W. Roberts to Agnes Martin, March 17, 1937, "The School Bank" general correspondence file folder, box 47, PSFS Archive.

172. Bank Lady column, *The School Bank* 1 (March 1932), 4, box 46, PSFS Archive.

173. PSFS's high school newspaper ads and magazine editorials lauded self-denial and accumulation but did not advise students how to become wise spenders. See, for example, *The School Bank* 3 (February 1934), 4, box 46, PSFS Archive; "This Little Penny Joined the School Bank and Grew and Grew and G-R-E-W," high school newspaper ad, ca. 1936–1937, box 15, Pictorial Collection, PSFS Archive.

174. For more on the growing interest in children's mental hygiene and psychological adjustment, see Grant, *Raising Baby by the Book*, 10, 168–169. For a discussion of the interest in personality formation, see Mintz and Kellogg, *Domestic Revolutions*, 123.

175. Fisher, "Are Allowances Really Practical?" 85–86.

176. Martha Wolfenstein, "Fun Morality: An Analysis of Recent American Child-Training Literature," in Margaret Mead and Martha Wolfenstein, eds., *Childhood in Contemporary Cultures* (Chicago: University of Chicago Press, 1955), 168–178.

177. Helen G. West, "Preschool Budgets," *Better Homes and Gardens* 17 (May 1939), 91.

178. For fuller discussions of the compatibility of twentieth-century Protestantism with a consumerist outlook, see Leach, *Land of Desire*; T. J. Jackson Lears, "From Self-Denial to Self-Realization: Advertising and the Therapeutic Roots of the Consumer Culture, 1880–1930," in Richard Wightman Fox and T. J. Jackson Lears, eds., *The Culture of Consumption: Critical Essays in American History, 1880–1980* (New York: Pantheon, 1983), 1–38; and Susan Curtis, *A Consuming Faith: The Social Gospel and Modern American Culture* (Baltimore: Johns Hopkins University Press, 1991).

179. "Parents Questions and Discussion," *Child Study* 9 (May 1932), 263.

180. Keith, "Children Never Steal," 21.

181. Glen Elder, *Children of the Depression: Social Change in Life Experience* (Chicago: University of Chicago Press, 1974).

182. Hawes, *Children Between the Wars*, 127.

3. HEROES OF THE NEW CONSUMER AGE

1. Advertisement, *Printers' Ink* 141 (December 1, 1927), 183.

2. Advertisement, *Printers' Ink* 76 (September 26, 1911), 5.

3. John Sekora, *Luxury: The Concept in Western Thought* (Baltimore: The Johns Hopkins University Press, 1977); Victoria de Grazia, *The Sex of*

Things: Gender and Consumption in Historical Perspective (Berkeley: University of California Press, 1996), 1–8, 13–15; Margaret Finnegan, *Selling Suffrage: Consumer Culture and Votes for Women* (New York: Columbia University Press, 1999), 10–11, 32–33; Elaine Abelson, *When Ladies Go A-Thieving: Middle-Class Shoplifters in the Victorian Department Store* (New York: Oxford University Press, 1989).

4. For more on admen's ambivalence toward their predominantly female audience, see Roland Marchand, *Advertising the American Dream: Making Way for Modernity, 1920–1940* (Berkeley: University of California Press, 1985), 66–72, 84–87; Ellen Gruber Garvey, *The Adman in the Parlor: Magazines and the Gendering of Consumer Culture, 1880s to 1910s* (New York: Oxford University Press, 1996), 175–183; Patricia Johnston, *Real Fantasies: Edward Steichen's Advertising Photography* (Berkeley: University of California Press, 1997), 234–235. For interpretations that stress advertisers' recognition of women's consumer sovereignty, see Regina Lee Blaszczyk, *Imagining Consumers: Design and Innovation from Wedgwood to Corning* (Baltimore: The Johns Hopkins University Press, 2000); Regina Lee Blaszczyk, "Cinderella Stories: The Glass of Fashion and the Gendered Marketplace," in Roger Horowitz and Arwen Mohun, eds., *His and Hers: Gender, Consumption, and Technology* (Charlottesville: University Press of Virginia, 1998), 139–164; James Williams, "Getting Housewives the Electric Message: Gender and Energy Marketing in the Early Twentieth Century," in Horowitz and Mohun, eds., *His and Hers*, 95–114. Women copywriters worked mostly on women's product accounts and were unlikely to handle boy market accounts.

5. Mark A. Swienicki, "Consuming Brotherhood: Men's Culture, Style, and Recreation as Consumer Culture, 1880–1930," *Journal of Social History* 31 (Summer 1998): 773–808; Blaszczyk, *Imagining Consumers*, 16–18, 20, 31–32, 46–47, 49, 271. Entertainment entrepreneurs in the first two decades of the early twentieth century were far bolder in imagining middle-class men as consumers. See Woody Register, *The Kid of Coney Island: Fred Thompson and the Rise of American Amusements* (New York: Oxford University Press, 2001). For a fascinating analysis of *Esquire* magazine's efforts to promote a "new model of self-indulgent" masculinity in the 1930s, see Kenon Brezeale, "In Spite of Women: *Esquire* Magazine and the Construction of the Male Consumer," *Signs* 20 (Autumn 1994): 1–22.

6. Virginia Scharff, *Taking the Wheel: Women and the Coming of the Motor Age* (Albuquerque: University of New Mexico Press, 1991), 35–66, 111–134. The quote appears on page 129.

7. There is a vast and growing literature on redefinitions of masculinity that accompanied the rise of managerial capitalism. Among the most helpful are Angel Kwolek-Folland, *Engendering Business: Men and Women in the Corporate Office, 1870–1930* (Baltimore: The Johns Hopkins University Press, 1994); Gail Bederman, *Manliness and Civilization: A Cultural Histo-*

ry of Gender and Race in the United States, 1880–1917 (Chicago: University of Chicago Press, 1995); E. Anthony Rotundo, *American Manhood: Trans-formations in Masculinity from the Revolution to the Modern Era* (New York: Basic Books, 1993); Jeffrey P. Hantover, "The Boy Scouts and the Validation of Masculinity," in Elizabeth Pleck and Joseph Pleck, eds., *The American Man* (Englewood Cliffs, N.J.: Prentice-Hall, 1980), 285–301; Michael Kimmel, *Manhood in America: A Cultural History* (New York: Free Press, 1996).

8. Marchand, *Advertising the American Dream*, 162. Rachel Bowlby comes to similar conclusions about male writers whose livelihoods depended on catering to feminine taste, in *Just Looking: Consumer Culture in Dreiser, Gissing, and Zola* (New York: Methuen, 1985).

9. Warren Susman, "'Personality' and the Making of Twentieth-Century Culture," in *Culture as History: The Transformation of American Society in the Twentieth Century* (New York: Pantheon, 1984), 271–285; T. J. Jackson Lears, "From Salvation to Self-Realization: Advertising and the Therapeutic Roots of the Consumer Culture, 1880–1930," in Richard Wightman Fox and T. J. Jackson Lears, eds., *The Culture of Consumption: Critical Essays in American History* (New York: Pantheon, 1983), 1–38.

10. Jackson Lears, *Fables of Abundance: A Cultural History of Advertising in America* (New York: Basic Books, 1994); Lendol Calder, *Financing the American Dream: A Cultural History of Consumer Credit* (Princeton: Princeton University Press, 1999).

11. Advertising proof sheet, 1910, box 197, Ayer Collection; "Let These Friends Develop Your Boy," advertising proof sheet, 1917, box 197, Ayer Collection.

12. Advertising proof sheet, 1910, box 197, Ayer Collection.

13. "The Boys Are the Buyers," advertising proof sheet, 1923, box 198, Ayer Collection; "A Course in Advertising FOR BOYS AND YOUNG MEN," advertising proof sheet, 1917, box 197, Ayer Collection.

14. For more on the advertising education campaigns in *Collier's* and *Good Housekeeping*, see Pamela Walker Laird, *Advertising Progress: American Business and the Rise of Consumer Marketing* (Baltimore: The Johns Hopkins University Press, 1998), 353–357.

15. "Gee! This train's ahead of itself," advertising proof sheet, 1925, box 200, Ayer Collection.

16. Advertisement, *Printers' Ink* 80 (September 5, 1912), 11.

17. Advertisement, *Printers' Ink* 80 (August 22, 1912), 13.

18. Advertisement, *Printers' Ink* 80 (August 29, 1912), 9.

19. Advertisement, *Printers' Ink* 80 (September 12, 1912), 78.

20. Ibid.

21. "Greasing the Wheels of Progress," advertising proof sheet, 1927, box 200, Ayer Collection.

22. Advertisement, *Printers' Ink* 102 (March 7, 1918), 13.

23. Advertising proof sheet, 1920, box 198, Ayer Collection.

24. "Suppose you were going to buy a camera," advertising proof sheet, 1918, box 198, Ayer Collection.

25. Advertising proof sheet, 1926, box 200, Ayer Collection.

26. Advertising proof sheet, 1918, box 198, Ayer Collection.

27. Marchand, *Advertising the American Dream*, 251–252.

28. Marchand, *Advertising the American Dream*, 251, 253.

29. Advertisement, *Printers' Ink* 117 (November 24, 1921), 7.

30. Advertisement, *Printers' Ink* 133 (October 8, 1925), 7.

31. "Choosing the car," advertising proof sheet, box 197, Ayer Collection; *American Boy* ad, *The Thompson Blue Book on Advertising* (New York: J. Walter Thompson Co., 1909), 122, JWT Archives.

32. "When father was a boy—," advertising proof sheet, 1920, box 198, Ayer Collection.

33. The argument that *American Boy* sold boys as well as other family readers was repeated throughout the Billy Byer series of 1918. See, for example, "Who tipped you off to those dandy shoes" and "Billy Byer Goes 'Over the Top' at High School," advertising proof sheets, 1918, box 198, Ayer Collection.

34. In *Creating America: George Horace Lorimer and the Saturday Evening Post* (Pittsburgh: University of Pittsburgh Press, 1989), 65–71, Jan Cohn notes that *Saturday Evening Post*'s publishers discovered in 1908 that the magazine became much easier to finance when it began welcoming a female readership and supplementing its narrow range of male-oriented advertised goods with household goods aimed at women.

35. Advertisement, *Printers' Ink* 149 (October 17, 1929), 5.

36. Advertisement, *Printers' Ink* 149 (October 3, 1929), 7.

37. Advertisement, *Printers' Ink* 141 (December 1, 1927), 7.

38. "Deciding the Advertising Contest," *American Boy* 15 (December 1913), 24.

39. *Special Curtis Edition of News Bulletin* 78 (May 14, 1921), 6, J. Walter Thompson Company Newsletter Collection, Main Series, JWT Archives. Advertising revenues totaled $501,830 for *Youth's Companion*, and $442,225 for *American Boy*. The top five magazines generated considerably higher revenues, with *Saturday Evening Post* at $36,181,200, *Literary Digest* at $12,719,770, *Ladies Home Journal* at $11,148,360, *Pictorial Review* at $6,907,687, and *Woman's Home Companion* at $4,965,200.

40. "Boy Scout Contest Lasts Another Month," *The Kodak Salesman* 10 (September 1924), 6, Ellis Collection.

41. Advertisement, *Printers' Ink* 100 (September 13, 1917), 13.

42. "Merchandising Mississippi Steamboats to Boys," *Printers' Ink* 136 (September 2, 1926), 95–96.

43. "What the Coupon Brings," *Printed Salesmanship* 48 (February 1927), 515–523.

44. E. Evalyn Grumbine, *Reaching Juvenile Markets: How to Advertise, Sell, and*

Merchandise Through Boys and Girls (New York: McGraw-Hill Book Company, Inc., 1938), 79.

45. Bernard Grimes, "Radio's Most Critical Audience," *Printers' Ink Monthly* 28 (June 1934), 49.

46. Laura Mulvey, "Afterthoughts on 'Visual Pleasure and Narrative Cinema' Inspired by *Duel in the Sun*," in Constance Penley, ed., *Feminism and Film Theory* (New York: Routledge, 1988), 72. For an interesting analysis of how gender identification shapes children's identification with characters and plot lines in late-twentieth-century children's television programs, see Ellen Seiter, *Sold Separately: Parents and Children in Consumer Culture* (New Brunswick, N.J.: Rutgers University Press, 1993), 186–189.

47. Julia Grant, "'Homo-sexuals in the Making': Gender, Childhood, and Masculinity, 1890–1940," paper delivered at the Society for the History of Childhood and Youth conference, July 2001, Milwaukee, Wisconsin.

48. Ruth Oldenziel, "Boys and Their Toys: The Fisher Body Craftsman's Guild, 1930–1968, and the Making of a Male Technical Domain," *Technology and Culture* 38 (1997): 63.

49. Advertisement, *American Boy* 113 (October 28, 1920), 7.

50. Advertisement, *Printers' Ink* 155 (May 21, 1933), 5.

51. For a full elaboration of the advertising profession's assessment of its contributions to progress, see Laird, *Advertising Progress*, 329–361.

52. *The J.W.T. Book: A Series of Talks on Advertising* (New York: J. Walter Thompson Co., 1909), JWT Archives.

53. *News Bulletin* 98 (May 1923), 1–3, JWT Archives.

54. Advertisement, *Printers' Ink* 133 (November 19, 1925), 7; advertisement, *Printers' Ink* 133 (November 5, 1925), 7.

55. Advertisement, *Printers' Ink* 137 (November 18, 1926), 7.

56. S. C. Lambert, "Building a Business on Children's Good Will," *Printers' Ink* 112 (July 29, 1920), 89.

57. Eric J. Segal, "Norman Rockwell and the Fashioning of American Masculinity," *Art Bulletin* 78 (December 1996): 633–646.

58. Advertisement, *Saturday Evening Post*, August 25, 1917, 60, reprinted in Segal, "Norman Rockwell," 640.

59. Segal, "Norman Rockwell," 641, 646.

60. Advertisement, *Printers' Ink* 137 (December 16, 1926), 7.

61. Advertisement, *Printers' Ink* 133 (November 19, 1925), 7.

62. Advertisement, *Printers' Ink* 145 (November 8, 1929), 89.

63. Advertisement, *Printers' Ink* 141 (December 15, 1927), 7.

64. Bederman, *Manliness and Civilization*, 10–13; Rotundo, *American Manhood*, 248–250; Peter Filene, *Him/Her/Self: Gender Identities in Modern America*, 3rd ed. (Baltimore: Johns Hopkins University Press, 1998), 77–79.

65. Bederman, *Manliness and Civilization*, 13; Rotundo, *American Manhood*, 251–253; David Macleod, *Building Character in the American Boy: The Boy*

Scouts, YMCA, and Their Forerunners, 1870–1920 (Madison: University of Wisconsin Press, 1983), 44–49.

66. Quoted in Macleod, *Building Character in the American Boy*, 48.

67. Rotundo, *American Manhood*, 253.

68. Bederman, *Manliness and Civilization*, 16–17; Kimmel, *Manhood in America*, 182–183; the phrase "robust, manly, self-reliant boyhood" was used by Boy Scout leader Ernest Thompson Seton, quoted in Macleod, *Building Character in the American Boy*, 49.

69. Bederman, *Manliness and Civilization*, 17. For more on the changing meaning of the term "sissy," see Peter Stearns, "Girls, Boys, and Emotions: Redefinitions and Historical Change," *Journal of American History* 80 (June 1993): 48–49.

70. Rotundo, *American Manhood*, 224–225.

71. Stephen W. Meader, "Selling the Tom Sawyers: No Kid Stuff—Your Fifteen-Year Old Won't Tolerate It," *Printers' Ink* 159 (June 16, 1932), 51–52.

72. Ernest Rowe, "Two Specialties, to Round Out Season's Sales," *Printers' Ink* 120 (August 24, 1922), 143.

73. Rotundo, *American Manhood*, 255–257; Macleod, *Building Character in the American Boy*, 52–54.

74. Rotundo, *American Manhood*, 256.

75. Register, *The Kid of Coney Island*.

76. Advertisement, *American Boy* 11 (December 1909), inside front cover.

77. Advertisement, *American Boy* 11 (February 1910), back cover; advertisement, *American Boy* 11 (March 1910), inside front cover.

78. Advertisement, *American Boy* 17 (September 1916), back cover. The Markham Air Rifle Company, makers of King air rifles, saw a "sharp increase" in business as a result of the campaign. More than 3,000 boys requested copies of the Briggs Book, which reprinted the series of cartoon ads and presented a history of the air rifle, along with a price list for the full King line. The initial success of the cartoon advertising campaign persuaded J. Walter Thompson to extend its run for an entire year. *News Bulletin* 32 (January 24, 1917), 1, Newsletter Collection, Main Series, Nov. 28, 1916–February 26, 1917, box 1, JWT Archives.

79. Advertisement, *American Boy* 18 (November 1916), 33.

80. Bederman, *Manliness and Civilization*, chapters 3 and 5.

81. John Kasson, *Houdini, Tarzan, and the Perfect Man: The White Male Body and the Challenge of Modernity in America* (New York: Hill and Wang, 2001), 10.

82. Bederman, *Manliness and Civilization*, 95–101.

83. Advertisement, *American Boy* 18 (March 1917), 42. Air rifle manufacturers were not the only companies to capitalize on anxieties that too much passivity and indoor activity were sapping boys of their vitality. In the 1910s Kodak depicted picture-taking as a fitting "sport" for the active, adventurous boy. For examples, see advertisement, *Youth's Companion* (May 14,

1914), 263, Ellis Collection; advertisement, *Youth's Companion* (May 29, 1913), n.p., Ellis Collection. One ad even intimated that boys who photographed enjoyed all the benefits of sharpshooting without any of the risks: "There are no game laws—and no accidents—for those who hunt with a Kodak." See advertisement, *Youth's Companion* (July 16, 1916), 379, Ellis Collection.

84. For more on the popularity of Tarzan, see Kasson, *Houdini, Tarzan, and the Perfect Man*, chapter 3.

85. K. B. White, "Booklets That Teach Boys How to Play," *Printers' Ink Monthly* 5 (November 1922), 33.

86. Frank E. Fehlman, "Copywriting Needs a Rebirth," *Advertising and Selling* 16 (December 10, 1930), 25.

87. Meader, "Selling the Tom Sawyers," 52.

88. Laird, *Advertising Progress*, 295–297.

89. "When father was a boy—," advertising proof sheets, 1920, box 198, Ayer Collection. In *American Boy* trade press ads, the technologically minded boy consumer functioned as a symbol of progress, marking how far modern boyhood had advanced beyond previous generations. Instead of the barefooted boy of father's day, who caught fish with a string tied to a sapling, the modern boy outfitted himself with fishing boots, a "trademarked steel rod, . . . jewelled reel, . . . fly book," and bait box. Instead of giving picture shows, as his father had, using "crude, home-made 'panoramas' or the magic lantern with its grotesque colored slides, usually 'made in Germany,'" the modern boy gave "real motion picture exhibitions at home, taken and projected with [his] own apparatus."

90. Susan Douglas, *Inventing American Broadcasting, 1899–1922* (Baltimore: The Johns Hopkins University Press, 1987), 191.

91. Ruth Oldenziel similarly notes that the advertisers and organizers of the Fisher Body Craftsman's Guild socialized boy guild members as technophiles who pursued "their new consumer roles as knowledgeable producers and builders." See Oldenziel, "Boys and Their Toys," 77–78.

92. Jess H. Wilson, "Does Your 'Research' Embrace the Boy of Today?" *Printers' Ink* 118 (March 16, 1922), 34.

93. Charles Jacobson, interview by author, August 12, 2001.

94. See the following *American Boy* advertising proof sheets housed in the Ayer Collection: "That's right, Mike—talk back at him," 1925 or 1926, box 200; "Choosing the Car," box 197; "Give the Boys the Credit," 1923, box 198, "But gosh, mother, she won't run on just looks," box 198.

95. Advertisement, *American Boy* 29 (September 1928), 47.

96. Advertisement, *American Boy* 28 (June 1927), 27.

97. Kwolek-Folland, *Engendering Business*, 80–88.

98. Meader, "Selling the Tom Sawyers," 51.

99. Meader, "Selling the Tom Sawyers," 52. A 1925 *American Boy* advertisement captioned "Pretty snarky, but will it write?" also described the boy

consumer as a loyal warrior: "The affection and loyalty a boy has for his pocket possessions, like pens and pencils, is almost beyond belief. He'll defend them from the slurring and kidding attacks of his friends . . . until eventually the whole bunch will want one 'just like Dick's.'" See box 200, Ayer Collection.

100. Advertising proof sheet, July 1924, box 198, Ayer Collection.

101. Advertisement, *American Boy* 18 (November 1916), 25.

102. Lambert, "Building a Business," 89, 90.

103. Macleod, *Building Character in the American Boy*, 101–105.

104. Lambert, "Building a Business," 90; Lambert touted the boy's "gang spirit"; the phrase "gang spirit and high-pressure enthusiasm" appeared in *American Boy*'s ad captioned, "Pretty snarky, but will it write?"

105. Advertisement, *American Boy* 17 (May 1916), 49.

106. Advertisement, *American Boy* 22 (November 1920), 43.

107. Advertisement, *American Boy* 30 (June 1929), 47.

108. Lambert, "Building a Business," 90.

109. Ad copy quoted in Lambert, "Building a Business," 90–91.

110. Timothy Spears, *100 Years on the Road: The Traveling Salesman in American Culture* (New Haven: Yale University Press, 1995), 7, 17, 193–220.

111. Advertisement, *American Boy* 26 (January 1925), 30.

112. Advertisement, *American Boy* 104 (February 1930), 39.

113. "Why Read Advertisements: Advertising Talk No. 4," *American Boy* 18 (August 1917), 24.

114. Edward Edson Lee, "Advertising Andy," *American Boy* 23 (January 1922), 9.

115. For other installments in the Edward Edson Lee serial, see "Adventures in Ouija Boards," *American Boy* 23 (February 1922), 13–14, 30; "Aunt Tilly's Taffy Tarts," *American Boy* 23 (March 1922), 17–18, 44–45; "Fresh Roasted," *American Boy* 23 (April 1922), 22–23, 45–47; "Ayer-Planed," *American Boy* 23 (May 1922), 17–18, 44–47; "The Forman Contract," *American Boy* 23 (June 1922), 22–23, 47–49; "Andy's Greatest Victory," *American Boy* 23 (July 1922), 19–29, 47–48.

116. Advertisement, *American Boy* 27 (March 1926), 51.

117. Advertisement, *American Boy* 26 (April 1925), 47.

118. Rather than relying on systematic market research surveys, in the 1920s advertisers typically gathered data about children's consumer preferences through advertising contests that solicited testimonial letters.

119. Advertisement, *American Boy* 30 (March 1929), 67.

120. Advertisement, *American Boy* 30 (May 1929), 32.

121. Advertisement, *American Boy* 30 (April 1929), 39.

122. Sinclair Lewis, *Babbitt* (New York: Penguin, 1996), 15.

123. Lewis, *Babbitt*, 17.

124. Lewis, *Babbitt*, 71, 73.

125. Lewis, *Babbitt*, 74.

4. ATHLETIC GIRLS AND BEAUTY QUEENS

1. See, for example, the ads placed in the October 1924 issue of *Everygirl's* and the May 1925, June 1925, April 1926, May 1926, and January 1927 issues of *American Girl*, microfilm roll #38, JWT Archives.

2. *News Letter* 83 (June 4, 1925), 2, Newsletter Collection, Main Series, box 3, JWT Archives; "Account History: The United States Rubber Company" (April 8, 1926), 9, JWT Archives.

3. This theme appears in the May 1927, June 1927, and November 1927 advertisements placed in *American Girl*, microfilm roll #38, JWT Archives.

4. Roland Marchand, *Advertising the American Dream: Making Way for Modernity, 1920–1940* (Berkeley: University of California Press, 1985), 208–217.

5. Kathy Peiss, *Hope in a Jar: The Making of America's Beauty Culture* (New York: Metropolitan Books, 1998), 133–166; Lois Banner, *American Beauty* (Chicago: University of Chicago Press, 1983), 207–208; Nancy Cott, *The Grounding of Modern Feminism* (New Haven: Yale University Press, 1987), 152, 172–174; Elaine Tyler May, *Great Expectations: Marriage and Divorce in Post–Victorian America* (Chicago: University of Chicago Press, 1980), 60–72.

6. Peiss, *Hope in a Jar*, 135.

7. Advertisement, *American Girl* 9 (November 1926), 53. For similar ads, see the Borden's Milk advertisements in *American Girl* 9 (September 1925), 32, and *American Girl* 9 (October 1926), 47.

8. For more on early-twentieth-century girlhood and its departure from Victorianism, see Nancy Tillman Romalaov, "Mobile and Modern Heroines: Early Twentieth-Century Girls' Automobile Series," in Sherrie A. Inness, ed., *Nancy Drew® and Company: Culture, Gender, and Girls' Series* (Bowling Green, Ohio: Bowling Green State University Popular Press, 1997), 75–88; Laureen Tedesco, "Making a Girl Into a Scout: Americanizing Scouting for Girls," in Sherrie A. Inness, ed., *Delinquents and Debutantes: Twentieth-Century American Girls' Cultures* (New York: New York University Press, 1998), 19–39; and Sally Mitchell, *The New Girl: Girls' Culture in England, 1880–1915* (New York: Columbia University Press, 1995).

9. Joan Jacobs Brumberg, *The Body Project: An Intimate History of American Girls* (New York: Vintage, 1997), 97.

10. Brumberg, *Body Project*, 101.

11. Brumberg, *Body Project*, 102, 104.

12. To their credit, juvenile advertisers discouraged the most damaging manifestation of the culture's growing body consciousness: the slimming craze that spurred college and high school girls to reduce weight until their bodies mirrored the slender, flat-chested silhouette of the flapper idealized in movies and popular magazines. Not surprisingly, food advertisers were the chief critics of the dieting "fad." See Kellogg's Corn Flakes advertisement, *Everygirl's* 16 (April 1929), inside front cover; Ovaltine advertisement,

Everygirl's 17 (October 1929), back cover. For more on the slimming craze, see Brumberg, *Body Project*, 99.

13. Advertisement, *Everygirl's* 14 (September 1926), 27.

14. The first quote appears in advertisement, *American Girl* 10 (October 1927), 37; the second quote appears in advertisement, *Everygirl's* 12 (May 1925), 19.

15. An ad in *American Girl* announced that Cantilever Shoes were "an official shoe for Girl Scouts"; see advertisement, *American Girl* 12 (April 1929), 47. Ads in *Everygirl's* also noted that Cantilever Shoes were especially suited for Camp Fire Girl activities; see *Everygirl's* 13 (September 1925), 19; *Everygirl's* 14 (October 1926), 21.

16. Advertisement, *Everygirl's* 13 (February 1926), 21. The adjective "boyish" appeared in a Cantilever advertisement in *Everygirl's* 13 (September 1925), 19.

17. Harvey Green, *Fit for America: Health, Fitness, Sport, and American Society* (New York: Pantheon, 1986), 225–226. For more on Progressive-Era athletic culture for girls, see Sherrie Inness, "'It Is Pluck, But—Is It Sense?': Athletic Student Culture in Progressive-Era Girls' College Fiction," in Lynne Vallone and Claudia Nelson, eds., *The Girl's Own: Cultural Histories of the Anglo-American Girl, 1830–1915* (Athens, Ga.: University of Georgia Press, 1994), 216–242.

18. Susan Cahn, *Coming on Strong: Gender and Sexuality in Twentieth-Century Women's Sport* (New York: Free Press, 1994), 31–32, 46.

19. Cahn, *Coming on Strong*, 31–32.

20. Pamela Laird, *Advertising American Progress: American Business and the Rise of Consumer Marketing* (Baltimore: The Johns Hopkins University Press, 1998), 297.

21. Peiss, *Hope in a Jar*, 105.

22. Marchand, *Advertising the American Dream*, 175–179; Peiss, *Hope in a Jar*, 134–158; Jennifer Scanlon, *Inarticulate Longings: The Ladies' Home Journal, Gender, and the Promises of Consumer Culture* (New York: Routledge, 1995), 207–209.

23. Mitchell, *New Girl*, 103–138; Tedesco, "Making a Girl Into a Scout," 35.

24. Tedesco, "Making a Girl Into a Scout," 22.

25. For an example of advertising that addressed the tomboyish impulses of athletic, outdoor girls anxious to overcome the disadvantages imposed on their sex, see the Hood Gym Shoes advertisement, *American Girl* 13 (June 1930), 43.

26. Advertisement, *Everygirl's* 13 (March 1926), 23.

27. Advertisement, *American Girl* 11 (April 1928), 45.

28. Advertisement, *American Girl* 13 (February 1930), 31.

29. Advertisement, *Scholastic* 16 (March 15, 1930), 25.

30. The unforgiving female gaze has strong parallels with the kind of indirect aggression and social cruelties that scholars have identified in present-day

girl culture. See Rachel Simmons, *Odd Girl Out: The Hidden Culture of Aggression in Girls* (New York: Harcourt, 2002).

31. Marchand, *Advertising the American Dream*, 208–217; Mike Featherstone, "The Body in Consumer Culture," *Theory, Culture, and Society* 1 (September 1982): 29; Warren Susman, "'Personality' and the Making of Twentieth-Century Culture," in *Culture as History: The Transformation of American Society in the Twentieth Century* (New York: Pantheon, 1984), 271–285.

32. Hazel Rawson Cades, "A Twelve-to-Twenty Talk," *Woman's Home Companion* 52 (September 1925), 72.

33. Joan Jacobs Brumberg, "Coming of Age in the 1920s: The Diaries of Yvonne Blue and Helen Laprovitz," in Susan Ware, ed., *New Viewpoints in Women's History: Working Papers from the Schlesinger Library Fiftieth Anniversary Conference, March 4–5, 1994* (Cambridge, Mass.: Schlesinger Library, 1994), 218, 221–222.

34. Kelly Schrum, "Some Wore Bobby Sox: The Emergence of Teenage Girls' Culture, 1920–1950" (Ph.D. diss., Johns Hopkins University, 2002), 209, 241.

35. Brumberg, *Body Project*, 68.

36. Peiss, *Hope in a Jar*, 25.

37. Brumberg, *Body Project*, 70.

38. Kathy Peiss, "Making Faces: The Cosmetics Industry and the Cultural Construction of Gender, 1890–1930," *Genders* 7 (Spring 1990): 142–169; Peiss, *Hope in a Jar*, 141–142; Brumberg, *Body Project*, 104.

39. For more on advertising industry debates about the virtues of photography vs. drawing, see Patricia Johnson, *Real Fantasies: Edward Steichen's Advertising Photography* (Berkeley: University of California Press, 1997), 66–68, 142, 144.

40. Cahn, *Coming on Strong*, 48–50.

41. Advertisement, *American Girl* 11 (October 1928), 41.

42. *Woman's Home Companion* advertisement, *Everygirl's* 13 (September 1925), inside back cover. For an interesting discussion of the "The Sub-Deb" beauty column that appeared in the *Ladies' Home Journal*, see Schrum, "Some Wore Bobby Sox," chapter 4, esp. 204–206, 231–234.

43. "This is how you marked your ballot," *American Girl* 9 (December 1926), 2.

44. Margaret Jennings Rogers, "From True to New Womanhood: The Rise of the Girl Scouts, 1912–1930" (Ph.D. diss., Stanford University, 1992), 163; Brumberg, *Body Project*, 101.

45. Robert S. Lynd and Helen Merrell Lynd, *Middletown: A Study in American Culture* (New York: Harcourt, Brace, and World, Inc., 1929), 138, 241. In surveying the magazine reading habits of 391 girls, the Lynds found that 367 read women's magazines while only 16 read juvenile magazines. The tabloid *True Story* also circulated widely among high school students.

46. Cades, "A Twelve-to-Twenty Talk," 72.

47. Elizabeth Woodward, "The Sub-Deb," *Ladies' Home Journal* (November 1940), 6, quoted in Schrum, "Some Wore Bobby Sox," 205.

48. Grace T. Hallock, "*Beginning* Your Mirror and You," *American Girl* 9 (September 1926), 29.

49. Hazel Rawson Cades, "She Wears Her Clothes Well," *Woman's Home Companion* 54 (June 1927), 80.

50. For more on democratic discourses in twentieth-century beauty culture, see Peiss, *Hope in a Jar*, 145–146, and Banner, *American Beauty*, 205–207.

51. Advertisement, *Everygirl's* 13 (September 1925), inside back cover.

52. Cades, "A Twelve-to-Twenty Talk," 72.

53. Advertisement, *American Girl* 11 (October 1928), 41.

54. Advertisement, *American Girl* 13 (February 1930), 31; advertisement, *American Girl* 11 (October 1928), 41.

55. Hallock, "Your Mirror and You," 29.

56. Gay Head, "Boy Dates Girl: First Aid," *Scholastic* 35 (September 25, 1939), 36. Elizabeth Woodward's "Sub-Deb" column in the *Ladies' Home Journal* also stressed the importance of scrutinizing the face for flaws; see Schrum, "Some Wore Bobby Sox," 205, 231–234.

57. This broad historical shift is elaborated in Susman, "'Personality' and the Making of Twentieth-Century Culture," 271–285, and T. J. Jackson Lears, "From Salvation to Self-Realization: Advertising and the Therapeutic Roots of the Consumer Culture, 1880–1930," in Richard Wightman Fox and T. J. Jackson Lears, eds., *The Culture of Consumption: Critical Essays in American History, 1880–1980* (New York: Pantheon, 1983), 1–38.

58. Hazel Rawson Cades, "How Can I Get a Job?" *Woman's Home Companion* 56 (December 1929), 84.

59. Cades, "A Twelve-to-Twenty Talk," 72.

60. Paula Fass notes that during the 1920s "more than 40% of one sample of California high-school boys had the use of the family car whenever they wished, and almost one-quarter owned their own. . . . The proportion having unlimited access to the automobile increased with high-school grade. Less than one-third of these youths never had the use of the car"; see Paula Fass, *The Damned and the Beautiful: American Youth in the 1920s* (New York: Oxford University Press, 1977), 218.

61. Ray Giles, "Catching Up with the Billion Dollar High School Market," *Advertising and Selling* 14 (February 19, 1930), 28, 56–57.

62. Fass, *The Damned and the Beautiful*, 211. Some scholars have noted that the elements of the modern high school peer society were in place at the turn of the century in communities where high schooling was common enough to attract a diverse student body. See Reed Ueda, *Avenues to Adulthood: The Origins of the High School and Social Mobility in an American Suburb* (Cambridge: Cambridge University Press, 1987).

63. Grace Palladino, *Teenagers: An American History* (New York: Basic Books, 1996), xv.

64. This figure comes from Fass, *The Damned and the Beautiful*, 124, 211. Fass notes that high school enrollments increased 650 percent between 1900 and 1930, with the largest absolute increase occurring during the 1920s.

65. Kelly Schrum, "'Teena Means Business': Teenage Girls' Culture and *Seventeen Magazine*, 1944–1950," in *Delinquents and Debutantes*, 136–137.

66. W. Ryland Boorman, *Personality in Its Teens* (New York: Macmillan Company, 1931), 74.

67. Lynd and Lynd, *Middletown*, 162–163, 215; According to David Macleod, by 1904, fraternities and sororities were present in nearly half the larger high schools. Between 1907 and 1913, thirteen states barred high school secret societies on grounds that they "foster[ed] smoking, drinking, and ribaldry, discourag[ed] academic achievement, and disrupt[ed] school unity." See David Macleod, *The Age of the Child: Children in America, 1890–1920* (New York: Twayne, 1998), 151.

   Exclusion from high school sororities and fraternities created bitter disappointment among teens. Airing their opinions on a 1936 radio broadcast, a group of Ohio high school students complained that select social clubs fostered "inferiority complexes" among students who lacked the financial standing to become members. "Those who don't have the money to run with the crowd feel out of it," Harold asserted. Further, because sororities and fraternities created their own dating networks, Harold explained, nonmembers found themselves "out in the cold." See I. Keith Tyler, *High-School Students Talk It Over: A Report of Actual Discussions by High-School Students About War, Motion Pictures, the High School, Radio, and Parents as Given on the Ohio School of the Air* (Ohio State University: Bureau of Educational Research, 1937), 33.

68. Lynd and Lynd, *Middletown*, 137, 212–214, 216.

69. Adverting proof sheet, 1917, box 197, Ayer Collection.

70. Advertisement, *American Boy* 27 (August 1926), 43.

71. The ad quoted is a Conn Saxophone advertisement, *American Boy* 28 (November 1926), 41. Oddly, an advertisement for Hohner Harmonicas, clearly addressed to boys, appeared in *American Girl* 13 (June 1930), 51. Ads for band instruments found a welcome place in *American Boy*, whose editors recognized musical accomplishment as "one of the surest ladders" to popularity in high school and college. "We know a man," began one "Friendly Talks with the Editor" column, "who was . . . as prominent an athlete as there was in his day, but to-day he is remembered affectionately by his classmates, not because of his prowess on the gridiron, but because he knew a million songs and . . . was always willing to sing them to the accompaniment of the guitar"; see *American Boy* 27 (October 1926), 22. For nonathletic boys, musical talent provided an alternate source of social esteem, sanctioned by dominant cultural authorities and peers alike. Indeed, the "prestige of playing in one of the high school bands or

in the well-known local boys' band," the Lynds discovered, dictated boys' preferences for brass and wind instruments—just the types advertised in *American Boy*. See Lynd and Lynd, *Middletown*, 244, n. 33.

72. Advertisement, *American Boy* 26 (January 1925), 31; advertisement, *American Boy* 26 (March 1925), 43; advertisement, *American Boy* 26 (June 1925), 41.

73. Advertisement, *American Boy* 103 (October 1930), 39.

74. Charles Atlas's recommendation to drink milk and shun coffee and tea mirrored the advice given in Postum ads and school health textbooks. For more on Charles Atlas and his appeal to young men, see Elizabeth Toon and Janet Golden, "'Live Clean, Think Clean, and Don't Go to Burlesque Shows': Charles Atlas as Health Advisor," *Journal of the History of Medicine* 57 (January 2002): 39–60.

75. John Kasson, *Houdini, Tarzan, and the Perfect Man: The White Male Body and the Challenge of Modernity in America* (New York: Hill and Wang, 2001), 30–38.

76. For more on the difficulties advertisers faced in addressing men as consumers of cosmetics and personal grooming aids, see Peiss, *Hope in a Jar*, 158–166.

77. Frank E. Fehlman, "Copywriting Needs a Rebirth," *Advertising and Selling* 16 (December 10, 1930), 25.

78. Boorman, *Personality in Its Teens*, 127–128, 131. Nonathletic boys like Farland Robbins, who worried that he ought to train more systematically, made especially prime targets for advertisers. "Every fellow wants a sound body and immunity to disease," he wrote the *American Boy* editors in 1929. Robbins feared, however, that he might be putting his health at risk, because his extracurricular activities and "extra heavy course in school" did not permit time for school athletics. "I'd like to see an article called 'Do You Keep Training?' It might start by giving reasons for training, then tell what to eat, how much sleep a fellow ought to have according to his age, and suggest a program for fun and exercise." Advertisers would certainly have found a receptive audience in Robbins, given their unrelenting focus on "training" for bodily vigor and business success. See "In the Morning Mail," *American Boy* 30 (April 1929), 64.

79. Lewis Erenberg, *Swingin' the Dream: Big Band Jazz and the Rebirth of American Culture* (Chicago: University of Chicago Press, 1998), 53–54.

80. Advertisement, *American Boy* 106 (June 1932), 33.

81. Advertisement, *Scholastic* 28 (April 18, 1936), 31.

82. Advertisement, *Scholastic* 28 (May 9, 1936), 27; advertisement, *Scholastic* 30 (April 10, 1937), 27; advertisement, *Scholastic* 29 (September 19, 1936), 39; advertisement, *Scholastic* 29 (October 10, 1936), 31.

83. Advertisement, *Scholastic* 29 (November 14, 1936), 25. In this ad, an acne-plagued boy took a good ribbing when found inspecting his pimply face in

the locker room mirror: "Lookit little whoosis admirin' himself," a clear-skinned boy teased.

84. Advertisement, *Scholastic* 28 (May 9, 1936), 27. Fleischmann's Yeast promised that consuming three yeast cakes a day would eliminate poisonous wastes from the blood and the skin disorders they caused, earning the enmity of consumer advocates, who criticized the company for making false and exaggerated health claims. Though controversial as an acne remedy, Fleischmann's Yeast staked out less controversial territory in marketing to adolescent boys. While acne traditionally had been viewed as a girls' disease, in part because of long-standing cultural associations of feminine beauty with flawless skin, by the late 1930s, articles in medical journals and the popular press began to recognize acne as an "adolescent agony" which undermined self-confidence in boys and girls alike. See Green, *Fit for America*, 112, 312; Brumberg, *Body Project*, 60–61, 71, 81.

85. Margaret Weishaar, "PSYCH-ING *Mrs. Smith*: Two Special Feminine Urges Make Her a Spender," *People* (October 1937), 4–7, J. Walter Thompson Newsletter Collection, Domestic Series: New York Office, box 9, JWT Archives.

86. Advertisement, *American Girl* 12 (May 1929), 45. Royal Baking Powder's offer for a free cookbook of "Menus That Win Popularity for the Young Hostess" guaranteed similar results: "To be a charming hostess is the aim of every American girl. If she can plan and prepare a simple supper for her boy and girl guests, she is sure to be the leader of the crowd." See Royal Baking Powder advertisement, *American Girl* 12 (October 1929), 41.

87. "Talking It Over with Aunt Cherry," *Everygirl's* 17 (December 1929), 24.

88. For more on Progressive-Era discourses that stressed natural means as a route to beauty, see Banner, *American Beauty*, 202–204. Advertisement, *Everygirl's* 19 (November 1931), 26.

89. Advertisement, *Everygirl's* 17 (April 1930), 31.

90. Advertisement, *American Girl* 13 (June 1930), 35.

91. Beth L. Bailey, *From Front Porch to Back Seat: Courtship in Twentieth-Century America* (Baltimore: The Johns Hopkins University Press, 1989), 26–31; Mary C. McComb, "Rate Your Date: Young Women and the Commodification of Depression Era Courtship," in *Delinquents and Debutantes*, 44–48.

92. John Modell, *Into One's Own: From Youth to Adulthood in the United States, 1920–1975* (Berkeley: University of California Press, 1989), 104.

93. Advertisement, *Everygirl's* 17 (May 1930), 24.

94. Advertisement, *American Girl* 13 (October 1930), 35.

95. Imitation of advice columns was also a common technique in women's magazines; Scanlon, *Inarticulate Longings*, 43–45, 170.

96. Advertisement, *American Girl* 13 (October 1930), 35.

97. Advertisement, *American Girl* 14 (May 1931), 32.

98. Advertisement, *American Girl* 14 (May 1931), 32.

99. Advertisement, *American Girl* 14 (August 1931), 31; advertisement, *Everygirl's* 19 (October 1931), 24.

100. Advertisement, *Everygirl's* 19 (September 1931), 31.

101. Pamela Haag, "In Search of 'The Real Thing': Ideologies of Love, Modern Romance, and Women's Sexual Subjectivity in the United States, 1920–1940," in John C. Fout and Maura Shaw Tantillo, eds., *American Sexual Politics: Sex, Gender, and Race since the Civil War* (Chicago: University of Chicago Press, 1993), 161–191.

102. Advertisement, *American Girl* 14 (November 1931), 31.

103. Gay Head, "Boy Dates Girl: Offsides or Take Me Out to the Football Game," *Scholastic* 29 (October 10, 1936), 22.

104. Advertisement, *St. Nicholas* 57 (October 1930), 951.

105. McComb, "Rate Your Date," 54–55.

106. Mary Brockman, *What Is She Like?: A Personality Book for Girls* (New York: Charles Scribner's Sons, 1936), 173.

107. "Student Forum," *Scholastic* 31 (November 13, 1937), 37.

108. For criticisms of the looks-obsessed foibles of adolescent girls, see Gay Head, "Boy Dates Girl: Dress Your Best; or, Clothes Make the Man," *Scholastic* 29 (November 14, 1936), 20; Gay Head, "Boy Dates Girl: Jam Session," *Scholastic* 35 (December 4, 1939), 29. In the 1930s, when high school girls began frequenting drug stores to purchase cosmetics, family fights over lipstick use became commonplace, especially in immigrant families, where makeup was viewed as a sign of declining morals and parental authority. For more on teenagers' use of cosmetics, see Peiss, *Hope in a Jar*, 55, 171, 188–189.

109. Susan Douglas observes similar contradictions in the alternately liberating and oppressive messages that adolescent girls of the baby-boom generation received. See *Where the Girls Are: Growing Up Female with the Mass Media* (New York: Times Books, 1994), 21–42.

110. Lynd and Lynd, *Middletown*, 83, 83 n. 21, 141.

111. Elizabeth Benson, "Are Children People? What a Young Girl Thinks About Children and Grown-Ups," *Everygirl's* 14 (November 1926), 9.

112. Advertisement, *American Girl* 10 (March 1927), 61.

113. Advertisement, *American Girl* 10 (October 1927), 34; advertisement, *American Girl* 10 (January 1927), 42; advertisement, *American Girl* 12 (October 1929), 32; advertisement, *American Girl* 12 (April 1929), 38.

114. For all the talk of girls' spending excesses, boys in reality were more likely than girls to experience conflict with parents over spending. Among Muncie youth, 37 percent of high school boys indicated that "spending money" was a source of family discord compared to 29 percent of the girls. Though such percentages did not represent a yawning gap, that boys would experience more family conflict over spending money is not sur-

prising given their responsibility for shouldering the burden of dating expenses. See Lynd and Lynd, *Middletown*, 141.

115. Advertisement, *American Girl* 9 (June 1926), 42.
116. Advertisement, *American Girl* 10 (March 1927), 61.
117. Advertisement, *Everygirl's* 16 (April 1929), 23.
118. Lynd and Lynd, *Middletown*, 185–186.
119. Lynd and Lynd, *Middletown*, 164 n. 15.
120. Quoted in Robert S. Lynd and Helen Merrell Lynd, *Middletown in Transition: A Study in Cultural Conflict* (New York: Harcourt, Brace, and World, Inc., 1937), 452.
121. Lynd and Lynd, *Middletown in Transition*, 445–446, 452.
122. Lynd and Lynd, *Middletown in Transition*, 171 n. 52, 199–200.
123. Advertisement, *Everygirl's* 18 (December 1930), 19; *American Girl* 13 (November 1930), 39.
124. Gay Head, "Boy Dates Girl: Home, Sweeter Home," *Scholastic* 31 (January 22, 1938), 15.
125. Advertisement, *American Girl* 16 (October 1933), 39.
126. Advertisement, *American Girl* 16 (March 1933), 45.
127. For immigrant daughters "reared in the morality of family obligation," such sacrifices were, of course, nothing new, but the call to put family needs ahead of the self was now spreading up the social scale. Elizabeth Ewen, "City Lights: Immigrant Women and the Rise of the Movies," *Signs* 5 (1980): 56.
128. Gay Head, "Home, Sweeter Home," 15.
129. Peter Stearns, "Girls, Boys, and Emotions: Redefinitions and Historical Change," *Journal of American History* 80 (June 1993): 61.
130. Advertisement, *American Girl* 14 (August 1931), inside front cover; advertisement, *American Girl* 15 (April 1932), inside front cover.
131. "Talking It Over with Aunt Cherry," *Everygirl's* 18 (August 1931), 20.
132. "Talking It Over with Aunt Cherry," *Everygirl's* 19 (December 1931), 18.
133. "Talking It Over with Aunt Cherry," *Everygirl's* 17 (July 1930), 20.
134. Gay Head, "Boy Dates Girl: Be Yourself," *Scholastic* 30 (February 20, 1937), 29.
135. For student praise of Head's gender portrayals, see "Reader's Forum," *Scholastic* 33 (January 7, 1939), 3; "Reader's Forum," *Scholastic* 34 (February 11, 1939), 4.
136. Gay Head, "Boy Dates Girl: Offsides; or, Take Me Out to the Football Game," *Scholastic* 29 (October 10, 1936), 22–23.
137. Natalie T., letter, "Student Forum," *Scholastic* 29 (October 31, 1936), 26.
138. DeWitt Porter, letter, "Student Forum," *Scholastic* 29 (October 31, 1936), 26.
139. Quoted in Lynd and Lynd, *Middletown*, 141.
140. Margaret McFadden, "Anything Goes: Gender and Knowledge in the Comic Popular Culture of the 1930s" (Ph.D. diss., Yale University, 1996), 86–144.

141. Gay Head, "Boy Dates Girl: Girl of Our Dreams," *Scholastic* 31 (October 2, 1937), 9.

142. Gay Head, "Boy Dates Girl: Jam Session," *Scholastic* 35 (December 4, 1939), 29, 35.

143. Gay Head, "Boy Dates Girl: Monsieur Beau-We-Care-For," *Scholastic* 31 (October 9, 1937), 10.

144. Gay Head, "Boy Dates Girl: Stags at Bay," *Scholastic* 33 (December 3, 1938), 12.

145. Schrum, "Some Wore Bobby Sox," 226–228.

146. Beth Twiggar diary, quoted in Schrum, "Some Wore Bobby Sox," 213.

147. Reed Ueda notes that turn-of-the-century high school students had much invested in proving to parents and peers that "they were not foolish innocents." See Ueda, *Avenues to Adulthood*, 134.

148. *The Whatsit*, in *True Story* 38 (March 1938), 99.

149. *The Whatsit*, in *True Story* 38 (May 1938), 87.

150. Gay Head, "Boy Dates Girl: Dress Your Best; or, Clothes Make the Man," *Scholastic* 29 (November 14, 1936), 24.

5. REVITALIZING THE AMERICAN HOME

1. Paula Fass, *The Damned and the Beautiful: American Youth in the 1920s* (New York: Oxford University Press, 1977), 217–218.

2. Henriette Walter, *Girl Life in America* (New York: National Committee for the Study of Juvenile Reading, 1927), 139.

3. Steven Mintz and Susan Kellogg, *Domestic Revolutions: A Social History of American Family Life* (New York: Free Press, 1988), xx, 107–132; Fass, *The Damned and the Beautiful*, 89–118; Robert Griswold, *Fatherhood in America: A History* (New York: Basic Books, 1993), 88–118; Elaine Tyler May, *Great Expectations: Marriage and Divorce in Post-Victorian America* (Chicago: University of Chicago Press, 1980); Margaret Marsh, *Suburban Lives* (New Brunswick, N.J.: Rutgers University Press, 1990).

4. Kathy Peiss explores how middle-class reformers attempted to desexualize working-class recreations in *Cheap Amusements: Working Women and Leisure in Turn-of-the-Century New York* (Philadelphia: Temple University Press, 1986), 163–184; Peiss examines the legitimation of middle-class public recreations in "Commercial Leisure and the 'Woman Question,'" in Richard Butsch, ed., *For Fun and Profit: The Transformation of Leisure Into Consumption* (Philadelphia: Temple University Press, 1992), 105–117; Lynn Spigel, *Make Room for TV: Television and the Family Ideal in Postwar America* (Chicago: University of Chicago Press, 1992), 23–26; Lary May, *Screening Out the Past: The Birth of Mass Culture and the Motion Picture Industry* (New York: Oxford University Press, 1980); M. Alison Kibler, *Rank Ladies: Gender and Cultural Hierarchy in American Vaudeville* (Chapel Hill: University of North Carolina Press, 1999).

5. Elaine Tyler May, "Myths and Realities of the American Family," in Antoine Prost and Gerard Vincent, eds., *A History of Private Life: Riddles of Identity in Modern Times*, vol. 5 (Cambridge, Mass.: Harvard University Press, 1991), 549.

6. For an overview of changing ideas and theories of play, see Dominick Cavallo, *Morals and Muscles: Organized Playgrounds and Urban Reform, 1880–1920* (Philadelphia: University of Pennsylvania Press, 1981); Donald Mrozek, "The Natural Limits of Unstructured Play, 1880–1914," in Kathryn Grover, ed., *Hard at Play: Leisure in America, 1840–1940* (Amherst, Mass., and Rochester, N.Y.: University of Massachusetts Press and the Strong Museum, 1992), 210–226; Bernard Mergen, *Play and Playthings: A Reference Guide* (Westport, Conn.: Greenwood, 1982), 57–102; Gary Cross, *Kids' Stuff: Toys and the Changing World of American Childhood* (Cambridge: Harvard University Press, 1997), chapter 5.

7. Shirley Wajda, "A Room with a Viewer: The Parlor Stereoscope, Comic Stereographs, and the Psychic Role of Play in Victorian America," in *Hard at Play*, 112–138.

8. Spigel, *Make Room for TV*, 14–16.

9. John Kasson, *Amusing the Millions: Coney Island at the Turn of the Century* (New York: Hill and Wang, 1978), 101.

10. Kasson, *Amusing the Millions*, 101–104; Cavallo, *Muscles and Morals*; Mrozek, "Natural Limits of Unstructured Play"; Jane Addams, *The Spirit of Youth and the City Streets* (Urbana: University of Illinois Press, 1972; reprint of 1909 edition), 4.

11. Arthur R. Jarvis Jr., "The Payne Fund Reports: A Discussion of Their Content, Public Reaction, and Affect on the Motion Picture Industry, 1930–1940," *Journal of Popular Culture* 25 (Fall 1991): 127–140.

12. Ethel Puffer Howes, "Home—A Project," *Child Study* 7 (December 1929), 73–74.

13. Elizabeth Cleveland, "'If Parents Only Knew—': The Vital Importance of Play," *Children: The Magazine for Parents* 3 (March 1928), 12.

14. The White House Conference on Child Health and Protection, *The Delinquent Child* (New York: The Century Co., 1932), 214.

15. Agnes Wayman, "Play Problems of Girls," *Playground* 20 (January 1927), 546–551.

16. Ruth L. Frankel, "Child Leisure—A Modern Problem," *Hygeia* 9 (July 1931), 613–616.

17. Ruth Danehower Wilson, "Are Your Children Overdoing?" *Parents' Magazine* 4 (December 1929), 71.

18. Cleveland, "'If Parents Only Knew,'" 13.

19. Leslie Paris, "Children's Nature: Summer Camps in New York State, 1919–1940" (Ph.D. diss., University of Michigan, 2000), 297–302.

20. Josette Frank, "The Outside World Comes Into the Home," *Child Study: A Journal of Parent Education* 16 (May 1939), 192.

21. Mrs. Robert E. Simon, "Week-Ends to Fit the Family," *Child Study* 7 (December 1929), 71–72.

22. Zilpha Carruthers Franklin, "Saturday and Sunday—Assets or Liabilities," *Child Study* 7 (December 1929), 66.

23. Karin Calvert, "Children in the House, 1890–1930," in Jessica H. Foy and Thomas J. Schlereth, eds., *American Home Life, 1880–1930* (Knoxville: University of Tennessee Press, 1992), 81.

24. Katherine Beebe, "The Child's Place in the Home," *Outlook* 59 (February 12, 1898), 429–430.

25. Beebe, "Child's Place in the Home," 430; Charlotte Perkins Gilman, "Housing for Children," *Independent* 57 (August 25, 1904), 434–438; Helen Christine Bennett, "The Playroom," *Harper's Bazaar* 45 (February 1911), 90; Elizabeth McCracken, "The Child in the Apartment," *House Beautiful* 40 (July 1916), 100–101; Sarah Hood Gilpin Bright, "Putting the Playroom Downstairs," *House Beautiful* 45 (June 1919), 360; Francis Duncan Manning, "A Child's Play Shelf," *Ladies' Home Journal* 36 (March 1919), 77.

26. Bennett, "Playroom," 90.

27. Manning, "A Child's Play Shelf," 77.

28. Calvert, "Children in the House," 81–82.

29. Mintz and Kellogg, *Domestic Revolutions*, 123.

30. Emma Kidd Hulbert, "Every Child Needs a Playroom," *Children: The Magazine for Parents* 3 (November 1928), 24, 47.

31. Quoted in David Macleod, *The Age of the Child: Children in America, 1890–1920* (New York: Twayne, 1998), 71.

32. Marian Abt Bachrach, "Is There Room in Your House for Your Children?" *House Beautiful* 59 (January 1926), 51.

33. Ethel Reeve, "Furnishing the Playroom," *Garden and Home Builder* 45 (August 1927), 608.

34. D. D. Hutchison, "An Honest-to-Goodness Playroom," *House Beautiful* 68 (September 1930), 239–241.

35. Karen Halttunen, "From Parlor to Living Room: Domestic Space, Interior Decoration, and the Culture of Personality," in Simon Bronner, ed., *Consuming Visions: Accumulation and Display of Goods in America, 1880–1920* (New York: Norton, 1989), 181.

36. Halttunen, "From Parlor to Living Room," 189.

37. Bachrach, "Is There Room in Your House?" 51.

38. Penelope Baldwin, "Children in the House," *Garden and Home Builder* 43 (April 1926), 160–162.

39. Reeve, "Furnishing the Playroom," 553.

40. Dorothy Gladys Spicer, "Pictures for the Playroom," *American Home* 15 (January 1936), 48.

41. Charlotte G. Garrison and Alice Dalgliesh, "What Toys for Your Children?" *Children: The Magazine for Parents* 2 (November 1927), 21.

42. Gertrude Oram, "New Toys and Old," *Parents' Magazine* 7 (December 1932), 15.

43. Minetta Sammis Leonard, "Buying Toys with an Eye on the Future," *Parents' Magazine* 6 (November 1931), 24–25.

44. "Keep Up Interest in Year-Round Toy Business with June Play-Day Event," *Dry Goods Reporter* 49 (April 10, 1920), 37, 40; "Stress Educational and Practical Theme to Encourage Toy Buying," *Dry Goods Reporter* 49 (November 27, 1920), 31.

45. Buddy "L" catalog, Toys box 1, n.d., ca. 1920s or 1930s, Warshaw Collection.

46. Advertisement, *American Boy* 17 (October 1916), 27. Similar arguments about the virtues of home billiard tables were made as early as 1898, though the unwholesome pleasures home billiards were designed to keep boys from were "the club, the play-house, the restaurant, and . . . the gambling-room." See *Handbook of Rules of Billiards* (New York: The Brunswick-Balke-Collender Co., 1898), 9, Billiards box 1, Warshaw Collection. Ironically, despite such warm appeals to companionate family relations, advertising of home billiard tables actually increased the popularity of public billiard halls, much to the surprise of pool hall owners. See John Allen Murphy, "The Miniature Product—How and Why It Is Marketed," *Printers' Ink Monthly* 6 (February 1923), 56. Perhaps most chagrined were the editors of *American Boy*, which contained numerous ads for home billiard tables and eschewed pool halls as "disreputable" places, while lauding billiards as a "gentleman's game" when played at home, at the local YMCA, or at father's club. See "Friendly Talks with the Editor," *American Boy* 17 (April 1916), 1.

47. Advertisement, *Saturday Evening Post* (March 7, 1931), Eastman Kodak (Consumer) box 1, 1930, J. Walter Thompson Company Domestic Ads, JWT Archives; advertisement, *American Boy* (December 1930), Eastman Kodak (Consumer) box 1, 1930, J. Walter Thompson Company Domestic Ads, JWT Archives; "Show Kodaplays and Sell Kodatoys: Demonstration Programs Big Success," *Kodak Salesman* 16 (December 1930), 11, Ellis Collection.

48. "Home-Made Playhouses," in *Mother's Own Book* (New York: The Parents' Publishing Association, Inc., 1928), 174–175.

49. Hulbert, "Every Child Needs a Playroom," 24.

50. "We don't view with alarm . . . ," *Children: The Magazine for Parents* 1 (November 1926), 15.

51. George Hecht, quoted in Joseph Hawes, *Children Between the Wars: American Childhood, 1920–1040* (New York: Twayne, 1997), 82.

52. Benjamin C. Gruenberg and Sidonie Gruenberg, "The Parent Faces a New World," *Parents' Magazine* 6 (October 1931), 23.

53. White House Conference on Child Health and Protection, *The Young Child in the Home: A Survey of Three Thousand American Families* (New York: D. Appleton-Century Company, 1936), 78.

54. "Why Children Go Wrong," *Children: The Magazine for Parents* 2 (June 1927), 19–20.

55. "How Much Are Parents to Blame?" *Children: The Magazine for Parents* 2 (January 1927), 20.

56. Clara Savage Littledale, "The Home Behind the Child," *Parents' Magazine* 12 (November 1937), 11.

57. "Parents' Questions," *Child Study* 7 (December 1929), 83.

58. Frank Lee Wright, "Father, as Others See Him," *Children: The Magazine for Parents* 3 (March 1928), 15, 63.

59. "Father and the Children," in *Mother's Own Book*, 202.

60. For an extended discussion of the new fatherhood, see Griswold, *Fatherhood in America*, 88–142.

61. Ernest R. Groves, "Modern Youth Needs Modern Parents," *Children: The Magazine for Parents* 3 (October 1928), 11.

62. Weaver Pangburn, "Home Recreation," reprint of radio talk for Better Homes in America, *Playground* 21 (July 1927), 197. Better Homes in America was a national nonprofit organization that built and displayed model homes under the auspices of the U.S. Department of Commerce.

63. Peggy Pond Church, "Stay Young with Your Children," *Parents' Magazine* 4 (September 1929), 28, 80.

64. Sidonie Matsner Gruenberg, "Be Glad You Are a Modern Parent!" *Children: The Magazine for Parents* 3 (November 1928), 68.

65. Elizabeth Cleveland, "A Spice for Virtue," *Children: The Magazine for Parents* 1 (December 1926), 18–20.

66. Happy Goldsmith, "Salesmanship for Parents: Business Psychology Adapted to Home Problems," *Children: The Magazine for Parents* 1 (October 1926), 19–21.

67. See also "'Selling' Food to Children," in *Mother's Own Book*, 59–64.

68. Roland Marchand, *Advertising the American Dream: Making Way for Modernity, 1920–1940* (Berkeley: University of California Press, 1985), 229–232.

69. "Home Play Week in Rock Island, Illinois," *Playground* 22 (August 1928), 269; "Play Leadership in a Department Store," *Playground* 22 (August 1928), 265.

70. Pangburn, "Home Recreation," 198. For more on the Better Homes in America campaign, see Karen Altman, "Consuming Ideology: The Better Homes in America Campaign," *Critical Studies in Mass Communication* 7 (1990): 286–307.

71. Charles A. Gates, "Child Versus Home or Child and Home?" *Journal of Home Economics* 22 (August 1930), 645.

72. Natt Noyes Dodge, "Come Out and Play!" *Parents' Magazine* 9 (June 1934), 31.

73. For a discussion of the high accident rates involving children and automobile traffic, see Viviana Zelizer, *Pricing the Priceless Child: The Changing Social Value of Children* (New York: Basic Books, 1985), 31–32.

74. James Ford, "Planning and Equipping the Home for Children," in Blanche Halbert, ed., *The Better Homes Manual* (Chicago: University of Chicago Press, 1931), 196.

75. Florence Fitch, "The Beauty of a Well-Ordered Home," *Journal of the National Education Association* 16 (January 1927), 17–18.

76. *Young Child in the Home*, 61, cited in Cross, *Kids' Stuff*, 128.

77. Robert S. Lynd and Helen Merrell Lynd, *Middletown: A Study in American Culture* (New York: Harcourt, Brace, and World, Inc., 1929), 147–148.

78. "Parents' Questions," 82.

79. Pauline Duff, "Furnishing the Whole-Family House," *Parents' Magazine* 5 (December 1930), 31.

80. Fitch, "Beauty of a Well-Ordered Home," 18.

81. Hazel Rawson Cades, "Tell It to Your Daughters," *Woman's Home Companion* 54 (May 1927), 115.

82. Marsh, *Suburban Lives*.

83. Fanny Kissen, "Boys Study Homemaking," *Parents' Magazine* 5 (March 1930), 29.

84. Helen Woodbury, "Preparing for Leisure," *Parents' Magazine* 8 (January 1933), 49.

85. Ernest Elmo Calkins, "Children as Hobbies," *Parents' Magazine* 9 (December 1934), 56.

86. Helen Sprackling, "A Family Playroom," *Parents' Magazine* 7 (October 1932), 51.

87. Donna R. Braden, "'The Family That Plays Together Stays Together': Family Pastimes and Indoor Amusements, 1890–1930," in *American Home Life*, 148.

88. Sprackling, "A Family Playroom," 22, 49–51.

89. "The Parents' Magazine Rec Room," *Parents' Magazine* 9 (December 1934), 29, 61.

90. Benjamin C. Gruenberg and Sidonie Matsner Gruenberg, "The Family and Its Leisure," *Parents' Magazine* 7 (April 1932), 25, 54.

91. For a more extended discussion of Burgess's ideas, see Griswold, *Fatherhood in America*, 92–94.

92. Charlotte Ross Mochrie, "Gifts for Eight to Sixteen," *Parents' Magazine* 10 (December 1935), 78.

93. Gary Cross, *An All-Consuming Century: Why Commercialism Won in Modern America* (New York: Columbia University Press, 2000), 126.

94. Frankel, "Child Leisure," 613–614.

6. RADIO CLUBS AND THE CONSOLIDATION OF CHILDREN'S CONSUMER CULTURE DURING THE GREAT DEPRESSION

1. A study found that listening to juvenile radio programs peaked at 9–12 years of age. H. P. Longstaff, "Effectiveness of Children's Radio Programs," *Journal of Applied Psychology* 20 (April 1936), 213.

2. This view is argued in Stephen Kline, *Out of the Garden: Toys and Children's Culture in the Age of TV Marketing* (London: Verso, 1993) and quoted and critiqued in Henry Jenkins, "Introduction: Childhood Innocence and Other Modern Myths," in Henry Jenkins, ed., *The Children's Culture Reader* (New York: New York University Press, 1998), 24. William Leach shares Kline's view that children lack any real agency, arguing that "children do not have the capacity to define clearly their own rights and desires. Only adults have this power. Only adults can articulate the meaning of childhood and make it good or intolerable." See William Leach, "Child-World in the Promised Land," in James Gilbert et al., eds., *The Mythmaking Frame of Mind: Social Imagination and American Culture* (Belmont, Calif.: Wadsworth, 1993), 210.

3. Grant McCracken, *Culture and Consumption: New Approaches to the Symbolic Character of Consumer Goods and Activities* (Bloomington: Indiana University Press, 1988); Mary Douglas and Baron Isherwood, *The World of Goods* (New York: Basic Books, 1979); Daniel Miller, *Material Culture and Mass Consumption* (New York: Basil Blackwell, 1987), chapter 9. Some excellent examples of cultural studies approaches to the history of childhood can be found in Miriam Formanek-Brunell, *Made to Play House: Dolls and the Commercialization of American Girlhood, 1839–1930* (New Haven: Yale University Press, 1993); Ellen Seiter, *Sold Separately: Parents and Children in Consumer Culture* (New Brunswick, N.J.: Rutgers University Press, 1993); Jenkins, *Children's Culture Reader*.

4. Jenkins, "Introduction," 25.

5. Harold Wengler, "Transmuting and Delivering a Bowl of Cereal (Hot)," *News Bulletin* 139 (August 1929), 19, JWT Archives.

6. The advertisements appeared in *Ladies' Home Journal, Woman's Home Companion, Pictorial Review, McCall's, Delineator,* and *Good Housekeeping*; JWT Archives.

7. Cream of Wheat advertisement, December 1928, microfilm reel #5, JWT Archives.

8. Cream of Wheat advertisement, March 1929, microfilm reel #5, JWT Archives.

9. Cream of Wheat advertisements, December 1928, January 1929, May 1929, microfilm reel #5, JWT Archives.

10. Child experts' collaboration with Cream of Wheat affirmed not only the rising influence of experts in American culture but their growing accommodation of consumerism as well. For an interesting discussion of home economists' collaboration with advertisers, see Laura Shapiro, *Perfection Salad: Women and Cooking at the Turn of the Century* (New York: Farrar, Straus, and Giroux, 1986).

11. Cream of Wheat advertisements, September 1928, December 1928, January 1929, microfilm reel #5, JWT Archives.

12. Cream of Wheat advertisement, March 1929, microfilm reel #5, JWT Archives.

13. Cream of Wheat advertisement, September 1928, microfilm reel #5, JWT Archives.

14. Cream of Wheat advertisement, January 1929, microfilm reel #5, JWT Archives.

15. William Graebner, *The Engineering of Consent: Democracy and Authority in Twentieth-Century America* (Madison: University of Wisconsin Press, 1987).

16. Cream of Wheat advertisement, May 1929, October 1928, microfilm reel #5, JWT Archives.

17. The concept of enticement as parenting technique became a recurring theme in advertisements of children's products during the 1920s and 1930s, one that Roland Marchand has dubbed the "Parable of the Captivated Child." This parable moralized that parents could mold child behavior without harsh discipline or excessive coaxing if they captivated the child with the right product—or in Cream of Wheat's case, the right consumer club plan. See Roland Marchand, *Advertising the American Dream: Making Way for Modernity, 1920–1940* (Berkeley: University of California Press, 1985), 228–232.

18. Cream of Wheat advertisement, microfilm reel #5, JWT Archives.

19. Cream of Wheat advertisement, November 1928, April 1928, microfilm reel #5, JWT Archives.

20. E. Evalyn Grumbine, "This Juvenile Market," *Printers' Ink* 168 (July 19, 1934), 16.

21. E. Evalyn Grumbine, "Age Groups of Children," *Printers' Ink Monthly* 30 (April 1935), 71; E. Evalyn Grumbine, "This Juvenile Market," *Printers' Ink* 168 (July 26, 1934), 50.

22. E. Evalyn Grumbine, "This Juvenile Market," *Printers' Ink* 168 (August 2, 1934), 68.

23. "Snort, Punk," *Time* 34 (October 9, 1939), 64.

24. Hadley Cantril and Gordon Allport, *The Psychology of Radio* (New York: Harper and Brothers Publishers, 1935), 236.

25. E. Evalyn Grumbine, *Reaching Juvenile Markets: How to Advertise, Sell, and Merchandise Through Boys and Girls* (New York: McGraw-Hill Book Company, Inc., 1938), 21; Stanley D. Roberts, "Breaking Open a New Market," *Printers' Ink* 159 (May 26, 1932), 4; Lester B. Colby, "Half a Million Youngsters Enroll in Cracker Jack's Air Corps," *Sales Management* 25 (January 10, 1931), 80; "Children Are Joiners," *Printers' Ink* 160 (August 18, 1932), 68–69.

26. Azriel L. Eisenberg, *Children and Radio Programs: A Study of Three Thousand Children in the New York Metropolitan Area* (New York: Columbia University Press, 1936), 138.

27. Grumbine, "Age Groups of Children" (April 1935), 38; E. Evalyn Grumbine, "Age Groups of Children," *Printers' Ink Monthly* 30 (March 1935), 28–29.

28. Grumbine, *Reaching Juvenile Markets*, 109–110.

29. *Howie Wing* broadcast scripts, John Cody, November 3, 1938, microfilm reel #157, JWT Archives; quoted in Ray Barfield, *Listening to Radio, 1920–1950* (Westport, Conn.: Praeger, 1996), 116.

30. Jean Shepherd, *In God We Trust: All Others Pay Cash* (New York: Doubleday, 1966), 54. According to the *New York Times Book Review*, Jean Shepherd's account, though "billed as a novel," closely resembled the "oral memoir the author has been ad-libbing beautifully for around ten years" on his late-night radio show. A promotional advertisement for the novel in the same issue of the *New York Times Book Review* also testified to the book's verisimilitude: "Ralph's fervent, bittersweet memoirs of things as they really were will strike a reminiscent chord in each of us." See *New York Time Book Review* 71 (October 23, 1966), 17, 57.

31. E. Evalyn Grumbine, "Children's Radio Programs: 'How to' Experiences of Successful Users," *Printers' Ink* 184 (September 15, 1938), 61–62.

32. Grumbine, "This Juvenile Market" (July 19, 1934), 12, 16; Barfield, *Listening to Radio*, 120.

33. J. Bryan III, "Hi-Yo Silver!" *Saturday Evening Post* 212 (October 14, 1939), 134.

34. *Jolly Bill and Jane* scripts, December 8, 1932, February 24, 1933, February 27, 1933, microfilm reel #6, JWT Archives.

35. Quoted in Barfield, *Listening to Radio*, 114.

36. Post Toasties advertising proofs, July 1, 1932, October 20, 1932, box 77, DMB&B Collection; Grumbine, "Age Groups of Children" (April 1935), 71.

37. Selma Heller, interview by author, September 8, 2001.

38. Horace A. Wade, "What Kind of Advertisements Do Boys Like?" *Printers' Ink Monthly* 2 (December 1920), 32, 99.

39. Cantril and Allport, *Psychology of Radio*, 64, 237.

40. Gary Cross, *Kids' Stuff: Toys and the Changing World of American Childhood* (Cambridge: Harvard University Press, 1997), 83.

41. Cross, *Kids' Stuff*, 101–103.

42. Cross, *Kids' Stuff*, 82.

43. Cross, *Kids' Stuff*, 109.

44. Cross, *Kids' Stuff*, 118.

45. Eisenberg, *Children and Radio Programs*, 125; Longstaff, "Effectiveness of Children's Radio Programs," 217.

46. *Howie Wing* broadcast scripts, December 28–29, 1938, February 2–3, 1939, May 2, 1939, microfilm reel #157, JWT Archives. Cream of Wheat also issued special pleas to enlist more girls in its Buck Rogers Solar Scouts, informing them of "25th-century equipment made especially for girl Solar Scouts!" *Buck Rogers* broadcast scripts, March 9, 1936, p. 18, and March 13, 1936, p. 18, microfilm reel #8, JWT Archives.

47. Longstaff, "Effectiveness of Children's Radio Programs," 217.

48. *Howie Wing* broadcast scripts, November 1, 1938, and December 13, 1938, microfilm reel #157, JWT Archives.

49. "Radio Gets 2,000,000 Boys Into 'Flying Clubs' for Oil Companies," *Sales Management* 36 (June 1, 1935), 688.

50. *Buck Rogers* broadcast script, March 23, 1936, pp. 17–18, microfilm reel #8, JWT Archives.

51. Post Toasties advertising proof, March 20, 1936, box 77, DMB&B Collection.

52. Post Toasties advertising proofs, February 25, 1937, and May 27, 1937, box 78, DMB&B Collection.

53. Cross, *Kids' Stuff*, 110.

54. Margaret McFadden, "America's Boyfriend Who Can't Get a Date: Gender, Race, and the Cultural Work of the Jack Benny Radio Show," *Journal of American History* 80 (June 1993): 133–134; Susan Douglas, *Listening In: Radio and the American Imagination, from Amos 'n' Andy and Edward R. Murrow to Wolfman Jack and Howard Stern* (New York: Times Books, 1999), 105–107, 114–119.

55. Lawrence Levine, "American Culture and the Great Depression," in *The Unpredictable Past: Explorations in American Cultural History* (New York: Oxford University Press, 1993), 227; David Ruth, *Inventing the Public Enemy: The Gangster in American Culture, 1918–1934* (Chicago: University of Chicago Press, 1996), 144–145.

56. Mark West, *Children, Culture, and Controversy* (Hamden, Conn.: Archon Books, 1988). For an insightful discussion of the dialogue surrounding children and television in the 1950s, see Lynn Spigel, *Make Room for TV: Television and the Family Ideal in Postwar America* (Chicago: University of Chicago Press, 1993) 50–60.

57. Worthington Gibson, "Radio Horror: For Children Only," *American Mercury* 44 (July 1938), 294, 296.

58. Thomas R. Henry, "'Terrorism' on the Radio!" *Journal of the National Education Association* 24 (May 1935), 145.

59. Arthur Mann, "The Children's Hour of Crime," *Scribner's Magazine* 93 (May 1933), 313, 315.

60. "The Children's Hour," *The Nation* 136 (April 5, 1933), 362.

61. Don Gridley, "Children and Radio," *Printers' Ink* 175 (April 9, 1936), 106; "Advertising to the Child to Reach the Parents," *Printers' Ink* 165 (October 12, 1933), 70; Bernard Grimes, "Radio's Most Critical Audience," *Printers' Ink Monthly* 28 (June 1934), 23, 49.

62. Cantril and Allport, *Psychology of Radio*, 64.

63. Cantril and Allport, *Psychology of Radio*, 235, 243.

64. "Protest: Adults Condemn Air Hair-Raisers for Youngsters," *Newsweek* 4 (December 1, 1934), 27–28.

65. For more on organized protests, which included signing petitions, writing to the broadcasting company, boycotting, or writing the sponsor, see H. P. Longstaff, "Mothers' Opinions of Children's Radio Programs," *Journal of Applied Psychology* 21 (June 1937), 278–279.

66. Susan Smulyan, *Selling Radio: The Commercialization of American Broadcasting, 1920–1934* (Washington, D.C.: Smithsonian Institution Press, 1994), 127–129.
67. Smulyan, *Selling Radio*, 70–71.
68. Smulyan, *Selling Radio*, 76–77.
69. Smulyan, *Selling Radio*, 83.
70. For more on the commercialization of radio comedies, see Douglas, *Listening In*, 120–121.
71. Mann, "Children's Hour of Crime," 315.
72. Mrs. William H. Corwith, "Harmful Children's Radio Programs," *Ladies' Home Journal* 56 (April 1939), 4, 93.
73. Mann, "Children's Hour of Crime," 313.
74. Longstaff, "Mothers' Opinions," 270–273.
75. Henry, "'Terrorism' on the Radio!" 145.
76. Joseph Heller, interview by author, September 9, 2001.
77. "Protest," 27.
78. Longstaff, "Mothers' Opinions," 270–273.
79. Post Toasties' advertising proof, October 20, 1932, box 77, DMB&B Collection.
80. Longstaff, "Effectiveness of Children's Radio Programs," 212–213.
81. Longstaff, "Mothers' Opinions," 270–273.
82. Grumbine, *Reaching Juvenile Markets*, 116.
83. "Kellogg, Fils, Enlists 'Pirates' to Gain Cereal Lead from W.K.," *Sales Management* 30 (May 15, 1932), 202.
84. Sinclair Lewis satirized such preoccupations with rank in advertising schemes and middle-class culture in *Babbitt* (New York: Penguin, 1996; 1922), 192.
85. Charles G. Muller, "Put a Practical Idea Back of the 'Buy Now' Plan," *Printers' Ink* 154 (February 12, 1931), 10, 12. During the first two months of the campaign, children's efforts doubled sales of Grandma's Molasses in areas that received the radio broadcast and put five men to work. Their success was rewarded with a certificate of honor—a prize that children could treasure as a measure of their collective endeavors and compassion for families with unemployed fathers.
86. *Buck Rogers* broadcast script, February 28, 1936, p. 22, microfilm reel #8, JWT Archives.
87. *Buck Rogers* broadcast scripts, March 6, 1936, p. 20, and March 31, 1936, p. 16, microfilm reel #8, JWT Archives.
88. Shepherd, *In God We Trust*, 51–56.
89. Quoted in Barfield, *Listening to Radio*, 115.
90. Shepherd, *In God We Trust*, 53.
91. Grumbine, *Reaching Juvenile Markets*, 115.
92. Grumbine, *Reaching Juvenile Markets*, 108.
93. Grumbine, *Reaching Juvenile Markets*, 109.
94. Grumbine, *Reaching Juvenile Markets*, 111.

95. Vivienne Jacobson, interview by author, August 12, 2001.

96. Grumbine, *Reaching Juvenile Markets*, 115.

97. Grumbine, *Reaching Juvenile Markets*, 114.

98. Harold F. Clark, "What Does Junior, and His Sister, Want to Win in a Prize Contest?" *Sales Management* 41 (November 15, 1937), 54; E. C. Knight, "Whatsit Mean? When 4,000,000 Children Read the World's Largest Newspaper," *Advertising and Selling* 30 (December 2, 1937), 36.

99. Clark, "What Does Junior, and His Sister, Want," 54, 56; Knight, "Whatsit Mean?" 36.

100. Clark, "What Does Junior, and His Sister, Want," 56.

101. Clark, "What Does Junior, and His Sister, Want," 54, 56.

102. The *Whatsit*, in *True Story* 37 (December 1937), 53.

103. The *Whatsit*, in *True Story* 37 (October 1937), 55.

104. Levine, "American Culture and the Great Depression," 228–229.

105. The *Whatsit*, in *True Story* 38 (February 1938), 53.

106. The *Whatsit*, in *True Story* 39 (September 1938), 97.

107. Knight, "Whatsit Mean?" 36.

108. Etna M. Kelley, "Magazine Characters Create New Brand for Children's Products," *Sales Management* 39 (December 1, 1936), 896–897.

109. The *Whatsit*, in *True Story* 37 (November 1937), 55.

110. Arthur Mann, "Children's Crime Programs: 1934," *Scribner's Magazine* (October 1934), 245.

111. "Child Radio Fans," *Literary Digest* 115 (April 1, 1933), 14; "Radio for Children—Parents Listen in," *Child Study* 10 (April 1933), 195.

112. Sidonie Matsner Gruenberg, "Radio and the Child," *Annals of the American Academy of Political and Social Sciences* 177 (January 1935), 126–127.

113. Josette Frank, "The Children's Programs!" *Parents' Magazine* 14 (February 1939), 69.

114. Gladys Denny Shultz, "Comics—Radio—Movies," *Better Homes and Gardens* 24 (November 1945), 23.

EPILOGUE

1. William Leach describes the cult of the new as a "cardinal feature" of the culture of consumer capitalism in *Land of Desire: Merchants, Power, and the Rise of a New American Culture* (New York: Pantheon, 1993), 3.

2. Advertisement, *American Boy* 16 (November 1914), 29; advertisement, *American Boy* 26 (January 1925), 23.

3. Spencer Downing, "What TV Taught: Children's Television and Consumer Culture from Howdy Doody to Sesame Street" (Ph.D. diss., University of North Carolina, Chapel Hill, 2004).

4. Steven Mintz and Susan Kellogg, *Domestic Revolutions: A Social History of American Family Life* (New York: Free Press, 1988), 200.

5. Steve Manning, "Students for Sale," *The Nation* 269 (September 27, 1999), 11–18; Liz Seymour, "'A' Is for Ad as Firms Gain Hold on Campus," *Los*

Angeles Times (November 23, 1998), A1, A19; Denise Gellene, "Consumer Education: Marketers Target Schools by Offering Facts and Features," *Los Angeles Times* (June 4, 1998), D1, D6.

6. Quoted in Steven Manning, "The Corporate Curriculum," *The Nation* 269 (September 27, 1999), 17.

7. Seymour, "'A' Is for Ad," A1.

8. The author is indebted to conversations with Margaret Finnegan for this insight.

9. Vanessa Hua, "Parents Give Credit Card Barbie a Low Rating," *Los Angeles Times* (April 2, 1998), D1, D5.

10. For more on licensed character toys, see Gary Cross, *Kids' Stuff: Toys and the Changing World of American Childhood* (Cambridge, Mass.: Harvard University Press, 1997), 106–120.

11. Lynn Spigel, "Seducing the Innocent: Childhood and Television in Postwar America," in Henry Jenkins, ed., *The Children's Culture Reader* (New York: New York University Press, 1998), 125–126.

12. Cross, *Kids' Stuff*, 197–215, 222–223.

13. Ellen Seiter, *Sold Separately: Parents and Children in Consumer Culture* (New Brunswick, N.J.: Rutgers University Press, 1993).

14. Spigel, "Seducing the Innocent," 128–129.

15. Charles Solomon, "The Gen-P Gold Mine," *Los Angeles Times* (October 2, 1999), F1, F16, F18; Sandy Banks, "Pokemon Turns Playground Into a Mini–Wall Street," *Los Angeles Times* (October 17, 1999), E1–E2.

16. Report by Brooke Gladstone, "All Things Considered," NPR transcript, November 17, 1999, 2.

17. Gladstone, "All Things Considered," 3.

18. Leslie Earnest, "'Tweens: From Dolls to Thongs," *Los Angeles Times* (June 27, 2002), A1.

19. Joe Austin, "The New Girl Cinema: History, Independent Film, and Representation" (paper delivered at the Society for the History of Childhood and Youth conference, Milwaukee, Wisc., July 27, 2001).

20. Report by Brooke Gladstone, "All Things Considered," NPR transcript, November 18, 1999, 4–5; Denise Gellene, "Internet Marketing to Kids Is Seen as a Web of Deceit," *Los Angeles Times* (March 29, 1996), A1, A20.

21. Steve Manning, "Branding Kids for Life," *The Nation* 271 (November 20, 2000), 7.

22. James McNeal, *The Kids Market* (Ithaca, N.Y.: Paramount, 1999), 29.

23. Rand Youth Poll, 1999, cited in Kathy Kristof, "Do Your Kids Know That Money Doesn't Grow on Christmas Trees?" *Los Angeles Times* (December 3, 2000), C3.

24. Katharine Lowry, "The Great Allowance Debate: Experts and Parents Don't Always Agree," *USAA Magazine* (August/September 1996), 12.

25. Gladstone, "All Things Considered," November 17 1999, 1.

26. The "'gimme' syndrome" was coined by a parent in a question-and-answer session with Dr. David Elkind entitled "Kids and Material Goods," on *Kids These Days*, undated transcript, Lifetime Entertainment Services, 1996.

27. John Deering, untitled cartoon, *Arkansas Democrat-Gazette*, reprinted in the *Los Angeles Times* (March 8, 1995), B7.

28. Jeannine Stein, "Sophisti-kids," *Los Angeles Times* (September 23, 1999), E1, E3.

29. Tim Padgett, "Keeping It Simple," *Time* (August 6, 2001), 48–49.

30. For more on parents' perspectives, see Lowry, "Great Allowance Debate," 12–14.

31. *School Savings Bank: A Laboratory Course in Personal Money Management* (Minneapolis: Farmers and Mechanics Savings Bank, 1947), miscellaneous pamphlets file folder, box 46, PSFS Archives.

32. *Hold It! You Belong in This Picture . . .* (Minneapolis: Farmers and Mechanics Savings Bank, 1947), miscellaneous pamphlets file folder, box 46, PSFS Archives.

33. "Percent Banks Reporting Highest School Savings Participation by Grade," *Results of 1964 School Savings Survey* (American Bankers Association, 1965), 3, miscellaneous pamphlets file folder, box 46, PSFS Archives.

34. David Tucker, *The Decline of Thrift in America: Our Cultural Shift from Saving to Spending* (New York: Praeger, 1991), 143.

35. Arthur Allen, "Young Buyers, Beware," *Los Angeles Times* (May 24, 2000), E2; Manning, "Branding Kids for Life," 7.

36. Seymour, "'A' Is for Ad," A19.

SOURCES FOR ILLUSTRATIONS

CHAPTER 1

Figure 1.1. Cream of Wheat advertisement, *McClure's Magazine*, 1916, Cereal box 1, Warshaw Collection.

Figure 1.2. Shredded Wheat pamphlet, 1910, Cereal box 2, Warshaw Collection.

Figure 1.3. Wrigley's Gum advertisement, *McCall's Magazine* (February 1913), Gum box 1, Warshaw Collection.

Figure 1.4. Whitman's Chocolates and Confections advertising trade card, 1902, box 11, Ayer Collection.

Figure 1.5. Lux advertisement, *American Girl* 11 (July 1928), 33.

Figure 1.6. "The Junior Store," *Printers' Ink Monthly* 26 (June 1933), 49.

Figure 1.7. Cream of Wheat advertising proof sheet, January 1928, microfilm reel #5, JWT Archives.

Figure 1.8. Puffed Grains cereal advertisement, *Youth's Companion* 94 (May 20, 1920), 111.

Figure 1.9. New Departure Coaster Brake advertisement, *American Boy* 17 (May 1916), 23.

Figure 1.10. Roy Sims, "How Jimmy Got His Bike," cartoon, *American Boy* 113 (December 1939), 27.

Figure 1.11. Elgin Watches advertisement, *Child Life* 8 (April 1929), 150.

Figure 1.12. Remington Typewriter advertisement, *American Boy* 25 (May 1924), 31.

CHAPTER 2

Figure 2.1. Photograph, Holmes Junior High School, Philadelphia, PA, ca. 1920s, box 9, PSFS Pictorial Collection, Hagley Museum and Library.

Figure 2.2. Photograph, PSFS school accounts counter, ca. 1920s, box 9, PSFS Pictorial Collection, Hagley Museum and Library.

Figure 2.3. Bank president trade card triptych, Accession 92.229, Pictorial Collection, Hagley Museum and Library.

Figure 2.4. Photograph, PSFS thrift pageant, 1936, box 9, PSFS Pictorial Collection, Hagley Museum and Library.

Figure 2.5. Photograph, thrift pageant at Manayunk Playground, Philadelphia, August 15, 1924, box 16, PSFS Pictorial Collection, Hagley Museum and Library.

Figure 2.6. Photograph, 1925, box 16, PSFS Pictorial Collection, Hagley Museum and Library.

Figure 2.7. Florence Farish, "Penny Bank Budget," *Woman's Home Companion* 66 (May 1939), 106.

Figure 2.8. PSFS advertisement in ten Philadelphia high school newspapers, October–November 1931, box 15, PSFS Pictorial Collection, Hagley Museum and Library.

CHAPTER 3

Figure 3.1. *American Boy* advertising proof sheet, 1920, box 198, Ayer Collection.

Figure 3.2. *American Boy* advertisement, *Printers' Ink* 80 (September 5, 1912), 11.

Figure 3.3. *American Boy* advertising proof sheet, 1926, box 200, Ayer Collection.

Figure 3.4. *American Boy* advertisement, *Printers' Ink* 137 (November 18, 1926), 7.

Figure 3.5. King Air Rifle advertisement, *American Boy* 18 (March 1917), 42. This is a reproduction of a vintage advertisement and does not reflect the manner in which air guns are currently marketed.

Figure 3.6. Burgess Batteries advertisement, *American Boy* 29 (September 1928), 47.

Figure 3.7. RCA-Radiola advertisement, *American Boy* 28 (June 1927), 27.

Figure 3.8. Brunswick Tables advertisement, *American Boy* 18 (November 1916), 25.

Figure 3.9. Ferry's Seeds advertisement, *American Boy* 27 (March 1926), 51.

CHAPTER 4

Figure 4.1. Keds advertisements in January and November 1927 issues of *American Girl*, microfilm roll #38, JWT Archives.

Figure 4.2. Cantilever shoe advertisement, *Everygirl's* 12 (May 1925), 19.

Figure 4.3. Postum advertisement, *Everygirl's* 13 (March 1926), 23.

Figure 4.4. Postum advertisement, *American Girl* 12 (April 1929), 39.

Figure 4.5. Lifebuoy advertisement, *American Boy* 106 (June 1932), 33.

Figure 4.6. Keds advertisement, *Everygirl's* 17 (May 1930), 24.

Figure 4.7. Keds advertisement, *American Girl* 14 (March 1931), 37.

Figure 4.8. Libby advertisement, *American Girl* 16 (October 1933), 39.

CHAPTER 5

Figure 5.1. "Playrooms for Modern Children," *Arts and Decoration* 36 (December 1931), 47.

Figure 5.2. Kodatoy advertisement, *Saturday Evening Post* 204 (March 7, 1931).

Figure 5.3. Frances Duncan Manning, "A Child's Play Shelf," *Ladies' Home Journal* 36 (March 1919), 77.

Figure 5.4. "We don't view with alarm . . . ," *Children: The Magazine for Parents* 1 (November 1926), 15.

CHAPTER 6

Figure 6.1. Cream of Wheat advertisement, *Delineator* 114 (May 1929).

Figure 6.2. Cream of Wheat wall chart, Cereal box 1, Warshaw Collection.

Figure 6.3. Post Toasties advertisement, *Country Gentleman* 104 (September 1936), 33.

Figure 6.4. Front page of *Whatsit, True Story Magazine* 40 (July 1939), 117.

Figure 6.5. The girls modeling *Whatsit* fashions and the Bloomingdale's advertisement both appear in Etna M. Kelley, "Magazine Characters Create New Brand for Children's Products," *Sales Management* 39 (December 1, 1936), 896, 897.

Figure 6.6. Cartoon in *Whatsit, True Story Magazine* 37 (November 1937), 55.

INDEX

Note: Numbers in *italics* denote illustrations.

American Boy, Family spending, Masculine consumer desire

"Boy Dates Girl" advice column (*Scholastic*), 80, 140, 150, 154, 156–158

Boyhood, constructions of, 26, 105, 111, 112

Boy's Life, 17, 32, 87, 88, 103, 104, 109

Boys Magazine, 97

Boys: anxieties about overcivilization of, 110, 111–112, *113*; as gang leaders, 119, 121; gang instinct of, 119; middle-class, 111, 114; rigid gender identification of, 5, 104–105

Boy Scouts, 8, 32, 55, 64, 104, 110, 114, 119

Boy's World, 27

Brand-name products: American Flyer trains, 52, 54; Arbuckle Coffee, 20; Aunt Jemima pancake mix, 32; Barbie, 219; Belding silk thread, 21; Black Cat hosiery, 107; Brunswick billiard tables, *120*; Buddy "L" dump trucks, 170; Burgess Super B batteries, 115, *116*; Cantilever shoes, 131, *132*; Clark's O. N. T. Spool Cotton, 19; Clinton Safety Pins, 21; Coca-Cola, 225; Cocomalt, 195, 220; Cream of Wheat, 21, *22*, 23, 44, *45*, 185, 186, 187, *188*, *189*, 193, 223; Daisy Air Rifles, 42,111; De Soto automobile, 35; E. A. Kids furniture, 223; Elgin watches, 47,50, *51*; Fab suds, 32; Fairy Soap, 19; Fels-Naptha Soap, 146; Ferry's Seeds, 123, *124*; Fisk bicycle tires, 119, 121; Fleischmann's Yeast, 144; Garbage Pail Kids; 220; Hoover vacuums, 55; Hormel soup, 201; Instant Postum, 131, 134, 136, 137, 143, 150; I. V. C. Vitamin Pearls; 191; Ivorine, 21; Ivory Soap, 23, 43; Keds shoes, 28, 127, *128*, 131, 143, 146, 147, *148*, *149*; Kellogg Toasted Corn Flakes, 103; Kellogg's All-Bran, 146; Kellogg's Corn Flakes, 195; King Air Rifles, 111, 112, *113*; Kodak Brownies, 29, 34; Kodak Hawk-Eyes, 34; Kodaks, Boy and Girl Scout, 34; Kodatoy movie projector, 31, 170, *171*; Korn Kinks cereal, 6, 26; Lexington Minute Man Six autos, 95; Libby's canned foods, 40; Libby's Evaporated Milk, 154, *155*; Lifebuoy soap, 32, 42, 46, 144, *145*; Lionel trains, 54; Lux soap, 32, 33; Mackintoshs's Toffee, 23; Mennen's Borated Talcum Baby Powder, 21; New Departure Coaster Brake, *49*; Ovaltine, 195, 205; Palmolive soap, 45; Pears' Soap, 21; Pepsi, 225; Pettijohn's, 23; Pierce-Arrow coasters, 121; Pops Cereal, 204; Post Toasties, 190, 194, 196, *197*, 202; Postum Cereal, 103, 131, 134, *135*, *138*, 143, 150; Puffed Grains cereal, 48; RCA Radiola 20 radios, 115, *117*; Remington typewriter, *53*; Shredded Wheat, 23, *24*, 41, 42, 43, 130; Singer sewing machines, 153; Skookum apples, 42; Stacomb Hair Cream, 143; Structo engineering toys, 47; Toddy drink mix, 43; Toxic High stickers, 220; Twinkies shoes, 54; U.S. Giant Chain Tires, 121; Wheaties, 202, 206, 220; Whitman's Chocolates and Confections, 23, 25; Woodbury's Soap, 133; Wool laundry soaps, 21, 223; Wrigley's Spearmint gum, 23, 25, 43

Briggs, Claire, 111, 112

Brockman, Mary, 150

Brumberg, Joan, 130, 136

Buck Rogers, 190, 219

Buck Rogers Solar Scouts, 196, 204–205

Bullock's, 210

Burgess, Ernest, 181

Burnett, Frances Hodgson, 107

Burns and Allen Show, 198

Burrell, Carolyn Benedict, 56, 71

Business ideology, 1920s, 115, 118

Cades, Hazel Rawson, 136, 139, 140, 141, 180

brand-conscious shoppers, 18, 36, 40, 215; impact of Depression on, 17; letters to editors, 38–39; support for thrift education, 64; *see also American Boy, American Girl, Boy's Life, Everygirl's, St. Nicholas, Youth's Companion*

Children's Bureau, *Infant Care* bulletins, 72

Children's Online Privacy Act, 221

Child saving, 59, 62, 64; *see also* Progressive reformers

Child Study Association of America, 73, 200, 202, 212, 213

Child-study clubs, 72, 174

Chrysler Motor Company, 35

Church, Peggy Pond, 176

Cleveland, Elizabeth, 164, 165, 176

Cody, John V., 191

Cohen, Lizabeth, 2

Coke in Education Day, 225

Colliers, 36, 97

Compulsory education laws, 6, 7, 8, 23

Consumer credit, 85–86, 219

Consumer cooperatives, 84–85

Consumer desire, revaluation of, 14, 74, 86–88, 90–91, 94, 106–107, *108*, 109, 123, 124–125

Consumer disappointment, children's, 14, 36, 203, 205–207

Consumer education movement, 46, 55, 84–85

Consumer Reports, 219, 225

Consumer's Research, 46

Coolidge, Calvin, 87

Corporate-sponsored clubs: Buck Rogers Solar Scouts, 196, 204, 205; Cream of Wheat's H.C.B. Club, 183, 185–187, *188, 189*; Fisk Auto-Wheel Coaster Club, 119, 121; Howie Wing Cadet Air Corps, 191, 195, 196; Inspector Post Junior Detective Corps, 14, 183, 190, 194, 202; Jimmie Allen Clubs, 196; Jolly Junketeers Club, 191; Junior G-Man Corps, 196; Little Orphan Annie's Secret Circle,

14, 182, 192, 195, 205; Pierce-Arrow Coaster Club, 121; U.S. Giant Chain Cycle Tires' Thriftville Boys Bicycle Club, 121; Wrigley's Lone Wolf Tribe Club, 190, 192

Corwith, Mrs. William H., 201

Cosmetics, 129, 133, 158

Cream of Wheat Company: H. C. B. Club, 183, 185–187, *188, 189*; school promotions, 44, *45*

Crosby, Percy, 93

Cross, Gary, 195

Crowell, Chester, 83, 84

Cultural anthropology, 184–185

Cultural studies, 184–185

Dahl, Roald, 222

Dating: boys' complaints about, 150–151, 157; cost of, 157; etiquette, 150, 156–157

Dating culture, 76, 142, 150–151; advertisers' interpretations of, 127, 134, 143, 144, *145*, 146–147, *148*, 150–151; rating-and-dating system, 146–147, *148*

de Gracia, Victoria, 94

Dell, Nancy, 147, *149*, 150

DeMille, Cecil B., 129

Democratic social engineering, 78, 187

Department stores, 27, 28, 29, 31, 178, 210, *211*

Depression, Great, 55, 163; children's heightened awareness of class distinctions during, 7, 130, 153, 156–157, 263n67; democratization of consumer culture during, 7; family conflicts over spending money during, 76–78; gender conservatism of, 150–151, 154–157; growth of high school attendance during, 142; humor during, 209; impact on advertising, 39, 144, *145*, 202–203; impact on children's financial outlooks, 85, 91–92; impact on children's money training, 13–14, 76–78, 80, 85–86, 90–91;